D1497843

The Bible Cause

The Bible Cause

A History of the American Bible Society

JOHN FEA

OXFORD
UNIVERSITY PRESS

OXFORD
UNIVERSITY PRESS

Oxford University Press is a department of the University of Oxford. It furthers
the University's objective of excellence in research, scholarship, and education
by publishing worldwide. Oxford is a registered trade mark of Oxford University
Press in the UK and certain other countries.

Published in the United States of America by Oxford University Press
198 Madison Avenue, New York, NY 10016, United States of America.

Library of Congress Cataloging-in-Publication Data
Fea, John, author.
The Bible cause : a history of the American Bible Society / John Fea.
pages cm
ISBN 978-0-19-025306-6 (hardback : alk. paper)   1. American Bible
Society—History.   I. Title.
BV2370.A7F43 2016
267'.130973—dc23
2015027208

1 3 5 7 9 8 6 4 2
Printed by Sheridan, USA

CONTENTS

ACKNOWLEDGMENTS

When one is tasked with writing a book of this size and scope, and given a year to do it, there are a lot of people to thank.

At Messiah College, Kim Phipps, Randy Basinger, and Peter Peters continue to support me as a writer, scholar, historian, and blogger.

The American Bible Society has been nothing but encouraging during this project. I want to thank President Roy Peterson and his staff for reading a draft of this book and making several useful suggestions. Philip Towner of the Nida Institute for Biblical Scholarship and Father Paul Soukup of the ABS Board of Directors gave me the green light to pursue this project in the way it needed to be pursued. Jason Malec, Paris Lofaro, and John Greco were supportive of this project even as they made sure I stayed on schedule. Kristin Hellman, director of Library Services at ABS, went above and beyond the call of duty to provide me with the materials I needed to make this book a reality. I am saddened that she has not made the move to Philadelphia. Mary Cordato, the ABS bicentennial historian, was a joy to work with. In addition to the hundreds of pages that she scanned for me, the numerous questions that she answered in person and via e-mail, and her willingness to share her office with me, Mary has been a constant source of encouragement and an indispensable guide to the history of this very complicated institution.

I benefitted greatly from interviews with Roy Peterson, Geof Morin, Steve King, Bob Briggs, Phil Towner, John Erickson, Lea Velis, Gene Habecker, David Burke, Bob Hodgson, and Lamar Vest. I especially want to thank John and Nancy Erickson for the gracious hospitality that they showed me in Crawford, Nebraska.

I could not have written this book in such a short span of time if it was not for the very talented and extremely hard-working Katie Garland. I can't imagine ever having a better research assistant. This is the fourth book that Katie and I have worked on together. It is now time for her to write her own! I am also grateful to my Messiah College research assistants Katy Kaslow and Alyssa Vorbeck for carrying such a large portion of the research load. I am glad that Katy managed to get a senior honors thesis out of this research. I apologize to Alyssa for having to listen to me talk endlessly about girls' volleyball. History Department work-study students Rachel Carey and Greg Slye also offered research assistance at different points during the project. Kelly Henderson, Laura Passmore, Jonathan Werthmuller, Megan Piette, Megan Ekstrom, Abby Blakeney, Rachel Carey, and Abigail Koontz performed the tedious work of transcribing interviews.

My editor at Oxford University Press, Cynthia Read, believed in this project from the moment she read the proposal. She and her staff have been a pleasure to work with and I hope I get a chance to do it again. Jonathan Den Hartog, Mark Noll, Paul Harvey, and the many other historians whom I interact with via Twitter and "The Way of Improvement Leads Home" blog have offered helpful advice and encouragement along the way.

My family has been very gracious and inordinately patient with me while I worked on this book. John Fea and Joan Fea, my parents, put up with me for seven weeks in the summer of 2014 while I was conducting research in New York. Allyson and Caroline Fea never stopped cheering me on: "Dad, you can do it!" Joy Fea shared the burden of this book with me at every step of the journey. I will never be able to thank her enough for her love and support.

The Bible Cause

Introduction

John Erickson sits at a table in his home in Crawford, Nebraska, on a chilly March 2015 morning. He is sipping bottled water and talking about the thirty-six years he spent working for the American Bible Society (ABS). Erickson is a living legend in ABS circles. He arrived in 1965 and has served the Society as Secretary of Asia, as an innovative fundraiser, and as a general officer responsible for the international work of the ABS. He finished his career as general secretary of the United Bible Societies, a fellowship of some 135 national Bible societies from across the globe. Erickson has been retired from Bible work for about two decades now, but there is little that he does not remember. His photographic memory seems to be both a blessing and a curse. Erickson talks as if it all happened yesterday—the trips around the world, the programs he was responsible for creating and implementing, and the relationships he cultivated with coworkers and mentors. "The Bible Cause is about *people*," he likes to say. He says it over and over again. And then he says it one more time—leaning forward in his chair for added effect. He has strong opinions, but they are always seasoned with a healthy dose of Lutheran humility. When John Erickson says that the Bible Cause is about *people* he speaks with the authority of a man who practices what he preaches. Whether it is the president of the Bible Society of India or an entry-lever staffer, Erickson has served them all with uncommon grace.

One week later, Roy Peterson, the current president of the American Bible Society, is seated in his corner office on the fifth floor of "Bible House"—the unofficial name given to the ABS headquarters at 1865 Broadway in New York City. He is dressed casually for a CEO of a major nonprofit organization—a navy blue V-neck sweater and blue khakis. On this particular day he is excited about spending the evening at Lincoln Center where he will be viewing an early screening of television commentator Bill O'Reilly's new movie, *Killing Jesus*. Peterson is a busy man these days. A few months earlier he announced that the ABS would be leaving Manhattan, the place where it has been located for almost two centuries, and relocating to Philadelphia. The decision to move was a controversial one. Many of the hardworking men and women who make up the ABS have strong connections to the New York Metropolitan area. Most of them will not be making the trip down the New Jersey Turnpike to the City of Brotherly Love. But Peterson believes—and he is very convincing—that the mission of the ABS can be fulfilled in a more effective and cost-efficient way in the place where the United States was born. Peterson has only been at the ABS for one year, but he displays an air of confidence, coupled with an abiding Christian faith, that comes from his experience leading Wycliffe Bible Translators, a major evangelical Bible translation ministry.

Erickson and Peterson have never met, but if they do ever get together over coffee or a meal they will be a lot to talk about. Like Erickson, Peterson also believes that the mission of the American Bible Society is about people. They both want men, women, and children to be confronted with the message of the word of God and have their lives changed in the process. Yet Peterson's vision for the ABS is more expansive than the one Erickson talks about from his home on the Nebraska panhandle. He is concerned about how the "power structures of our culture—government, media, and education"—have led us down a path toward secularization. He mentions the "radical attack" on religious liberty, the decline of a Christian "worldview" among young people in the United States, and the destruction of the traditional family through divorce and other forms of vice. The only way to rescue the United States from this "downward spiral"—to change the culture, if you will—is by getting more and more Americans engaged with the Bible.

John Erickson and Roy Peterson are very good at appealing to the history of the ABS when they talk about how the organization should approach its third century of operation. Erickson likes to bring up Eric North, the general secretary of the ABS from 1928 to 1956. As we will see, North and Bible translator Eugene Nida are probably the two most important people in the twentieth-century history of the organization. Erickson is fond of referencing his predecessor's 1938 article "The Purposes and Processes of the Bible Society." In that piece North writes: "The most important process which the Society carries on, is not at the Bible House in New York, nor at the Bible Houses in Tokyo, Rio, Peiping, Manila, or Cristobal. The major work is done *where the man without the Scriptures is met by the man with the Scriptures*." For Erickson it's really very simple. Whenever the ABS has followed North's advice, it has succeeded. But when it has strayed from this kind of face-to-face encounter over the word of God, it has lost its way.

Peterson is new to the ABS. As a result he does not know the history of the organization as well as Erickson. But this has not stopped him from finding a useable past of his own. He is attracted to Elias Boudinot, the man responsible for the founding of the ABS in 1816. According to Peterson, Boudinot wanted people to have the Bible in their own language, and the scriptures distributed to as many people as possible, but he also wanted the ABS to help men and women use the Bible to draw closer to God and become virtuous citizens—the kind of citizens that are necessary for a republic to survive. Boudinot and his peers, Peterson says, "knew that you can't build a nation built upon democracy without moral values and he saw the destructive nature of that without the word of God." Peterson is convinced that the work Boudinot started must continue or else America will "lose the values with which we built this country." If the ABS and other organizations like it fail in this task, the result will be the "deterioration of our families and our nation and you [will] see the drifting from moral values." This vision is more than just about one man meeting another man with a copy of the scriptures. It is about sustaining the vision of the American founders, of which Elias Boudinot was one.[1]

Erickson and Peterson both embody the spirit of the Bible Cause as it has developed over the last two centuries. Though the American Bible Society has seen many changes during that period—changes that will be chronicled in the pages that follow—two things have remained the same. First, the American Bible Society has always believed that the Bible, as the word of God, offers a message of salvation for humankind and thus must be distributed as widely as possible in a language and form that people will understand. Laton Holmgren, one of the General Secretaries who led the ABS through most of the 1960s and 1970s, put it this way: "If possible, every man on earth must be told of the Savior in his own tongue and given the opportunity to surrender his life to Him." Second, the American Bible Society has never lost touch with its cultural mandate: to build a Christian civilization in the United States and, eventually, around the world. One will not find this written in any of the official documents of the ABS, but it is a theme that cannot be missed in the annals of the Society's past. The relationship between the American Bible Society and the United States is evident in a 1904 fundraising appeal that appeared in the *Bible Society Record*, the Society's official publication. It read: "The social fabric of modern states has no surer foundation than the Bible, especially in a republic like ours, which rests upon the moral character and educated judgement of the individual. No thoughtful man can doubt that to decrease the circulation and use of the Bible among the people would seriously menace the highest interest of civilized humanity." The letter was signed by Theodore Roosevelt, Grover Cleveland, and William Jennings Bryan, among others.[2]

God and country. The United States of America and the Bible. Rare is the case when one is treated as less important to the mission of the ABS than the other. What follows is the story of the American *Bible* Society and the *American* Bible Society.

The Bible Cause chronicles the history of the American Bible Society from its founding in 1816 as one of several Christian benevolent societies created in the decades following the American Revolution, to its current status as a nonprofit Christian ministry with a $300 million endowment that engages people "with the life-changing message of God's word." In December 2013 I was contacted by Chris Thyberg, who was at the time working as a project manager with the Nida Institute for Biblical Scholarship, the intellectual and academic arm of the ABS. Chris asked me if would consider writing the 200th anniversary history of the American Bible Society. Chris knew that I would not be interested in writing some sort of celebratory coffee-table book, but when he promised "full academic freedom" and added that the ABS wanted a book published by a "reputable academic press" in the hopes that it would make "a real contribution to the history of the Bible and its role and place in America," I was intrigued. Chris put me in touch with Philip Towner, the dean of the Nida Institute. In the first week of the New Year I was on the phone with Towner and Paul Soukup, SJ, a communications professor at Santa Clara University and the chair of the ABS Translation and Scholarship Committee. After a visit to the American Bible Society to meet with Mary Cordato, the ABS bicentennial historian, and Kristen Hellman, the archivist and director of Library Services, I agreed to write the book. In order to make sure that the project would remain an honest piece of scholarship, I did not take any remuneration for my work, although the ABS did agree to cover my travel expenses. The goal was for the book to be completed in time for the 200th anniversary celebration in May 2016.[3]

One hundred years ago, Henry Otis Dwight, a Civil War veteran, newspaper correspondent, and missionary to Constantinople, wrote the two-volume *The Centennial History of the American Bible Society*. Another history of the ABS was planned for the 150th anniversary, but it was never completed. The author of that book was supposed to be Kenneth Scott Latourette, the renowned historian of global Christianity and Sterling Professor of Missions and Oriental History Emeritus at Yale Divinity School. He was close to eighty years old when the ABS approached him about the project. Latourette agreed to write the book, but he told Robert Taylor, general secretary of the ABS, that he did not have the time to come to New York to conduct the research. When retired General Secretary Eric North learned about this, he volunteered to do the research for Latourette. The ABS provided North with a staff of assistants and the project was on its way. An agreement for publication was secured with Harper & Row Publishers, and the book was scheduled to be released in 1966.[4]

According to Taylor, who would eventually write his own short, popular, paperback history of the ABS titled *Wings for the Word*, North's research moved along much slower than expected, forcing Latourette to "accept the material in pieces." As a result, Taylor thought that the manuscript, or at least the parts that he reviewed, "lacked the broad sweeping review of events which characterized Dr. Latourette's earlier works." The research for the book continued to fall behind and Latourette could not meet the deadlines that the ABS had set for him. When it was clear that the book would not be ready in time for the 150th anniversary, Harper & Row cancelled the contract. In his 1974 reflections on the events surrounding the proposed 150th anniversary history, Taylor made two comments that have stuck with me throughout the course of this project. First, when he realized that Latourette was not going to complete the book he had started, he tried to look on the bright side: "The production of a [150th anniversary] history has now made the research task much lighter for the preparation of an ABS history at the time of the Society's 200th Anniversary." Taylor was correct. In the course of writing this book I was able to draw extensively on the research conducted by North and his team. Second, if Taylor were alive today, I think he would have sympathized with my task. "It is extremely difficult to write popular reading material about the ABS," he wrote. "This writing is a frustrating game."[5]

In writing *The Bible Cause* I have stayed as true as possible to a chronological narrative. I think Taylor's comments about the difficulties in writing about the history of the ABS stem from the fact that institutions do not usually make for the most thrilling reading. On this front, I have taken a tip from John Erickson and tried to bring as many *people* into the story as possible. Those who are interested in the way that an institution functions will find plenty of material in these pages about organizational structure, business plans, and vision statements, but I have deliberately chosen to downplay this aspect of the ABS's past so that I can focus more fully on the anecdotes and stories that bring the Society's history to life.

Readers should also know that I have in no way tried to be comprehensive. I wish that time and space would have permitted me to say more than I did about the international outreach of the ABS. Chapters that cover ABS projects in the Levant, China, Japan, Korea, and Mexico touch mostly on the Society's work in the period before the establishment of the United Bible Societies in 1946, and even then only scratch the surface of what happened in those places. There is still much more to be said about the global outreach of the ABS, especially as it relates to Africa and Latin America. I look forward to the work of future historians who will tackle these subjects.

Those who read *The Bible Cause* carefully will not be able to miss the way in which the two aforementioned themes—the ABS's work to use the Bible as a means of heralding the "good news" of Jesus Christ and its use of the Bible to build a Christian civilization—are threaded through the narrative. The ABS's pursuit of these goals has remained constant, even during some of its radical seasons of change. But the spreading of the Gospel and the building of a Christian nation should also be understood in the context of four other aspects of ABS history.

First, the American Bible Society has always been a Christian organization that is interdenominational in scope. From its earliest days as a Protestant benevolent society in the early American republic, the ABS has tried to work with as many expressions of Christian faith as possible. This, of course, does not mean that the ABS was immune to the limits of Christian cooperation that have defined the American religious experience, especially in terms of its relationship with Roman Catholicism. *The Bible Cause* traces how the ABS has tried—sometimes successfully, sometimes not—to create a community of Christians whose love for the Bible transcends its commitment to a particular creed, confession, or denominational identity.

Second, the American Bible Society has always sought to work from a position of religious and cultural power in the United States. The ABS never let its constituency forget that it was the *American* Bible Society. The Society never operated from the fringes of American life. While it has been willing to work with any Christian body interested in promoting the Bible, the ABS has always gravitated toward the particular expression of Christianity that its board and staff believed to be the moral guardians of America's status as a Christian nation. This was rather easy in the nineteenth century, a time when evangelical religion held cultural power. But in the twentieth century, particularly after the Fundamentalist-Modernist controversies of the 1920s, this required more of a conscious decision. As we will see, for most of the twentieth century the ABS made its peace with the Protestant mainline. This meant that it developed close connections not only with the Ecumenical Movement as embodied in the National Council of Churches, but with American presidents, businessmen, and celebrities who were associated with these historic denominations. Since the 1990s, as the power of mainline Protestantism to shape the culture waned, the ABS cast its lot again with evangelicalism.

Third, the American Bible Society has always been at the forefront of innovation, both in American Christianity and the nation as a whole. The ABS was and is cutting-edge. It was the first publisher in the United States to use steam-power presses. It quickly embraced Braille, talking Bibles, direct marketing, postage seals, music videos, and digital scripture products. The two Bible translations that it has produced—Today's English Version and the Contemporary English Version—were the first to apply the translation theory of "dynamic equivalence." This spirit of innovation continues today as the ABS staff seeks out new ways to get people engaged with the message of the scriptures.

Fourth, the American Bible Society has struggled over the years to define its organizational identity. Is the American Bible Society a benevolent society? A business? A ministry? A service organization? All of these questions have, at some point in the history of the ABS, been answered in the positive. Today it is a ministry. For most of the twentieth century it was service organization. In the early nineteenth century it was part of a national network of benevolent societies. Because it has always placed a premium on selling Bibles rather than giving them away, some have called it a business. If one follows closely the story that unfolds in these pages, it will be easy to see that the identity of the ABS is constantly evolving and has always been contested.

In the end, the history of the American Bible Society has been inseparable from the American experience. As an organization with leaders who always believed that they were presiding over a national institution, the ABS was present at nearly every significant moment in the history of the United States and many moments that were not significant. So now, with the preliminaries out of the way, let's explore American history as seen through the window of the Bible Cause.

The Bible Cause in America

In 1818, Elias Boudinot posed for a portrait to commemorate his role as the first president of the American Bible Society (ABS). The man who had two years earlier brought the ABS into existence by the sheer force of his will and the power of his reputation is pictured seated in a red upholstered chair with his right hand open, hovering over a copy of the Bible and what appears to be the Constitution of the ABS. His left hand clutches a cane, a reminder that he was seventy-eight years old and suffering from a severe case of gout at the time the portrait was painted. His illness, coupled with the usual maladies of old age, meant that he was unable to travel from his Burlington, New Jersey, home to New York City for the first meeting of the ABS in 1816. In fact, he probably spent most of his five-year term as president (1816–1821) in bed, attending a few annual meetings to encourage those working on behalf of the Bible Cause and to hear his presidential address read by another ABS officer. Samuel Lovett Waldo and William Jewett's larger-than-life portrait of Boudinot has hung in every New York City headquarters of the ABS after the organization moved into its first building on Nassau Street in 1821. Until 2015, visitors could find it in the first-floor boardroom of the ABS building at 1865 Broadway (just off of Columbus Circle), where it provided a sense of historical continuity to the staff as the ABS approached its 200th anniversary.

Though Boudinot's résumé does not hold a candle to that of George Washington, John Adams, Thomas Jefferson, or Benjamin Franklin, he was still an active participant in the creation of the early American republic. The ABS presidency was the final act in a career of public service that spanned nearly half a century. Boudinot was born in 1740 to a French Huguenot (French Protestant) father and Welsh mother. As a young man he studied law under the direction of Richard Stockton, a Princeton attorney, signer of the Declaration of Independence, and the father of his future wife, Hannah Stockton, whom he would marry in 1762. Boudinot settled with his bride in Elizabeth-Town, New Jersey. He opened a law practice and was elected to a seat in the New Jersey Provincial Assembly just in time for that body to overthrow Royal Governor

William Franklin in 1776 and declare New Jersey an independent state. As the Revolutionary War got underway, General George Washington appointed Boudinot Commissary General for Prisoners, a position that gave him the responsibility of both caring for British prisoners of war and interrogating them for intelligence that might help Washington predict the movement of the British Army.

In 1777, the same year he was appointed Prison Commissary, Boudinot was chosen to represent New Jersey in the Second Continental Congress. Five years later, as the war was coming to a close, he served a one-year term as president of the Continental Congress. The presidency was a largely ceremonial position, but Congress's choice of Boudinot shows the respect he had garnered from his fellow patriots. After the United States Constitution was ratified in 1789, Boudinot served New Jersey in the US House of Representatives. As a staunch supporter of the Washington administration and the growing Federalist faction surrounding the first president, he spent most of his time in Congress defending Treasury Secretary Alexander Hamilton's plan to put the nation on solid economic footing through the promotion of manufacturing and the creation of a National Bank. In 1795 George Washington called again. He appointed Boudinot director of the United States Mint, a post he held until his retirement from public life in 1805.[1]

Boudinot devoted the last twenty years of his life to writing religious tracts and supporting charitable causes. One of those causes was the New Jersey Bible Society, an organization that he helped to found in 1809. The New Jersey Bible Society was one of several new voluntary organizations that cropped up in the early nineteenth century for the purpose of distributing Bibles. Most of these societies were modeled after the British and Foreign Bible Society (BFBS). Founded in 1804, the BFBS brought British Protestants of all denominations together in the work of printing and distributing Bibles in the United Kingdom and around the world. The BFBS worked closely with satellite Bible societies, known as "auxiliaries," located on nearly every continent of the globe. It funded Bible distribution programs and translation efforts through monetary grants.

Boudinot was a logical choice to serve as the first president of the New Jersey Bible Society. He was a member of the revolutionary generation, had an unblemished political reputation, and always fused his political ambitions with a deep and abiding Christian faith. Boudinot was born in Philadelphia during the religious revival known as the First Great Awakening and was baptized by none other than the "Grand Itinerant" himself, George Whitefield. He was an active member of the Elizabeth-Town, New Jersey, Presbyterian Church during the patriotic pastorate of Rev. James Caldwell, the so-called fighting parson, and counted himself part of a larger circle of Presbyterian clergy and revolutionaries affiliated with the College of New Jersey at Princeton. Boudinot sat on the College's board of trustees and kept a regular correspondence with President John Witherspoon (the only clergyman to sign the Declaration of Independence) and the young men who studied religion and politics at Princeton under his care.[2]

Boudinot was no stranger to promoting the Bible in public life. On several occasions he used his pen to defend orthodox Protestantism against threats from "infidels," and was an avid student of Biblical prophecy. In 1801, fearful that heretics and unbelievers were infiltrating American society and influencing its youth, he published a book-length critique of Thomas Paine's *The Age of Reason*, which he perceived as an attack on traditional Christianity. Boudinot called his book *The Age of Revelation or The Age of Reason Shewn to be an Age of Infidelity*. He addressed it to his daughter Susan. "In short," Boudinot told his daughter, "were you to ask me to recommend the most valuable book in the world, I should fix on the Bible as the most instructive, both to the wise and the ignorant." In *The Age of Revelation* Boudinot defended traditional Christian doctrines such as the divine inspiration of the Bible, the virgin birth and deity of Christ, and Christ's or Jesus's resurrection from the dead.[3] The book never came close to the popularity of *The Age of Reason* and was largely forgotten, but it still reveals the depth of his theological acumen and his willingness to uphold the Christian character of the nation against intellectual threats from deists like Paine.[4] Boudinot's next two books focused on Biblical prophecy. In 1815 he published *The Second Advent*, a study of the Second Coming of Jesus Christ. After twenty-five years of studying the Bible, Boudinot concluded that Napoleon Bonaparte was probably the antichrist described in the Book of Revelation. He also suggested that the Second Coming was likely to occur before the dawn of the twentieth century. A year later Boudinot published *A Star in the West*. In 312 pages of dense biblical commentary and prophetic analysis of current events, Boudinot argued that Native Americans had descended from Jewish ancestry and were likely the ten lost tribes of Israel. He claimed that the book was the culmination of over forty years of research on the fate of the Jews during last days of the world.[5]

Boudinot's New Jersey Bible Society was not the first Bible Society in the United States. In the winter of 1808, a small number of Philadelphia religious and business leaders gathered to found the Philadelphia Bible Society. The group included Benjamin Rush, the famed Philadelphia doctor and signer of the Declaration of the Independence. Though the Philadelphia Bible Society was not an official auxiliary of the BFBS, it kept close ties with the London-based organization, called itself an "infant institution" of the BFBS, and accepted financial support from the London-based society. The BFBS considered the Philadelphia Bible Society an "emanation" of its work around the world.[6] Bishop William White, the rector of the nationally known St. Peter's and Christ Church and a former chaplain of the Continental Congress, was chosen as the first president of the Philadelphia Bible Society. The original vision of the Society was to publish Bibles without notes or commentary and distribute them, free of charge, to those in Philadelphia and the surrounding region who did not own a personal copy of the scriptures. News of the establishment of the Philadelphia Bible Society spread quickly up and down the east coast. Within a year of its creation similar Bible societies were founded in New York, Connecticut, Maine, and Massachusetts.

The first Bible societies were organized on the belief that there were a large number of people living in the United States who did not own a copy of the Christian scriptures, but would benefit from having access to the Bible. Most of these societies saw the Bible as a tool of evangelism. Their leaders believed that with the help of the Holy Spirit, any reader of the Bible could decipher its meaning and be transformed by its message. Most of the societies sold Bibles, but all of them, in cases of real need, offered Bibles to individuals free of charge. They also provided Bibles to charity schools, prisons, orphan asylums, hospitals, alms-houses, the United States military (especially during the War of 1812), churches, missionary societies, and Sunday schools. The work of distribution was conducted by volunteer agents—usually local ministers or devout laypersons—appointed by a given society's board of managers. Smaller Bible societies, such as the New Hampshire Bible Society, the Female Bible Society of Philadelphia, and the Bible Society of the District Columbia, distributed anywhere between 100 and 500 Bibles per year. The larger societies, such as the Philadelphia, New York, and Massachusetts Bible Societies, could distribute as many as three to five thousand Bibles annually.[7]

A few of the larger Bible societies had the financial resources to publish their own Bibles through the purchase of stereotype plates. These plates were made from plaster of Paris molds that enabled printers to print large works without having to reset the type every time they wanted to republish a volume. Plates were expensive, but they would pay off in the long run for societies that distributed a considerable number of Bibles each year because they allowed printers to keep the Bible in standing type.[8] Prior to the use of stereotype plates, Bible societies had to either export cheap Bibles from the BFBS or purchase expensive Bibles from printers in the United States. In 1812 the Philadelphia Bible Society purchased a set of plates from the BFBS at a cost of $3,500. The Baltimore Bible Society followed Philadelphia in the purchase of plates, but the New York Bible Society decided that plates were, at least for the moment, too expensive.[9]

Many of the early Bible societies in America distributed Bibles beyond their geographical bounds. For example, the Philadelphia Bible Society and the

New York Bible Society supplied a few hundred French Bibles to the settlers of the newly formed Louisiana territory. The Philadelphia Bible Society supplied Bibles to the destitute in Ohio, Illinois, Missouri, Indiana, and among the Highlander settlements around Fayetteville, North Carolina. The New York Bible Society donated funds to the BFBS to publish and translate Bibles for English missionary William Carey and his work in India. New York's board of managers imagined extending its society's influence across North America as well as to the thousands of sailors who moved in and out of New York harbor each year. Other local and state Bible societies funded Bible translation and distribution efforts in the West Indies, Canada, Smyrna, the Sandwich Islands, Cuba, and Mexico. As Protestant organizations, it was imperative that these Bible societies provide copies of the Bible in the native tongue. The number of non-English speakers in the early American republic was growing and the Bible societies tried to meet their spiritual needs by publishing Bibles in French, German, Dutch, and Spanish.[10]

As Bible societies began to cast their vision across the continent and around the world, it was only a matter of time before friends of the Bible Cause began to contemplate the creation of a national Bible society. One of the earliest proponents of such a society was Samuel J. Mills, a missionary with the Massachusetts Missionary Society. In 1812 Mills joined fellow missionary John Schermerhorn on a year-long tour through the southern and western portions of the United States. Their mission was evangelistic, but they were also charged with gaining information about the spiritual and moral state of the frontier. Schermerhorn gathered data about the religious and geographical climate of the places they visited—Virginia, Ohio, Indiana, Kentucky, Tennessee, Mississippi, Illinois, Missouri, and Louisiana. Mills was much more interested in the state of Bible ownership in these frontier areas and even helped establish local Bible societies along the way in Nashville, Tennessee, and Natchez, Mississippi.[11]

Following his trip, Mills proposed the creation of a national Bible society in a letter to Jedidiah Morse, the editor of *The Panoplist*, one of the prominent religious journals of the day. Morse published Mills's proposal in the October 1813 edition. Mills praised the work of local Bible societies, but said that the reach of these societies was disproportionate to the number of people living in the west who were destitute of Bibles. For example, Mills claimed that there were 40,000 to 50,000 French Catholics in Louisiana who did not own Bibles, but the Philadelphia Bible Society, the New York Bible Society, and the other large societies on the east coast did not have the financial resources to pull off such a distribution. (The Philadelphia Bible Society and New York Society were only sending a few thousand Bibles to Louisiana per year.) Soon, Mills predicted, the nation would expand into Spanish-speaking regions, creating an even greater demand for the Bible. State and local societies could purchase inexpensive Bibles from the BFBS, but they took too long to be shipped— sometimes up to six months. "As a Christian nation," Mills wrote, "we are not likely to labor at all according to our ability, for the relief of the needy in our own country and abroad, until we have some general bond of union." He proposed a national Bible society made up of Protestants of all denominations. It would be based in Philadelphia and its membership would include delegates from every state and local Bible society in the country.[12]

We do not know if Mills discussed his idea for the creation of a national Bible society with Elias Boudinot. It is likely, however, that Boudinot read Mills's letter in *The Panoplist*. This may have had been why the president of the New Jersey Bible Society was the first to make an official call for a national Bible society. In August 1814 the board of managers of the New Jersey Bible Society approved the founding of a society "for uniting the people of God, of all denominations, in the United States, in carrying on the great work of disseminating the Gospel of Jesus Christ throughout the inhabitable world." They called delegates from Bible societies all over the country to meet at a "central place to be agreed on." Boudinot published the New Jersey Bible Society resolution and sent it to Bible societies in each state of the union. His circular asked each society to send two delegates to Philadelphia on the Monday of the third week of May 1815 for the purpose of organizing a body that would be tentatively called the General Association of Bible Societies in the United States. The society would "disseminate the Scriptures of the Old and New Testament, according to the present approved edition, without note or comment, in places beyond the limits of the United States, or in them."[13]

Not everyone was thrilled about the establishment of a national Bible society. The Philadelphia Bible Society led the opposition. The board of managers did not think that a national organization could distribute Bibles any more effectively than the state societies. Local societies had a better understanding of the Bible needs of the people in a particular region. And if a national organization was little more than a configuration of local societies, then what was the point of having such a society to begin with? State Bible societies were more than competent at delivering the word of God to places outside of their geographical bounds. Moreover, the timing was not right for a national society. The country was in a "difficult economic state" in the wake of the recent war with England, and as a result Americans would not be willing to support new charities. The managers of the Philadelphia Bible Society also worried about competition between a new national organization and the state and local Bible societies that refused to join it. These kinds of "jealousies" would make the Bible Cause appear divided and "foolish" in the eyes of the world. In the end, the Philadelphia Bible Society thought that the state and local Bible societies were working just fine: "It is not hazardous then to touch the wheel that moves well, even though our benevolent intention be to accelerate its motion." These criticisms were included in a document circulated to Bible societies throughout the United States for the purpose of convincing them to ignore the New Jersey Bible Society's proposal.[14]

Shortly after the Philadelphia Bible Society published its formal objections to a national Bible society, Boudinot wrote a point-by-point rebuttal from the bed in the back room of his Burlington, New Jersey, home. He had been suffering from gout and was unsure how long he would live, telling his brother Elisha that "my powers of mind, appear to me to be fast failing, and I am warned thereby of the uncertainty of life and the certainty of Death."[15] Boudinot would have agreed with the words of an anonymous clergyman who published a similar essay in support of a national society: "The very fact of there being so many separate and independent societies is proof enough that they are individually weak; that no one can have the ability of extending its operations much beyond the limits of the district in which it is located." Using words that echoed the sentiments of those politicians (such as Boudinot) who also defended the United States Constitution, the clergyman added, "Can there be a union of the people for political purposes, and not one for those of a moral and religious nature?" After all, this was not a debate over the "ends" of "Bible work" in America, but how it should be carried out.[16]

In his response to the Philadelphia Bible Society, Boudinot referenced the BFBS. This was a national Bible society founded in the midst of a global war between England and France, and it appeared to have weathered these storms just fine. Boudinot called the BFBS the "most important human establishment Christianity had yet produced or the world has *ever seen*." It was a masterful ploy, since the managers of the Philadelphia Bible Society had long conceived of their organization as an extension of the BFBS. Boudinot also quoted Mills and Schemerhorne's estimation that over 200,000 Bibles were needed for "immediate distribution" in the Western states, an order that could only be handled by a national organization with a reach similar to the BFBS. When it came to the Philadelphia Bible Society's concern over the potential of animosity and disunity among the various Bible societies in the United States, Boudinot took the high road. The purpose of such a national society was to overcome such petty jealousies by forcing those involved in Bible distribution to "forget our differences and recognize our common relation to the same divine master and our common obligation to support His cause in the world." If the Philadelphia Bible Society did not want to join a national society, Boudinot hoped that its managers would, at the very least, allow the society to function without publicly opposing it. Boudinot compared the organization of a national Bible society to the creation of the First National Bank.

He was not only a staunch supporter of the bank from the floor of Congress in the early 1790s, but he also served on its board of directors for over twenty years. Boudinot reminded his critics that when the bank was first proposed it drew heavy criticism from those who did not think such a national economic institution would be effective. But over the course of time those critics of the bank turned out to be wrong. The First National Bank *was* a success, and Boudinot was now confident that a national Bible society would follow a similar pattern.[17]

Boudinot's rebuttal to the Philadelphia Bible Society convinced the managers of several state and local Bible societies to change its minds about uniting their efforts with other societies in the formation of a national organization. Other Bible societies, however, stayed with Philadelphia. It was the New York Bible Society and the Massachusetts Bible Society that provided the death blow to the New Jersey Bible Society's proposal. In response to Boudinot's circular letter, the managers of the New York Bible Society concluded that they "were not able to discover any advantages likely to result from the contemplated institution which could not be compassed by a more simple, expeditious, and less expansive process." The Massachusetts Bible Society managers claimed to be "strongly impressed with the weight and sufficiency" of the objections put forward by the Philadelphia Bible Society.[18]

Boudinot was angry with the way the leadership of the Philadelphia Bible Society expressed its opposition. He could understand differences of opinion—he had participated in some of the country's most intense political wars to date—but he could not tolerate the Philadelphia Bible Society's successful attempt "to interfere & endeavor to prejudice all the other societies & forestall their sentiments, against so important a measure for the spread of the gospel of the Son of God." He found such action to be "extremely wrong." Boudinot claimed that several Bible societies had offered him support privately, only to later reject his idea for a national Bible society after reading the Philadelphia circular.[19] As a good Christian and republican who sought to avoid division and schism, Boudinot remained silent, venting only to his close friends in the Bible Cause. He told Alexander Proudfit, the president of the Washington County Bible Society in Salem, New York, that he had heard from an unnamed source that the Philadelphia Bible Society's resistance to a national Bible society was "occasioned by a Jealousy of certain persons lest their influence should suffer, if such a measure should take place."[20]

Boudinot decided that he would not go forward with his plans for a national Bible society until twenty Bible societies agreed to send delegates to Philadelphia for his proposed May 1815 meeting. He estimated that thirteen or fourteen societies supported his proposal. Five or six more rejected the proposal. And another four or five supported the measure but did not have the financial resources to send delegates to a convention. Without the support of

Philadelphia, New York, and Massachusetts he had little chance but to render his proposal "abortive." As might be expected, Boudinot saw the providential hand of God in it all. He told Proudfit that the work of a national Bible society must come in God's timing, not his timing. For now he would "joyfully submit to his will," hoping that one day God would raise up a Solomon to build the "temple" that David was unable to erect.[21]

Just when it looked as if a national Bible society would not happen, Samuel Mills returned from a second missionary journey to the West. He once again traveled under the auspices of the Massachusetts Missionary Society, but he was joined by a new partner: Daniel Smith. Mills and Smith reported on the "flourishing" state of Bible Societies in Ohio. In St. Louis they estimated that at least 13,000 Bibles were needed in order to provide one for every family. Thirty thousand more Bibles were needed to do the same in Kentucky. They expressed similar demands in Tennessee, Indiana, Illinois, Mississippi, and Missouri. Mills and Smith described in much detail the depressed spiritual state of these areas. Not only did they lack Bibles; there were few religious books in the region and even fewer ministers. The need for French and Spanish Bibles in Louisiana and Mississippi had skyrocketed since Mills's last visit. Once again they concluded that the Philadelphia Bible Society and the New York Bible Society had made valiant efforts to meet these needs, but it was not enough. In July 1815 Mills was on the east coast speaking and consulting with the region's Bible societies and churches about the best way to meet the religious demands of the frontier. As he had done following his first missionary tour, Mills preached that the only way to effectively supply Bibles to the West was through the creation of a national Bible Society. He lamented that the "whole country," from "Lake Erie to the gulf of Mexico," is "as the valley of the shadow of death." He calculated that 76,000 families lacked Bibles. The efforts of state and local Bible societies were "scattered," "feeble," and "by no means adequate" to deal with this spiritual crisis. Several of Mills's and Smith's letters from the frontier, along with the summary of his missionary trip written for the Massachusetts Missionary Society, were published in Jedidiah Morse's *The Panoplist.*[22]

The work of Mills and Smith caught the attention of John Caldwell, the new secretary of the New York Bible Society. Caldwell was the son of James Caldwell, the fighting parson of the American Revolution and Boudinot's former pastor at the Elizabeth-Town, New Jersey, Presbyterian Church. Both of John's parents were killed during the course of war in New Jersey, presumably for their patriotic convictions. Boudinot gave an address at James Caldwell's funeral and cared for several of his children, including John. When John turned thirteen years of age, Boudinot sent him to France to study under the patronage of the Marquis de Lafayette. Shortly after the publication of the

Mills-Smith report in *The Panoplist*, Caldwell wrote a letter to Boudinot to tell him that he thought the board of managers of the New York Bible Society might be reconsidering the idea of a national Bible society. Caldwell was a supporter of a national Bible society and seems to have provided an answer to the Philadelphia Bible Society's objections that satisfied the members of the New York board. Sensing the time was right, Caldwell urged Boudinot to make a second call for a meeting to establish a national society. He even agreed to host the event in New York.[23]

With New York in his corner, Boudinot and the New Jersey Bible Society were ready to take Caldwell's advice and move forward with another call for a national Bible Society. On January 17, 1816, Boudinot issued a circular letter addressed to "THE SEVERAL BIBLE SOCIETIES IN THE UNITED STATES OF AMERICA." The missive included the New York Bible Society's resolution to unite behind the cause. Boudinot announced that a meeting would be held in New York City on May 11, 1816. He hoped to attend the meeting "should it please a merciful God to raise me from the bed of sickness to which I am now confined." Morse published Boudinot's circular letter in the February 1816 edition of *The Panoplist* with a note praising these new developments. Caldwell, who had just started a new religious journal the *Christian Herald*, published Boudinot's circular in its first issue.[24]

The Philadelphia Bible Society remained opposed to Boudinot's plan, but it was now not the only opponent of a national organization. John Henry Hobart, the Episcopal Bishop of New York, had founded the New York Bible and Common Prayer Book Society in 1809 as an organization narrowly focused on distributing the Bible and Prayer Book to New York Episcopalians. Hobart, like many High-Church Episcopalians of his stripe, was suspicious of benevolent efforts that ignored the theological and ecclesiastical differences between denominations. In April 1815 he issued a pastoral letter to the Episcopalians under his care expressing his disapproval of the entire national Bible society experiment. While Hobart taught that the Bible was a source of divine truth, it needed to be distributed and read alongside the Book of Common Prayer. He believed that the purpose of distributing the Bible was to create good Episcopalians. Hobart worried that the larger and stronger denominations— such as the Presbyterians—would eventually overwhelm the smaller groups. Episcopalians needed to look out for themselves.[25]

This time around, despite the opposition, most Bible societies rallied to Boudinot's cause. One of those supporters was William Jay, the recording secretary of the Westchester Auxiliary Bible Society in Westchester, New York, and the twenty-six-year-old son of John Jay. William Jay had never met Boudinot, but this did not stop him from writing to his father's friend a few weeks before the May meeting of delegates. Jay had composed his own defense of a national

Bible society and he asked Boudinot if he wanted to read a copy.[26] Upon receiving the letter Boudinot was ecstatic. His doctors had just given him permission to "set up in my bed" for "two or three hours a day" and he used part of that time "against medical advice" (apparently the green light from his doctor did not apply to writing) to respond to young Jay's proposal. Boudinot told Jay that he planned on publishing his essay, which eventually appeared in print as *A Memoir On the Subject of a General Bible Society for the United States of America By a Citizen of the State of New York*. Drawing on the missionary report of Mills and Smith, Jay believed that the need for Bibles in the United States was so great that the work of publication and distribution could not be confined to "Independent Bible Societies alone." Using the annual reports of several state and local Bible societies, he compared the number of Bibles that these societies distributed each year with the potential reach that a national society akin to the BFBS might have in the same geographic region As expected, he found the state and local societies wanting. These societies were not in a financial position to translate the Bible into non-English languages or support Bible distribution in foreign countries. Shortly after Boudinot published Jay's *Memoir*, John Caldwell began to publish excerpts in the *Christian Herald*.[27]

It now appeared that Boudinot's convention was going to happen. Caldwell tried to make every accommodation possible to convince Boudinot to come to New York, including having his wife prepare two beds for him in the first-floor "back parlour" of his New York City home.[28] But Boudinot's health problems were too great. Eight days before the meeting Boudinot announced that he would not attend. His gout was so severe that he was unable to stand. In a letter to Caldwell, Boudinot thanked him for offering a place to stay, but added that God had "thought it proper to put a sovereign Veto" on his "anxious endeavors to meet you." The meeting of delegates would have to go on without him. Joshua Wallace, an officer in the New Jersey Bible Society, would attend the conference in his place. Boudinot wrote a long letter to Wallace a few days before the convention to instruct him on everything from the best method of calling the group to order to the content of his opening remarks. The elder statesman of the Bible Cause in America was worried. There were still some Bible societies aligned with the Philadelphia Bible Society, and Bishop Hobart's criticism was growing stronger among New York Episcopalians.[29] The May meeting appeared to be the one and only chance of getting a national Bible society organized. "If we don't get this done now," Boudinot told Wallace, "it will be difficult to get everyone together again." He encouraged his proxy not to waste any time after calling the meeting to order. He was to propose the creation of a national Bible society as soon as possible before any naysayers arrived at the convention and muddied the waters.[30] As Boudinot prayed for a successful meeting, the supporters of a national Bible society packed their bags for New York.

2

The American Bible Society

The delegates began to arrive in New York City on Wednesday, May 8, gathering at 11:00 a.m. in the Consistory Room of the Dutch Reformed Church on Garden Street. The room was filled with some of the country's leading scholars, ministers, and Protestant laypersons. Nathaniel Taylor, one of the most influential New England theologians of his generation, represented the Connecticut Bible Society. Gardiner Spring, the pastor of the Brick Presbyterian Church in New York City and a theological opponent of Taylor, joined John Caldwell as a delegate from the New York Bible Society. Jedidiah Morse took a break from his duties as editor of *The Panoplist* and pastor of the First Congregational Church at Charlestown, Massachusetts, to attend the convention. Lyman Beecher traveled to New York City from Litchfield, Connecticut, presumably leaving young Henry Ward (age three) and Harriett (age two) at home. The Otsego County, New York Bible Society sent a twenty-seven-year-old writer named James Fennimore Cooper.[1]

Joshua Wallace, the New Jersey delegate replacing the bedridden Elias Boudinot, was chosen president of the convention. Beecher and Rev. J. B. Romeyn of the Dutch Reformed congregation in New York served as recording secretaries. Eliphalet Nott, the president of Union College in Schenectady, New York, opened the proceedings with an invocation as fifty-six delegates from Bible societies across the country prayed along silently. The group then traveled about half a mile north through New York City streets to the relatively new City Hall (it had been built in 1812) where a large room—delegate Samuel Bayard of New Jersey called it "one of the most commodious rooms of the City Hall"—awaited them.

Upon arrival, Wallace brought the group to order and, as Boudinot had instructed him, called for the creation of a "general Bible Institution" with a national scope. Debate was minimal. The delegates agreed unanimously with Wallace's proposal. Bayard, obviously enthused by the vote, slipped out of the room and scribbled a short letter to Boudinot (to be followed by a more extensive letter the following day) informing him that things were moving forward.

Meanwhile, a committee that included Nott, Beecher, Morse, and William Jay was appointed to write a constitution. The meeting adjourned with plans to reconvene on Saturday, May 11, at 11:00 a.m.[2]

The constitutional committee met at the New York home of John Mason and took a mere five hours to accomplish its work. By the afternoon of May 10, subcommittees were busy polishing the language of the new constitution and preparing a formal address to announce the creation of the American Bible Society. The members of these subcommittees worked well into the night, and by the morning of May 11 they walked triumphantly back to City Hall to present the constitution to the reconvened convention of delegates. A large crowd was waiting.[3] A group of New York Quakers had heard about the gathering in City Hall and arrived on Saturday morning to ask to be appointed delegates to the convention from the Society of Friends. Another attendee asked the delegates to invite New York's Roman Catholics to join the new society. Both requests were granted. Following the conclusion of these small items of business, the constitution was read aloud and the official formation of the American Bible Society was announced. Wallace called for the question: "Does this Convention determine that it is expedient to form a National Bible Society?" Those in attendance responded "Yea" with a "loud acclamation." He then asked if there was anyone present who disapproved of the measure. The room fell silent. The Constitution received unanimous approval. Samuel Mills, who was attending the convention as an observer, smiled with delight from his seat in the back of the room. His dream for a national Bible society had become a reality. Wallace would later write, "Tears of Joy and Exultation were the Expression of the General Sentiments." He added that the "Unanimity of Sentiment" and "Spirit of Christian Love & affection" displayed at the meeting was "almost miraculous."[4] Of course most of those who opposed the creation of such a national Bible society—such as New York Episcopal Bishop John Henry Hobart and the men of the Philadelphia Bible Society—were not present that day in New York.

The convention then turned to electing the first ABS Board of Managers. The ABS would be an organization of laymen. Those chosen were some of New York's most prominent businessmen, lawyers, and doctors. They were wealthy men with connections to the world of transatlantic trade. Most of them were selected for their philanthropic work and their involvement in the early nineteenth-century network of voluntary societies described by historians as the "benevolent empire." One of the members of the Board of Managers, Leonard Bleecker, was a Revolutionary War veteran and a former director of the Bank of Manhattan who served as treasurer of the Free School Society of New York, president of the New York Samaritan Society, and vice president of the American Tract Society. Matthew Clarkson was a war veteran, a merchant, and a politician. Like Bleecker, he served a stint as the president of the Bank of New York. Clarkson was also a trustee of the New York Free School, a charter member of the New York Humane Society, and president of the Board of Trustees of the New York Hospital. Henry Rutgers, whose family owned much of what today is New York's lower East side, was also elected to the ABS Board of Managers on May 11. After a brief career in politics Rutgers turned toward charity work. He was the president of the Free School Society of New York City, a benefactor of Queen's College in New Brunswick, New Jersey (later Rutgers University), and an underwriter of the publication of religious books, most notably Philip Doddridge's famous devotional tract *The Rise and Progress of Religion in the Soul of Man.*[5]

Finally, the convention elected officers. These were mostly ceremonial positions, and while some of the men appointed took their roles more seriously than others, they were all chosen for their moral character, commitment to the Bible Cause, and public reputation. As expected, Elias Boudinot was selected as the first president of the ABS. Twenty-three vice presidents were picked from among some of the nation's leading politicians. Eleven of the men who were chosen agreed to serve, including John Jay and former Federalist presidential candidate Charles Coatesworth Pickney. In the coming years John Quincy Adams, DeWitt Clinton, Rufus King, Marquis de Lafayette, and Francis Scott Key would be added to this list. The day-to-day work of the Society would be carried out by John Mason, who was appointed Corresponding Secretary for foreign affairs, and J. B. Romeyn, who was appointed to the same post for domestic affairs. Samuel Varick, a Revolutionary War confidant of George Washington and a former Mayor of New York City who would later be chosen as the third president of the ABS, took the position of treasurer. John Pintard, a New York businessman and philanthropist, agreed to serve as recording secretary and accountant.

The Constitution of the American Bible Society was drawn from the Constitution of the British and Foreign Bible Society (BFBS) in London and William Jay's proposed constitution was published as *A Memoir On the Subject of a General Bible Society for the United States of America.* With the War of 1812 just barely over, it might seem strange that a Bible society founded in the United States was modeled after a British institution, but the men gathered in New York in May 1816 believed that the work of distributing the Bible transcended political and military conflicts between nations. Moreover, most of the founders were Federalists. Elias Boudinot, John Jay, Charles Pinckney, Caleb Strong, John Cotton Smith, Eliphalet Nott, Rufus King, John Rice, Jedidiah Morse, and Samuel Bayard were all veterans of the political battles of the 1790s. They had been on the front lines defending the idea of a strong national government against the localism of their political rivals, the Jefferson Republicans.

Federalists were Anglophiles. They championed all things British, especially when it came to building national institutions. The fact that these men called for a national society to bring order and unity to the Bible Cause was not a surprise.[6]

The "sole object" of the American Bible Society was to "encourage the wider circulation" of the Bible "without note or comment" in the English version "now in common use." Anyone who read the Constitution knew that the phrase "version now in common use" was a reference to the Authorized Version, commonly called the King James Version. But the Constitution's reference to publishing Bibles "without note or comment" would be a point of discussion and debate for decades to come. ABS Bibles did not include commentary, study notes, or any kind of critical apparatus that might privilege the view of one denomination over others. The founders of the ABS understood denominational differences as one of the many "jealousies" or "factions" that could undermine the Bible Cause in America. As Peter Jay (brother of William and son of John) put it, "our object is to distribute the Holy Scriptures without note or comment. At this, no politician can be alarmed, no sectary can be reasonably jealous. We shall distribute no other book, we shall teach no disputed doctrine."[7]

The Constitution also required the ABS to purchase its own set of stereotype plates so that it could publish Bibles at cost and sell them to those who were "destitute" of the word of God. The BFBS helped get the ABS started on this front by loaning the Board of Managers a set of stereotype plates for a French translation of the Bible and an additional 1,000 printed sheets from its previous press runs.[8] The ABS would also purchase its own stereotype plates. Nearly all of them were housed in New York City, but a few were sent to the Kentucky Bible Society in the hopes that Lexington might become an outpost for publishing, storing, and distributing Bibles for frontier settlers.[9] The work of selling and distributing Bibles domestically would rest on local Bible societies, commonly known as auxiliaries. The ABS sold Bibles to its auxiliaries at discounted rates. The auxiliaries then distributed the Bibles throughout the regions under their care and agreed to turn over any surplus funds received through sales or donations to the parent society in New York. The auxiliaries could withdraw from the ABS at any time and their managers could spend their money as they saw fit, as long as they were donating surpluses to the ABS.[10] With the creation of the ABS, the Bible Cause in the United States was more centralized than it had been before, but it was not centralized to the point of taking power away from the auxiliaries. This arrangement, which gave authority to the national society and power on the ground to the local societies, was the plan that everyone involved in the Bible Cause was willing to endorse.

The founders of the American Bible Society were nationalists. We have already seen that many of them had strong ties to the Federalists, but even those who were not on the public stage during the politically tumultuous 1790s favored a strong national government over a republic in which power was invested locally. Older Federalists associated with the ABS, such as Boudinot and Jay, had opposed the decentralized nature of the Articles of Confederation in favor of a national constitution. They had supported Alexander Hamilton's plan for building and strengthening national institutions over the more states-centered focus of Thomas Jefferson and his followers. But by the end of the War of 1812 even the Jeffersonian Republicans had embraced a vision for the United States that was national in scope. They were known as National Republicans, and their agenda was represented best by President James Madison's Seventh Annual Message to Congress on December 5, 1815. Madison called for an expansion of the military, a reconstitution of the National Bank, tariffs to protect American manufacturing, a plan to strengthen the country's transportation infrastructure, and even a national university to be housed in the District of Columbia. This was an agenda that most of the founders of the American Bible Society—whether they were old Federalists, National Republicans or future members of the Whig Party—could embrace.[11]

As the United States began forging its national identity, the founders of the ABS were doing the same thing for the Bible Cause in America. The writers of the ABS Constitution stated that "concentrated action is powerful action." The creation of a national society was the only way to bring those working on behalf of the Bible Cause to a sense of "national feeling and concurrence." Auxiliaries would control distribution, but the American Bible Society would be the glue holding all of these state and local societies together. The work of Bible publishing and distribution would now transcend geographical limits.[12] But the founders of the ABS had grander visions than just uniting state and local Bible societies under one roof. They also believed that the ABS would make a contribution to the moral character of the United States and thus play a major role in the construction of an American national identity that went beyond the construction of roads, the passing of tariffs, the encouragement of manufacturing, and the renewal of a National Bank. It was imperative that the United States be unified as well around Protestantism and the social virtues that logically flowed from its teachings. Such a homogeneous nation would be made up of Christians who would at times sacrifice their individual rights for the greater good of the republic. For example, when the students at Hampden-Sydney College in Virginia formed a Bible society and collected fifty dollars for the cause, the Board of Managers of the ABS were pleased that these young men were "laying restraints on youthful indulgences and practicing self-denial" in this way. If more young men in America could participate in this kind of charitable giving, "we shall entertain good hopes concerning our Republic."[13] This understanding of a Protestant republic was utopian in

nature. If everyone had access to a Bible, "prejudice" and "narrowness of education" would be overwhelmed by a patriotic and unified spirit of self-sacrifice.
The word of God was the only way for the nation to heal itself of the wounds it
had suffered from decades of self-interested factionalism.[14]

On this point the ABS vision parted ways with one of the eighteenth
century's most well-formed statements on the relationship between self-
interest and national identity. In Federalist #10 (1788), James Madison, writing in defense of the US Constitution, argued that all human beings were
self-interested and were thus naturally prone to undermine national unity
through the forming of factions based on such self-interest. Since the causes
of faction could not be removed, the nation needed a strong central government to control them. For the founders of the ABS the selfishness inherent
within political factionalism was a theological problem, a manifestation of
the sin nature. They thought such sinful tendencies could be extracted from
the hearts of men and women through a supernatural work of the Spirit. Thus
rather than letting a thousand factions bloom (as long as one did not trump
the others) under the watchful eye of a strong national government, as
Madison argued in Federalist #10, the ABS founders believed that factions
could be eradicated entirely by exposing as many Americans as possible to
the teachings of the Bible. The success of American nationalism, which the
ABS founders understood in terms of a republican spirit of disinterested-
ness, depended on the word of God.[15]

The founders' belief that they were nation-builders was seen clearly in
1818 when the ABS Board of Managers asked the US Congress for an exemption from tariff duties on the foreign paper (purchased mostly from France)
used to publish Bibles and stereotype plates purchased abroad. In addition,
it requested a postage exemption for letters sent to and from ABS officers.[16]
Why would the ABS seek such an exemption? According to Samuel Bayard,
the author of the petition to Congress, the ABS was in the business of shaping the "national character." If the US government was serious about diffusing
knowledge that "informs the understanding" and "improves the heart," then it
would accept the ABS's request for this exemption. Bayard appealed to an 1813
case in which the US Congress excused a "vaccine institution" in Baltimore
from having to pay postage on flyers urging people to get vaccinated. Congress
stated that by sending the flyers the vaccination institution was serving the
public good and should thus receive free postage. Bayard argued that if a threat
to public health merited such an exemption, the "promotion of religion and
morals, and the consequent improvement of society, is no less important in a
national view." Similarly, if the United States was willing to invest large sums
of money in the creation of manufacturing jobs, then why not also show some
concern for the moral and spiritual needs of workers? Industrial jobs offered

"the bread that perishes," but the Bible provided the "Bread of Life." The government should be in the business of underwriting the promotion of Christian virtue.

Bayard even went so far as to argue that the small amount of revenue the government would lose by providing an exemption to the ABS paled in comparison to the eternal benefits one might receive from possessing a Bible. "Every dollar taken from these funds," Bayard wrote, "is taking a Bible from the poor." He also turned to American history. In George Washington's famous 1796 farewell address he referenced religion as one of the key components of a strong and happy republic. In the United States that George Washington envisioned, Bayard suggested, Congress should jump at the chance to aid in the publication and distribution of the Bible by granting the ABS an exemption from tariffs and postage duties.

Bayard ended his plea by interpreting the religion clauses of the First Amendment. The ABS's request for an exemption on tariffs and postage was not a violation of the First Amendment. The Amendment's disestablishment clause was designed to protect the United States against *an establishment of religion*. This meant that the Amendment forbade the existence of a state-sponsored church in the way that Catholicism was the established church in France or Anglicanism was the established church in England. Bayard concluded that this clause had never been meant to be applied to the publishing and circulation of the Bible. It was inconceivable that the framers of the Bill of Rights would reject such an exemption request from an organization responsible for the dissemination of the Bible when the principles of Christianity found in the scriptures were the "purest system of morals and duty that ever was prescribed to man." The First Amendment applied solely to the "union of ecclesiastical with civil power," which had the potential of leading to the "tyranny" of one denomination over others. And moreover, how could a voluntary society like the ABS, made up of members of several different denominations, be a threat to form a national religious establishment? Bayard took this argument even further. By imposing taxes on the importation of paper used to make Bibles, the government would be diminishing the number of Bibles published and disseminated throughout the country. Such a practice would, in essence, limit the "free exercise of religion" afforded to citizens under the First Amendment. If Congress was willing to fund chaplains for the Congress and the armed forces, then it must believe that the promotion of religion was important to the success of the republic. Then why not provide an exemption for the ABS?

In the end Congress never took up Bayard's petition (nor a similar petition from the Philadelphia Bible Society), but the very fact that the ABS made such a case sheds light on its understanding of the relationship between

Protestantism and the burgeoning American nationalism of the post–War of 1812 era. The ABS was confident that the US government could be swayed to see religion as an important contributor to the public good.[17] Though no one in the ABS would claim that America was a Protestant nation in a legal sense, it was certainly a Protestant nation—or on the way to becoming one—in a cultural sense. James Blythe of the Kentucky Bible Society captured this sentiment clearly when he told the American Bible Society that "the religion . . . of your Bible is the established religion of your country, established not by law, but written upon all your institutions, from the humblest court of justice to Congress Hall."[18]

The founders of the ABS believed that they were ushering in a new era of human history. In a speech before the sixth annual meeting, Peter Jay told a receptive audience that the Protestant Reformation had introduced civil and religious liberty into the world and dispelled the "empty forms" and "cloud of ignorance" that characterized the Catholic Middle Ages.[19] The Protestant Bible was translated into languages that could be read and freely interpreted by ordinary people without the aid of the Church. The right to read the Bible for oneself and draw one's own conclusions about its meaning was the essence of religious liberty. The Protestant Bible was present at the earliest settlement of the British colonies. The Pilgrims of Plymouth, the Puritans of the Massachusetts Bay, and the Quakers of Pennsylvania all built their societies on its teachings.[20] The founders of the American republic believed that the Bible taught principles of order and peace that would "strengthen the bands of society by its powerful influences on the social affections." The Bible was the source of the laws that kept the United States moral, and it was the means of restraining the passion-driven impulses of democracy that led to licentiousness.[21]

At the same time that the United States began to exert itself in the larger world through enhanced trade, a major victory over England in the War of 1812, and its self-proclaimed role as protector of the western hemisphere as exemplified in the Monroe Doctrine, the champions of the Bible Cause were exalting the nation's growing role as a beacon of Christianity to the rest of the world. George Griffin, a prominent New York lawyer, told the first annual meeting of the ABS that the world had "a right to expect, that the American nation would arise in majesty of its collected might, and unite itself with the other powers of Christendom in the holy confederacy for extending the empire of religion and civilization." Griffin concluded that "this auspicious era has now arrived."[22] Nine years later, James Kent, the recently retired chancellor of the State of New York, told those present at the ABS annual meeting that Providence had blessed the United States with "extraordinary prosperity," raising the country to an "exalted pitch of national glory." He claimed that the nation was "commanding the admiration of the world through its internal improvements and spirit of enterprise." Kent's words baptized American exceptionalism and imperialism with a dose of evangelical Protestantism. He believed that the Bible Cause was "attending a commanding attitude" at this point in human history. Its progress was "irresistible," its "success sure."[23]

The soaring optimism of the ABS founders existed alongside a sense of urgency driven by the belief that Jesus Christ could return at any moment. Peter Jay, for example, believed that a period of "millennial happiness on earth" was coming soon and would be "literally fulfilled" when the "knowledge of the Lord shall cover the earth, as the waters cover the sea."[24] His father John Jay, the second president of the ABS, never attended an annual meeting due to health concerns, but regularly used his yearly presidential addresses (read by another ABS officer in attendance) to expound upon the unique role that the Society would play in God's future plans. Jay knew that no one could predict the time of Christ's return, but he was confident that the Second Coming would be "preceded and denoted by appropriate and significant indications." One of the most important of these indications was the "conversion of the Gentiles" to Christianity. In his 1822 presidential address Jay referenced British missionaries in Africa and India working to convert the Gentiles to Christ. A year later he would apply the same argument to the "many savage nations" that were "hearing the gospel more than they ever have before." He saw the Protestant benevolent societies (such as the ABS) emerging from the spiritual hothouse of the Second Great Awakening as a sign that "the Redeemer is preparing to take possession of the great remainder of his heritage."[25]

Jay's millennial thought was slightly different than that of Elias Boudinot. While Jay saw the work of the American Bible Society as a means of ushering in the Second Coming and an impetus for the moral improvement of the world, Boudinot believed that the return of Jesus Christ was imminent and Protestants thus needed to offer the free gift of eternal life to as many people as possible before it happened. In an address to the New Jersey Bible Society he warned his hearers to be "watching and praying, with our lamps trimmed and burning" because "the bridegroom is coming" and his voice "is almost sounding in our ears."[26] God had a plan for the United States, but that plan was not yet clear. America's fate depended on how the country responded to God's revelation in the Bible. Because the United States was a Protestant nation it would not be punished as severely as the Catholic nations of Europe. In fact, these European nations had already suffered under the cruel reign of Napoleon. Boudinot compared the United States to two of the Asia Minor churches described in the third chapter of the Book of Revelation. If America stayed the course and remained obedient to God and his holy word, it would end up like the Church in Philadelphia. God praised the Philadelphia Church for its faithfulness to his teachings and promised to keep its members from "the hour of temptation." So far the United States was on the right track. But if America did not remain faithful to the teachings of the Bible it would end up like the Church of Laodicea, a congregation that had departed from God's principles and had "lost its first love." Because this church's piety was neither "cold nor hot," God announced that he would "spue thee out of my mouth."[27]

As Boudinot and the other ABS founders thought about their place in human history, they were convinced that between 1790 and 1815 the United States' relationship with God was in danger of moving from the privileged position of the Church of Philadelphia to the condemned status of the Church of Laodicea. In the decades following the American Revolution there were many public figures in the United States offering an alternative understanding of human history defined more by the secular progress of the Enlightenment than the millennial and providential progress of Protestantism. Once again, Thomas Jefferson and his followers were the villains. Following Jefferson's presidential victory over John Adams in 1800—a triumph that Jefferson called the "Revolution of 1800"—many Christians feared that the Virginian's unorthodox religious beliefs posed a threat to the Protestant consensus of the United States. The fear was a real one. Jefferson was a champion of the separation of church and state, he opposed the New England religious establishments that many Federalists believed brought moral order to society, and he personally rejected cherished Protestant doctrines such as the inspiration of the Bible, the deity of Jesus Christ, and the resurrection. Six years after the ABS was founded, Jefferson told his correspondent Thomas Cooper that "unitarianism . . . will, ere long, be the religion of the majority from north to south, I have no doubt."[28]

In addition to Jefferson, Thomas Paine posed a threat to the Protestant nation that the ABS founders hoped to build. Writing in *The Age of Revelation*, his response to Paine's *Age of Reason*, Boudinot was "mortified" to learn that Paine's published assault on Christianity was having an influence on young people and "unlearned citizens." He viewed Paine's ideas as a type of infection that was slowly eating away at the Protestant culture of the United States. The only antidote was the Bible. In the preface to *The Age of Revelation* Boudinot promised that he would do his part in "opposing the flood of infidelity that was deluging our land."[29] The course of history needed to be redirected away from what Spencer H. Cone, the pastor of the New York Baptist Church, described as "the age of Voltaire, and Hume, of Gibbon, and Paine."[30] As Jeremiah Day, the president of Yale College, put it in an address to the ABS, scientists of the Enlightenment age in America set out to uncover knowledge, but the Bible would reveal mysteries that could only be "unfolded to the enraptured view of the redeemed."[31] This was a better kind of progress—moral progress rooted in the teachings of the Christian scriptures.

On Monday, May 13, 1816, just two days before the ABS constitution was approved, about 1,000 New Yorkers, prompted by announcements made in churches across the city, gathered at City Hall to celebrate the creation of the American Bible Society. Jacob Radcliff, the mayor of New York City, presided over the event. J. B. Romeyn, the secretary for domestic correspondence, read the ABS Constitution. Eliphalet Nott, Peter Jay, and John Mason, among others, addressed the crowd.[32] Over the course of the next year 930 individuals would contribute to the work of the American Bible Society. Most of these supporters came (788) from New York, but word was spreading outside the city's bounds. Fifty-eight Bible societies from across the country were contributing to the cause, and forty-one of those societies formally aligned with the ABS as auxiliaries. The managers of these Bible Societies wrote with congratulatory remarks, pledging their support to the ABS and expressing delight over this new initiative to advance God's work in the United States. Congratulatory letters also arrived from the British and Foreign Bible Society and national Bible societies in Russia and Germany. The latter organization inadvertently sent its letter to William White in Philadelphia. Even God has a sense of humor.[33]

On June 5, 1816, about three weeks after the meeting of delegates in New York, Elias Boudinot accepted the presidency of the ABS. In his acceptance letter he expressed his conviction that the formation of the Society was a work of God "to accomplish his will on earth as it is in heaven." The letter was a final missive from a tiring servant of God and country who had just won his last great public victory. Though Boudinot would manage to attend several future annual meetings of the ABS, and would soon donate 4589 acres of land in Luzerne County, Pennsylvania to the Society and an additional $10,000 in the form of 100 shares of the Bank of America, his health was deteriorating.[34] In the spring of 1821 Ward Stafford, a newly appointed agent of the American Bible Society, visited Boudinot at his Burlington home before embarking on a Bible distribution tour of Delaware, Maryland, and Virginia. Stafford described the ABS president as "feeble," but he still managed to get Boudinot to sign a letter of introduction. The president could not sit up in bed or write his name. He probably dictated the letter to his daughter, Susan Bradford.[35] Boudinot died in October, but not before setting in motion what would become one of the largest and most influential Christian organizations in American history.

Toward a Christian Nation

In November 1822, the American Bible Society moved into its first permanent headquarters on 72 Nassau Street between Beekman and Ann Streets. (During its first six years of existence the ABS rented spaces throughout the city.) The new home of the ABS was located in a part of New York City experiencing a small renaissance. A dense collection of houses that the *New York Mirror* described as "very offensive to the eye" was about to give way to "several lofty and commodious edifices," transforming the neighborhood into an "animated and lively scene" attracting a "resort of busy throngs." The ABS building was located a few hundred feet north on Nassau, right next to Clinton Hall, a library and lecture hall built in 1830 by the New York Mercantile Library Association for the scientific and literary improvement of its members. When an ABS employee stepped out of the front door of the Bible House he or she could glance upward and see the steeple of the Brick Presbyterian Church. A short northeast walk past Clinton Hall led to the Chatham Street schoolhouse, the Brick Presbyterian graveyard, and a public park.[1]

The Nassau Street property had four floors and was large enough to accommodate offices for the ABS general agent, the recording and corresponding secretaries, and the treasurer. It contained a Bible library, a storage room for paper, and a depository that could hold 100,000 Bibles. The third and fourth floors of the building housed the Society's binding and printing operations, although the sound of presses was a constant annoyance to those occupying the offices below. The building was purchased partly through the financial support of ABS officers and members of the Board of Managers, including Elias Boudinot, Peter Jay, William Jay, Henry Rutgers, Arthur Tappan, Richard Varick, and Stephen Van Rensselaer.

In a few short years the ABS expanded its operations by purchasing two lots, located directly across the street from the Bible House, from Daniel Fanshaw, one of the New York City printers who handled the Society's work. All of the printing operations moved to a new building constructed on these lots, freeing up more space at 72 Nassau Street for the bindery. One can imagine some of the ABS's 200 employees crossing Nassau Street pushing wheelbarrows or pulling carts full of freshly printed and dried sheets from Fanshaw's shop that were ready to be stitched and bound. By 1829 the Society had one of the most productive printing outfits in the country. Fanshaw's building had twenty hand presses and eight Treadwell presses powered by a steam engine on the first floor. The Treadwell press was the newest and most efficient press in the industry. It did not require hand power to operate, did little damage to stereotype plates, and saved the Society money on paper and labor. With the acquisition of the new buildings and Fanshaw's equipment upgrades, the Board of Managers estimated that the ABS could now produce up to 600,000 Bibles per year.[2]

In its early years of operation the ABS sold three kinds of Bibles, available in calf or sheep bindings, printed on different grades of paper, and varying in price from $3.00 to 60 cents, depending on the quality of the paper. The ABS also sold two different kinds of New Testaments, bound in sheepskin and ranging in price from 35 cents to 22 cents. By the 1830s the Society added to its catalog at least nine additional English Bibles and Testaments in various shapes and sizes, including a popular pocket version. The Society also owned foreign-language stereotype plates, enabling it to print Bibles in French, Spanish, and German. The depository carried Bibles purchased from other printers in the United States and abroad, in Gaelic, Welsh, Dutch, Mohawk, Hawaiian, and Seneca.[3]

Once ABS Bibles were printed, stitched, and bound they were packed up, stamped with the familiar "A.B.S." monogram, and shipped to the local and state Bible societies responsible for their distribution. Without these auxiliaries the ABS would not have been able to carry out its mission. In 1849, thirty-three years after the founding of the ABS, the organization had 1,200 different auxiliaries scattered across the United States (compared to 350 auxiliaries in 1823). Auxiliaries purchased Bibles produced at the ABS headquarters in New York and sold them or gave them away free of charge in their districts. The money gained from sales and donations went toward day-to-day operations, but the auxiliaries were required to send any surplus money to Nassau Street. The financial support that the auxiliaries provided would enable the ABS headquarters to distribute Bibles overseas or directly to population groups— such as Native Americans or the blind—that were not represented by a specific auxiliary.[4]

The ABS owed much of its distribution success to a burgeoning American infrastructure. The construction of the Erie Canal and other canals reduced by months the time it took to send Bibles from New York to growing river and lake cities like Buffalo, Pittsburgh, Cleveland, and St. Louis. ABS packages traveled down the Ohio or Mississippi and along the tributaries extending from these mighty rivers. A representative from the Pittsburgh Bible Society described ABS packages as floating "messengers of salvation," making visits to the "huts of the poor and destitute" on the frontier.[5] Fitting with a nation committed to building itself through travel across rivers, lakes, and canals, the ABS and its auxiliaries often used water metaphors to describe the distribution process. The Bible traveled along "little streams" that flowed into the "mighty river" of the Christian nation that the ABS hoped to forge. The distribution of the Bible was like the opening of a great "flood gate" that poured through the "arid regions" of the country, serving as a "streamlet to water every plant." The managers of the Indiana Bible Society, using a passage from the Book of Ezekiel, described the process of distribution as "Holy Water" issued from the "Sanctuary" that "spread wide and flowed deep, and all things lived whereso-ever the waters came."[6] Both literally and figuratively, the ABS was using water to link remote and scattered settlements into a Bible nation.

Auxiliaries that received a package from the Bible House on Nassau Street were entrusted with religious, moral, and financial responsibilities. The work of bringing the Bible to those in need was not to be taken lightly. The ABS leadership believed that the Bible prepared individual souls for a personal relationship with God and an eternal resting place. But Bible distribution was also important for the betterment of *this* world. Its message, when applied in everyday life, could produce good citizens, improve the condition of fami-lies, inspire men and women to exercise their God-given rights and love their neighbors, curb vice and encourage virtue. "The character and the condition of the entire community," wrote the ABS Board of Managers, "depends in no small degree upon the manner in which our auxiliaries and friends perform the work of Bible distribution." If individuals ignored the "Oracles of God" entire communities—both local and national—would be "seriously affected for evil."[7]

Unlike other Christian organizations that sold books and tracts through retail bookstores, the domestic work of the ABS was conducted almost exclu-sively through its auxiliaries. Such a system enabled the Society to reach parts of the country with the Bible that did not have a bookstore or easy access to printed materials. Fitting with its commitment to printing the word of God "without note or comment," ABS Bibles did not include images, illustrations, or other curiosities. As a result they were the lowest-priced Bibles in the coun-try. Other printers and bookstores could not compete with the ABS. If they wanted a piece of the Bible market in America they would have to specialize in luxury Bibles filled with artwork, maps, and commentary.[8]

The auxiliaries fulfilled the mission of the ABS at the grassroots level. Every state in the Union had a Bible society and most states had smaller, more local, county and town-based auxiliaries known "branch societies." Volunteers working for these branch societies infiltrated the life of their towns and neigh-borhoods. For example, in order to be as effective as possible in the distribution of Bible, the Montgomery County Bible Society in Pennsylvania encouraged its branches to assign one or two managers to canvas local school districts and identify those who could read and those who could not. Since Bibles were lim-ited, it was essential that they be distributed only to those who would ben-efit from owning one. The Vermont Bible Society urged all of its members to imagine themselves as agents of the American Bible Society as they distrib-uted books in their communities. If they did not know someone in need of a Bible they could encourage neighbors to join the Society or donate to the Bible Cause. The Lancaster County (PA) Auxiliary Bible Society reminded its mem-bers to concentrate their efforts not on the "moral desolation of Africa," but on the "moral desolation of Lancaster"—the "spiritual wretchedness of hundreds within the reach of your daily walks."[9]

The auxiliary system was not perfect. At times it could be woefully inef-ficient. The ABS officers were always complaining about the failure of auxilia-ries to hold regular meetings, pay for the Bibles that they ordered, or provide the ABS with its surplus revenue. In 1828 the Board of Managers, anxious about the rising cost of paper, printing, and binding, claimed that the auxilia-ries owed the Society over $50,000. "What is to be done?," the managers asked. "Shall some of the *thirty* presses stop? . . . Shall Auxiliaries send for Bibles to supply the destitute around them, and be told that they cannot be supplied with these sacred messages?" The auxiliaries needed to step up and fulfill their duties. In 1836, ABS Corresponding Secretary John Bingham visited auxilia-ries in the Midwest and wrote several letters back to Nassau Street complain-ing about the "apathy" in Bible distribution that he encountered along the way. Some auxiliaries did not have local depositories, and others had ordered pack-ages of books that, for whatever reason, had been sitting unopened for years. Bingham urged auxiliaries to make sure that every village had a good stock of Bibles available to the public, preferably housed in an accessible location "indi-cated by a sign of BIBLE DEPOSITORY."[10]

Bibles were not the only printed materials produced at 72 Nassau Street. The Society's *Annual Report* was published and distributed to auxiliaries around the country. In 1818 the ABS began to publish the *Extracts from the Correspondence of the American Bible Society*, a periodical that included let-ters from Bible societies around the world and reports from auxiliaries. The *Extracts* would eventually become the *Bible Society Record* and serve as the organization's official publication. The ABS understood the *Annual Report* and the *Extracts* (and later the *Record*) as important tools for building its organization and enlisting men and women in the Bible Cause. The appen-dix of the *Annual Report* presented, in the words of Bingham, "a somewhat comprehensive view of the state and progress of this cause in all countries." He thought that auxiliaries could do a much better job of circulating the *Annual Report* so that more clergy would read it and unite with "what the great Author of the Bible" was doing to extend his "blessing over the world."[11] At the heart of the ABS publications were stories about the way God was working in the nation and the world through the distribution of the Bible. These stories and reports prompted Christians around the country to imagine themselves as part of the larger Bible Cause. The secretary of the Bible society in Harrison County, Kentucky, put it best when he wrote: "Though buried deep in the western world, and by that fact cut off from a knowledge of much that is doing in the Bible cause, yet we are rejoiced to hear, by the . . . *Extracts*, what exertions are making to spread the knowledge of God, and his salvation, among the inhabitants of our fallen world." He concluded that "our feelings and our judgments are more than ever enlisted in the work."[12]

The stories that filled the pages of the *Annual Report* and the *Extracts* were meant to encourage the faithful with sensational accounts of the struggles faced in Bible distribution. Though the water continued to flow, and local communities—in a literal and imagined sense—were integrated into the Christian nation that the ABS was attempting to build, some of the more remote corners of the country, where bridges were yet to be built, roads were rough and muddy, and rivers and streams froze during the winter, were still difficult to reach with the word of God. Not everyone in the United States had access to the growing transportation infrastructure, yet it was essential— for individual souls and for the good of the nation—that those who dwelt in these remote outposts were not left behind. Daniel Bushnell, who distributed Bibles in southern Ohio, regularly departed from the roads and turnpikes and occasionally climbed fences and traversed corn fields "at the cost of considerable time" to bring Bibles to families living in the "dark corners." John Young, another ABS agent, brought Bibles to the inhabitants of fifteen islands off the coast of Maine. His work required him to cross small bays and harbors and walk along blind meandering paths "over rocks and ledges, abounding with hill and dale."[13]

Though most of this difficult distribution work was performed by volunteers affiliated with auxiliaries, the ABS occasionally appointed its own agents. These agents visited auxiliaries, encouraged them in their work, and started Bible societies in areas where they had yet to be formed. The members of the auxiliaries usually welcomed these agents, but they were also occasionally concerned that agents from the east coast would not adapt well to local conditions. Those laboring on behalf of the Bible Cause in Texas were very specific about the kind of skills and talents an agent needed to be successful in their state:

He should be a man who can sleep under a tree, or in a log cabin, without door, floor, or windows, upon a mattress without feathers, and with scanty clothing, who can make himself at home in any family, eat dodger and drink cold water or strong coffee without milk, as well as all kinds of animal food, and not find fault if it is not got up (as we Yankees call it) in as good style as he would like it. He must be emphatically a working man, for a lazy minister or agent would do but little among that people. The great body of them are not religious, and have apparently only an external regard for Christianity, and a man from the American Bible Society, or any other benevolent Society who should go among them professedly to do them good, and exhibit marks of indolence, would be greatly detrimental to the cause of Christ in that nation. He must be courageous. Not afraid to brave storms, nor to swim rivers and creeks when necessary.[14]

P. M. Ozanne, an agent for the South-Western Bible Society in New Orleans, working in the Gulf Coast parish of Lafourche, was charged with distributing Bibles in the Louisiana bayou. He spent his hot and breezeless summer days paddling up the narrow waterways in a small canoe delivering Bibles to Indian and white families in French-speaking settlements. On one particular journey in the summer of 1860 he was forced to leave his canoe, hide it for safekeeping, and walk three miles in the woods along a narrow cow trail with weeds growing as high as five or six feet. Ozanne must have been a sight to see as he moved through the damp bayou wilderness with a bundle of books under one arm and the other arm clearing the weeds and driving off the mosquitos and flies. His travail was worth it. Ozanne eventually encountered two men who could read. He sold them a Bible and a Testament and invited them to attend Protestant services the following Sunday. For the American Bible Society, every soul was important.[15]

The *Extracts* also relayed stories of generous giving. The editors did not miss opportunities to tell heartwarming stories of ordinary people, without wealth or status, who gave money to support the Bible Cause. A "poor old man" from New Hampshire stopped a local agent on the street, called him to his door, and donated twenty cents. A young girl gave five cents to the Society and told the agent that "she would rather give it to the Bible Society than spend it for trifles." An elderly woman had no money, but she "had a desire to promote the good cause" so she "cheerfully" donated a bunch of thread to the ABS. An agent from New Hampshire arrived at a house and met a young boy, with his money in hand, ready to purchase a Bible. Upon entering the house the boy's five brothers were also waiting to purchase a Bible with money that they had saved. When the youngest child in the house, a three-year-old boy, begged his mother to buy him a Bible like the books just purchased by his older siblings, she told him that she had no money to buy him one. The boy responded with a small tantrum, pleading and crying until his brothers and sisters pooled their money and came up with nine cents to buy him a copy of his own.[16]

Even as agents covered difficult landscapes on behalf of the ABS and its auxiliaries, and men, women, and children made financial sacrifices to support its mission, enemies to the Bible Cause were still out there, and they needed to be challenged. With this in mind, the editors of the *Extracts* and the secretaries of the auxiliaries who wrote annual reports and letters to the parent society in New York, could not resist a good story describing the triumphant (always triumphant) encounter of a Bible agent with the rare "infidel" or "atheist" who was prone to "use Tom Paine" for a Bible and preferred the *Age of Reason* over the word of God.[17]

One such story came from J. J. Hughes, the ABS agent in Alabama. As he traveled through Walker, Tuscaloosa, Marion, and Fayette counties, Hughes visited thousands of some of the nation's poorest white families. Though he had worked in Alabama for over two years, he was still a curiosity to the people of the territory. One day, while local residents were enjoying themselves at a log-rolling, the subject of this "queer stranger" arose. Who was this man "going from house to house, giving the old folks books, talking to them about their souls, praying with them, and catechizing their children?" One log roller, with a reputation for violence, was not happy with Hughes's presence in the region and made a threat on his life. When Hughes got wind of the threat he was intent upon visiting the man in his home. Alabamians who were sympathetic to Hughes's mission begged him not to go. One woman even tried to stop him from getting on his horse. But Hughes was determined. He responded that "the Lamb, in meekness, was more powerful, than the Lion in a rage."

After a few miles of riding through some mountainous terrain Hughes arrived at the house of his nemesis. It was rainy and cold and Hughes was wet from his difficult journey. When the man opened the door Hughes admitted that "I hardly ever had such a conflict between fear and duty." As the agent shivered, the man lorded over him, "pale and tremulous with rage." In a brief moment of courage, Hughes asked if he could warm himself by the fire. The man "gruffly" granted his request. As Hughes dried off, the man's wife appeared with some breakfast. In a gesture of hospitality that surprised the Bible agent, the man asked Hughes to stay for the meal. When Hughes asked the family if he could pray a blessing before they began to eat, the man responded, "if you think it will do any good." As they ate their venison the conversation turned toward Hughes's mission. The man was adamant that he did not want a Bible. He and his family had "gotten along very well, so far, without one, and could do so still." While they were talking "some fine healthful looking boys" entered the room. Hughes seized the moment, asking the man if his sons could read. When Hughes learned that they were indeed literate, he offered to give the boys a copy of the Bible. The man did not stop him. Hughes then read a chapter from the Bible and said a prayer for the family.

It was as this point in the visit that everything changed. As Hughes prayed the man's eyes flooded with tears. His wife began sobbing aloud and the boys all started to cry. The man asked Hughes if he was planning to preach the next Sunday at the local church. He said he would like to attend. The man eventually did go to the service and wept through the entirety of Hughes's sermon. The next week he followed Hughes eighteen miles to hear him preach at a church in a neighboring town. When Hughes met the man on the road to the town he was a "picture of sadness and horror." He had a Bible under his arm and his face was swollen from crying. "Oh my dear friend," he said to Hughes, "I never wanted to see any man half as much as I want to see you." The man had spent several sleepless nights reading the Bible and, for the first time in his life, had led his family in prayer. He told Hughes that when he first heard about his presence in the region "I was fully determined to whip you," but he now thanked God that he had encountered the ABS agent. He had "never saw a man I loved so much."[18]

Several auxiliaries, with the full support of the ABS headquarters in New York, targeted special groups—such as Native Americans and mariners—that did not naturally fall under the state and local geographical bounds of the traditional auxiliaries. For example, the ABS provided Bibles to missionaries involved in work among Native Americans (the Board of Managers often referred to them as "our brethren of the woods") and the auxiliaries that these missionaries formed in the course of their labors. In 1817 the ABS distributed a Delaware translation of the Epistles of John made by a Moravian missionary.[19] In the 1820s the ABS gave 500 copies of the Gospel of Luke in Mohawk and 750 in Seneca to Indian missionaries for distribution among these groups. In 1839 the ABS printed Dakota translations of the Gospel of Mark and in 1842 translations of several other New Testament and Old Testament books were given to missionaries at the Lac qui Parle Mission in present-day Minnesota. S. R. Riggs, a missionary at Lac qui Parle, encouraged the Dakota Indians to make and sell moccasins to raise money so that ABS Bibles could be distributed among Indian groups that were "poorer than the Dakotas."[20] Despite these efforts, the ABS outreach to Native American groups was never strong in the early nineteenth century. The Board of Managers was convinced that the Bible needed to be distributed among the natives as a means of civilizing and Christianizing them, but many missionaries presiding over the auxiliaries formed among Indian tribes and nations believed that the best way to reach Indians with the word of God was to teach them to read English rather than to translate the Bible into their native tongues. As was specified in its Constitution, the ABS often deferred to the missionaries and auxiliaries to make these local decisions.[21]

ABS auxiliaries also reached out directly to the seamen and mariners working on ships and on the docks in major port cities. These men were notorious for vice, irreligion, and congregating together in urban areas where they gambled, visited prostitutes, and drank their fair share of alcohol.[22] Marine Bible societies were formed throughout the country to provide them with Bibles in the hopes that they would turn their lives to God through evangelical conversion. The merchants who funded these efforts were also aware that a sober, industrious, and Christian sailor made for a better employee. The Board of Managers of the Portland Marine Bible Society in Portland, Maine, was convinced that the Bible "counteracts all tendencies to intemperance, to theft, to desertion, to perjury, to mutiny, to piracy, and to murder."[23] The New York Marine Bible Society, a branch society of the New York Bible Society, was the largest and most influential of these mariner societies. It had its own book depository supplied with Bibles printed in multiple languages. Sailors would come to the depositories before or after long voyages to obtain a copy of the Bible and purchase other religious reading materials.[24] Some seamen found comfort in the Bible, often memorizing passages during voyages. It was common for sailors to return to port desperate to replace a Bible lost at sea. In one instance, a sailor on a brig leaving New York accidentally dropped his Testament overboard. According to L. P. Hubbard, the Bible agent of the New York Marine Bible Society, he and his shipmates nearly fell into the harbor in an attempt to recover the lost Bible. "Perceiving that they were hazarding their lives, the tide being very strong," Hubbard wrote, "I advised them to desist, but to no purpose, for they seemed determined to have it, and at last brought it up, much to their gratification, not so much for pecuniary values as because it was the word of God."[25]

As the Founding Fathers faded off the scene in the early nineteenth century, the next generation of American nation-builders set out to connect a growing number of disparate states, territories, and frontier settlements into a unified country. They accomplished this task in a variety of ways. Improvers built roads, bridges, and canals to enhance trade and link isolated places into a national community of markets and consumption. Print connected the patriotic celebrations of local towns and villages to similar festivities occurring hundreds of miles away. Soon a common affection for the nation—one that transcended state or local concerns—began to emerge in the ever-expanding United States. The American Bible Society was an active participant in this process of nation-building. The Society utilized transportation improvements to distribute Bibles throughout the nation.

It used print to connect rural and remote places to the Bible Cause. And it cultivated among thousands of Americans an emotional and imagined connection to the larger political entity known as the United States. But there was something different about the kind of nation-building promoted by the American Bible Society. The Board of Managers, the ABS officers, the leadership of state and local auxiliaries, and anyone else committed to the Bible Cause, worked and prayed for a nation that was decidedly Christian in character. Their approach was at the very center of nation-building efforts in the years between the War of 1812 and the Civil War. Only by understanding this Christian nationalist mission can we make sense of why the ABS, in 1829, was prepared to undertake the most ambitious project in American religious history to date. We now turn to that story.

4

A Bible for Every American Family

On February 4, 1829, Alexander Proudfit, the fifty-nine-year-old minister at the Associate Reformed Presbyterian Church in Salem, New York, and an officer in the Washington County, New York Bible Society, wrote a letter to 72 Nassau Street proposing that the ABS undertake the bold and ambitious plan of providing a Bible to every family in the United States. The magnitude of such a benevolent effort was probably mind-boggling for some of the members of the ABS Board of Managers and staff, but Proudfit was confident it could be done. He and his colleagues had just supplied a Bible to every family in Washington County, so why couldn't every auxiliary in the nation follow suit? It was time, Proudfit wrote, for a "more expanded view" to be set in motion. He urged the Board of Managers to consider this "mighty and magnificent project" at its next meeting. In the meantime, the members of the Washington County Bible Society agreed to raise $5,000—an extraordinary sum for a small benevolent society—to get the effort started. A Bible in the home of every US family would bring "light" to "perishing thousands," "prosperity to our highly favoured nation," and "perpetuity to our civil institutions."[1]

The ABS treated Proudfit's letter as more than just an outrageous request from a "remote Auxiliary" in the woods of upstate New York. Proudfit was a founder. He was present at City Hall on May 11, 1816, when the ABS was organized, and he had a national reputation for his work as an Indian missionary and a supporter of theological education.[2] Proudfit's letter also came at a time when several ABS auxiliaries were making distribution efforts similar to the one recently concluded in Washington County. In May 1825, the Monroe County, New York, Bible Society sent volunteers, with "roll and inkhorn in hand," to every house in the county for the purpose of identifying those families without a Bible. After the data was collected the Society's volunteers took to the road, Bibles in hand. Within a year, 1,200 families had a Bible that did not have one before.[3] The members of the Nassau-Hall Bible Society, mostly students at the College of New Jersey at Princeton, resolved to supply a Bible to every family in the state of New Jersey and do it in one year. Within weeks the boys from Nassau Hall had the support of branch auxiliaries in Hunterdon, Somerset, Monmouth, and Sussex counties. Like the promoters of the Bible Cause in Monroe County, the goal was to visit every family in New Jersey, ascertain the number of people in each family who could read, create a list of those families without a Bible, and provide them and any "adult individuals" with a copy of the holy book. When the story of the dedicated students at Princeton was published in the *Extracts* it "stirred up" other auxiliaries to follow their example. Twenty-seven other auxiliary and branch societies—from Maine to Illinois—would announce similar plans.[4]

The ABS Board of Managers considered the proposal from the Washington County Bible Society on April 2, 1829, and agreed to make a final decision later in the month. In the meantime, in order to see if such a project was feasible, it made a thorough assessment of the Society's financial state, examined the efficiency of its printing operation, and consulted with prominent clergy and laypersons who had a vested interest in the Bible Cause. The board concluded that if the ABS was to carry out Proudfit's plan it would need more space. When two lots became available on Nassau Street adjacent to the Bible House the board assigned one of its members, Arthur Tappan, the noted businessman, philanthropist, and abolitionist, to help them with the purchase. Tappan agreed to offer the current occupants of the lot $1,000 in exchange for the surrender of their lease, but he had one caveat: He would only help the ABS with its land deal if the board adopted Proudfit's resolution. And if the ABS did indeed decide to supply every family in the United States with a Bible, Tappan would donate an additional $5,000 toward the cause.[5] One week later, at another meeting of the Board of Managers, the "highly interesting communication of the Washington County Bible Society" was adopted. The ABS would call the project "the General Supply," and it would begin "immediately."[6] A formal announcement was made through a circular pamphlet sent to ten thousand ABS supporters of the Bible Cause, including members of the clergy and all the Society's auxiliaries.[7]

The Gospel was advancing in the United States and the General Supply was one way that the ABS could contribute to its progress. Milnor, in a long address following the passing of the official resolution, suggested that if the ABS had proposed such a nationwide distribution even two years earlier, the Society "would have been smiled at as Utopians." But now, due to the "rapidly progressive march of Christian enterprise," such an effort was in the realm of possibility. The General Supply would be part of the unfolding drama of Christian history. It would be the "grandest memorial of the triumph of Christian faith and effort which the annals of the Church in this age of exertion, shall record." The fact that so many auxiliaries had already attempted to supply the inhabitants in their vicinity with Bibles was proof that the work of God in redeeming the world and Christianizing America was making significant strides. Milnor estimated that 800,000 American families did not own a Bible. Could such a spiritual lacuna be remedied? The ABS was up to the task.[8]

Of particular concern to the ABS were the families in the newly developing western territories. Most of the eastern auxiliaries had either already supplied every family with a Bible or were well on their way toward achieving this goal, but the Bible Cause in the west needed help. The ABS, as we have seen, was born out of a concern for the West. The General Supply was merely an extension of Samuel Mills's original vision for a national Bible society. The Board of Managers portrayed the West as a barren place, void of the word of God. The vast "multitudes" of settlers moving westward during the 1820s and 1830s did not have the "invaluable privileges" of schools and churches. "Public worship" was virtually "unknown," and children grew up without an understanding of basic morality. The ABS had a moral and Christian duty to bring Bibles to these God-forsaken places, whether the settlers wanted the book or not. This, according to the Board of Managers, was an "incalculable moment in the National welfare." The "stability of our free Government and our civil privileges" rested upon providing Bibles to western settlers. The Bible was the source of the "virtue and intelligence" necessary for the United States to survive.[9]

The success of the General Supply would also be contingent upon the ABS's ability to produce enough Bibles to distribute to the estimated 800,000 souls who needed the word of God and its message. The printing of these Bibles would fall upon Daniel Fanshaw, the strong backs of his team of printers and laborers, and the Treadwell steam power presses recently installed in the new shop across the street from 72 Nassau Street. Shortly after Fanshaw moved into the building in 1828, the Board of Managers doubled the number of Treadwell presses (from four to eight). And now that the General Supply was underway eight more Treadwells were ordered, scheduled to be delivered sometime in the summer of 1829. At the time that the General Supply was announced, the ABS depository had 200,000 Bibles and Testaments. These books were "seasoned and dry" and ready for delivery to the auxiliaries. With the arrival of the additional Treadwell presses, Secretary James Milnor estimated that the ABS could produce 500,000 to 600,000 Bibles per year. And once the ABS built two new buildings on Arthur Tappan's lots on Nassau Street, the number of Bibles produced each year would reach the 800,000 mark.[10]

The equipment and the labor were in place to get the General Supply started, but a distribution project of this magnitude had never been tried and the members of the Board of Managers knew that in order to sustain it they would need additional support from the auxiliaries. It was now time for the nearly 700 ABS auxiliaries to get their affairs in order. The General Supply would be a grassroots effort—every auxiliary need to do its part. Outstanding debts to the ABS needed to be paid and each auxiliary was asked to make a renewed commitment to the distribution of the Bible in their regions and neighborhoods. For some auxiliaries, this might require hiring agents to carry out the work. The ABS encouraged the auxiliaries to seek out members of the clergy, students at theological seminaries and colleges, and pious laymen who could work at little expense to serve as temporary distributors during the General Supply. In addition, the ABS Board of Managers urged the auxiliaries to raise money for the production costs in New York. Many state and local Bible societies accepted the challenge. Letter after letter rolled into the Bible House from auxiliaries eager to join the work of the General Supply.[11]

The ABS provided the auxiliaries with instructions detailing the most effective way to distribute the Bible in their locales. In an 1830 article in the *Extracts* titled "How to Supply a County with Bibles," the ABS suggested a multi-step approach. The first step was to call the auxiliary society together for a meeting. While this might seem obvious, the ABS had been dealing with auxiliaries for about fifteen years and the Board of Managers knew that the mere existence of a state or local Bible society was no guarantee that its members gathered on a regular basis. If a county did not have an auxiliary, it was the duty of those in the area who were sympathetic to the Bible Cause to form one. Once a meeting was called or a Bible society founded, the ABS encouraged those present to divide their particular county or region into districts and appoint two "thorough men" to each district to "ascertain the number of destitute families." Two or three weeks after the original meeting, the auxiliary should call another meeting to let the district committees report on their progress. Once the number of people without Bibles was known, the auxiliary should collect money and immediately order Bibles from 72 Nassau Street. (If the auxiliary did not have enough money to purchase the Bibles its board should ask the ABS for a line of credit.) Finally, once the Bibles arrived, the committee should give one to every destitute person. If every auxiliary followed these guidelines the General Supply would be a success. As we will see, this was easier said than done.[12]

The General Supply clock began ticking in May 1829. Eight hundred thousand Bibles. Two years. If the influx of letters in the months following the announcement of the General Supply is any indication, the project was off to a good start. Auxiliary after auxiliary reported that they were on board with this massive effort.[13] The Seneca County, New York Bible Society committed to raising $1,000 for the cause. The Pittsburgh Bible Society pledged $300; the Newburg, Massachusetts Bible Society $600; Schenectedy County, New York Bible Society $1,000; and the Dutchess County, New York Bible Society offered to raise $5,000. Other auxiliaries shared their needs and requested

Bibles. The Bloomington, Indiana Bible Society had 175 "destitute." Half of the families in the vicinity of the Hamilton, Illinois Bible Society were without Bibles. The Petersburg, Virginia Bible Society asked the ABS for 2,000 Bibles to meet its need. The staff at 72 Nassau Street worked frantically to fulfill these orders, no matter the size. Within the first months of the General Supply a pattern was beginning to emerge. Long-established states, counties, and communities—many of which had either already supplied their region or were close to finishing—tended to give donations to the ABS, while auxiliaries on the frontier settlements in the west and southwest requested Bibles.[14] The General Supply had lit a fire under these state and local auxiliaries and the excitement for the cause was palpable. Gifts poured into New York. The ABS staff was energized and motivated. In the summer of 1829, fifty-two New York employees of the ABS, most of them print shop and bindery laborers, pooled their money and made a forty-six dollar donation to the cause. Gifts also came from unexpected places. Four young boys in New York each donated seventy-five cents. A clergyman agreed to set aside all of the money he received from marriage fees, funerals, and baptisms until he raised fifty dollars for the General Supply. A woman from Franklin County, Massachusetts donated a string of gold beads (worth about two dollars) and another "young lady" from Columbia County, New York, gave a gold ring valued by the ABS at about fifty cents.[15] Every little bit helped.

In addition to the ongoing news of donations and renewed commitments from the auxiliaries, reports from the field of distribution were essential to measuring the progress of the General Supply. These reports arrived from the boards of local auxiliaries and from special agents appointed by the ABS to aid in the promotion of the General Supply. These agents were usually sent to regions of the United States in which the Bible Cause needed help due to the limited number of inhabitants or the lack of auxiliaries. For example, the Mississippi Bible Society was eager to participate in the General Supply, but its organization consisted of only a few individuals living in and near the city of Natchez. The state did have a few county and branch societies, but they were either too small or too inactive. Distribution to the distant and remote parts of the state was impossible without outside help.[16] The ABS already had seven such agents under its employ at the time the General Supply was announced, but more were needed. If the applications received by the ABS for new agents are any indication, there were many clergy and theology students who were desirous of becoming ABS agents during the General Supply. In the years between 1829 and 1831 the ABS received at least thirty-one such applications. Those applying believed that something big, something historic, something providential, was happening in the ongoing annals of Christendom and they wanted to be a part of it.[17]

Each agent developed a different approach to rousing the auxiliaries and identifying the destitute. Indeed, much of 1829 was spent planning and strategizing. In Pennsylvania, ABS agent William Arnian proposed the creation of a "moral map" of the state and the surrounding regions so he could identify which local auxiliaries were actively pursuing the goals of the General Supply and which ones were not. As he traveled throughout the state his moral map would "shape my courses to those points where little or nothing is doing or where the little that once was doing is dead or dying."[18] Herbert Thompson had his own strategy for canvasing Kentucky. He urged the members of local auxiliary boards to visit their respective city halls and peruse the township records for two or three "Gentleman" from each school district who would be "most disposed to favour the objects of the Society." These men would be appointed as "visitors" and travel from door to door throughout their towns with a "subscription paper" to record the names of those members of the community who purchased a Bible. When the Bibles arrived from the ABS the visitor would be responsible for distributing them to everyone on the list.[19] John Mason Peck, the ABS agent assigned to Illinois, made a "rapid tour" of the state and noted those auxiliaries that needed to be "roused to action." He sent a letter to every auxiliary in Illinois to set up a meeting in the nearest county seat for the purpose of explaining the General Supply and encouraging participation in it. Peck met every week or two with the managers of auxiliaries, provided them with copies of the ABS *Annual Report* and *Extracts* to connect them with the larger work of the Society, and trained volunteers in the best way of distributing Bibles to the destitute. He even purchased, at his own expense, a "light traveling two wheeled vehicle with a small rearborn body" so that he could help the auxiliaries bring Bibles to the state's remote settlements. "In our level open, prairie country," Peck wrote, "such a vehicle would meet but little impediment."[20]

As the auxiliaries and the agents did the work of distribution, John Brigham, the Corresponding Secretary of the ABS, orchestrated the General Supply from his office on the first floor of 72 Nassau Street. Brigham was a Congregational clergyman from Massachusetts and a former missionary to South America with the American Board of Foreign Missions. He had been on the job at the ABS for three years when the General Supply commenced. A tireless correspondent, Brigham kept track of efforts to meet the demand for Bibles in every state and territory of the union.[21] He posted short articles in the *Extracts* asking auxiliaries to provide him with information about the progress of distribution. What states and counties were already supplied? What auxiliaries were optimistic about finishing by May 1831? How many Bibles would each auxiliary need to complete the General Supply in their region? What percent of the Bibles distributed would be sold, and how many would need to be distributed gratuitously? What kind of donations could the ABS headquarters expect from the auxiliaries? Brigham was the mastermind behind the General Supply, and he left no stone unturned in trying to get a Bible in the hands of every American family.[22]

In March 1830, as the General Supply neared the halfway point, Brigham and the Board of Managers took stock of its progress. Bibles were flying off the shelves of the ABS depository. Fanshaw's steam presses were getting the job done—enough Bibles were being produced. But there was great concern that the fundraising and distribution efforts were not moving as quickly as the board had hoped. Donations to the ABS were not meeting printing costs, and the ABS was forced to borrow money to keep the Treadwells going. Yet the board remained optimistic. If the auxiliaries kept collecting donations, and they continued to pay their past debts, the ABS was confident that this problem could be easily solved. Wishful thinking indeed.[23] But would it really be possible to get a Bible to every American family? At the midway point the Board of Managers could report that New Jersey, Pennsylvania, and Maryland had finished the work of the General Supply. Every family in these states had a Bible. New Hampshire, Vermont, Massachusetts, Rhode Island, Connecticut, and New York were almost finished with the work. Maine and Ohio were making good progress. The real problem, as the ABS expected from the beginning, was in the southern and western states and territories. Virginia, North Carolina, South Carolina, Kentucky, Mississippi, Louisiana, Missouri, and Illinois were just getting started with the distribution process. Alabama, Indiana, Michigan, Arkansas, and Florida had not even begun. Panic had not yet set in at 72 Nassau Street, but Brigham and his team were concerned. The General Supply still had a chance to be a success if "friends of the Bible *will do their duty.*" The pressure was on.[24]

Meanwhile, the auxiliaries and agents continued their labors. The winter of 1830–1831 was rough one. Heavy rains and snow made travel extremely difficult. The auxiliaries in East Tennessee could only deliver half of the Bibles they hoped to deliver because of the "extreme badness" of the roads, making it impossible for carriages to travel. Sumner Mandeville, the ABS agent in the region, complained about the wintery mix of rain, snow, and ice, claiming that "such a winter has scarcely ever been known in this country." Since the weather prevented people from getting to church, Mandeville was forced to cancel many of his meetings with local auxiliaries. He spent most of his time riding through the chilling rains only to arrive to find no one present at the appointed site of an auxiliary meeting. His horses were not faring well. He wore one of them out, had another one go "entirely blind" as a consequence of "hard riding," and expected his current horse to be "dead in a day or two."[25]

In southern Illinois ABS agent Solomon Hardy found the severe weather nearly unbearable. The cold and wind were so severe on the prairies that he was unable to travel. He had to deal with three-foot high snow banks that interrupted the mail routes. The weather was playing havoc on his wife's health, and he eventually thought that he was growing too old for such rigorous work. "I try to do the best I can," he wrote to Brigham, "but it seems to me I do but little. I know too that I have not so strong a constitution for the rough work of swimming creeks and 'doing all weathers' as some have." The waters were too high and Hardy's motivation was too low. "With regard to the progress of the work," he wrote Brigham, "I can say but little."[26]

Yet the agents continued their heroic work. An unnamed ABS agent working in the West rode 2,000 miles in six months. During that time he visited twenty different county auxiliaries, delivered seventy or eighty sermons and addresses, and raised $1,400 for the cause. John Vinton, an agent of the New Hampshire Bible Society, spent twenty-six days along the Canadian border in remote Coos County. He traveled 260 miles and visited every town and settlement in this sparsely scattered region. In the process he founded five female Bible associations and appointed eleven local agents. He met some interesting characters along the way, including an elderly woman who had read the entire Bible fifty-two times in thirteen years and a man who gave up a fifty-year tobacco habit in order to afford the membership fee of the New Hampshire Bible Society.[27]

No place suffered from a lack of grassroots organization more than Alabama. In March 1830 the Alabama Bible Society, in the hopes of throwing its full support behind the General Supply, called a statewide convention to rally supporters and develop a plan to supply the state with Bibles. It did not go well. Few of the lay delegates and very few members of the clergy showed up for the convention. As Joseph Cunningham, one of the managers of the Alabama Bible Society, told Brigham, "for some time after that meeting, our hopes evidently sunk." By September 1830 Cunningham was in panic mode. He estimated that Alabama had "5,000 perishing souls" in need of the word of God, but with only eight months remaining in the General Supply it was highly unlikely that Alabama would reach them with Bibles unless they received help from New York. He did not want the General Supply to fail because Alabama did not deliver. Cunningham asked Brigham to go the bookshelf in his Nassau Street office, take his copy of *Finley's Atlas* off the shelf, and turn to the section on Alabama. Such an exercise would give him a better sense of the size of the state and what it might take to supply those in some of the remote regions with Bibles. Cunningham told Brigham that the possibility of Alabama's failure "has pressed upon me at night, until my head could no longer recline at ease upon my pillow."

He begged Brigham to send an ABS agent and relayed a very detailed plan for how he might salvage the General Supply efforts in the state. May 1831 was right around the corner. The job of placing a Bible in every American home could be stressful.[28]

As the General Supply approached its final six months, the ABS had a record-high nineteen agents in the field.[29] The reports received were not encouraging, especially in the south and west. The ABS Board of Managers could rejoice in the fact that more people had access to a Bible than ever before, but the chances of the Society meeting its goal to supply a Bible to every American family over the course of two years now looked slim. Agent George Sheldon reported that the distribution of Bibles in Ohio had cost him "immense *travail* in body & mind," but "the work had not failed in a single county in which I gave the original impulse." Sheldon, however, was not able to cover every county in two years and there were some regions of Ohio that failed to receive books on time.[30] In East and Middle Tennessee, Mandeville was happy with his progress, but in March, just months before the General Supply deadline, he had "not yet heard of any County being entirely supplied." He was confident that some counties would meet the deadline, but others, largely due to the lack of manpower and poor internal distribution of Bibles, would not make it in time.[31]

In other places the Bible Cause was an organizational mess. When ABS agent Reuben Taylor arrived in Illinois and took an account of the state's progress, he found that little had been done in the work of the General Supply. Even the secretary of the Illinois Bible Society could not provide him with any information about how the cause was moving forward in the state. Some local societies were eager to get started with the work of distribution, but they did not have access to Bibles. Taylor learned that a box of ABS Bibles had been sitting at St. Louis for months, prompting postal officials to send the secretary a "sharp letter" urging him to come and take them away. Other auxiliaries seemed to show no interest in the General Supply. Taylor had little patience for such "cold indifference." He was so disgusted with the "drones" responsible for local Bible distribution in Illinois that he chose to leave the state, but not before he had harangued the leaders of several auxiliaries for the "impropriety of their conduct." According to Taylor, the General Supply could easily be accomplished in Illinois if the auxiliaries would perform their duties. He concluded that the "business of the Bible Society is badly managed in the State of Illinois," and added that the Illinois Bible Society is "worse than useless."[32]

As the two-year deadline arrived in May 1831, Brigham and the ABS once again took stock of what was accomplished. The Bible had been distributed to every family in New Hampshire, Vermont, New Jersey,

Pennsylvania, Maryland, Michigan, and Mississippi. Maine, Massachusetts, Rhode Island, and Connecticut were "nearly" or "quite finished" with the work. In New York, two or three remote counties were still unsupplied. The reports for the rest of the nation were far from encouraging. Forty out of sixty-four counties in North Carolina were supplied and two ABS agents were in the field trying to finish the work. There was "still more work to do" in South Carolina, Georgia, Kentucky, Ohio, and Tennessee. Indiana and Illinois were only "half completed" and only four counties had been supplied in Missouri. Louisiana was three-fourths supplied, Alabama was "not more than half supplied" and there was still "much to be done" in Arkansas Territory and Florida Territory.

The General Supply had failed. Though the work of distribution would continue, the ABS attempt to supply a Bible to every American family in two years was unsuccessful. The auxiliaries and friends of the Bible Cause did not act quickly enough or take the work seriously enough, and the weather of late 1830 and early 1831 brought snow and flooding that made traveling difficult, slowed the transportation of books, and suspended the operations of the auxiliaries.[33] One year after the ABS self-imposed deadline to supply a Bible to every American family, the Board of Managers reflected on its efforts. There was still hope that the General Supply could be completed, but the two-year experiment was over. The population of the United States was changing too quickly. The ABS estimated that up to 200 families destitute of a Bible had moved into each county in the nation since the May 1831 deadline. Brigham found it difficult to let the project go. He continued with his calculations. By June 1833, he reported that Missouri had managed to complete its supply, but distribution was still moving slowly in Illinois, Kentucky, Tennessee, Mississippi, Louisiana, Alabama, and Georgia.[34]

In the end, the General Supply brought a "season of great excitement and exertion" to the Bible Cause in America. The potential of a Christian nation of Bible readers seemed like a real possibility. But since the General Supply came to end, the auxiliaries had fallen into apathy. Never again would they reach the level of enthusiasm that characterized the first year of the General Supply. Bible distribution in the United States had dropped by one-third in the two years since May 1831. Indeed, such apathy was "the greatest of all evils" that stemmed from the work of the General Supply. Though the ABS would work through auxiliaries for many more decades to come, the board was beginning to lose confidence in the effectiveness of these local and state societies.[35] But despite the failure to meet its goal, the General Supply went a long way toward fulfilling the ABS mission to Christianize the United States through the distribution of the Bible. The General Supply put the ABS on the map as the largest and most powerful benevolent society in the country. Its reach was unprecedented. For the rest of the century the ABS would play a leadership role in the vast empire of voluntary associations forming throughout the country for the purpose of reforming American habits, Christianizing the people, and building the nation. The character of such an empire will be subject of our next chapter.

5

The Business of Benevolence

The American Bible Society's quest to place a Bible in the hands of every American—and, in the process, promote a Christian United States—did not occur in a vacuum. The ABS was part of a larger movement of Christian benevolence taking hold in the decades prior to the Civil War. As the ABS leadership continued to believe that God would bring the United States out of the Jeffersonian darkness and into a post–War of 1812 Christian republic, they often understood themselves as just one cog in a larger machine at work to spread the Gospel of Jesus Christ and bring moral reform to the country. Though the US Constitution made it clear that there would be no official state church or religious establishment in the nation, benevolent societies sought to forge an unofficial *moral* establishment.[1] The ABS Board of Managers believed that its mission of publishing and distributing Bibles intersected nicely with the goals of other societies devoted to the cause of Christian reform. In fact, some affiliated with the ABS thought it was the *most important* benevolent society in the country because all of the other reform movements drew their moral imperatives from the teaching of the Bible. As the Rev. C. Cummins of the Jamestown Bible Society in Xenia, Ohio, put it, "the Bible is not to be brought up in the rear of temperance and other moral reforms. It must be put in front of them all." Abraham Hasbrouck, a Dutch Reformed clergymen in Ulster County, New York, made the superiority of the ABS clear in a speech at the 1831 annual meeting: "Although the other benevolent institutions of the day have produced, and are still producing, great and lasting good," he stated, "American Bible Society stands among them all, conspicuous and pre-eminent."[2]

At the start of the Civil War, close to half of the population of the United States were evangelical Christians, and most of these evangelicals were sympathetic to the work of benevolent societies. By 1837 there were 159 such societies in the United States. Between 1789 and 1829 the nation's thirteen largest benevolent societies—most of them unaffiliated with a specific denomination—spent more than $2.8 million to promote a more Christian and moral nation. In the same period, the US government spent $3.6 million to build a transportation and communication infrastructure (roads, bridges, canals, etc.). Lyman Beecher, perhaps the most vocal champion of a Christian nation and a founder of the ABS, believed that such interdenominational societies should supplement the churches as a "sort of disciplined moral militia."[3]

The emergence of benevolent societies was inseparable from the evangelical zeal sweeping the United States during a series of religious revivals often called the Second Great Awakening. Millions of Americans in this period joined churches, received Jesus Christ as savior through the experience of the New Birth, and rededicated themselves to a life of Christian service and church membership. Revivals occurred sporadically, but forcefully, throughout the country. In the South and West massive religious awakenings took place in camp meetings such as the one at Cane Ridge, Kentucky, in 1801, where up to 25,000 people gathered together in the small frontier town to pray, fast, and listen to evangelistic sermons. The revival fires occurred so often in western and central New York that Charles Finney, one of the awakening's chief promoters, called the region "the burned-over district." The revivals particularly affected Methodist and Baptists congregations and had a significant impact on African Americans from those denominations. Methodist and Baptist itinerant preachers offered ordinary Americans— especially on the frontier—a free-will understanding of salvation that was in tune with the democratic spirit of the age. Whatever hopes that eighteenth-century religious skeptics and Enlightenment thinkers had for a more secular nation were dashed by this massive outpouring of evangelical Christianity.[4]

The work of the American Bible Society often served as a catalyst for local revivals. The Bible, when illuminated by the power of the Holy Spirit, had the potential of triggering spiritual awakenings. Reports from ABS auxiliaries made a definitive connection between the distribution of Bibles and revivals. The leaders of the Lynchburg Bible Society could not deny a "coincidence in the progress of . . . the Bible cause, and Revivals of Religion." In 1845 Dr. Cooley, an ABS agent working in Massachusetts, described a religious revival that broke out in the town of Tolland. Members of the local congregational church were meeting each evening for prayer, clergy in town were having serious conversations with townspeople about the state of their souls, and several young people were converted. The best explanation for this revival, according to Cooley, was the hundreds of Bibles that had recently been distributed in the region by the ABS. "Does not all past experience prove," he wrote in a letter to 72 Nassau Street, "that in no way are revivals of religion promoted and their power and purity more effectually sustained than by giving prominence to the Holy Scriptures!"[5]

Access to the Bible could not only activate a revival of religion, but it could also sustain one. Cephas Washburn, a Christian missionary in Arkansas Territory, led an evangelical revival among the Cherokee Indians in 1832. After some early struggles teaching the Cherokee how to read and appreciate the Bible, Washburn had a breakthrough when an awakening occurred among the tribe. This brought an intense spiritual interest among the Cherokee under his care and many more Indians wanted to learn how to read, specifically for the purpose of understanding the word of God. Eventually an auxiliary Bible society was formed in the mission. One Cherokee woman was so overwhelmed upon receiving an ABS Bible that she wrapped it in silk and carried it close to her chest at religious meetings. According to Washburn, the care she gave to the Bible—unwrapping it to read a verse or two and then wrapping it back up—coupled with the tears that flowed from her eyes and the gleam in her eyes whenever she read it, was a testimony to other Cherokee in the tribe. "Her example and exhortations, joined to her prayers," Washburn added, "were the means . . . of a revival of religion in the neighborhood, which resulted in the conversion of thirteen individuals."[6]

Those touched by the Holy Spirit during these revivals set out to be "salt and light" in the world around them. They evangelized neighbors and strangers in the hopes of bringing them into the church and preparing their souls for eternal life. But the practice of being a Christian witness in the world also required converts—new and old, women and men—to address a host of social problems that they believed to be undermining the moral fabric of American society. Evangelicals applied the social requirements of their faith to fight poverty, drunkenness, sexual immorality, crime, disrespect for the Sabbath, and slavery, to name just a few of their causes. They promoted Christian learning in Sunday schools and employed the ever-expanding networks of evangelical publishing to reach millions with the gospel message through the distribution of the Bible and religious tracts. The benevolent societies were created to harness evangelical zeal into the virtuous action necessary to forge a Christian society and usher in the Kingdom of God.[7]

Evangelicals concerned with the moral reform of American life concentrated much effort on the religious education of children and young people through Sunday schools. Some of the earliest Sunday schools in America were formed in the eighteenth century to provide biblical instruction to the children of the urban poor, many of whom spent their Sundays roaming city streets looking for trouble. Children would gather in churches to sing hymns, pray, read the Bible, and hear a short sermon. They were rewarded for regular attendance and their hard work memorizing Biblical passages. If records of enrollment in Sunday school classes are any indication, the efforts of these schools were successful. By 1832 there were over 300,000 boys and girls attending

Sunday schools in the United States, or about 8 percent of the young people eligible to attend such classes. The numbers were even higher in urban areas. For example, in the same year, close to 28 percent of Philadelphia children were attending Sunday schools. Because these schools focused on reading and writing, many of them drew large numbers of free blacks—both children and adults. Starting in 1824 a benevolent organization called the American Sunday School Union was formed to stimulate the movement across denominations and provide literature for Sunday schools operating around the country.[8]

The American Bible Society and the Sunday School Movement shared many of the same activist convictions. In 1827 the ABS authorized the publication of a "small testament" for Sunday schools with the goal of meeting the spiritual needs of the "thousands of poor children . . . in our large towns."[9] From this point forward, the Society supplied Bibles to any Sunday school organization in need. For example, in 1831, the ABS provided the American Sunday School Union with 20,000 copies of the New Testament in support of a massive effort to establish schools in the Mississippi Valley. In the 1830s the ABS distributed over 14,300 Bibles and over 57,700 Testaments around the country, with most of them going to the American Sunday School Union and the Methodist Episcopal Church. In the 1850s these numbers rose to 27,729 (Bibles) and 134,237 (Testaments). Rev. Charles McIlvane of Brooklyn, in a message to the annual meeting of the ABS, compared the Society's educational outreach to Cambridge University in England. The only difference was that "our University is in the business of benevolence."[10]

Through much of the antebellum period ABS headquarters in New York received constant reports from Sunday schools in need of Bibles and moving letters from agents about their rapid growth. One of the more sentimental requests came in 1847, when the ABS received a small tin savings bank filled with $2.17 in change. It was sent by a small girl requesting three dozen Bibles for her Sunday school class. The money enclosed in the bank did not cover the cost of the Bibles, but the ABS sent them anyway. In 1854, H. W. Pierson, the ABS agent in Southern Kentucky, visited all seven of the "Coloured Sabbath Schools" in Louisville. He was impressed with slaves and free blacks of all ages attending these schools and noted that a great majority of the teachers were black, but he lamented the general lack of teachers and Bibles.[11]

It is hard to ignore the significant overlap between the proponents of the Bible Cause and the supporters of the Temperance Movement. Benjamin Rush, Lyman Beecher, Stephen Van Rensselaer, and Arthur Tappan, to name a few, were active in both communities of reform. These men believed that temperance was needed to counter American's addiction to alcoholic beverages. In the mid-1820s Americans consumed about seven gallons of alcohol per person each year (compared to 2.8 gallons in 1995). People drank whiskey for breakfast, lunch, and dinner in the early republic, much in the way that they drink coffee or other caffeine-laced beverages today. Alcoholic beverages were cheap (costing less than coffee or tea) and were healthier than drinking water. Alcohol was blamed for its effect on families, young people, crime, the strength (or weakness) of the American military, and poverty.[12] In the first few decades of the nineteenth century there were several local attempts—mostly in New England—to curb the destructive effects of alcohol on American life, but the movement became national when Lyman Beecher published six sermons on temperance in 1827. For Beecher, temperance was a "the sin of our land." America's alcohol problem was a moral one, but it had eternal consequences. It would lead to behavior that would separate individuals from God. He made a direct connection between the depravity of the culture and the need for salvation—a fitting message in the midst of the Second Great Awakening. Beecher concluded that "ardent spirits" should be "banished" from the "list of lawful articles of commerce, by a correct and efficient public sentiment." In 1826, temperance advocates formed the American Temperance Society to urge citizens to engage in total abstinence from alcoholic beverages. By 1835, the Society could boast five thousand chapters and a million members.[13]

For the American Bible Society, the problem of alcohol in American life was easily solved through the life-changing message of the word of God. The managers of the Jefferson County, Virginia Bible Society encouraged drinkers to use the money spent on alcohol to purchase a Bible. "The price of even *one pint*, of the cheapest kind of spirituous liquor," they argued, "would enable you to be a member of a Bible . . . Society, and have something else for Sunday Schools." It was time to stop drinking whiskey so the ABS could send "the *water of life* to thirsty souls." Cephas Washburn worked hard to stop the Indians in his Cherokee mission from turning to the bottle. One sign of success was when the Cherokee ceased trading their recently received Bibles for whiskey.[14] In 1840 James McElroy, a Bible colporteur (or book peddler) working for the Virginia State Bible Society, encountered a young man who had acquired the "ruinous habit of intemperance" during his stint in the US Army. His appetite for peach brandy was so strong that he had built a distillery for its manufacture at his house near Staunton. According to McElroy, the man's addiction was having negative effects on his relationship with his wife and six children and was generally "dragging him down into wretchedness and ruin." One morning, after he awoke from a "long fit of debauch," he found a new Bible placed in the house by an agent of the Virginia State Bible Society, presumably McElroy himself. As he read the Bible his resolution to break from his intemperance was strengthened. He began to pray for forgiveness, asking God to save him from "the drunkard's eternity." McElory concluded that the more encounters like this multiplied, the better chance of ridding the nation of this threat to Christian civilization.[15]

The work of the American Bible Society in promoting a Christian nation would have been impossible without the work of women. They were the driving force behind the great wave of benevolent institutions founded in the decades preceding the Civil War. A significant portion of the grassroots distribution and fundraising was done by middle-class women: the wives of businessmen, merchants, lawyers, and clergymen. Women were active in local auxiliaries run by men and also formed their own female Bible auxiliaries throughout the country. Two years after its founding, the ABS was already reporting that "female charitable societies have spread throughout the land with an almost electrical rapidity, and they contribute no small part of the sums which are annually raised for benevolent objects."[16] By 1817 at least fifteen female Bible societies had declared themselves auxiliaries of the ABS. By 1838, eighty-two female societies had affiliated with the Society.

Women formed and joined Bible societies, and other societies like them, as a way to express their faith in public life in a way that was not available to them in the eighteenth century. The Founding Fathers understood women's roles in society through their commitment to republican virtue. In other words, women had an important part to play in the development of American morality by training their sons to exemplify a love for God and country. Such "republican motherhood" gave women a role in the creation of a moral citizenry, but it did not allow them to bring their deepest religious convictions to bear on the life of the republic. The Second Great Awakening and the rise of nineteenth-century benevolent societies changed all of that. Women who embraced evangelical faith in the midst of the revivals found an outlet in a host of Christian reform movements, including the various auxiliaries of the American Bible Society.[17]

The men in charge of the American Bible Society believed that women had "natural tendencies" that made them especially fit for charity work—their "female character can never shine with so bright a lustre as when employed in relieving the wants of the distressed." The grassroots outreach of the ABS depended upon their superior "social disposition," "keener sensibility," and advanced skills at "ascertaining the wants of a neighborhood." Men possessed strength, valor, and the capability to perform the "severer toils of life"—toils that might require facing danger. Women, however, were tender. They were able to "soften the severity of the male character and sympathize more full" with those in need. The male leaders of the East Tennessee Bible Society, for example, believed that women's "natural modesty" was proof that God had created them to stay home in the "proper sphere he has assigned them," rather than "travel through the country on public business." The belief that women were best suited to the "limits of town or neighborhood" made them ideal volunteers.[18]

Those connected to the Bible Cause argued that the special characteristics women possessed were instilled in them by God, making them different from men. Women, for example, played a special role in the life of Jesus as portrayed in the gospels. They had the "happy privilege" to "sit at the feet of their Lord, and to hear the words of grace which flowed from his lips." They washed the feet of Jesus with their tears and dried them with their hair. In God's providence, women were honored to be the first witnesses to the resurrection. As the male ABS leadership noted in 1822, "they are employed as angels of mercy to carry the word of . . . salvation." Such an understanding of female virtue was not unique to the American Bible Society. The theologians, clergymen, and authors of the day thought that women were made by God to exemplify Christian virtue to a degree that men could not. Because of their status in society, protected from the corruption of the political arena and the marketplace, women did not commit as many violent crimes, and did not drink alcohol to excess. A quick glance at the membership rolls of Protestant churches during the Second Great Awakening era reveals that evangelical religion, and the benevolent work that stemmed from it, had a feminine quality.[19]

The leaders of the ABS also believed that the distribution of the Bible would have a profound effect on the cause of women's rights in the United States and abroad. Edward D. Griffiths, in his speech before the fourth annual meeting of the ABS, suggested that if one took a map of the world and circled all of the countries where women were not prisoners or slaves, the area enclosed would be the regions where "the rays of revelations shine." The women of the Female Auxiliary Bible Society of Springfield, Illinois, gave thanks for "our own happy position in a Christian land" as compared to the "degradation and wretchedness of females in those countries where the Bible is unknown." American women, they claimed, lived in an "elevated and privileged station" which they traced directly to the influence of Christianity and the Bible. These middle-class women of Springfield expressed "feeling" and "sympathy" on behalf of women living in parts of the world where women had less freedom. To these women they offered the "precious gift" of the Bible in the hopes of "ameliorating their condition."[20]

Hundreds of auxiliary societies around the country translated their understanding of the nature of women into the practice of Bible work. The largest and most prominent of the female auxiliaries was the New York Female Auxiliary Bible Society (NYFABS), founded on May 11, 1816, by four hundred prominent New York women at the City Hotel in Manhattan. The Society was run by thirty-six female "managers" (including the wives of John Caldwell, John Jay, and Richard Varick). Women could join the Society for the price of two dollars a year. In the first twenty years of the Society's existence, the women of the NYFABS focused on both the distribution of the Bible in New York and the raising of funds for the American Bible Society. Over 180 women carried out the mission of the NYFABS during the 1820s and by 1855, the NYFABS had developed "committees" in over eighty New York City churches.[21]

In the decades preceding the Civil War, the leadership of NYFABS focused much of its attention on the poorer women and immigrants in the city. It began hiring women, known as Bible Readers, to carry out this work. Bible Readers would be assigned a specific neighborhood, such as the forty-six blocks that made up the heavily populated Seventh Ward on the Lower East Side, for the purposes of visiting families and distributing Bibles. The first of these female Bible Readers, whose name is not mentioned in the NYFABS records, visited 1,000 families in the Seventh Ward in a three-month period. She gave away Bibles, invited women and children to church and Sunday school, and even established a sewing school in the neighborhood. A few NYFABS women developed a plan to gather "little circles" of about twelve women together for "tea meetings" so that they could read and explain the Bible to them. In 1862 alone, these female "distributors" and "readers" made more than 7,000 visits. The Society reported that the women who attended these meetings returned home "with a new feeling of being cared for."[22]

Not all Protestants in the United States believed that benevolent societies were the best way to advance a Christian nation and address social problems. In 1827 E. R. Fairchild, an agent of the ABS in Indiana, wrote to the Bible House about some of the difficulties he was experiencing carrying out the work of the Society in this outpost. Fairchild met with opposition from Protestants who had "very strong prejudices" against the work of benevolent societies, including the ABS. F. R. Goulding, an ABS agent working in Georgia in 1842, encountered similar opposition, although he was more specific about its nature. Goulding told the ABS Corresponding Secretary that it was difficult to find anyone in Georgia who owned a Bible or any kind of religious book distributed by one of the many interdenominational tract societies working around the country. "This may be accounted for," he noted, "by the fact that in that region the *Anti-missionary Baptists* are numerous and stout in their ignorance and error." An ABS agent in Illinois described the antimission Baptists as an "extensive opposition."[23]

The antimission Baptists were opposed to the work of the American Bible Society—and for that matter all benevolent societies—for several reasons. First, they believed that nondenominational benevolent work was unscriptural. As devout adherents to a literal interpretation of the Bible, antimission Baptists and those of other religious groups with similar convictions, thought that the only truly biblical way of conducting Christian benevolence was through organizations connected with established Protestant denominations. Second, the adherents of the antimission movement tended to live in frontier settlements in the Midwest and South. The ABS found that opposition was particularly strong in Illinois and Indiana, although opponents of nondenominational benevolent societies could be found all over the backcountry. Those affiliated with the antimission movement associated benevolent organizations with wealthy north-easterners more concerned with the financial stability of their organizations than with Christian missions. One antimission critic wrote a letter to the ABS describing it as little more than a "money-making institution" intent upon selling Bibles to poor people who could not afford them. Fairchild reported that he encountered a man who had "strong prejudices" against the ABS because he believed the organization was designed to "deceive people, and get away their money." The ABS claimed to be a benevolent society, the antimission leaders argued, but in reality it was a business made up of businessmen, the kind of men who were out to exploit the settlers of the frontier in order to advance their money-making schemes.[24]

Third, the antimission faction tended to reject the Calvinism behind many of the benevolent societies. They favored a more democratic, free-will approach to religion. But what worried them most were the political implications of Calvinism as it related to religious liberty. Congregationalists and Presbyterians, with their historic Calvinist commitment to Christianizing culture (from John Calvin to John Winthrop), would use their benevolent societies to promote a religious establishment that would ultimately pose a threat to the separation of church and state. This fear, accompanied with the economic, cultural, and political power that the members of the ABS Board of Managers had in the nation, drove their opposition. The concerns of the antimission groups were real.[25] Benevolent societies, led by wealthy and powerful evangelical Protestants, were in the business of creating a Christian nation. Lyman Beecher's thoughts in an address to the Charitable Society for the Education of Indigent Pious Young Men for the Ministry of the Gospel, could not have put it more clearly:

> The integrity of the Union demands special exertions to produce in the nation a more homogeneous character and bind us together with firmer bonds . . . A remedy must be applied to this vital defect of our national organization. But what shall that remedy be? There can be but one. The consolidation of the State Governments would make a despotism. But the prevalence of pious, intelligent, enterprising ministers through the nation, at ratio of one for 1000, would establish schools, and academies, and colleges, and habits, and institutions of homogeneous influence. These would produce a sameness of views, and feelings, and interests, which would lay the foundations of our empire upon a rock.[26]

Beecher wanted a homogeneous Christian culture of educated and "enterprising" men.

C. R. Fairchild claimed that the antimission opposition to the work of the ABS in the Midwest was "excited and strengthened in a great degree" by a periodical, based in Philadelphia but circulated widely throughout the "Western country," called *The Reformer* (1820–1835). The antimission movement was promoted by several periodicals published in the midst of an explosion of religious print in the early American republic, but no religious periodical was more caustic. *The Reformer* was started by a group of antimission Christians, but it reached its height under the editorship of Theophilus Gates, a nonsectarian intellectual who had rejected his Calvinist upbringing in favor of a vision of Christianity void of any organization or structure. He believed that the essence of Christianity was to be found in the practice of the teachings of Jesus in everyday life, not in the adherence to Calvinist orthodoxy. His periodical had a strong populist flavor, appealing to antimission Christians and all Americans who opposed the nation's evangelical turn during the Second Great Awakening. Its readers included free thinkers and skeptics as well—men and women who felt that their liberty was threatened by the attempts of benevolent societies to exert ecclesiastical and cultural power over America through the establishment of a Christian nation.[27]

Every issue of *The Reformer* was loaded with scathing attacks on benevolent societies. Its authors challenged the notion that Christianity—particularly Presbyterianism—must become the official religion of the nation. Gates feared that President John Quincy Adams, a Calvinist and strong supporter of national morals (and an honorary ABS vice president), would use his authority to promote "the pompous and arrogant assumptions of the proud representatives of John Calvin." Calvinists, Gates believed, wanted to end the separation of church and state in America and were planning to use benevolent societies—with their "national" and "American" titles—to do so.[28] The editors of *The Reformer* argued that the ABS reports on the Bible needs of the United States were heavily exaggerated. Gates questioned ABS assertions that there were "whole neighborhoods in which there was not a single copy of the Bible." He found this hard to believe, since, as he put it, "almost every storekeeper in the country keeps Bibles to dispose of, and no one that valued the Bible more than all his property would long be without one." According to Gates, such reports were published to convince unsuspecting Christians to donate more money to the ABS, which, in turn, would empower them further to infiltrate the government and establish a Presbyterian nation. Soon, the editor worried, the leadership of the American Bible Society would lobby to make it a law requiring all Americans to pay religious tithes for the support of religion—a clear violation of the disestablishment clause of the First Amendment.[29] In the end, Gates and the antimission Baptists were the first to point out that the ABS leadership was in the business of selling Bibles for the purpose of promoting a Christian civilization. This, of course, did not sit well with these self-appointed guardians of the separation of church and state. But what kind of Christian nation was the ABS promoting? As we will see in the next chapter, it was a decidedly Protestant one.

6

The Bible is the Religion of Protestants

In 1829, an American Bible Society agent working in the western United States met a young female Irish immigrant—let's call her Mary—who, he claimed, was "rigidly educated in the Roman Catholic faith." Before arriving in America Mary was planning to spend her life in an Irish convent, but when her father decided to migrate he brought her with him. Upon arrival Mary continued to practice Catholicism under the watchful eye of her father, who the ABS agent described as a "very wicked man, but bigotedly attached to the forms and ceremonies of his church." She was trained to believe that there "was salvation in no other." Mary's spiritual life took a drastic turn when a young neighbor boy who was playing in her house dropped a portion of a New Testament he had carried with him. She picked up the pages and began to read, concealing the book from her father, who had taught her that it was a sin to read the scriptures "without note or comment." In the course of her reading Mary became convinced that Catholicism "would not answer in the last great day." She came to grips with the sinful state of her soul and became anxious about her salvation, all the while keeping her spiritual searching away from her father for fear of punishment. Without a teacher to explain what she was reading, Mary pressed on, guided only by the words of the small New Testament portion. As the anxiety-induced tears rolled down her face, she eventually came to grips with "the pardoning love of God, through a crucified Saviour" and found that the pages of the Bible—those "leaves from the tree of life"—had healed her "wounded spirit."

A revival had commenced in Mary's town and she decided, unbeknownst to her family, to attend several of the meetings. As Mary watched, new converts paraded to the front of the church to make public professions of faith, and she "felt an ardent desire" to do the same. The agent counseled Mary, but she knew that as soon as word of a conversion reached her father he would "immediately banish her from his house." She even feared that his rage might lead him to "take her life." As the agent wrote, "I had never before thought it possible for an individual, in this land of freedom, to be placed in circumstances so trying."

As the ABS agent continued to talk with Mary he was surprised at just how much she knew about the Protestant way of salvation, despite the fact that she had no one to instruct her and no books to read beyond the Testament that "had fallen into her hands" and "the teachings of that Spirit which had indicted the Word." Eventually Mary did make a profession of faith and joined the local Protestant church. The ABS provided her with a full Bible—Old and New Testaments—to replace the portion she had been reading. She received it with "tears of gratitude." Mary continued to hide her newfound faith, and her new Bible, from her father, and prayed that someday he too might come to saving faith in Christ.[1]

Mary's story tells us several things about the American Bible Society in the decades preceding the American Civil War. The ABS believed that the Bible had the spiritual power to send people like Mary on an entirely new trajectory of life. It was no mere coincidence that Mary stumbled across this Bible on the floor of her house. It was a providential act of God. The agents working on behalf of the Bible Cause were appointed to deliver the word of God wherever it was needed, but they also believed that the Bible was a supernatural book that could lead people to salvation without the aid of a preacher or teacher. Mary's story was published in the monthly *Extracts* to show that the Bible, without any commentary, could bring people into the Kingdom of God, defeat a growing Catholic menace, and advance the cause of Protestantism in America. Though ABS agents often took opportunities to preach and teach, most of the time they merely dropped off a copy of the Bible at a house, on a train or a ship, or to someone they met on the road—and let the Spirit do the rest. The ABS agent who encountered Mary was not only recording yet another story of personal salvation, but he was relaying an uplifting account of another soul saved from tyrannical Catholicism. Mary's strong-willed father, a man who she believed might kill her for becoming a Protestant, was representative of all that was wrong with Rome. Indeed, the agent had never thought it was possible "in this land of freedom" for the life of an "individual" to be placed in jeopardy because of her religious convictions.

The American Bible Society rarely dabbled in the work of Protestant theology. This was an organization of lay leaders (mostly businessmen), not professional theologians. It did not work with churches or denominations—at least not yet. The Society was tasked with distributing the Bible without note or comment through its auxiliaries and letting the Holy Spirit deliver its life-changing message. Yet one would be hard pressed to argue that the ABS did not operate with certain generic theological assumptions about its work. As Rev. T. V. Moore of the First Presbyterian Church of Richmond told a gathering of Bible leaders at the organization's thirty-fifth anniversary in 1852, "there are certain doctrinal positions which unquestionably underlie her (ABS) organization, without which that organization must speedily fall to the ground."

For example, at the time of Moore's speech, the ABS affirmed that the very words of the Bible were inspired by God giving it an "absolute sufficiency as a rule of faith and practice." Since the Bible was a direct revelation from God, it was true and without error. The ABS went so far as to state that God is "embodied" in the very words of Scripture and "the light of His unutterable brightness is enshrined in these wondrous syllables." This view of verbal plenary inspiration implied that anyone who could read would be able to use common sense to understand the meaning of its words.[2]

But at the core of the ABS mission was the distribution of the Bible "without note or comment." As we have seen, the ABS tried to rise above the sticky doctrinal issues that distinguished one denomination from another and focus its attention on what united all Protestants—a belief in the redemptive power of the word of God. The American Bible Society printed and distributed the King James Version of the Bible without commentary or marginalia. In 1824, Jeremiah Day, president of Yale College, explained the importance of this practice:

> Should not the Scriptures . . . be accompanied with notes and comments? So far as commentators enable us to understand what we read, we may be grateful for their aid. But we are not to look for improvements on a revelation from heaven. The volume of immutable truth is not to be wrought into a more perfect form by metaphysical refinement. It will not be in a higher degree, the wisdom of God, and power of God to salvation, when translated into the technical language of modern theological systems.[3]

The message was clear. The Bible was not meant to be interpreted. The Bible's salvific message was self-evident in the words of the inspired text.[4]

ABS publications were fond of using the phrase "the Bible doing its work" to describe the effects the book had on sinners and potential converts. For example, as he prepared to send his son off to college a Christian father worried that the young scholar would lose his faith during the course of the experience. So he purchased "an elegant copy" of the Bible and, without his son's knowledge, placed it at the bottom of his trunk. Shortly after the son's arrival at college the father's worst fears were realized. "The restraints of a pious education were soon broken off," and the young man "proceeded from speculation to doubts, and from doubts to denial of the reality of religion." One day, while "rummaging through his trunk," he found the "sacred deposit" that his father had placed there. In a spirit of indignation, the young man decided that he would use the Bible to clean his razor after his daily shave. Each day he used the blade to tear a leaf or two out of the "Holy Book" until half of the volume was destroyed.

But one morning, as he "was committing this outrage" to the text, several verses met his eye and struck him "like a barbed arrow to his heart." These verses were like a "sermon" to him, awakening him to the wrath of God and leading him to "the foot of the cross." There was no need to provide rational answers to the young man's skepticism—the "Sacred Volume" had "done its work." It had led him "to repose on the mercy of God, which is sufficient for the chief of sinners."[5]

The words of God without "note or comment" even had the power to bring spiritual vitality to the insane. In 1852, an ABS agent visited a Maryland Hospital for the Insane and began reading the Gospel of John to one hundred and forty inmates gathered for Sunday morning services. Before he could finish reading the passage, one of the inmates arose and "gave vent to his feelings in prayer." Another wept. A third patient raised his hands in the air. A man who held a "prominent and responsible position in the community" stood up, "gazed intently" at the agent, and then turned to the audience in a way that seemed to suggest his "gloomy habit of his mind was at least momentarily removed." The lesson, of course, was that these mental patients responded to the word of God in a powerful way, "but little was said in explanation of the portion selected." The Bible, "bore its own testimony, it made that impression of its divine origin, on the minds of those treated as irrational, and separated from the rest of man as injurious to themselves or others." The agent was quick to note that his story did not mean that in all cases "insanity" would be "lulled to rest by the reading of a few passages of the God's Word," but it was worth mentioning, he added, that "the book must be divine which could make its impression through the veiled intellect, or carry its consoling influence to the seared affections of the wildest insanity."[6]

In 1840 ABS agent Sylvester Holmes stumbled upon a woman near Nashville, Tennessee, trapped in an abusive marriage with a "whiskey lover" who became enraged whenever she read her Bible. One day the husband, presumably in a drunken stupor, decided he was going to burn his wife's Bible. He ripped it from her hands and threw it into the fire where it was "consumed to ashes." As soon as the Bible began to burn, the "wretched" husband lost the use of his hand and could not speak.[7] In a similar story, a German man living in Syracuse, New York, took the Bible he received from an ABS agent and threw it into a fire, but he "could not make it burn." He eventually took the Bible out of the fire and, "in its singed state," began to read it, leading him to request another Bible from the agent.[8] Another agent in New York encountered a man, "full of cursing and bitterness," who would not permit a Bible to be left in his house. Since the agent did not want to leave the man's farm without depositing a copy of the word of God, he decided to leave a copy in the barn. (After all, he concluded, "our Blessed Savior once lay in a manger.") The very presence of the Bible in the nearby barn caused the unregenerate owner to think constantly of his "rashness and guilt." After several days his spiritual "distress became so great, that he went out to the barn in search of the rejected volume." He turned to the gospels and read the story of Jesus's birth in a lowly manger. He repented of his sins and "consecrated himself to God through faith in Jesus Christ."[9]

The managers and agents of the ABS lived in an enchanted world where books in barns could convict men of sin and those who burned sacred scriptures suffered negative consequences. This was a world in which men and women could pick up a copy of the Bible on a ship or railcar and immediately turn to a verse or passage that spoke to a specific need. Though there were some who probably believed that the Bible was a kind of talisman or amulet, most ABS agents believed that the Bible's apparent magical powers could be easily explained by an appeal to the third person of the Trinity—the Holy Spirit. When those in charge of the ABS talked about the Bible "doing its work," what they were really saying was that the Holy Spirit was illuminating the Bible in such a way that touched the hearts of those who encountered it and its message. Though the influence of the Spirit's work in shedding light on the message of the Bible could come quickly and abruptly, as in the case of an evangelical revival, it usually had a "slow, silent, effective influence" on the reader. This was the same kind of spiritual power that "moves the deep tides of the oceans and holds and guides the planets in their spheres." If the ABS could just get the pure word of God, without note or comment, in the hands of every person in America, a slow and steady spiritual and moral transformation would capture the nation.[10]

In keeping with its "no note or comment" policy, the ABS avoided translations that seemed to favor the theological beliefs of specific denominations. The first major test to this policy was the proper way to translate the Greek word *baptizo*. In 1835, the British Baptist Mission in Calcutta, India, appealed to the ABS for help in funding a second edition of a translation of the New Testament in the Bengali language. The Mission turned to the ABS after the British and Foreign Bible Society (BFBS) refused to fund the translation because *baptizo*—the Greek word for "baptism"—was translated in a way that implied the practice of immersion. The BFBS believed that this translation favored a Baptist understanding of the sacrament and thus excluded denominations that believed in sprinkling or pouring as a form of baptism. The representatives of the Baptist mission in Calcutta thought that the BFBS, in refusing to publish the translation, was displaying its own denominational preferences. They were quick to point out that ten of the twelve members of the BFBS committee on translations were paedo-Baptists. In order to get the necessary funds needed for the publication of their Bengali New Testament,

the members of the Calcutta mission would "look to America for more liber-
ality than at home."[11]

The ABS appointed a special committee to study the request from
Calcultta. It concluded that the ABS would only sponsor Bible translations
that all Protestant denominations could "consistently use and circulate." It
reaffirmed its commitment to publishing Bibles "without note or comment"
in English, and, as far as foreign translations were concerned, appealed to a
clause in its Constitution that forbade the ABS from supporting translations
that promoted "local feelings, party prejudices," and "sectarian jealousies."
Fourteen of the fifty-six members of the Board of Managers opposed the
resolution—most of them Baptists. Following the decision, Spencer Cone, a
Baptist who served the ABS on this special committee, resigned his post as
the Corresponding Secretary of the ABS and several Baptist members of the
Board of Trustees followed his lead. The dissenters organized a new Bible society called the American and Foreign Bible Society, which quickly printed a
copy of the New Testament that translated *baptizo* with the word "immerse."
Meanwhile, the ABS leadership did spin control with its Baptist constituency.
It explained that its decision not to fund the Bengali New Testament was made
on the basis of the ABS's denominationally neutral translation policy and not
as a rejection of immersion as a form of baptism.[12]

The ABS took a decidedly Protestant and American approach to the Bible.
The Bible was a book of liberty. It not only taught individuals how to be free
from the bonds of sin and the devil, but it was wholly compatible with the kind
of political liberty that flowed naturally from the American Revolution. In
December 1830 the ABS published a circular, written by "an intelligent layman," titled "The Bible: A Religious Constitution." The circular was a manifesto on the subject of religious freedom written by an author who was clearly
sympathetic to the Bible Cause. He argued that a person's right to religious
liberty came not from a "compact with his fellow-creatures," but was rather
a "matter between him and God." The Bible was the source of religious freedom in the sense that it "guarantees the conscience of the Christian against
the encroachments of ecclesiastical ambition." In fact, the "Sacred Scriptures"
were nothing short of a "bill of rights dictated by the Holy Spirit—a charter
granted by the Deity himself!" The Bible was a Christian "Magna Carta." It
was a book to which ordinary people should appeal whenever their rights were
threatened.[13]

The ABS commitment to distributing a Bible without note or comment,
and its belief that the Bible was essential to the freedoms enjoyed by citizens of
the United States, led the Society to see Catholicism as a serious threat. In the
decades prior to the Civil War the ABS made it clear to its constituency that
the Roman Catholic Church was a false version of Christianity. If not checked,

it had the power to undermine the American republic. At the time of its founding, the ABS seemed willing to include Roman Catholics in the interdenominational Bible Cause. Catholics were welcomed at the founding of the ABS in May 1816 and in its early years the organization worked closely with the Catholic bishop of New Orleans in the distribution of French-language Bibles in Louisiana. It also published Spanish versions of the Bible translated from the Latin Vulgate and distributed Bibles to Catholic congregations in Argentina and other parts of South America. Though ABS Bibles were popular in these Catholic regions of the world, the Society's decision to publish them without the so-called Apocryphal or deuterocanonical books, and without Catholic commentary or notes, ultimately presented an obstacle to distribution.[14]

But between 1830 and 1870 the Catholic population in America increased by 1,300 percent, from about 318,000 in 1830 to 4.5 million in 1870. Between 1846 and 1851 over 1 million people fled Ireland during the infamous potato famine. By 1850, Catholicism was the largest religious body in the United States.[15] The ABS was very aware of these demographic trends. Located in New York City, its staff had a first-hand look at the social and cultural transformation. The New York Bible Society, for example, noted that "Irish Roman Catholics" constituted "almost the entire population" in some parts of the city. In an 1847 report the New York society described the Irish immigrants as "extremely ignorant and generally bigoted." They had beliefs and practices that were foreign to Protestant America such as transubstantiation, the use of holy water, and the practice of praying to the Virgin Mary.[16]

ABS publications during the 1840s and 1850s described "the rapid influx of foreigners" bringing with them "the prevalence of infidelity, of Papacy, Mormonism, and other soul-destroying delusions" that could only be countered by the spread of the "*volume of truth* without delay over all our land." An ABS agent in Iowa wrote, "Catholics, aware of the future importance of Iowa, are pouring in their population with a rapidity truly alarming to those who have come here to find a home for themselves and families." ABS agents feared that "the Papists" were making the city of Indianapolis "one of their strongholds." It was time for all Bible-loving Protestants to "redouble their efforts" in the dissemination of the Holy Scriptures as the "surest means" of keeping the Protestant settlers of Indianapolis "free from the errors of Popery." After all, "Rome cannot take root in soils impregnated with the salt of divine truth."[17]

The ABS was also concerned that Catholic social teaching was incompatible with Protestant notions of American progress. In 1843, ABS president John Cotton Smith believed that Roman Catholics were using the religious freedoms afforded to them by the United States to spread beliefs that undermined modern life. Catholics fought against the use of the King James Version in schools, built churches that served as "monuments of papal superstitions," and manipulated the "American system of free elections." William Adams, another ABS supporter, argued that the places in the world where Catholics had a stronghold were often characterized by "decay, degradation, and suffering." These were places where "commerce droops, agriculture sickens, and useful arts languish." He contrasted the woeful state of Catholic countries with those that championed the Protestant faith: "Pass over the Alps into Switzerland, and down the Rhine into Holland, and over the channel to England and Scotland, and, what an amazing contrast meets the eye!" These countries, according to Adams, were known for their "industry, neatness, [and] instruction for children." These were modern nations—countries that had embraced Enlightenment progress in the form of liberty and free economic growth. They were modern because they allowed people to read the Bible, "and happy are the people who are in such a case."[18]

Catholics, on the other hand, believed that individualism—particularly as it informed Protestant interpretations of the Bible—eroded the authority of the Church. As long as American progress was rooted in the autonomous liberty of the individual, the Catholic Church would reject it in favor of a more collective approach to Christianity. Smith, of course, saw things differently. He believed he was living in a new age of liberty in the United States. The legacy of the American Revolution was coming to fruition in the form of greater political participation, increased economic opportunities, and the rapid rise of evangelical Christianity. He refused to stand by and allow "the boasted light of the nineteenth century" to be "overspread with the darkness of the sixteenth"—a darkness which had been overcome by the Protestant Reformation. "Romanism" was a religion characterized by the "dungeons and tortures" of the Inquisition and a long history of "papal denomination." Protestantism, the religion of the Bible, was a religion of freedom. Catholicism was a threat to democracy and all forms of religious liberty. It substituted the truth of God for the theological reflections and inventions of men.[19]

What was most disturbing for the ABS was the refusal of Catholic priests to allow their parishioners to read the King James (the "Authorized") Version. According to the Council of Trent, the official Catholic Bible was the Latin Vulgate. Public readings, sermons, and translations needed to be based on its text. Moreover, the Roman Catholic Church forbade laypersons from interpreting the Vulgate. This was the responsibility of the "Holy Mother Church." The only English-language Bible permitted by the Catholic Church was the so-called Douay Version, a translation made by English Catholic exiles in 1582 (New Testament, published in Rheims, France) and 1609 (Old Testament, published in Douay, France).[20] Priests in the United States took the Council of Trent's decrees seriously, making the ABS's work of Bible distribution very difficult in heavily Catholic communities. Dozens of ABS agents complained in letters to New York, that priests were forbidding their parishioners from accepting Bibles with the organization's imprint. An ABS agent in Ulster County, New York, described a common practice among the Catholic laity he encountered: "I have visited the most difficult districts personally, and on presenting a Bible, the first thing is to look at the title page and then return the book." One woman asked for an ABS Bible, but added that she would need to conceal it from her priest or else he will "lay a penance upon me that I shall not be able to bear." This story fits well with the ABS belief that the Catholic laity were "afraid to receive the Bible."[21] Some Catholic priests went so far to advise parishioners to burn copies of the King James Version. ABS publications reprinted several articles related to the "Champlain Bible burning" of 1842. Champlain was a town near the Canadian border with a large population of French Catholics. When the Jesuits in the town learned that the ABS had distributed Bibles to Catholics, they required all those who possessed one of these Bibles to make a confession and turn over their Bibles to be burned in a public bonfire. A similar incident occurred in Buffalo around 1850, although in this case the burning was stopped by "the interference of a good woman" who promised to take the Bibles and distribute them among the city's Protestants.[22]

The ire of the ABS faithful was particularly stirred when the Pope himself decided to comment on the prevalence of Protestant Bible societies. In 1844, Gregory XVI issued an encyclical warning Catholics about Protestant attempts to convert them. Though he believed that all Protestant denominations were a threat to Catholicism around the world, Gregory specifically called out "the Bible Societies" as worthy of specific attention. He described them as an "army, uniting together for one common object, namely to publish the books of the Holy Scriptures translated into every vernacular tongue, in an infinite number of copies, and to distribute them indiscriminately . . . as to induce every one to read them without the aid of an interpreter or guide." Later in December 1849, Pius IX issued a similar encyclical. He pointed to "recent improvements in the art of printing" as being responsible for the "various insidious measures, of which malicious enemies of the church, and of society, endeavor to avail themselves for seducing the people . . . to their wicked designs." Catholics should "be on their guard," he added, "*against the poison*, which cannot fail to be *imbibed by the reading of such books*." Pious also reminded Catholics that "no person whatever is warranted to confide in his own judgment, as to [the Scriptures'] true meaning, of opposed to the holy mother church, who alone and no other, has received the commission from Christ . . . to decide upon the true sense and interpretation of the Sacred Writing." The American Bible Society published both of these Encyclicals in the *Bible Society Record*, and, as might be expected, used them to show the backwardness of Catholic nations when compared to the freedom and progress of Protestant nations.[23]

The ABS concerns about defeating the Catholic threat and spreading Protestantism in the West often intersected with national politics. In June 1845, the United States became embroiled in a border dispute with Mexico. The Rio Grande River served as the border between Mexico and the newly annexed state of Texas. President James K. Polk sent General Zachary Taylor to Texas with 3,500 soldiers to ward off a possible Mexican invasion. When the Mexicans refused to negotiate with Polk (who not only wanted the Rio Grande border, but the territories of New Mexico and California as well), the president sent Taylor and his troops to the banks of the Rio Grande in an area that Mexico believed it possessed. In April 1846 a skirmish broke out in this region. Polk took the skirmish as an act of Mexican aggression and in May convinced Congress to declare war. Polk's claims about what exactly happened in this disputed territory were controversial, and many questioned whether the Mexicans had indeed acted first, but the Mexican-American War—"Mr. Polk's War"—had commenced.[24]

ABS leadership followed closely the events on the Rio Grande. Well before the hostilities broke out, the Society was distributing Bible in Texas. The new Republic of Texas, which was created by American settlers who had won their independence from Mexico in 1836, would serve as a "door through which, in the providence of God, the Gospel could be introduced into Mexico." Roman Catholicism was the official religion of Mexico and many of the Americans who settled there in the 1820s and 1830s, including Stephen F. Austin, one of the heroes of the revolution, had converted to the Catholic faith as part of their settlement agreement. The Texas Bible Society, an auxiliary of the ABS, understood the Texas Revolution to be a victory for Protestantism over Catholicism. The managers reminded the ABS in 1841 that their republic had "just been rescued from the dominion of Popery." The Texas Bible Society made sure that every family in the republic was supplied with a Protestant Bible and even asked the ABS to open a Bible depository in Galveston. But Catholic power was great. An ABS agent in Texas wrote that Catholics were establishing churches and "seminaries of learning" at a rapid rate.[25]

When the Mexican-American War broke out in 1846, ABS agents reported "evidence of great destitution of the Bible" in East Texas. George West wrote from Jefferson County, Texas, "there is perhaps a greater famine of the word of God in some of these counties than any others in the United States." The few Protestant Bibles in the region were either "worn out" or "destroyed." The ABS was prepared to fill the void. Like many evangelical Protestant benevolent organizations, it saw an opportunity to "vindicate her character as the true angel of mercy to the world, and to show that not by might, nor by power, but by the Spirit of God, the wounds of Texas must be healed; and never was there a time which so loudly called on the Christian sower to go forth and sow."[26] The ABS responded by supplying Bibles to the American army in Mexico, the first of many opportunities the Society would have over the course of the next 150 years to provide Bibles for the military. Auxiliaries throughout the country gave Bibles to soldiers preparing to enter the Mexican theater. In 1847 the ABS sent 400 Testaments, earmarked for soldiers traveling down the Mississippi River on their way to Mexico, to Bible societies in Cincinnati and New Orleans, and another 1,350 were designated for troops leaving Indiana.[27]

In December 1845 an ABS agent in Granville, Massachusetts, reported to the ABS headquarters in New York news of a religious revival occurring in the town. As was quite common whenever an agent presided over such an awakening, he credited the renewed religious fervor to the distribution of the Bible. In a moment of spirit-filled exaltation, he ended his letter with a word of praise to God for all that was happening in Granville: "He has magnified the word above all thy name! The Bible! The Bible is the religion of Protestants!" Indeed, as the ABS made abundantly clear in the first forty years of its existence, the Bible was indeed the religion of the Protestants. The organization could testify again and again to the fact that the word of God, without note or comment, had done its work in the United States and done its work well. With the arrival of Catholics to American shores the ABS vision of forging a Christian, Protestant nation seemed to be in more jeopardy with each passing year, but the Board of Managers, the staff in New York, the agents in the field, and the faithful lay men and women who supported the organization, were confident that the Bible would continue to help Protestant light to triumph over Catholic darkness and American liberty to triumph over Catholic tyranny. Such confidence would be needed in the decades to come, as the United States—and the Bible Cause—would be rent asunder by civil war.

A Bible House Divided

In 1853 the ABS opened its new Bible House on Astor Place in New York City. It was a massive building. The Bible House cost $303,000 to build; it was six stories high, and its brick exterior walls fronted four different city streets. Much of the building was used for the production of Bibles, but there was also office space for ABS staff and secretaries and additional space for the staff of other New York benevolent societies. The ABS rented space at street level for "various business occupations." The building committee concluded that the new Bible House was "congenial to all who love the Bible, and in themselves a beautiful development of that Christian civilization and 'good will to men.'" The structure became the center of print culture not only in New York City, but in the entire nation. Over the course of the next thirty years it was a regular stop for tourists. Mark Twain visited the Bible House in 1867 and claimed that he "enjoyed the time more than I could possibly have done in any circus."[1] Its size and façade sent a clear message: Christian civilization in the United States would advance, and the American Bible Society would lead the way. But few of the ABS's staff could anticipate what was coming. The Bible House may have been a symbol of a growing nation founded upon the word of God, but eight years after its opening the Civil War would threaten the very idea of American nationalism. Could the Bible Cause transcend political and sectional strife and continue its mission as a national organization committed to bringing the message of the Bible to the people of the United States?

Before the ABS came to grips with the American Civil War, it had to weather a storm directly related to its policy on the distribution of Bibles to slaves. The ABS had a long history of opposition to the institution of African slavery in the United States. Many of the organization's founders—including Boudinot and John Jay—opposed slavery. Jay's son William drafted the founding constitution of the New York Anti-Slavery Society in 1833 and remained active in the organization, serving in various leadership roles, until his death. As antislavery became an important moral and political issue in the United States, the ABS developed strong ties with the American Colonization Society (ACS).

The goal of the ACS was to emancipate American slaves and unite them with free blacks in Liberia, West Africa. The ACS was also founded in 1816 and it shared many of the same founders and officers as the ABS, including Samuel Mills, Jedidiah Morse, Bushrod Washington, Alexander Proudfit, and Theodore Frelinghuysen. The ABS frequently sent Bibles to Liberia to support the work of the ACS.[2]

Antislavery forces in America, particularly those who favored the immediate abolition of slavery, did not think the ABS was doing enough to bring Bibles to the slaves. In 1834, at the first meeting of the American Anti-Slavery Society (AASS), an organization that included some of the leading abolitionists in the United States, including William Lloyd Garrison and Arthur Tappan, the ABS was taken to task. Up until this point, the ABS did not have an official policy on the distribution of Bibles to enslaved men and women. Constitutional principles guided the Board of Managers and those principles applied to all people, white or black, slave or free. The Bible should be distributed without note or comment to anyone who could read it. And this must be the work carried out by ABS auxiliaries.

Because many ABS auxiliaries in the South were governed by slaveholders who were not interested in having their slaves exposed to the message of liberty and freedom taught in the Bible (contrary to the beliefs of many southern Christians, abolitionists believed that the Bible was an antislavery book), the leaders of the AASS pressed the ABS to distribute Bibles directly to slaves. In order to encourage a move in this direction, the AASS offered the ABS $5,000 to make sure that "every colored family in the United States be furnished with a copy of the Bible." Lewis Tappan, a founder of the ABS, suggested that the men of the AASS raise an additional $30,000 to help the Bible Society accomplish this task. Almost immediately, the members present at the meeting committed $14,500 to the cause. By the end of the first annual meeting, for reasons that are unclear, the amount of money to be raised was reduced to $20,000 and an additional stipulation was added: The ABS would need to accomplish the task of supplying all the slaves with Bibles in a period of two years.[3] If the ABS could come close to providing every white American with a copy of the Bible during its two-year General Supply, the leaders of the AASS were confident that it could do the same thing among the enslaved families of the South.

Shortly after its first annual meeting in May 1834, the AASS continued to press the ABS to accept its lucrative offer. It criticized the ABS General Supply for failing to include slaves—which the leadership of the AASS estimated to represent one-sixth of American families. They also saw the Bible as a means by which slaves might learn how to read. Such an argument challenged the ABS belief that the Bible was only useful to those who were already literate. "We do not say, 'teach them to read and *then* we will give them a Bible,'" the

AASS argued, "but here are Bibles which they may have *to read*." The AASS challenged every ABS auxiliary to place "one [Bible] in the hands of every five slaves, and then at length we shall see how much regard they have to the command of the Savior to carry the gospel to every Creature." Moreover, if the Bible could find a place on a southern plantation, and the slaves read it and acted on its message, it would inevitably force slaveholders to admit that the Bible does not condone this form of labor.[4] This was the AASS version of the "Bible doing its work."

The ABS responded quickly to the AASS's challenge. The Committee on Distribution thanked the AASS for the gift and affirmed its commitment to distributing the Bible "among their fellow destitute fellow men, of every name and nation wherever they can be reached." But the men of the committee also concluded that they were bound by the ABS constitution to keep the primary burden of distribution on the auxiliaries. From 1834 onward, this would be the official ABS policy. The ABS wanted to make it clear that its decision did not mean that the Society was "indifferent to the duty of furnishing the Bible to the slave"; it would be more than willing to "urge the auxiliaries to get the Bible in the hands of slaves." But in the end, the Society was constitutionally bound to let the auxiliaries "act as they judge most wise in their circumstances." Finally, the ABS affirmed that it distributed "many thousands" of Bibles to auxiliaries in the slaveholding South and many of them did end up in the hands of slaves, although it was doubtful that any of the slaves who received a Bible could read and few of their masters had any interest in teaching them.[5]

The ABS response drew widespread criticism from the antislavery community. In 1849 another antislavery society, the American and Foreign Anti-Slavery Society, invited a fugitive slave from Kentucky named Henry Bibb to address its annual meeting in New York. Bibb's speech echoed familiar themes. He noted that "the Bible Society . . . had not done all that it might have done" to bring Bibles to the slave population. Instead, it had given slaves "the go-by." Bibb made it clear to the philanthropists in attendance at the meeting that the leaders of several ABS auxiliaries in Kentucky were slaveholders. In fact, the man who sold him to New Orleans and, in the process, separated him from his family, was the secretary of an ABS auxiliary. The American and Foreign Anti-Slavery Society decided to throw most of its support behind the American Missionary Society, an organization that it believed was making a "systematic effort" to get Bibles and tracts to slaves.[6] The criticism grew stronger as the Civil War drew closer. At an antislavery rally in Ravenna, Ohio, the attendees included the ABS in a list of benevolent societies that "in consequence of the countenance and support they give to American slavery are unworthy of confidence & support of American Christians."[7] An abolitionist in Edgartown, Massachusetts, who wrote the ABS in 1858, had read about the

Society's refusal to accept the money of the AASS: "Did the A.A.S. ever make this offer?" he asked, "and if so did you refuse it and why?"[8] Through it all the ABS held its ground. It would refuse to distribute Bibles directly to slaves.

By 1861 the differences over Bible distribution to slaves took a backseat to the pressing political matters of the day. After Abraham Lincoln was elected in November 1860, the South finally acted on its longstanding fear that some-day a northern president would threaten the institution of slavery. Though Lincoln was no friend to the abolitionist camp, his moral and economic opposition to the spread of slavery still posed a direct threat to the southern way of life. Following his election Lincoln promised not to interfere with slavery in the South when he took office in March 1861, and his Republican Party members did everything they could to separate themselves from radical abolitionist behavior. But few southerners believed them. Rather than facing the prospects of a Lincoln presidency, southern states decided to secede from the Union. South Carolina led the way in December 1860. Mississippi, Florida, Alabama, Georgia, Louisiana, and Texas soon followed. These states would form the Confederate States of America in February 1861. When South Carolina troops opened fire on the Union military instal-lation on Ft. Sumter on April 12, 1861, the Civil War was underway. By the end of May, Virginia, Arkansas, Tennessee, and North Carolina had joined the Confederacy.

The American Bible Society prided itself on being a national organization. During the course of the war, employees of the ABS were forbidden to make public statements on the political affairs of the day.[9] At the time of the Civil War the Society continued to operate under the belief that the strength of the nation was directly linked to the influence of the Bible on its citizenry. In the months following secession, the ABS remained committed to staying the course in their southern distribution efforts. In his annual address published in May 1861, ABS president Theodore Frelinghuysen was certain that the Bible had the power to bring the nation back together again. He insisted that the Bible Cause was still unified: "We are still one—bound together by the bands of Christian kindness, animated by like hopes ... and cheered by the same sympathies." The Bible, he argued, "can harmonize discordant elements" and had the power to "unite extremes, to reconcile differences and compose peace . . . Nothing can withstand its influence." Some of the southern auxiliaries seemed to agree, at least initially. N. R. Middletown, the president of the Bible Society of Charleston, South Carolina, made it clear in a letter to the Bible House that "political differences should not be permitted to interfere with the existing relationship of the Societies." He added, "surely there is no reason why a work so entirely catholic as the one in which we are engaged should suffer in any way from dissensions in which it is no way involved. Political considerations should always be subordinated to the claims of the Word of God."[10]

As Lincoln set out to raise an army for the purpose of bringing the South back into the Union, the friends of the Bible Cause took the message of Frelinghuysen and Middleton to heart. It was the Bible, not the Army of the Potomac, which had the best chance of reuniting the broken nation. It was time for the ABS to "redouble" its efforts and "make greater exertions to diffuse the Sacred Volume throughout every portion of the country."[11] This, of course, was easier said than done. At the same time that some auxiliaries were reporting a renewed commitment to the work of Bible distribution, others admitted that the start of a Civil War was hindering the Bible Cause. An agent in Southern Iowa reported that he "was able to accomplish but little in the month of April owing to the political agitation." In northern Missouri, an agent wrote that "the month's labors were not particularly encouraging, owing in great measure to the excited state of the country." An agent in Michigan had difficulty collecting donations "oweing to the state of the country and monetary derangement." Instead of making a contribution to their favorite benevolent society, the people of Michigan were spending their money to supply local militia.[12]

The Civil War opened up a new mission field for the ABS. Here was an opportunity to reach more people with the life-saving message of the Bible than ever before. In 1863, 1864, and 1865 the Society distributed over 1 million Testaments per year. This was the first time in its history that its distribution numbers had reached the seven-figure mark and it would not happen again until 1918.[13] The instant need for Bibles in the months immediately following Ft. Sumter caught the staff of the Bible House off guard: "Orders . . . come from every part of the country in such abundance, that it has been nearly impossible to keep up our supply." The Bible House asked the auxiliaries to be patient as they replenished their empty warehouse. By April 1862, the ABS announced to its constituency that the "largest part" of its distribution to soldiers had "now been completed." Today, with the benefit of hindsight, such a pronouncement appears rather naïve. Yet like many Americans, the ABS was expecting a short war. The Board of Managers had no idea that they would be supplying Testaments to Civil War soldiers for another three years.[14]

Though the war led to increased donations from some auxiliaries, in the bigger picture the economic hardships placed on the ABS were great. The new demand for Bibles meant the Society needed to spend more money on paper, leather, printing, and other materials necessary to produce a soldier's Testament. By August 1862 the number of Testaments printed off the Bible House presses had risen to about 125,000 per month, and by the end of the war the ABS was churning out Bibles at a rate of nine volumes per minute.

These Bibles were going to the troops in the field, injured soldiers in makeshift military hospitals, and Confederates in Union prisons. In November 1862, the high demand and the rising cost of manufacturing in an unstable economy forced the ABS to raise its prices on Bibles by nearly 25 percent.[15]

Every box of ABS Testaments distributed during the Civil War came with a circular titled "Suggestions for Distribution of the Scriptures in the Army and Navy, Hospitals, Etc." These instructions encouraged distributors to deliver a Testament promptly to "every man who wishes it, and will use it properly." Distributors were warned against giving Bibles to soldiers who did not want one or who might "wantonly sell, or misuse, or destroy" it. The ABS required them to make careful notes of the process of delivery and relay any interesting stories to the Bible House "which illustrate the value of the Scriptures" in a time of war. These stories should include the Bible's "effects on morals, manners, religious character, conversions, reclamation of backsliders, happy deaths of Christians & c." Another circular included thirteen questions for Bible distributors. It asked for a record of the number of troops supplied with Testaments, the plan for distributing the books among those still in need, the literacy rate of soldiers receiving Testaments, the number of soldiers who refused to receive a Testament, the number of military hospitals supplied, and the "general spirit" of those who received a copy of the scriptures.[16]

These circulars and questionnaires served two purposes. First, they allowed the ABS to distribute Bibles as frugally as possible. With the prices of printing Bibles rising every day, the ABS wanted to make sure that those soldiers who received a Bible were actually going to use it. Second, they served as a testimony to the work of God among the soldiers. As always, the ABS staff wanted to make sure that they could promote stories of the Bible "doing its work" in the camp. Civil War stories filled the pages of the *Bible Society Record* as a means of encouraging ABS supporters in their spiritual lives and prompting readers to donate money to the cause. By collecting anecdotes about how its books were being used in the field, the ABS was able to tell its own story about the Civil War, a story with the Bible and Christianity, and not the violence of battle or immorality of the camps, at the center.

In the first two years of the war, the ABS distributed Bibles to northern soldiers in the traditional fashion—through local auxiliaries and agents. This strategy proved effective for providing regiments with Testaments before they headed off to war or for supplying soldiers in hospitals and prisons. But very few auxiliary volunteers or ABS agents could get close to soldiers in military camps situated near the front lines of battle. In order to bring the Bible to soldiers where they needed it most, the ABS forged a working relationship with the US Christian Commission. Founded by the Young Men's Christian Association (YMCA) in November 1861, the Christian Commission was a national evangelical benevolent organization created to distribute supplies, stationery, medical services, and especially religious publications to the troops. During the course of the Civil War over 5,000 volunteers, united behind the purpose of persuading soldiers "to become reconciled to God through the blood of His Son," worked for the Christian Commission.[17] The Commission had headquarters in Washington, Baltimore, Chicago, St. Louis, Annapolis, and Frederick, Maryland, and worked closely with a network of Union chaplains and volunteers in military hospitals. The ABS began providing Bibles to the Christian Commission sometime in the fall of 1862.

The ABS also targeted its Civil War distribution efforts toward places where runaway slaves were welcomed by the Union Army as contraband of war. For example, in November 1861 when the Union Army occupied Beaufort, a town on Port Royal Island in the South Carolina low country, white slaveholders fled for their lives, leaving behind thousands of black slaves. Northern benevolent societies quickly moved into Beaufort to help the former slaves adjust to their newfound freedom. In what became a "rehearsal" for the Reconstruction Era that would follow the Civil War, slaves, under the auspices of what came to be known as "the Port Royal Experiment" began working the plantations left by their former masters. Schools were set up for the education of these freedmen. And, of course, these freedmen needed Bibles. The ABS worked with both the Christian Commission and the American Missionary Association to provide Bibles to freedmen in Beaufort, Hilton Head, St. Helena, and the surrounding island region. F. S. Williams, a minister working for the American Missionary Association, described freedmen crowding around boxes of Bibles and Testaments, eager to "see the books from the Norf." Williams noted that these former slaves—"every man, woman, and child"—were "determined" to use their Bibles to learn how to read. In Beaufort, nearly four thousand freedmen were attending federally sponsored schools in 1864 where they were using ABS Testaments—2,000 of them—"as a textbook for daily reading."[18]

While the distribution to the soldiers and the civilians of the Union was moving forward with great success, the ABS reaffirmed its commitment to distribute Bibles to the destitute in both the North and the South. But war made it extremely difficult for the ABS to be anything other than a *Northern* benevolent society. In January 1863 an ABS agent in Virginia lamented, "the largest part of my former field is still held by the enemy, and in the other part the surface of society is so much disturbed by war as to prevent any regular Bible work." Other agents, especially those with roots in the South, resigned. It was not uncommon for Confederate soldiers to destroy boxes of ABS Bibles simply because they were sent by a northern benevolent society. As ABS Corresponding Secretary James McNeil, a southerner who would eventually leave New York and join the Confederate Army, wrote, "surely an embargo will not be deliberately laid upon the Word of God."[19] Communication was key to the Bible Cause in the Civil War. The ABS needed to maintain contact with its southern auxiliaries in order to receive and fulfill their orders for Bibles. Cut telegraph lines, mangled railroad tracks, and the general political and military unrest in the country hindered the movement of Bibles from North to South. In September 1861, the ABS complained that "we are bound . . . to supply the wants of the South. But we have now no access to the Confederate States whatever." Adams Express, the company the ABS commonly used for its delivery needs, refused to transport anything below Washington, DC. It was easier for the ABS to send Bibles to Constantinople than it was, at least at the start of the Civil War, to get boxes of Testaments past the Confederate lines. And since the South lacked major printing presses and book binding operations, the demand for Bibles in the region was high. According to one estimate, only one of every six Confederate soldiers owned a Bible or Testament.[20]

The Confederacy attempted to meet the need for Bibles in several ways. The Confederate Bible Society was organized in Augusta, Georgia, in 1862. Over the course of the war it printed two versions of the New Testament for use among the troops, but it was never able to keep up with the great demand for Bibles among southern soldiers.[21] The Virginia Bible Society sent Rev. Moses D. Hoge to England, where he convinced the British and Foreign Bible Society to make Virginia a grant of 10,000 Bibles, 50,000 Testaments, and 250,000 Gospels and Psalms for distribution among the Army of Northern Virginia. These Bibles were shipped to the South in small installments by blockade runners. Hoge's travels became legendary in the annals of Virginia history. The Union blockade forced him to travel to England via Nassau, Cuba, and St. Thomas. On his return home Union naval guns fired at his ship while it was docked in Wilmington, North Carolina. Hoge's dramatic journey led to an ongoing relationship between the Confederacy and the British and Foreign Bible Society, resulting in a steady shipment of Bibles to the South.[22] When the ABS offered to supply Virginia, the Virginia Bible Society declined its offer, claiming that "there exists, therefore, no longer any necessity to apply to the American Bible Society for either grants or sales."

During the Civil War the ABS relied heavily on the Maryland Bible Society, an ABS auxiliary, to help it bring Bibles to the South. The government of Maryland supported the Union, but as a slave state it maintained connections with the Confederacy. Maryland Bible Society President Thomas Quinan worked closely with ABS Corresponding Secretary William Taylor to bring Bibles into Virginia and other portions of the South. Quinan reported success smuggling ABS Bibles into Virginia through "benevolent women" who were able to cross enemy lines without being stopped. At other times he brought Bibles into the region by taking advantage of the common belief among the South that Maryland was sympathetic to the cause of the Confederacy. Quinan informed Taylor that he and his colleagues were in a state of "constant watchfulness to avail ourselves of every opening to send our book to them" and he would continue to "practice the wisdom of the 'Serpent with the harmlessness of the dove'" as he worked up new ways to get the Bible behind enemy lines. Because of the work of Quinan and the Maryland Bible Society, Baltimore gained a reputation as a place where Southern clergy, missionaries, and chaplains could come to purchase Bibles without having to deal with the political fallout and shipping restrictions of working directly with the Bible House in New York.[23]

Another partner in this work was the Memphis and Shelby County Bible Society of Tennessee. This auxiliary, under the direction of President Ethel Thomas, provided tens of thousands of Bibles to Confederate soldiers under the commands of Braxton Bragg and Albert Sidney Johnston. It is unclear whether or not these generals knew that their armies were being supplied by the ABS, nor is it clear whether or not they cared.[24] Another breakthrough in the South occurred in August 1863 when Basil Manly, the president of the Southern Baptist Sunday School Board, addressed a letter by flag of truce to the Maryland Bible Society requesting that the Baltimore-based organization purchase 25,000 Testaments from the ABS for use in southern Sunday schools. Manly, of course, wanted to meet what he perceived to be a spiritual need among the children of his denomination, but he was also aware that such a purchase would go a long way to "assure the Christian people of the South that the American Bible Society is still faithful to its constitution."[25]

One of the more interesting parts of the ABS distribution efforts was the sale of Bibles in exchange for cotton. Since the Union would not accept Confederate currency as a form of donation or payment for Bibles, the Memphis and Shelby County Bible Society in Tennessee circumvented this problem by offering the ABS bales of cotton. Cotton was purchased by southern philanthropists and friends of the Bible Cause with Confederate money, and the bales were shipped off to New York. In February 1865, an anonymous donor gave the Memphis and Shelby Society six bales of cotton to help defer the cost of electrotype plates used to print Bibles at the Society distribution depot in Nashville. Whatever was left after the plates were paid for was used to provide boxes of Bibles and Testaments for Confederate troops. Similarly, the Memphis society received a request from Monticello, Arkansas, proposing to exchange ten bales of cotton for Bibles and Testaments that would be distributed to citizens and soldiers in the surrounding region. The Memphis and Shelby Society planned to have the cotton shipped directly to the Bible House as soon as possible. Porter was also optimistic that he could get "some cotton for the Bible cause" from Christians in Mississippi. The ABS was not prepared to receive cotton in exchange for copies of the scriptures, but the Board of Managers were more than willing to accept it as a form of payment if it meant getting Bibles past the Confederate military lines. Transporting cotton through a country torn by Civil War was difficult. The Memphis and Shelby Society needed the permission of Confederate authorities and generals. The ABS had to obtain special approval from the US Treasury Department. In some cases the cotton, once received in New York, was deposited in a US government warehouse "to the credit of the American Bible Society for special purposes."[26]

What role did ABS Bibles play in the life of Civil War soldiers? The answer to this question was of great interest to the Bible House staff. The success of their efforts could be measured in statistics, but data was useless without anecdotes about the way the Bible was changing individual lives in the field. Most Civil War soldiers believed that the Bible was the word of God. As a result, they read it. The evidence is overwhelming. Stories abound of soldiers reading the Bible in their tents before bedtime. Sometimes they would read together in groups, with each solider taking a turn. A chaplain of a New York regiment stationed near Alexandria, Virginia described some troops "sitting in sunny places reading their Testaments." As they perused the "Oracles of Truth," the chaplain reported, they often looked "up into each other's faces, conversing, thinking of home, and distant friends they might never see again." An agent in Ohio informed the Bible House that the New Testament was read by the troops more than any other reading material that found its way into the camp: "I have seen packages of tracts lying in the mud, and pamphlets put to various other uses than reading, but I have not seen one New Testament thrown away or otherwise misused." The members of a Wisconsin regiment were seen reading their Testaments in the breastworks before the Battle of Petersburg while bullets of rebel sharpshooters whistled overhead.[27] The ABS had the most success distributing a pocket-sized version of the New Testament. The troops found the nonpareil 32mo. (4.5 × 3.5 inches) soldier's edition especially useful because the entire Bible—Old and New Testament—was too bulky and cumbersome for everyday use and it was very difficult to carry it with them into the field of battle. These Testaments were also cheap (anywhere between thirty-five and seven cents each at the start of the war) and easy to distribute.[28]

Civil War soldiers read their Bibles as a source of spiritual comfort as they faced the serious possibility of death. While many chaplains, US Christian Commission volunteers, and ABS and auxiliary agents reported on the sins of drunkenness, profanity, Sabbath-breaking, and gambling (card playing, mostly) in the camps, they also described dramatic conversions and evidence of deep Christian piety among the troops. It is not too far of a stretch to say that both the Union and Confederate armies experienced a sustained and ongoing religious revival that lasted through the entire war.[29] For example, an ABS agent working with Union soldiers in the eastern theater of the war described a Massachusetts officer who during picket duty following a day of "carnage" on the battlefield noticed a blood-stained Bible sitting next to a dead Confederate soldier. When he examined the Bible more closely, he saw that the cover contained the bloody fingerprints of a soldier who was obviously gripping it tightly at the time of his death. When the officer saw how this southern soldier "drew light and comfort for his passage through the dark valley" from the word of God, he eventually began to read it for himself. This led him to ultimately "surrender himself to the authority of its divine Author." Stories of soldiers lying dead on the battlefield clutching an ABS Testament opened to a favorite verse (Psalms 19 and 23 were very popular) filled the pages of the *Bible Society Record*.[30]

Many soldiers viewed the Bible as a holy book with spiritual power apart from the words contained therein. Even if the Bible was not being read, it still had the mystical power to provide spiritual solace in the most frightening of times as long as it was somehow connected to one's body during the thick of the battle. It was common for soldiers heading off into battle to pull their pocket Testaments out of their knapsacks and place them in the breast pockets of their shirts. The object of such a move, according to the ABS, was "to have the Word of God with them if they should fall in battle, to be the lamp of their feet and the light of their path, even if called to the last march through the dark valley." One soldier in Yorktown, Virginia pulled a worn-out Testament from his pocket and told a chaplain that he had carried the book during the entire Peninsular Campaign. He pointed to the outside of his coat pocket where a hole was developing over his heart in the exact size of an ABS Testament. When the chaplain asked him if he had been reading the worn-out Bible, the soldier slapped his hand on the battered Bible and declared, "I would not take five dollars for that book! It has been with me thus far through the war!"[31] Oftentimes the armies used ABS Bibles as a means of identifying dead soldiers on the battlefield in the wake of a particularly bloody battle. One soldier described the Testament as a kind of "headstone." It was not only a symbol of a dead soldier's experience with Christian faith, but if he wrote in his Bible, as many were inclined to do, it might be the only means by which anxious parents and friends could identify the body.[32]

Sometimes a Bible in the shirt pocket could save a soldier's life by stopping an enemy bullet. As might be expected, these stories appeared over and over again in ABS publications. While it is unlikely that a pocket-sized ABS Testament was thick enough to protect a soldier from a direct hit from a mini ball, these books were probably capable of shielding soldiers from spent bullets—balls that were near the end of their useful range. The ABS and its auxiliaries were quick to compare the spiritual and physical protections that the Bible offered Civil War soldiers. The Bible could save a soldier's life and could save a soldier's soul. John Hampen Chamberlain, a Virginia artillery officer, jokingly wrote in a letter to his mother that he had yet to meet "the man whose life was saved by a pack of cards in his breast pocket."[33]

The work of supplying an army with the Bible was often complicated by the itinerant nature of military life. A soldier who was supplied with a Bible before leaving home might need additional Bibles as his war experience wore on. The ABS planned for such cases. Civil War soldiers were notorious for losing their Bibles and Testaments or forgetting to take them when they traveled to another camp. Water could easily ruin a Bible, making it unreadable. But such exposure to the elements was unavoidable as soldiers marched in the rain or waded across streams and rivers. Following the Battle of Murfreesboro, E. P. Smith of the Christian Commission spent the afternoon walking the Union camp and only found six Testaments. This meant that his work in distributing Testaments at the next camp would be light because so few had been lost in battle. But when the Army of the Cumberland arrived in Tullahoma, Winchester, and Selma, Tennessee, he realized that nearly all of the soldiers' books had been damaged by heaving fighting and pouring rains. Some soldiers had lost their Bibles when they burned their baggage to keep it from the Confederate troops under the command of Braxton Bragg. Smith asked the ABS to send him 5,000 more Testaments as soon as possible.[34]

During the Civil War era the mission and guiding principles of the American Bible Society was tested on several fronts. In the decades leading up to the war the Board of Managers clung to the original intent of the Society's 1816 constitution amidst intense pressure from abolitionists. Though most of the ABS leadership was sympathetic to the cause of bringing the scriptures to slaves, they clung to their founding principle that gave local auxiliaries the power to distribute Bibles as they saw fit. The Civil War also put the Bible House's ability to print and distribute massive numbers of Bibles in a short period of time to its ultimate test, but with the help of the US Christian Commission and local auxiliaries, the word of God found its way to the soldiers who wanted it. Finally, the Civil War challenged the ABS's identity as a truly *national* Bible society. For five long the years the Bible House lost some of its power in shaping the Christian course of the *United* States. It was now time to get some of that power back.

8

Rebuilding a Christian Nation

When the Civil War officially ended at Appomattox Courthouse on the morning of April 9, 1865, parts of the South looked like a wasteland. Farms had been trampled by Union soldiers. Major Confederate cities such as Richmond, Atlanta, and Columbia lay in ruins. Cotton fields were burned to the ground by fleeing Confederate soldiers. It would take a generation or more before the South recovered. To make matters worse, over 200,000 federal troops occupied the region. Meanwhile, in Washington, DC, the federal government debated how best to bring the South back into the nation and integrate over 3 million slaves into society. Dixie would never be the same.

As plans circulated about how to accomplish the mission of reconstructing the South, the American Bible Society started to reconnect with its southern auxiliaries and repair whatever damage was done to its national reputation. It was important to remind the local Bible societies in the South, and anyone else who would listen, that the ABS did not choose sides during the Civil War. The vagaries of war *did* get in the way of the effective distribution of Bibles to the Confederacy, but there was really nothing the ABS could have done to overcome these obstacles. Now the end of the war offered an opportunity to bring the Bible to a broken Southern culture in need of its message. The Lord works in mysterious ways, even using the "wrath of man to praise him." The ABS made it clear to its southern auxiliaries that its work in the former Confederacy had nothing to do with the plan of the so-called Radical Republicans or any other political groups with a blueprint to reconstruct the South. John Knox Witherspoon, an ABS agent in Camden, South Carolina, put it best when he told Corresponding Secretary William Taylor that the Bible society was best suited to prevent the "war of races" taking place in the United States because it had always shunned political involvement. Witherspoon lamented that too many of the teachers and government workers arriving in the South had become "tools of Political Organizations." These carpetbaggers had sowed "seeds of dissention and discord where peace and brotherly love should be the object of every one."[1]

The ABS believed that the Bible was indispensable to the "new birth of freedom" that Abraham Lincoln described so eloquently in his Gettysburg Address. "There can be no hopeful or true reconstruction of the country, nor any real pacification," the *Bible Society Record* announced, "without the Bible at the foundation of our government and civilization. We want, we must have, an open Bible in the hands of all the people, white and black." Unlike many Protestant denominations that split into northern and southern branches in the decades prior to the Civil War, the ABS did not have to worry about reuniting churches. It could focus instead on the work of national healing—the kind of healing that only the word of God could bring. Its role was to be the "Balm of Gilead for a nation's bleeding wounds, the lively Oracles of our country's peace, and the hope of salvation for a dying race." Civil war had plagued the nation because its people rejected the authority of the Bible in their lives. Only a return to its teachings would "calm the passions of the people, restore peace and quiet to the land, and secure unity, harmony, and general good will."[2]

The ABS approached Reconstruction with the explicit goal of supplying the entire country with Bibles, regardless of region or race. The need for such work should have been obvious to all good citizens of the United States. The distribution of the Bible would result in the restoration of civil government, the purification of society, a revival of the religious life of the nation, and the "union and unity" of both the churches and the states. *Bible Society Record* proclaimed, "providence has plainly ordained that we shall be one people, with one government, one civilization, one Bible, on Christian faith and destiny."[3] This was not a new idea in the Bible House, but it had a particular relevance in the late 1860s and 1870s.

The end of the Civil War coincided with the fiftieth anniversary, in 1866, of the ABS. Dr. Thomas DeWitt of the Collegiate Reformed Church in New York reminded the society's membership of the "peculiar significance in the fact that our year of Jubilee is that of returning peace to our country." In biblical times, DeWitt noted, the jubilee restored Israel's "broken bonds" and allowed them to reconnect with their "heritage." The ABS season of jubilee would restore the broken bonds of a nation wracked by war and allow citizens to reconnect with its Christian heritage. It was a new age of liberty in the United States, and the people needed to be reminded that the individual rights that they so enjoyed were rooted in the teachings of Scripture. They also needed a short history lesson on the relationship between the Bible and the American founding. The word of God had been present when the first settlers arrived, it was adopted by the first Congress, and it was the book on which George Washington "laid his honest hand" upon when he took the oath of office as the first president of the United States. How could anyone ignore the fact that the Bible provided "vitality and strength to the foundation and pillars of the American republic?"[4]

The Board of Managers thought it would be appropriate to celebrate fifty years with yet another General Supply. As we saw in chapter 4, the First General Supply, which was conducted by the ABS from 1829 to 1831, had the ambitious goal of providing a Bible to every household in the United States. The Second General Supply was initiated just prior to the Civil War, and as a result never gained the kind of national attention that the First General Supply received. But as the Civil War came to an end and the spiritual needs of the nation seemed great, the ABS decided it was time to once again try to distribute a Bible to every American family. This time, however, the destitute would include the families of freedmen.

True to form, the ABS relied heavily on auxiliaries to carry out the Third General Supply. The Board of Managers encouraged the auxiliaries to focus on bringing Testaments to young people, seamen, railroad hands, stage drivers, people who labored on the Sabbath, and, of course, to the freed men and women throughout the South. There was no special fundraising associated with these efforts, but the ABS encouraged donors to earmark financial gifts for the General Supply. Soon money was flowing into the ABS coffers from places such as Charleston, Mobile, and Savannah. This was a cause for rejoicing. The South was once again contributing to the Bible Cause and one ABS agent reported that "everywhere [in the South] the American Bible Society has been welcomed as a peacemaker and an evangelist."

But in other places of the South the General Supply did not meet with much enthusiasm. An Alabama agent reported in 1867 that many southern whites were uninterested in reconnecting with their northern parent society. Their interest in the Bible Cause had not waned, but they preferred to work with a uniquely southern Bible society, something akin to the short-lived Confederate Bible Society. The ABS also found it difficult to hire southern agents due to the fact that few qualified candidates were willing to risk their reputations by working for a northern effort to distribute Bibles to freed slaves. The ABS was quick to use the moniker "extremists" to describe those southerners who were opposed to its work in the region. But the problem of finding southern agents was a real one.[5] Until the Bible "did its work" in softening the negative attitudes toward northern benevolence, the ABS would need to deal with these "strong local feelings and prejudices" in the South. It encouraged Southerners and freedmen to create their own Bible societies and reminded them that the work of distribution belonged to the auxiliaries, not the parent society in New York. The ABS strategy was not unlike President Andrew Johnson's failed approach to Reconstruction, a plan that made it relatively easy for former Confederates to return to the Union. For the ABS, the success of Reconstruction would be measured by how many southern auxiliaries they could bring back into the ABS tent. The Board of Managers thus had no problem turning to agents who had sided with the Confederacy during the war. Twelve southern agents who left the ABS after their states seceded from the Union were quickly reappointed. Half of those men were reappointed to their old posts.[6] By 1868 the ABS announced that "the restoration of the American Bible Society" in the South "may now be regarded as accomplished; and that it has secured a stronger hold upon the Christian regard of the people, than at any former period." With more and more southern Bible societies coming back on board, the national Bible Cause had been restored. The ABS viewed its victory as so complete that it decided to stop publishing a separate section about "southern Bible distribution" in its annual reports.[7]

As the ABS announced its reunion with southern society, it was still faced with the task of providing a Bible for every American family. As was the case with both the First and Second General Supply, the ABS had to sustain interest in the Third General Supply through the constant distribution of Bibles and Testaments to its auxiliaries. This would not be easy. Rapid population growth, the influx of new immigrants from Europe, the "restless movements of families and whole communities in search of homes and wealth," and the opening of new territories made it difficult to track the progress of the General Supply. By 1869, the General Supply had not yet been completed due to the economic hardships faced by local auxiliaries and the ever-mobile American people. Such difficulties, the ABS staff reported, "have all enhanced the labor, the cost, and the duration of the work, and rendered it impossible to report its completion." In other words, the Third General Supply, like its predecessors, had failed. It had reached only 81 percent of those families targeted as "destitute."[8]

As freed slaves made their way in the post–Civil War South, they relied heavily on family and the church for guidance and support. Many slaves reunited with long-lost family members and pursued legal marriages. They were also free to form religious congregations and purchase land to build churches. These churches became the center of African American life in the South. They often housed schools, political meetings, and other types of community events. With the assistance of the Freedmen's Bureau, a federal agency responsible for uniting lost families, helping slaves find employment, and supervising schools, former slaves learned much-needed skills, including the ability to read. The Bureau encouraged freedmen to become self-sufficient farmers and often provided them with land to get started, but by the late 1860s most freedmen were working the land as sharecroppers. Under this system of labor landowners divided their plantations into smaller farms that were rented to freedmen in exchange for a share of their annual crop. And with the passing of the ratification of the Fifteenth Amendment in 1870, freedmen were given the right to vote, although in some southern states they had been voting in state and local elections as early 1867.[9]

The ABS was committed to distributing Bibles among the African American community. The Society believed that the civil rights of freed slaves were "indissolubly bound up with their possession of the Bible." In February 1865 the ABS employed Rev. Samuel Hall, a Presbyterian minister and agent with the Christian Commission, to survey the needs of the newly emancipated people in the South in order to determine how best to reach them with the Bible. Hall concluded that the need among the freedmen was urgent and advised the ABS to work with the Freedmen's Bureau to facilitate distribution. One of the primary reasons for such an approach, Hall concluded, was the fact that local southern auxiliaries were not in any position, at least not yet, to accept distribution from what they perceived to be a northern agency. Hall urged the ABS to treat the distribution of the Bibles among the freedman as a "special work from the parent society." Moreover, by distributing Bibles directly from New York to the former slaves, the ABS would avoid criticism from northerners similar to what it received when the Board of Managers refused to directly provide Bibles to slaves prior to the war. In other words, the ABS could squelch rumors that it was somehow propping up the work of southern auxiliaries that were unwilling to deliver Bibles to freed slaves. Hall concluded that "the sooner action is had in this matter the better."[10]

In the end, the ABS did not take Hall's suggestion, preferring instead to follow its traditional policy of leaving the work of distribution to its auxiliaries. Though it is likely that the ABS Board of Managers and the staff of the Bible House wanted to do everything in their power to bring the Bible to freedmen—and in many cases, as we will see, they were successful in accomplishing this task—their understanding of the reunification of the Bible Cause did go not far beyond attempts to restore relationships with white auxiliaries, even if the leadership of some of those auxiliaries refused to supply former slaves.[11] For example, when the Charleston Bible Society refused to supply freedmen with Bibles, there was little that the ABS could do about it. When faced with the potential of other auxiliaries declining to provide Bibles to freedmen, Corresponding Secretary William Taylor concluded that if white southerners refused to distribute Bibles among the freedmen, "the coloured people will be educated by others." For Taylor this was not an ideal situation, but he, like many before him, was handicapped by the original ABS Constitution as it related to the relationship between the ABS and its auxiliaries.[12] As was its habit, the ABS would not dwell on the limits of its distribution system, preferring instead to focus on stories of success.

The official publications of the ABS described a freedmen population that was hungry for the word of God. Former slaves preferred to pay for their copies of the Bibles and ABS agents encouraged them to buy whenever they could in the hopes that the purchase of a Bible would give the freedmen a sense of ownership. It was not uncommon for agents to describe the African American desire for Bibles as far exceeding the interest among white southerners or immigrants—"untaught foreigners who throng our shores." In order to facilitate the freedmen who were learning to read, the ABS distributed Bibles printed in large type. Thousands of ABS Gospels of John found their way to freedmen schools in the South. Some freedman held a "superstitious reverence" for the Bible. They desired to have a copy of the word of God "lying on the table of their humble cottage" as a "comfort highly prized."[13]

Though not all southern auxiliaries were willing to distribute the Bible to freedmen and women, many of them did. The Virginia Bible Society, for example, concluded in 1866 that "the negro population must be supplied, as far as practicable, with the word of God. Their welfare and our safety demand it." In Georgia, a white minister who gave Bibles away to freedmen was encouraged that the book was enabling them "to learn faster" in their local schools. He added that a small revival was occurring in these schools and a few blacks were preaching in their communities. Positive reports about distribution to the freedmen arrived at the Bible House from nearly every former Confederate state. African Americans were learning how to read with ABS Bibles in schools sponsored by the Freedmen's Bureau and were putting their Bibles to good use in new churches. During the Third General Supply several states reported that most of the Bibles distributed were going to blacks because they were most needy.[14]

But many southern auxiliaries, for reasons most likely related to racial tension, did not devote their time and energy to distributing the Bible among freedmen. John Vassam, a friend of the ABS, traveled into the South and reported back to William Taylor that ABS agents in the region "cannot rely all together on the means adopted by your auxiliaries" to supply the black population because the leadership of these auxiliaries were too busy raising money to support the needs of the white population. "I am sorry to say," Vassam wrote, "but few of our southern people take an active interest in furnishing them [freedmen] with the only true guide to heaven." William Miller, the presiding elder in the Pensacola, Florida Methodist Conference, wrote to ABS headquarters frustrated that he was having difficulty obtaining Bibles to supply the blacks in his region because, as he understood it, the southern auxiliaries "appear to be doing nothing to supply the wants of the people." Miller asked Taylor to send him ABS Bibles directly since the white auxiliaries were inflicted with racial bigotry. "You cannot realize," he wrote, "how Christian people and especially Christian ministers can treat their brethren on the account of prejudice."

Henry Gray, a former slave from Texas who started a school in Mississippi that taught slaves religion and literacy, had his request for Bibles denied by the Memphis and Shelby County Bible Society, so he obtained them from other benevolent organizations working in the area. Certain parts of the South remained an obstacle for Bible distribution because of their "prevailing indisposition to co-operate with any northern organizations." As a representative of one southern auxiliary confided to William Taylor, "we beg of you to let us alone for the present, even with your gifts." An agent working in Statesville, North Carolina, reported that the whites in his neighborhood displayed "intense disgust for all who devote themselves to the evangelization of the 'niggers.'" Thomas Quinan of the Maryland Bible Society warned Taylor that there were some members of his society who refused to distribute ABS Bibles among the freedmen because they did not want to "offend the South by urging our books upon them without their assent." An ABS agent in Atlanta reported in July 1865 that "leading members" of southern white Churches "are not prepared to acknowledge the defeat of the South and the emancipation of slavery as Providential. They are soured in their feelings, and will be sure to stand aloof for the present." As long as the ABS stayed true to the principle that it would not interfere with the work of its auxiliaries, thousands upon thousands of freed men and women would not have access to the word of God.[15]

The ABS realized that the supply of the freedmen in the South was a massive undertaking. As a result, it created a new position called the Agent to Superintend Bible Work among the Freedmen, and appointed William F. Baird to fill the post. Baird was an ordained clergymen in the Cumberland Presbyterian Church and had worked as an ABS agent with the northern army during the Civil War. He would not have any authority over the auxiliaries or the agents, but was simply there to come alongside them in the work of distribution and fundraising. Taylor urged Baird to avoid all contact with the work of the Freedmen's Bureau so as not to give the appearance that the ABS was operating in an official government capacity. In fact, Baird would rarely refer to himself as an agent of the American Bible Society so not to elicit the usual southern prejudice shown toward the representatives of northern benevolent organizations. Baird spent most of his time in the South working with southern auxiliaries, but he was also active in distributing Bibles to black soldiers serving in Reconstruction military units and mobilizing freedmen to form their own Bible societies.[16]

A number of "colored Bible societies," run entirely by African Americans, emerged in the period of Reconstruction. Many of these societies utilized black colporteurs. The determination of blacks to form their own societies was not unlike the work that the African American community was doing in forming their own churches. It was a clear act of self-determination on the part of the freed people and was one of several ways in which they used religion to exercise their newfound freedom. Bible societies run entirely by freedmen were established in Nashville and Knoxville, Tennessee and Columbia,

South Carolina. William Baird was influential in the creation of the Knoxville Colored Bible Society. In September 1865 he met a group of freedmen at an Old School Presbyterian Church. Upon his arrival, he found them singing hymns and praying. When an elderly African American man who was leading the group saw Baird enter sanctuary, he told him that "we are just putting in the time till you should come." Baird read a portion of the 119th Psalm, said a prayer, and began to envision a Bible society among this group of freed slaves. After those in attendance sung a rousing edition of "O For a Thousand Tongues to Sing," Baird delivered a short address and appointed officers for what he believed to be the first Bible society organized among the freedmen of the South.[17]

The ABS Board of Managers and staff responded ambivalently toward the growing number of colored societies. While they were more than willing to supply them with Bibles, they preferred to work with established auxiliaries and other benevolent societies. ABS agents, and even Corresponding Secretary William Taylor did not believe that freedmen had the skills to facilitate the work of Bible distribution and would ultimately waste all of the Bibles sent to them. For example, in 1873 an ABS agent in Texas wrote that few freedmen in his region were "competent to understand and carry out the detail of their supply." Thomas Rutlege, an ABS agent in Alabama and West Florida, tried to form a colored auxiliary in 1876, but concluded, without any additional commentary, that "the results will not justify the repetition of the experiment." Though few of these colored societies lasted very long, they did serve an important role among the community of freed men and women.[18]

Sometimes African American churches provided a more efficient alternative to colored Bible societies. During Reconstruction the church became the center of African American life. As Abraham Lincoln, in his famous Second Inaugural Address, noted that both the white North and the white South "read the same Bible" and "prayed to the same God," slaves understood the Civil War on completely different religious terms. They were less concerned with who was to blame for the war, or whether the South deserved God's wrath, and more focused on how God had used the conflict to free them from the bondage of slavery. The church was the place where freed slaves could celebrate this providential view of history and, in the process, exercise autonomy over their lives. As a result, former slaves began pouring out of southern white churches shortly after they learned about Lincoln's Emancipation Proclamation.[19]

Black churches were more than willing to work with northern benevolent associations such as the ABS. The pleas for Bibles that the ABS received from newly formed African American churches could be quite powerful. For example, in 1866, an unidentified "coloured minister in the South" introduced himself in a letter to the ABS as a pastor who had been "set at liberty from under the yoke of bondage from our earthly masters." He described the process by which he and about 200 of his fellow freedmen had built a church, a "flourishing Sunday School," and day schools for children staffed by black teachers. The pastor and his school teachers learned to read while they were slaves and now had a desire to teach the members of their congregation how to read as well. Could the ABS help them by providing Bibles for their school? In a probable reference to the local auxiliary in the area, the minister declared that "our white people still seem to think that the great light of truth should be kept back from us." It is unclear as to whether the ABS fulfilled the request. Through the late 1860s stories of African American churches similar to the local pastor mentioned above flooded into the Bible House. Rev. Richard Cain, a black minister in Charleston, received a batch of ABS Bibles to distribute among his congregation. He wrote, "the daughters of Africa light up on the presentation of these books, as if they had caught a glimpse of the better country for which they had longed prayed and constantly sighed on the days of bondage." Seventy-seven teachers in his congregation were teaching 977 children how to read.[20]

By 1870 the Republican Party, the architect of Reconstruction and the defender of freedmen's civil rights, was losing power in the South. Resentment of northern carpetbaggers resulted in key victories at the polls for the largely racist southern Democratic Party. By 1876, Republicans had control of only three southern states—South Carolina, Florida, and Louisiana. In the rest of the South former Confederates had returned to office. Southern Democrats used a variety of tactics to win political power. They intimidated Republican candidates and terrorized the blacks who voted for them. As these Democrats set out to "redeem" the South from Republican rule, they did everything possible to prevent blacks from voting and exercising the civil rights they had gained following the Civil War. In the decades that followed, state and local governments in the South passed discriminatory and racially motivated decrees that became known as Jim Crow laws. These laws led to the segregation of schools, restaurants, public transportation, theaters, drinking fountains, and public bathrooms. They were enforced at the national level by Supreme Court cases such as *Plessy v. Ferguson* (1896), which required black schools and other facilities to be "separate but equal." By the turn of the twentieth century many southern blacks had been disenfranchised through poll taxes and literacy tests, and lynching became a popular form of racial violence directed toward African Americans. Between 1867 and 1900, African Americans were rarely, if ever, mentioned in the stories, reports, and anecdotes that appeared in the *Bible Society Record*. While the ABS published endless articles about its work among Native Americans, Chinese, and Mexican immigrants in the West and new immigrants arriving in eastern cities, the ABS remained silent on the so-called Negro question.

The end of Reconstruction in the United States also brought economic woes to the nation. The ABS spent most of the 1870s trying to maintain its mission amid the fiscal panic of 1873. The panic began when Jay Cooke & Company, America's premier financial organization, overextended itself with investments in the Northern Pacific Railroad, causing thousands of business (including a number of railroads) to go bankrupt and banks to close across the country. The subsequent depression lasted five years and unemployment in the United States rose to 14 percent. Corporations responded to the crisis by cutting wages. When workers tried to unionize and strike in response to these cuts, they were shut down. Ultimately, the panic led to the end of Reconstruction. Republicans focused on dealing with the financial crisis and many lost interest in rebuilding efforts in the South.

ABS auxiliaries, especially those in the South, felt the pinch of the economic crisis. Epidemics, crop failure, and the falling price of cotton hindered the Bible Cause in Alabama and West Florida. The Bible Society of Louisiana was in debt as the people of the state remained "apathetic" to the cause. The ABS agent in Central Texas told the Bible House that the people were too poor to buy Bibles. In Western Texas virtually nothing was done on behalf of the Bible Cause, because the region was suffering under a "financial pressure unprecedented in its history." As might be expected, the economic slump was felt in the New York. The total yearly revenue of the ABS hit an all-time high in 1870 at $747,058, but had plummeted to $446,954, a whopping 40 percent decline, by 1878. Some of this decline can be attributed to a drop in the demand for Bibles in the wake of the Third General Supply, but much of it was related to the economic condition facing the country and the inability of ordinary Americans to purchase Bibles and, perhaps more importantly, make donations to the ABS.[21]

Despite its financial woes, the end of Reconstruction provided the ABS—and the nation as whole—a chance to once again reflect on its contribution to the greatness of the United States. The country celebrated its one hundredth birthday in 1876, and the ABS did not miss the opportunity to remind all who would hear of the ways it had kept the republic on the right path. The ABS Board of Managers was confident that the "chief glory of the nation" and the sources of its "enduring prosperity . . . must be attributed to the influence of the Bible." The centennial provided an opportunity to inter-twine the history of the nation, the history of the Bible in America, and the history of the ABS. The managers invoked Elias Boudinot and the founding of the ABS, and extolled its Bible distribution efforts among the "destitute." They also portrayed the ABS as an organization that always adapted to the changing nature of American life, pointing to its successful manufacturing techniques, its publication of Bibles for immigrants and Native Americans who did not speak English, and its efforts to reach the freedmen in the South. They even placed an ABS exhibit at the Centennial Celebration at the 1876 World's Fair in Philadelphia, with a particular focus on its foreign-language Bibles and growing international work. In the same year, the ABS annual meeting was moved to Philadelphia as a means of encouraging the membership and staff to consider the organization's role in the history of the nation.[22]

By the time of the centennial celebration in Philadelphia, the ABS had restored its national reputation. The ABS understood the restoration of its reputation as a benevolent organization committed to distributing the Bible to both North and South in terms of reconnecting with its southern auxiliaries once the hostilities of war came to an end. For the most part, the ABS succeeded in restoring these connections and it was able to announce that it would no longer treat the former Confederacy as a region in need of special attention. But reconnecting with southern auxiliaries meant that the ABS would be forced to let the distribution of Bibles to freedmen be carried out by members of auxiliaries who may not have been particularly keen, for racial reasons, in bringing the Bible to the black population in their midst. It would be easy to condemn the ABS for not doing more to reach the freedmen population and to encourage their southern auxiliaries to lay aside racial prejudice in the distribution of scriptures, but the decentralized structure of the ABS made this difficult, if not impossible. The ABS had no control over the distribution practices of their auxiliaries. As a result, the practice of bringing the word of God to all Americans would be carried out locally. In the meantime, the ABS would celebrate the reunion of North and South, its role in American history, and its work in sustaining a Bible nation with a clear conscience.[23]

9

The Bible Cause in an Age of Immigration and Expansion

With the southern auxiliaries reconnected to the parent society in New York, the ABS could now turn its attention to other areas of American society that needed to be exposed to the message of the Bible. As the US population expanded during the last quarter of the nineteenth century, the ABS worked on a number of initiatives to meet the needs of this diverse population, particularly in growing industrial centers and the ever-expanding West. Much of this work followed a now long-established pattern of cloaking Bible distribution in a veil of Protestant nationalism. Immigrants needed the Protestant Bible as part of the process of their overall assimilation to American ideals and values. Similarly, the inhabitants of the West—both white and red—needed to be Christianized as an essential part of spreading American democracy.

As the ABS recovered from the financial crisis of the 1870s, and before it faced a similar crisis in the early 1890s, it decided that it was time to embark on yet another General Supply. The so-called Fourth General Supply, which ran from roughly 1882 to 1890, was needed to meet the Bible needs of the expanding number of immigrants coming into the United States. In 1867, at the time of the Third General Supply, the population of the United States stood at about 37 million. In 1882 that number was now close to 53 million. In 1881 alone, the ABS concluded, nearly 600,000 individuals had landed on American shores and a "large portion" of them "were without any decided religious faith" or had been "imbued with skeptical and Communistic principles." The ABS feared that the United States was no longer a "homogeneous people." It was time to print the Bible in the language that many of these new immigrants could understand with the ultimate purpose of bringing the "gospel of salvation for the healing of the nations." The implication was clear—the United States could once again become a "homogeneous nation" if newcomers could be unified around the spiritual and moral message of the word of God.[1]

The Bible also needed to be put in the hands of every immigrant in order to secure the continued strength of "free institutions" in the United States. The success of the United States as a "beacon of hope and refuge for the oppressed from every part of the world" rested on getting a Bible to every adult and young person who arrived in the country. The motive for this new supply was couched in the language of Christian nationalism: "Patriotism demands it for the preservation of our liberty, union, and government of this republic, which owes its existence and prosperity to the open Bible and tolerant Christianity." The Bible was needed so that humanity could be kept from falling into disorderly "barbarism." The nation's "foundations" needed to remain "pure." The Bible would ultimately fix humanity's "ignorance" and "errors" by leading immigrants and others away from their sin and toward membership in the Kingdom of God.[2]

Unlike the previous General Supplies, the Fourth Supply was focused on urban areas. The Board of Managers urged colporteurs to make sure Bibles were carried "to the teeming population of the tenement districts of the large cities, where the population of a village is often concentrated into a single block." The more dense the population, they argued, the more corrupt a neighborhood will become "without the leavening influence of the Bible." The ABS anticipated that the Fourth General Supply would end in 1889, but it was extended an additional year because it was so difficult to measure the number of urban dwellers who still needed copies of the Bible. The influx of new immigrants to these urban areas made it hard to obtain an accurate canvass. ABS colporteurs would estimate the number of "destitute" families in a particular region, city, or territory, distribute the Bible in those places, and then return a year or two later only to learn that the number of destitute was now larger than when the region was originally canvassed.[3] Ultimately the Fourth General Supply, like the three previous efforts to supply every American with a copy of the Bible, had failed by the high standards the ABS had set for itself. Modern America was too diverse, too populated, and too transient for these kinds of mass distribution efforts to meet their set goals. The need for the Bible would remain great, and the ABS would continue to try to meet that need, but the days of General Supplies had come to end in 1890.[4]

Just as the United States seemed to have recovered from the economic anxiety of 1873, another financial meltdown struck the nation twenty years later. The panic of 1893 sent the American economy generally, and the ABS specifically, into a crisis. As with the earlier panic, this one was also caused by a railroad failure. The Reading Railroad, an important eastern rail line, went bankrupt, creating a domino effect among other railroads, businesses, and banks. The stock market subsequently plunged as European investors pulled their money from US banks. These problems were compounded by a number of labor strikes in the 1890s. The ABS was not immune to the panic any more than any other business or nonprofit organization. In 1894 donations began to drop and revenue would continue to fall until these important markers of the ABS's institutional health had been cut in half by 1898.

Discouraging reports of economic hardship began flooding into the Astor Place Bible House. In California and Nevada industrial laborers were out of work, railroad strikes were commonplace, and poor weather created what Rev. John Thompson, an ABS agent, described as "one of the hardest [seasons] financially during my superintendency of the work on this coast." Colporteurs in the West had to be let go "on account of financial stringency." The economic climate in Nevada was so poor that Thompson abandoned the state, deciding to stay in California where his work could have the largest impact during the financial crisis. In Illinois, E. G. Smith reported that the Bible Cause was faltering because the people of the state were distracted by "labor troubles and the cry from our drought-stricken and suffering neighbors on the western frontier." In Indiana mines, shops, and farms, the primary source of the state's wealth, were not delivering the extra income needed to support the Bible Cause. W. J. Vigus informed the Bible House that hundreds of manufacturing centers in the "Gas Belt" region were closed and early frosts had destroyed fruit crops. Drought destroyed the rest. And in Louisiana and Mississippi, Rev. J. W. McLaurin lamented that the financial crisis had come precisely at a time when the Bible was most needed in his region due to the growing number of "colored, Catholic, and foreign" who had recently arrived.[5] The crisis required the ABS in New York to limit its programs. For example, it discontinued its use of paid colporteurs. This was a particularly heart-wrenching decision, because colporteurs had become the primary means by which the ABS extended its outreach and distribution efforts into regions where auxiliaries were either weak or nonexistent. In the midst of the crisis the ABS expressed the "embarrassments" it was now laboring under. Important and longstanding initiatives had been brought to an abrupt halt due to lack of funds, the Society could no longer rely upon auxiliaries for financial support, and churches and denominations were not responding to appeals for money. It would take nearly a decade before the ABS returned to a position of financial stability.[6]

As the ABS tried to survive the worst depression in American history, it continued to work hard at bringing the Bible to immigrants. In 1892 the ABS Board of Managers, ever aware of the nation's changing demographics, described the United States as a "great foreign missionary field." The ABS perceived these newcomers as people sent by God to the United States. Their arrival presented a "grand opportunity" for American Protestants. Indeed, the board declared, "patriotism as well as Christianity makes their evangelization imperative." If immigrants were not "won over to Christianity" they would "affect disastrously our civilization." "Left to themselves," the managers added, "the numerous discordant elements must eventually result in the disruption of the bonds which now bind the nation together." They asked, "How are we going to give these strangers that come to our land the spirit of true Americanism?" Indeed, "the best lovers of our race believe that this American Republic is to be the field for the development of the highest civilization the world has ever known." But how might such grand aspirations for American civilization be fulfilled if "people are allowed to come to us in uncounted multitudes bringing with them their ignorance of the Bible, their false conception of true liberty, and their low moral standards?"[7]

The ABS pointed to a variety of ways cultural unity could be maintained among growing ethnic diversity. The government, for example, could educate immigrants in American political values, thus pointing them to a "higher civilization." Or they could teach them how to function as good cogs in the American capitalist machine. Dr. Howard B. Grose, an agent working in the newly created ABS Northwestern Agency, wrote that "for the most part the vote buyer, the saloon-keeper, the bribe taker, the Jew Sweater, the owner or agent of wretched or unsanitary tenements, are the ones who are teaching [immigrants] what America stands for." But all of these efforts—whether noble or debase—would ultimately prove to be "impotent." The only "hope for the future" of America was the God of the Bible. If these immigrants could be given copies of the word of God at the point of their entry into the United States they would carry the message of the Bible to their homes and settlements and be forced to come to grips with the claims of Jesus Christ on their lives.[8]

The Bible Cause among immigrants in New York City was promoted largely through the New York Bible Society (NYBS). Bible agents working for the NYBS met immigrants with Bibles in their own languages when these newcomers set foot on American soil. In 1879 alone, the NYBS distributed copies of Scripture to roughly 45 percent of the immigrants who arrived in New York through Castle Garden (the first immigrant station in the United States, preceding Ellis Island). Immigrants had the potential for either good or evil once they arrived in New York. As a result "no effort should be spared to bring them in contact with the word, which alone can teach self-government and make them 'free indeed.'" Or to put it differently, "those added to our population have been put in possession of that book which is the foundation of national prosperity, that they might learn their duties as future citizens of this great Republic."[9]

Once new immigrants arrived in the city, the NYBS continued with its work of distribution. In 1880 it distributed more Bibles than any other year since the Civil War. Agents of the NYBS traveled from tenement house to tenement house, covering the rooms from "floor to attic." The NYBS worked closely with other New York benevolent societies, including its own women's branch and denominational agencies, to canvass the city. Oftentimes NYBS agents came face to face with the poverty of New York City's immigrant population. The biggest struggle they faced in extending the Bible Cause to these communities was the inability of immigrant families to afford a Bible. Agents were willing to donate Bibles to destitute families, but they could not do this too often because sales were the primary way that the NYBS stayed financially solvent.[10]

New York City was not the only place where the ABS brought the Bible to the immigrant population. The supporters of the Bible Cause in Minnesota described it as a "missionary State" where "the tide of immigration is rolling fast and increasingly upon us." Industry and manufacturing in the state coincided with a large influx of immigration, mostly Germans. In Nebraska, the ABS used auxiliaries to reach prairie settlers and the "restless" and "homeless" immigrants working the mines. Rev. J. Horton of the Northwestern Agency informed the Board of Managers that one of every "four or five" inhabitants of Chicago in 1908 was a "native-born American." He worried about the Poles and Lithuanians of Chicago who spent their days laboring in the stockyards. They needed the word of God to lift them from their terrible living conditions where they existed "more like cattle than human beings," with twenty or twenty-five people living in a room that was 18 × 25 feet in size. Such an environment, Horton added, "produces low moral conditions."[11] In Indianapolis, ABS agent W. S. Elliot claimed that the Bible Cause was in a state of "innocuous quietude" until he and other ABS representatives arrived on the scene. Elliott reinvigorated a "noble band" of female volunteers and with their help began distributing Bibles to the city's 5,000 immigrants from Bulgaria, Croatia, Greece, Slovenia, Romania, Serbia, and Italy. He turned a local saloon-keeper into a business agent for the ABS and within a few months after his arrival hundreds of immigrants were coming to the bar to place orders for Bibles. Elliott also hired Vincenzo De Francesco, a recent convert to Protestantism, to serve as a colporteur among the Italian population of Indianapolis. In one instance, when DeFrancesco presented a copy of the Gospel of John to a woman who was ill, her husband found the Gospel portion and began to read it. He told De Francesco that reading that Bible had changed his life. The man had been a member of a "deadly society like the 'Black Hand,'" and his hands were stained with the blood of twelve men." He now, however, wanted to repent and become a Christian. Eventually the former mafia member hosted a weekly prayer meeting in his home.[12]

Many of these new immigrants found their way to the western United States. The West always loomed large in the imagination of those affiliated with the American Bible Society. As we saw in chapter 1, Samuel Mills, the preacher from the Massachusetts Missionary Society who traveled throughout the West at the start of the nineteenth century, was the first person to call for the creation of a national Bible society to meet the growing spiritual needs of frontier settlers. By the time the historian Frederick Jackson Turner declared the American frontier "closed" in 1893, the "West" included eastern migrants moving along the Oregon and Santa Fe Trails and over paths blazed by Lewis and Clark. After the Civil War the Pony Express made runs from Missouri to California, and in 1869 the golden spike was hammered into the ground at Promontory Point, signaling the completion of America's first transcontinental railroad. New territories and settlements were constantly springing up as the nation proclaimed its "manifest destiny" to establish white Protestant civilization in the region.[13] Distributing Bibles in the West proved to be one of the most challenging aspects of the ABS's mission in the late nineteenth century, because the people settling and living in the region were extremely diverse and spread out over vast acres of territory. If the Bible Cause was going to be successful in the West it would mean working with people who spoke a number of languages, from Spanish to Chinese to various Native American tongues. In 1873, as Reconstruction was winding down in the South, the Board of Managers announced that "the word of God, the people's Bible, must be diffused among the diverse and rapidly increasing, population of the West, as the political and social as well as the religious safeguard of the nation."[14]

The ABS plan for reaching the West was aided by transportation and infrastructure improvements. In the fifty years following the merger of the Central Pacific and the Union Pacific at Promontory Point, the nation's railroad system expanded by more than 250,000 miles. Railroads were symbols of progress. When an engine rolled through the plains or the Rockies it represented the triumph of American ingenuity and civilization. The growth of railroads would integrate the West into an ever-expanding industrial nation defined by manufacturing, big business, labor unions, economic risk-taking, and government subsidies. New settlements would crop up around the shanties that passed for depots.[15] Boxes of ABS Bibles would ride in freight cars along the seemingly endless miles of track in the West, but the Board of Managers also saw train travel as an excellent opportunity to distribute the word of God to passengers in need of reading material on their long journeys. The ABS placed Bibles in cast bronze receptacles within easy reach of passengers. The Society believed that the Bible would serve as an "antidote" to the "vicious literature" that could often be found in passenger cars. Since most middle-class Americans spent more time on trains than "in chapel," it made sense to reach them through railroad Bibles. The ABS's special "Railroad Editions" of the New Testament and Psalms were distinguished for their attractiveness, legibility, and "convenience of handling."[16]

The ABS had been distributing Bibles in California since settlers discovered gold at Sutter's Mill in 1849. In that year, Frederick Buel was appointed agent for California and was given the responsibility of supplying a "strange mingling of faces, complexions, garbs, and dresses." Buel could not help but compare his ministry in California with the day of Pentecost described in the New Testament book of Acts. Shortly after his arrival he gathered Presbyterian, Episcopalian, Methodist, and Congregationalist men together to discuss how the Gold Rush, Pacific trade, and western agriculture would bring more people to California and provide more opportunities for the Bible Cause. Eventually these men joined together to form the San Francisco Bible Society. Using metaphors appropriate for what was happening in the boom towns of the Gold Rush, Buel described California as a "powerful magnet" attracting thousands of people from "Catholic and Pagan lands, as well as from our own," to meet God in the "waters of the River of Life" where a "golden stream" would offer them the "pearl of great price." Buel was confident that the Bible would "lay the foundation for the rapid rise of a Christian republic on the Pacific."[17]

The work in California required physical stamina and a familiarity with the rugged terrain of the Sierra Nevada Mountains. In August 1859, Buel spent three months in the Sierras distributing the Bible to miners searching for gold in mountain streams. He wrote of his treacherous descents from the mountains, "zigzagging" down paths with "very sharp angles of inclination." About a year later, Buel again found himself winding down the slope of the mountain— this time as a passenger in a stagecoach, "traveling seven miles to gain two." As the stage was about two miles from the foot of the mountain, it tipped over and began rolling down the hill on its side. Buel quickly concluded that the "end of the overturnings would be in eternity" and decided to "commit himself to the hands of the Lord." Eventually, "after several successive bounds," the stage came to a stop and Buel climbed out, surprised that his limbs were still attached to his body. Though Buel, the stage driver, and a young woman and her baby were scratched up, everyone survived the incident.[18] Now here was a California story for the Bible House in New York.

Buel and his successors in California would face stiff opposition from the Roman Catholic Church. As we saw in chapter 6, many Catholics followed the orders of their priests and would not accept a copy of the King James Version of the Bible. There were also several recorded incidents of Catholic priests in California burning ABS Bibles. Yet Buel pressed on in the work of advancing Protestantism in a region with a long history of Spanish Catholicism. In 1870 he reported the deathbed conversion of a "Romanist" and several successful attempts at distributing ABS Spanish-language Bibles. When he proposed building a Bible depository in San Francisco, he was encouraged that many of his most curious inquirers about the project were Catholics. Buel believed that if Catholics could only read the word of God for themselves they would abandon the superstitious, anti-Biblical religion that held them captive to the tyranny of their local priests. In one case Buel squared off against a Catholic priest in San Francisco in what seemed like an Old Testament showdown between the prophet Elijah and the prophets of Baal. When Buel informed the priest that he planned to distribute ABS Bibles "throughout the length and breadth of the land," the priest encouraged him: "Go," he said, "carry the Bible where you please and we will go after you, and the more Bibles you scatter, the more Catholics we will make." Confident in the "power of Protestantism," Buel welcomed the challenge. "Let us scatter the truth to every family," he wrote to the ABS leadership in New York, "and if truth makes Catholics, let truth and error meet and grapple." In a "free and open encounter" the truth of the Protestant message would prevail.[19]

As Americans moved west, Chinese immigrants were arriving from the Pacific and moving east. In August 1850, Buel organized a ceremony in San Francisco to present members of this immigrant community with Bibles. With the mayor, the members of the Protestant clergy, and numerous citizens in attendance, Rev. S. W. Bonney, a former missionary to China and a friend of the ABS, made the presentation. At the appointed hour, about one hundred Chinese immigrants, dressed in "their native costume" and "bearing countenances and features which Americans are not accustomed to look upon," paraded across the city plaza in two lines to receive a copy of the Bible. Buel told New York that he had witnessed the first "collected representation of a people" who would soon be adding to the "population about to gather on these shores." He wrote that their "habits, characteristics, and customs" would eventually be "swallowed up and lost in the preponderating influence of Anglo American's character." The Chinese would "blend and unite with Americans" and contribute to the American race—a people with "characteristics of their own." Such racial assimilation would be good for the Chinese people. They came from a "dark land" where they were "walled in from all access to Christian influences, and wholly wrapped in a vail of idolatrous darkness."[20]

Buel's work with the Chinese population in the United States began in earnest in 1870. The Chinese were "heathen" in need of the word of God, but they were also productive members of society. The Board of Managers described them as having commendable "traits of character" that made them good servants, employees, laborers, ranchmen, gardeners, and railroad contractors. The ABS was prepared with Chinese-language Bibles, but many of these immigrants from the East could not read. In 1867, California Presbyterians established a mission to teach English to the Chinese populations, but teachers in this school and others like it struggled to translate religious terms such as "love," "sin," "repent," "believe," "pray," and "worship" into Chinese because the Chinese did not have any words with corresponding meanings. Many ABS agents found it easier to simply preach to the Chinese. Teaching them English was too difficult and time-consuming. By 1871, there were nearly 200 schools for Chinese immigrants in California and the ABS was supplying most of them with Bibles.[21]

After a few years of frustration, the ABS decided to reach out to these immigrants through Chinese colporteurs or former missionaries to China who knew the language. In 1872, the ABS hired two Chinese colporteurs. The ABS described Al Sing as a Chinese convert to Protestantism who "soon provided himself a zealous inquirer after the truth." Al had "abandoned heathenism," turned his "idols" over to an ABS agent for destruction, and eventually became a Christian minister. Similarly, Wong Chick Sing, another Chinese convert, tried to get his countrymen to give up "idol worship" and come out of the "great moral darkness into which they have plunged." His work met with much hostility among the California Chinese. "While many do not like to hear about Jesus, and are displeased at any word I say about idols," he told the Board of Managers in New York, "they think they are very smart to worship images, and to minister to devils." Wong Chick wrote that his fellow Chinese immigrants "treat me very badly sometimes," but he was confident that God would give him the strength and faith to "endure their wickedness for the sake of Jesus."[22]

The number of Bibles distributed to Native American people groups in the West was very low when compared to the number of white Americans, or even African Americans, that the ABS reached with the word of God, but the Society continued to make the translation of the Bible into Indian languages and the circulation of the scriptures among the Indian population a priority throughout the nineteenth century and into the twentieth century. Following the Civil War, the already hostile relationship between the US government and the native tribes of the West grew even worse. If the agents of the Bible Cause were going to make an impact on this population group, they would need to learn the best way to distribute Bibles in a war zone. As an ABS agent in Nebraska put it in 1865: "The recent Indian raids have so thoroughly disorganized our new settlements . . . that I am exceedingly perplexed as to the best methods for carrying on my agency."[23]

As white settlers began to move west of the Mississippi River, violent conflicts with Indian peoples were inevitable. Prior to the arrival of Europeans in the sixteenth century, the tribes in what would later become the western United States had occupied that territory for more than 20,000 years. Though the arrival of Europeans would have a profound effect on Indian religion and economic life, the western Indians remained isolated enough to protect themselves from the disease and subsequent cultural holocaust that brought most of the powerful eastern woodland Indians to their knees. The best estimates suggest that there were about 360,000 Native Americans living west of the Mississippi River at the end of the Civil War. Most of them lived on the Great

Plains. Several eastern tribes that had been sent by Andrew Jackson's Indian Removal Act (1830) to march west along the Trail of Tears had settled in what was called Indian Territory, a large tract of land that originally included present-day Oklahoma and parts of Kansas and Nebraska.

As Indian territory was taken by American settlers on a feverish quest for more land, treaties between tribes and the federal government were broken, and white hunters, with the support of the US Army, began killing off the buffalo; tribes were left with little alternative but to fight for their own survival and the survival of their way of life. For example, in 1864, a group of Colorado civilians known as the Colorado Volunteers killed 133 Cheyenne men, women, and children in what became known as the Sand Creek Massacre. Between 1865 and 1867 the Sioux waged war against the US Army in present-day Wyoming. Sioux and Cheyenne warriors brought a fateful end to American troops on a surveying expedition at Little Big Horn under the leadership of Lieutenant-Colonel George Armstrong Custer. When Apache Indians in the Southwest, led by their chief Geronimo, resisted being placed on reservations, they united with the Comanches and the Kiowas in 1874 to fight the American army in what became known as the Red River War. William Baird, who following his work with African Americans during Reconstruction began distributing Bibles in Indian Country, often visited the Chickasaw nation "armed with two pistols and a gun."[24]

While it was difficult for ABS agents to visit Indians in the midst of these wars, they could at least work on translating the Bible into Native American tongues. In 1869, the ABS published portions of the Old Testament in Dakota and the Gospel of Matthew in Creek. Some questioned whether these translations were worth the time and expense since there was a growing sentiment that natives needed to learn English as part of their assimilation process. But as long as missionaries in schools continued to teach Indians in their native tongues, the ABS would publish Bibles to meet their needs.[25] The ABS saw the Bible as fundamental to the process by which Indians would be incorporated into the nation. This practice of assimilation had a long history in US-Indian affairs, but it reached its height in the 1880s under the leadership of Henry Dawes, a senator from Massachusetts. Dawes pushed the United States down a path that he hoped would end with the total assimilation of the nation's Native American population. The defenders of assimilation wanted Indians to wear "civilized" clothing, engage in agriculture, send their children to school, and live in houses. But more importantly, they wanted them to become Protestants.[26]

The ABS agreed. "Where the Bible has been circulated and Christianity exerts any strong influence [on the Indian populations]," the Society affirmed, "the people are peaceful, docile, and progressive." In 1873, the *Bible Society Record* reprinted a speech from Rev. Alfred Riggs, a missionary among the Dakotas, on the relationship of the Bible to the civilization process. Riggs's speech addressed a much-debated issue in the practice of Bible distribution among Native Americans: Should the Indians be "civilized" before they were "Christianized"? Riggs and the ABS rejected this approach since they understood the practice of civilizing the Indians to be inseparable from teaching them how to read the Bible. "We have found the Bible the best civilizer," Riggs wrote, "our Protestant Christianity carries with it, wherever it goes, all the modern appliances of civilization. In fact, ours is mainly a Christian civilization. It has grown out of the word of God."[27]

The work of Protestant missionaries among the Indian groups of the trans-Mississippi United States, and consequently the work of the ABS, met with controversy in 1887 when John DeWitt Clinton Atkins, the Commissioner of Indian Affairs in the Department of the Interior, began to forbid the use of native languages in missionary schools. If the Indians were to become citizens of the United States, then the "rising generation will be expected . . . to read, write, and speak the English language and to transact business with English-speaking people." Atkins argued repeatedly that Indian vernacular would be "of no use to them" or "of no advantage" when they "take upon themselves the responsibilities and privileges of citizenship." The decree was an act of nation-building, for Atkins affirmed that "no unity or community of feeling can be established among different peoples unless they are brought to speak the same language, and thus become imbued with like ideas of duty." The order applied to all schools on Indian reservations, whether they be conducted by the federal government or a church. It required that "no books in any Indian language must be used or instruction given in that language to Indian pupils," since such teaching would be "detrimental to the cause of their education and civilization."[28]

The ABS affirmed the idea that the Native American population needed to learn English in order to function efficiently as US citizens and assimilate fully into American culture. ABS Bibles were used in Indian mission schools in the West as a tool for teaching Indians to read English, and the *Bible Society Record* often reported on the success of these education efforts by publishing letters it received from Indian pupils thanking the Society for Bibles. But the ABS was also in the business of publishing Bibles in Indian languages. Atkins's decree would mean that Native Americans in western schools who had not yet learned English might be deprived of access to the word of God. The ABS complained that missionaries to the Dakota were no longer allowed to read ABS-published Dakota Bibles during church services and added that more than a dozen private missionary schools were forced to close as a result of the edict. The Society mounted opposition to the Bureau of Indian Affairs based on the First Amendment right to free speech and the free exercise of religion. It argued that the Commissioner of Indian Affairs, by forbidding schools to read the Bible in the Indian vernacular or preventing the use of such Bibles in religious services, was violating the religious freedom of those Indians in the schools who did not understand English. "What becomes of freedom of speech," the ABS contended, "if a government officer can forbid a man's teaching in the only language he knows?" And "where is freedom of religion if a civilian has authority to say in what tongue the Bible shall be read in public worship?" The ABS was especially bothered by Atkins's belief that the Bible was somehow "detrimental to the civilization of the Indians." It demanded that local schools be given discretion to teach the "great commission" and "elementary principles of morality and religion" in the way that they saw fit.[29]

In September 1887, nearly 300 Dakota Christians and representatives from Protestant missionary agencies to the Dakota gathered together at the Santee Normal Training School and Indian Mission in Nebraska to discuss, among other things, the recent decree of the Bureau of Indian Affairs regarding the use of native languages in Indian schools. James Garvey, a Sioux, told those in attendance that "to make the best citizens you must Christianize the people, and to make them Christians you must give them the Bible in their own language. All of us have become white people through the gospel." Spotted Bear, another Christian Indian, wanted his children to be taught English, but he also wanted them to be able to read the Bible in Dakota. Walking Head, a local Indian from Santee, agreed: "We have the right to choose what language to learn to read in. It is the missionaries and the Dakota Bible that have brought us out of heathenism and up to this conference. We want both languages. We don't want Dakota forbidden." At the end of the conference the Dakota Christian Indians adopted a memorial "begging" President Grover Cleveland to "abolish" the order of the Indian Commissioner. They claimed that because of their study of the Dakota-language Bible many of their people "have been quieted down in Christian homes and civilized ways" and had become responsible members of society in their roles as ministers, teachers, government employees, farmers, and, "above all, true Christians."[30]

In November 1887, a committee representing several different New York-based Protestant missionary organizations, including the American Bible Society, visited Washington, DC, to meet with President Cleveland and Indian Commissioner Atkins. They came to the meeting hoping to win several concessions, including permission to provide oral instruction in morality and religion in native tongues. They argued that native languages and native-language Bibles were indispensable for training Christian Indian preachers to spread the Gospel among their fellow natives who would not have the opportunity to attend a missionary school. "It were enough to neglect the duty of enlightening these tribes," the committee contended, "but to place barriers and hindrances in the way, to seal up the only language which can possibly be the medium of gospel truth to their souls . . . is something which the American people must regard with a universal and emphatic protest." They left the meeting confident that the official orders about the use of Indian language in schools would be modified.[31] Unfortunately, Grover Cleveland and the Bureau of Indian Affairs saw things differently. All of the appeals made by this Protestant delegation were disregarded. The Bureau once again affirmed that no white teacher would be permitted to teach in Indian languages. The ABS Board of Managers concluded that "the Commissioner of Indian Affairs assumes to know better than the missionaries," and added, with a sense of urgency, that "no policy can be endured which forbids Christian men and women to teach Christian truth." To do so would be a violation of religious liberty, a civil right "which is unhampered in every other part of our land, and must hereafter be unhampered within all Indian reservations." The ABS concluded that "so long as the order stands, the Department of the Interior will be in a position of direct antagonism to the Christian sentiment of our land."[32] In a showdown between the federal government's program to assimilate the Indians through the English language, and the ABS (and other missionary agencies) program to assimilate the Indians through the teachings of the Bible in their native tongues, the federal government won.

The last several decades of the nineteenth century were tumultuous years for the domestic mission of the ABS. On the one hand, the Society was able to distribute approximately 7.3 million Bibles from 1880 to 1900. Though the Fourth General Supply failed to reach projected goals, the number of people exposed to the Christian scriptures was a testament to the powerful distribution machine housed in the Bible House at Astor Place in New York City. As the ABS entered the twentieth century, it was financially struggling from effects of the panic of 1893 and was trying to keep up with the ever-changing population of the United States. As more and more immigrants poured into American cities, the ABS interest in contributing to a "homogeneous" Christian nation merged well with the nativist attempts of the American middle class to assimilate immigrants into an American way of life. The souls of Catholic immigrants needed to be saved and they simultaneously needed to become part of a Protestant country where the ABS served as one of the primary gatekeepers. Like the influx of southern and eastern European immigrants to eastern port cities and the Midwest at the end of the nineteenth century, the American West also provided opportunities for the ABS to meet the spiritual needs of individual people and advance the cause of a Protestant nation. Whether it was Chinese immigrants in California or the Native American people groups west of the Mississippi, the Bible Cause went forward and the ABS continued to adapt and adjust to the demographic changes facing the United States as it approached the turn of the twentieth century.

The Levant

When the American Bible Society was founded in 1816, it was focused on distributing the Bible to people in the United States. The number of Bibles it sold or granted beyond its national boundary was small. Between 1816 and 1830 the ABS distributed over 16,000 Bibles or Testaments in Latin America (with the most—about 2,000—going to Colombia and Mexico) and about 21,000 in the rest of the world (with the most going to Canada and Hawaii). The ABS usually sent Bibles and money to overseas missions run by denominational organizations. For example, in the first several decades it donated money to translation projects in India and Burma and sent Bibles to agents of the American Board of Commissioners for Foreign Missions (ABCFM), the Methodist United Foreign Missionary Society, and the American Colonization Society. But the door was always left open for a more expansive distribution program. Article II of the original ABS Constitution stated that "this Society shall . . . according to its ability, extend its influence to other countries, whether Christian, Mahometan, or Pagan."[1]

By the end of the American Civil War, the ABS was sending Bibles to organizations—mostly other Bible societies and missions—in Western Europe, Russia, Japan, China, Turkey, Africa, and Latin and Central America. "Wherever American missionaries speak for Jesus," the Board of Managers wrote in 1865, "where American commerce spreads her snowy sails, wherever our immense immigration winds its way across the continent, from the Atlantic to the Pacific and around the globe, we trace the blessed volumes from this Bible House and we thank God and take courage." Missionaries would do the work of preaching the Gospel and building churches and the ABS would provide them with Bibles to aid them in their work.[2]

The goal of this missionary-ABS alliance was twofold. First, the people of the world, especially those outside of Western Civilization, needed the Christian Gospel because it held the promise of eternal life. Second, these same people needed to be civilized into a Western, even American, way of life. The spiritual needs of the world went hand in hand with Western ideas such as moderation, industriousness, and cleanliness. The Gospel would prepare souls for heaven, but it would also bring improvement to *this* life as well. As the ABS worked with missionaries and churches at home to civilize immigrants and Indians, the people of Africa, Asia, Latin America, and the Middle East needed similar lessons. In 1897, two years before Rudyard Kipling published his imperialistic poem "The White Man's Burden," the *Bible Society Record* printed a speech by a missionary calling for the need to bring literacy, reading, Christian songs, classical languages, the printing press, and the "ink bottle and the reed pen" to the people of the non-Western world. American Christians wanted to "lead them across a gulf which other nations have only traversed in the slow progress of centuries." Christian missions in the nineteenth century blended Protestantism and the American way of progress. The assumption was that the United States was a Christian nation. For the American missionary enterprise and the ABS, it was the natural extension of Manifest Destiny.[3]

In the 1830s the ABS Board of Managers, who had already been active in working with denominational missionary boards overseas, decided that the Bible Cause might advance more effectively if they sent some of their own agents abroad. Missionaries were busy saving lost souls and thus would not have time to do the work of Bible distribution effectively. The establishment of an overseas agency might prompt Christians to donate more money to the ABS, thus advancing its spiritual and cultural work. When the time finally came to put down roots outside the United States the ABS chose the Levant, a swath of territory in southwest Asia bordered by the Taurus Mountains to the North, the Mediterranean Sea to the West, and the Arabian Desert and Mesopotamia in the East.[4] Today the Levant region includes Cyprus, Hatay, Israel, Jordan, Lebanon, Palestine, Syria, Iraq, Sinai, Egypt, and Turkey.

When the ABS started its work in the Levant the Ottoman Empire controlled most of the region. Founded in 1299 by Oghuz Turks under Osmen Bey in northwestern Anatolia, the Ottoman state became the Ottoman Empire in 1453 when Mehmed II conquered Constantinople and absorbed the remains of the Byzantine Empire. The Ottoman Empire's territory continued to grow, and during the 1500s and 1600s, under the control of Suleiman the Magnificent, it had become a powerful multinational and multilingual political entity that controlled large parts of Europe, Asia, the Caucuses, and Africa. After Suleiman's death in 1566, the Empire declined due to incompetent leaders, inflation, and excessive taxation. By the 1800s, at the time the ABS began its work in the Levant, the Empire was on its last legs. The Crimean War (1853–1856) reduced its territory, and the Russian victory in the Russo-Turkish War (1877–1878) proved to be a devastating blow to Ottoman supremacy. While the Empire had always been religiously diverse, with a Muslim minority ruling over a Christian and Jewish majority, as the empire declined an increasing number of Christians either migrated out or declared independence as part of nationalist secession movements. When ABS representatives arrived in the mid to late 1800s, Muslims were firmly in the majority.

The ABS chose Smyrna as its first headquarters in the Levant largely because the BFBS and the ABCFM had already established themselves there and several translation and printing projects were already underway. It was centrally located between Greece, Asia Minor, and the Near East. Smyrna was also the home of Simeon H. Calhoun, a missionary with strong ties to the ABS. When the Society learned that the American Foreign and Missionary Society was interested in securing the services of Calhoun, the Board of Managers snatched him up quickly and made him the agent for its new Mediterranean Station in Smyrna. As an employee of the ABS, Calhoun divided his time equally between translating, printing, and distribution. His work required regular trips to Constantinople, Beirut, Jerusalem, and wherever a door for Bible work was open.[5]

Turkey, where Calhoun spent most of his time, was a diverse place. He estimated that the 1 million inhabitants were divided among Greeks (200,000), Armenians (150,000), Jews (80,000), Catholic Armenians (10,000), Franks (10,000), and about half a million Muslim Turks. Calhoun faced immediate opposition to his work. The Greek Orthodox clergy opposed the circulation of the Bible and on occasion demonstrated its dislike of the King James Version by burning it in public. In December 1837, Calhoun reported that the Patriarch of Constantinople, the head of the Orthodox Church, had written a circular letter to his clergy and laity to warn them against the "dangerous" activities and doctrines of "Luthero-Calvinist" missionaries who had arrived in their country to spread "the poison of their heresies into the ears of the members of the eastern church, in order to corrupt our spotless faith and to scatter the flock of Christ." The Patriarch pulled no punches in his critique of Western Protestants. At times his comments made the remarks of the Pope concerning Bible societies (see chapter 5) seem tame by comparison. He claimed that the Greek Church "is now making war upon you—ye Satanic heresiarchs, who have appeared in these last years from the recesses of hell and from the depths of the northern ocean." Faithful Orthodox Christians in Turkey were urged by their spiritual leader to collect and destroy "all the translations of the holy Scriptures into the Modern Greek tongue which are found in their dioceses."[6]

Whatever hopes Calhoun had for reaching the Greek Christians were dashed by the stubborn resistance of the clergy. In the New Testament city of Ephesus, Calhoun spent three days passing out Bibles until the local Greek bishop condemned the use of Protestant Bibles and "no more Greeks dared to call for them." In 1839, on a visit to Syria, he met the principals of a local missionary school who encouraged Calhoun not to abandon efforts among the

Greeks of Turkey. Soon the Greeks would awaken to the "superstitious observances of their church" and cease following their "ignorant priests" who were incapable of making "an intelligent or intelligible exposition of the simplest portions of the word of God." Some of these churches, Calhoun reported, did not even have pulpits![7] But at the end of his nearly thirteen years of service with the ABS in the Levant, Calhoun still bemoaned the difficulty of penetrating Eastern Christianity with the Bible. During a trip to Jerusalem during the Greek celebration of Easter he wrote that the "distribution of the Scriptures . . . among the pilgrims of the Greek Church is small. It would seem as though ecclesiastical opposition is manifesting itself in every direction." In Turkey and Syria there appeared "to be a growing determination to adhere more and more closely to the corruptions of the church and an increasing jealousy of foreign interference."[8]

American missionaries and benevolent societies like the ABS did very little work among Muslims in the region. The proselytization of Muslims was strictly forbidden in the Ottoman Empire for political reasons. The Sultan feared that Protestantism encouraged nationalism among minority groups such as the Armenians and Syriacs. It was not uncommon for Calhoun to write to the Bible House in New York with comments such as "among the Mohammedans in Persia, there seems to be no opening at the present for the distribution of the Bible." Calhoun commented on Islamic religious practices whenever he got the chance. In 1837, on a return boat trip from Greece with a few dozen Turks he was offended by their "often repeated prayers" and "many kneelings and prostrations in the most public parts of the vessel." For Calhoun, such practice was not religious devotion. It was just the opposite. Muslims did not understand prayer as "spiritual communion with God," but looked upon it rather as a "meritorious act," a means of pleasing God that ran counter to the Protestant doctrine of divine grace and justification by faith alone. Calhoun was impressed with Muslim devotion during the day-long fasts and evening festivals of Ramadan, but he could never shake his belief that his new neighbors were "practicing the religion of the false prophet" and "laboring under a delusion."[9]

Calhoun spent most of his time on the road, visiting mission stations throughout the Levant. Many of these missionaries were at work translating the Bible. Missionary-translators in Constantinople were revising an Armeno-Turkish Old Testament, a Hebrew-Spanish Old Testament, and a version of the Psalms in Modern Armenian, Arabic, and Ancient Syriac. All of these projects were funded, at least in part, by the ABS. Calhoun often traveled with boxes of Greek, Armenian, and Turkish scriptures in the hopes of distributing them through the region. When he wasn't traveling, he was presiding over the ABS depository in Smyrna and sending Bibles off to missionaries in Russia,

Jerusalem, Syria, Palestine, Persia, Cyprus, Patras, Broosa, Greece, and Mani. His primary role, as would be the primary role for subsequent Levant agents, was to serve as a liaison between the missionaries in the field and the Bible House in New York.

Yet Calhoun was never wholly satisfied with the work of distribution. He was a missionary at heart. He often chided the Board of Managers and the Bible House staff for measuring the success of their work in terms of the amount of money in the bank or the number of Bibles shipped around the world. In 1837 he made this abundantly clear to the ABS Board of Managers: "We have been and are yet looking altogether too much to the numbers sent out, to the funds raised, etc., etc., and too little to God." The ABS, however, had a slightly different understanding of its work in the Levant. The Bible society was a service organization. It was designed to support missionaries doing the work of evangelism. It did not prohibit its agents from spreading the good news of the Gospel, but this was not the Society's primary responsibility. In 1840, Calhoun returned to the United States on a short furlough. While he was home the ABS informed him that it would not support his work in the Levant with a full-salaried position unless he was willing to make his main priority fundraising and distribution rather than ministry. The Society cut his compensation and sent him back to the Near East as part-time employee of the ABS. Four years later Calhoun and the ABS parted ways. He stayed in the Levant as a missionary with the ABCFM.[10]

After Calhoun's departure, the ABS agency in the Levant ceased operations for a decade, although the Society continued to contribute Bibles and money for the ongoing translation work of the ABCFM. In 1854, the Board of Managers decided to reopen the agency and appoint Chester Righter as its agent. Righter, a seminary graduate with little life experience apart from a year of travel in Europe and the Near East, only lasted two years in the Levant before his premature death while touring a mission station in Asiatic Turkey. The ABS replaced Righter with Isaac Bliss, a missionary in Turkey. Under his leadership Constantinople became the new center of ABS operations in the region. Bliss got right to work with the daily tasks of supervising the disbursement of funds to missionary stations involved in translation work. He visited these stations to introduce himself and the work of the Bible Cause; oversaw the distribution of Bibles in the region; learned to speak Turkish, Armenian, and French; and even developed a basic understanding of ABS printing operations. Bliss possessed the business savvy that Calhoun did not. He made connections in the city with booksellers and street peddlers, convincing them to sell ABS Bibles in exchange for a small percentage of the profit. He even persuaded the Bible House in New York to allow him to hire two colporteurs to carry out the work of distribution in Constantinople. According to Bliss, the

Ottoman city was a "promising field" filled with hundreds of thousands of inhabitants and "numberless khans and coffee shops." Eventually the ABS provided funds for a region-wide colporteur system that extended Bible distribution to the Sea of Marmora region, Scutari, Bulgaria, and Bithynia.[11]

Bliss often complained to the Board of Managers in New York that the ABS needed more financial support in order to compete with the BFBS. The BFBS was a global organization. It had been in the Levant since 1808, well before Calhoun established the ABS agency in 1831.[12] Yet by the mid-nineteenth century the United States was also beginning to find its way in the world, especially in the area of international missions and benevolent work. As far as the worldwide Bible Cause was concerned, a clash between the ABS and BFBS was inevitable and Bliss had an ornery personality that was useful in such a competitive atmosphere.

When Bliss arrived in the Levant the BFBS had a Bible depot in Constantinople and was close to edging the ABS out of the region. BFBS translators were working on more relevant translations, including an Arabic translation of the ABS-owned Armeno-Turkish scriptures. When the BFBS asked Bliss if it could print its Arabic New Testament, he was not happy: "I must confess that I am amazed that *such an application should be made at all when they have but just refused our society permission to print our edition of the Ref. Testament in Bulgarian.*" The BFBS claimed a monopoly on Bible work in Bulgaria, even to the point of forbidding the ABS to print one of its own Bibles in Bulgarian. As far as the BFBS was concerned, the ABS would need to "seek some other field of labor." Bliss could not understand why the BFBS was so protective of Bulgaria when "the whole world . . . is in the hands of the B&F Society." He saw the BFBS as trying to "get all they can & keep all they get," and thus urged the ABS to reject its request to print the Arabic New Testament of the Armeno-Turkish Bible. All was not well among those laboring on behalf of the Bible Cause in the Levant.[13]

The BFBS and the ABS also argued over the pricing of Bibles. Though the two agencies were selling many of the same Bibles, their prices often differed, leading to competition for sales. Bliss thought that it was wrong for the ABS and BFBS to be "occupying a position of rivalry" and asked BFBS agent Robert Thomson to agree to similar prices and similar salaries for colporteurs. Thomson ignored Bliss's request. Several months later, the BFBS lowered its prices in Egypt on its large Arabic Bible so that it was 10 pisastres below the ABS price for the same Bible. Bliss was upset about this move, because the ABS had funded the translation of this particular Bible and had given the stereotype plates of the edition to the BFBS free of charge. One missionary in Egypt wrote to Bliss informing him that the BFBS colporteurs were selling copies of the large Arabic Bible while ABS supplies "remain on the shelf unsold."

Missionaries in the region found this price war to be detrimental to the spread of the word of God and urged the Bible societies to work together in coming up with a common price. Bliss and the representatives of the BFBS finally agreed to these requests.[14]

But tensions between Bliss (and by extension the ABS) and the BFBS continued throughout the agent's thirty-two-year (1857–1889) tenure in the Levant. Both national Bible societies had agents in the region and they were often doing their work in the same cities. When the location of the work of the ABS and the BFBS overlapped there were tacit agreements made about how to divide the territory, but since these agreements were not binding they were often ignored. In 1867 Bliss wrote to the Board of Managers in New York, telling them that "it was high time to consider the question whether it may not be well to correspond with the B. & F.B.Soc. as to the division of the Arabic field." At the time, the ABS was distributing in the areas of the Levant where American missionaries were working and the BFBS was working in those areas where British missionaries were present, but the British had far more missionaries in the region than the United States. Similarly, when BFBS agents claimed that all of Greece belonged to their agency, Bliss wrote another fiery letter back to New York, telling Corresponding Secretary Joseph Holdich that while he respected the "proper fields of our older and venerated Sister or Mother Society," the ABS needed the freedom to distribute "wherever we can find an open door & a demand for our labors," even if that meant moving into longstanding BFBS territory.[15]

In 1876, Bliss and Thomson exchanged some heated letters over these territorial disputes. Bliss was upset that Thomson had assigned a BFBS colporteur to work in Lebanon. Lebanon had always been ABS territory and Thomson knew it. Bliss already had five colporteurs in this part of Lebanon and he could not understand why Thomson would send one of his own at such a great expense to the BFBS when the work of distribution could be easily accomplished by the ABS colporteurs. Thomson, on the other hand, defended his decision on the grounds that there were British missionaries in Beirut and Lebanon who deserved to get their Bible from a fellow countryman.[16] Thomson and Bliss made efforts at reconciliation in the hopes of working out a fair division of labor in the Levant field, but neither side was willing to concede territory. Part of the debate involved distribution in Turkey. Bliss claimed that Thomson had agreed to concentrate the BFBS efforts in Northwest Turkey and avoid distribution in places where American missionaries had been entrenched for decades. In return, Bliss agreed not to send colporteurs into "British territory." Thomson, however, denied that any such pact was ever made and claimed that the BFBS had the right to distribute Bibles throughout the entire Turkish Empire, Greece, and any other field where there was a need. Thomson told

Bliss that "to send a colporteur even into a district that has been pretty well worked by others, does not seem to me either unjust or any disturbance to the work of others." With this letter, the friction between these two Bible societies had reached its peak.[17]

Meanwhile, despite these battles over territory and pricing with the BFBS, the work of Christianizing the Levant continued. Protestant Bible distribution was not easy in a culture dominated by Muslims and Eastern Orthodox Christians. In 1864, the Ottoman Empire shut down the ABS Bible depository (along with a number of other Protestant organizations in Constantinople) and arrested five Turks who had converted to Protestantism. The government accused American missionaries of publishing Protestant books from an underground printing press that also happened to be printing anti-Ottoman texts. Bliss was able to refute these claims by proving that most of the Bibles being distributed were actually printed in the West. Eventually the depository was reopened, but the converted Turks were left in prison. Because of this incident the ABS was forbidden to utilize colporteurs. This temporary shutdown of operations brought about a major decrease in distribution and once the ABS was allowed to start selling Bibles again many residents of Constantinople and the surrounding regions were unwilling, out of fear of more government reprisal, to purchase their texts. Bliss was a master at putting a positive spin on things. Despite the persecution, he told his superiors in New York that Protestantism was growing in the Levant. Four years after this incident, he reported that missionaries had established sixty "evangelical churches" north of Syria and there were about 16,000 Protestants now living in the Ottoman Empire. "Surely it is not too much to say," he wrote, "that the results already attained in the work of evangelization in Turkey have in number, variety & breadth of influence been very great."[18]

Bliss's pet project was the construction of a Constantinople Bible House. Missionaries in the Levant did not have enough space to store their books and as work in the region grew, the need for a better depository became more and more apparent. The current storage facility was inadequate. Space was limited, mice and rats often ate copies of the Bible, and the rent was high. Bliss's plan was to build a Bible House that would be owned by the Board of Managers and run by a committee of Bible agents and missionaries, with Bliss at its head. Such a Bible House would be a monument to the American efforts in the Levant and send a clear message to the BFBS about American power. Bliss told the ABS Board of Managers that the building was *not* designed, as some of them might have believed, "for the sake of gaining an advantage" over the BFBS, but he did believe that it was time that the ABS "take a position of equal importance & honour with that of the B&F." As one missionary noted, the proposed Bible House would "at once give a character of permanency &

efficiency to the work of the distribution of the Holy Scriptures" and "all evangelical labors."[19]

In June 1866, Bliss traveled back to New York to convince the Board of
Managers to support his vision. The board was sympathetic, and was even
willing to endorse the idea, but few of its members wanted to commit money
or establish such a permanent presence in a foreign country. Bliss was disappointed. This was a clear sign that the ABS had a "lack of confidence in me as
the representative of the whole thing." In the end, the board wished Bliss success in his efforts to build a Bible House, but if Bliss wanted a more permanent
center for the Bible Cause in Turkey he would need to build it himself.[20]

And build he did. Instead of immediately returning to the Levant, Bliss
stayed in the United States to raise funds for his Bible House. He set off on a
nationwide fundraising tour, managing to obtain meetings with New York's
wealthiest Christian businessmen and philanthropists. He spoke at some of the
most prominent churches in the country. By July 1867 he had raised $50,000,
enough to get the project underway. Five years later the Constantinople Bible
House was finished. *Harper's Weekly*, which was one of the most widely read
magazines in the United States, took notice: "Its site commanded a full view of
the magnificent harbor, the Golden Horn, and a portion of the Bosporus . . .
in every respect, a more advantageous site could hardly be found in the entire
city." The Bible House of Constantinople, as it was officially named, was eighty
feet in length by seventy-one feet in depth and four stories high. It was constructed out of stone in a "neat" and "plain" style that stood "as a strange contrast to the irregular and fantastic architecture which surrounds it." The Bible
House would be run by a group of seven trustees representing the various
Protestant Bible, charitable, and missionary societies of the United States that
had operations in Turkey. All of these representatives were given space in the
building. "It is a joy of our hearts," Bliss told the ABS, "it attracts general attention and few are the passers by [sic] who do not look up at it and ask for what
purpose such a building may be."[21]

In the final decades of Bliss's career in the Levant the ABS appealed to the US
government several times in an effort to secure greater rights for Americans in
Turkey. The limits placed on the ABS in the 1860s were eventually lifted, allowing Bliss to continue the Society's distribution work in the Ottoman Empire,
but suspicion on the part of the Turkish government remained. For example,
in 1874 the ABS had an unusually strong year of Bible sales in Constantinople.
When local Muslims learned about these increases in sales they brought the
news to the attention of the Ottoman authorities, who responded, "without
warning," by forbidding the sale of Protestant Bibles in the city. It also ordered
the seizure of all Turkish-language scriptures from the Bible House. Bliss
and other Protestant missionaries appealed to the American ambassador in

Constantinople, and the ban was lifted and the Turkish government apologized. The religious tensions, however, did not go away. Local government officials continued to seize Turkish Bibles from ABS colporteurs working in the city until the ABS finally received a special permit from the Turkish government granting permission to print the Bible in Armenian, Armeno-Turkish, and Osmanlee characters. This new freedom to print came with the caveat that the title pages of these Bibles had to identity that they were "Protestant books," so that Muslims who stumbled upon them knew that they were forbidden to read them. Bliss was not convinced that this would end the persecution so in 1881 he formed a committee to draft a letter to President Chester Arthur, followed six years later by a similar petition to Grover Cleveland, asking the United States to intercede and ensure that the ABS could go about its business in Turkey without interference. We do not know if these US presidents ever responded to the petitions, but very little changed. Ironically, this was a time when Turkey had an official policy of religious liberty. According to Bliss, such policies were seldom enforced to protect the work of Bible distributors.[22]

When Bliss died in 1889 the leadership of the ABS efforts in the Levant was passed to Marcellus Bowen, a Presbyterian clergyman with fifteen years of missionary experience in the Levant. During Bowen's tenure the tensions between the Turkish government and Protestant missionaries grew intense, placing the Bible Cause in jeopardy. During stretches when the ABS was unable to sell or distribute books Bowen was forced to cut wages of Bible House employees. He worried that the Ottoman government's attempt to discredit the ABS in the minds of ordinary people had been effective. Moreover, it became clear that the Empire's policy of religious toleration did not apply to colporteurs. ABS colporteurs selling Bibles in the streets of Constantinople continued to be arrested, prompting Bowen to wonder if the whole colporteur system needed to be abandoned since he could find few men willing "to run the risk that has to be encountered."[23]

Like Bliss, Bowen often appealed to the United States for help. He was not the only one. In fact, much of American foreign policy in Turkey during the late nineteenth century was focused on issues related to missionaries and religious freedom. In 1891 Bowen demanded that the preferences of ABS workers in Turkey were considered in the selection of the US minister to Constantinople. He even asked that the US Navy send a gunboat to protect the work of the ABS from what he believed to be a Turkish government hostile to the Bible Cause. The connection between American imperialism in the late nineteenth century and the distribution of the Bible in the Levant is hard to miss. Bliss eventually appealed to the US Department of Public Instruction, which helped the ABS secure a permit allowing it to import the Bible into the Ottoman Empire. Bowen worked to get permits for all of the colporteurs on the ABS payroll. These documents stated that ABS salesmen were working on behalf of the United States selling books "authorized by the Department of Public Instruction." Though Bowen was successful in convincing the American government to support the sale and distribution of Bibles in the Empire, in the end it did not seem to help much. Colporteurs continued to be arrested and kept for days in "filthy prisons, chained at times to murderers and other criminals of the foulest character," until word came from Constantinople officials that they could be released. This was not the kind of religious toleration that Bowen had hoped for, and it appeared that whatever support he received from the US government was insufficient.[24]

At the start of the twentieth century the Ottoman Empire was just a shadow of its former self. Internal corruption and bribery and wars with neighboring powers had diminished its size. The Empire became dependent upon foreign capital to keep its economy afloat. In 1908, a political reform movement known as the Young Turks led a rebellion against the absolute rule of Sultan Abdul Hamid II that restored the short-lived (1876–1878) Ottoman Constitution of 1876, a European-influenced form of government that established a Parliament as a necessary check to the power of the Sultan. Bowen observed the revolution from the Constantinople Bible House: "Gallows have been erected at different points in the city, and yesterday morning the people saw 13 bodies which had been suspended just at daybreak." Though he found the hangings of former Ottoman leaders to be a "gruesome spectacle," he told the ABS in New York that these executions are "likely to have a salutary influence." In the end, the Young Turks proved too inexperienced to rule effectively and began fighting among themselves. Bowen again added commentary: "The present regime is not gaining the confidence either of foreigners, or of the native Christian races." Distribution of Bibles stopped during revolution, but the Young Turks generally left the ABS alone and there was no outright opposition to its work.[25]

The 1908 Revolution was only the beginning of the political unrest and chaos that would ensue in the Ottoman Empire over the next several years, ultimately bringing an end to the Empire following World War I. Yet the post-1908 world opened up new opportunities for the ABS. Bowen was encouraged: "It must be well nigh impossible for the outside world, even in the exercise of its wildest imagination, adequately to measure the gulf that separates the Turkey of to-day from the Turkey of a year ago." What was once "one of the worst forms of absolutism in history" had quickly become a place of unprecedented religious freedom. Colporteurs wrote Bowen "cheerful letters" about the lack of opposition to the work of the ABS. In 1912, Bowen even presented a Bible to the Sultan Mehmed V, Bowen thanking him for allowing the ABS to do its work. He told the Sultan that he hoped he would be "impressed with the loftiness" of the teachings to be found within the scriptures. In classic ABS style, Bowen informed the Sultan that the Bible would go a long way toward the "spiritual development of your Majesty's subjects and the promotion among them of the spirit of peace and good will."[26]

The American Bible Society would continue its work in the Levant well into the twentieth century and it continues to bring Bibles and resources to this region through the outreach of the United Bible Societies. The Levant was a tough mission field filled with Muslims and Orthodox Christians and a government that, despite promises of toleration, was never fully comfortable with Protestants distributing Bibles. It appears to have been an odd choice of location for the Society's first attempt at establishing an overseas agency. But the Levant was a popular mission field where American and British missionaries had been laboring for several decades prior to the ABS arrival. In its first seventy-five years in the Levant the ABS learned three important lessons. First, the success of its mission in foreign countries was always at the mercy of local politics. If foreign governments, such as that of the Ottoman Empire, were not completely supportive of ABS efforts, the Bible Cause would not go forward. Second, as historian Peter Wosh has shown, the Levant experience made it abundantly clear that the ABS was not a missionary organization. The differences in approach between Calhoun and Bliss illustrate this point. The ABS was in the Levant primarily to sell Bibles and serve the denominations. While it certainly remained concerned with spreading Protestantism and American values in the Levant, it would do so through an effective business and marketing plan, leaving the practical work of ministry to the missionaries. Third, the experience in the Levant, especially in the era of Bliss, allowed the ABS to assert itself as an international player in the Bible business. Until it arrived in the Levant the ABS viewed its relationship with the BFBS as that of a doting child who was supposed to be always learning lessons from the great "mother society." It was now time for the ABS to exert its muscle, not unlike the way the United States was starting to flex its foreign policy muscles in the cause of imperialism. It would still be some time before the ABS led the way in the global Bible Cause, but its competition with the BFBS in the Levant was a clear sign that times were changing.

11

Mexico

By 1889, the American Bible Society was operating ten agencies around the world. In addition to its agency in the Levant, the Society had established a significant presence in Argentina, Mexico, Persia, China, Japan, Cuba, Brazil, Peru, and Venezuela. The ABS commitment to Latin America was strong, and there is perhaps no better place to explore its work in this region in the decades surrounding the turn of the twentieth century than in Mexico.[1] Prior to the American Civil War the ABS efforts in Mexico were sporadic at best. Agents provided Bibles to American troops during the Mexican-American War, but when the army left the country, the ABS, for the most part, followed it. In 1870 a special ABS committee recommended that the Society place five agents at Zacatecas to supervise Bible work in the region. These agents would be responsible for hiring a Mexican native to serve as the chief distributor in the country. The holder of this position would report to the committee in Zacatecas, who would then report to the Bible House in New York. Unlike the Levant, in which the ABS allowed Isaac Bliss to operate with a great deal of autonomy, the Board of Managers kept close tabs on the work in Mexico. Don Juan Amador, a recently converted Mexican Protestant, was chosen to serve as the chief distributor and was provided with funds to hire three colporteurs to help him in his labors. One of those colporteurs was Doña Francisca Alvarez de Castilla, the first female ABS colporteur in Mexico. Because the members of the board were not entirely convinced that native colporteurs would be effective in Mexico, they also reached out to the American and Foreign Christian Union to sell and dispense Bibles in parts of the country.[2]

Life was not easy for native colporteurs peddling a Protestant book in a Catholic country. In Sierra Hermosa one of Amador's colporteurs was threatened with violence from local authorities and wealthy residents of the town. Since no one would provide him with lodging, he chose to spend the night in the public plaza. At about midnight, as the colporteur slept, he was surrounded by a gang of masked men who stole all of his Bibles and Testaments (twenty-four of each) and burned them. The poor Bible distributor fled the city, narrowly escaping with his life. Yet he remained persistent. At some point following the book burning he returned to Sierra Hermosa. While once again sleeping in the plaza, he was awakened by the "hissing sound" of a slow match beneath the packsaddle he was using as a pillow. A bag of gunpowder was positioned under his makeshift pillow and was about to explode. Fortunately, he was able to leap to his feet and flee the scene before explosion occurred. Around the same time, Doña Francisco was selling Bibles in Hacienda del Carro when a few Catholic priests, disguised as potential customers, bought Bibles and took them to the town plaza where they conducted *a regular auto-da-fé* (a ritual of public penance of condemned heretics that was popular during the Spanish Inquisition), to the "delight of the ignorant fanatics and to the scandal of the better class of the community."[3]

Colporteurs knew that they would be persecuted, but this expectation rarely distracted them from their work. One Mexican colporteur wrote, "[I] cannot express my joy at being counted worthy to suffer threats of death on account of the Word of God." When he started selling Bibles in the town of Valparaiso someone warned him that a local gang was planning to attack him. Fearful for his life, the colporteur returned to his room, opened his Bible, and prayed that God would lead him to a passage that might bring some comfort. He randomly opened to Psalms 34 and 35, King David's song of thanksgiving to God for delivering him from his enemies. The colporteur read these psalms "with joy" and would later write that he "felt sure that the Lord had revealed to me that my enemies would not be suffered to lay their hands on me." Later that evening four soldiers came to his room and escorted him to see the mayor of the village. He was told to bring his Bibles. As they departed the house, the colporteur and his armed escorts were met by a crowd of villagers armed with sticks and stones. As they advanced to attack, the soldiers fought back the mob. They eventually made it to the house of the mayor who interrogated the colporteur, but found nothing wrong with the Bibles he was selling. A similar attack occurred the following week. This time the mayor's guards captured the "ringleaders" and imprisoned them "as murderers." Following this second incident the mayor assigned a soldier to serve as the colporteur's permanent escort for the rest of his stay in the village.[4]

As new fields of service were opened in Mexico, the ABS Board of Managers finally became convinced that they needed to have a more permanent agency. They started looking for a person who could work closely with Protestant missionaries in the country and who had the administrative skills to give the work in Mexico some "shape and consistency." The ABS established its agency in Mexico City. It was a logical choice. Mexico City was the nation's capital, and it was centrally located so that "it is most easy to radiate and reach the different parts of the country." A large number of Protestant missionaries were stationed in the city.[5] The first ABS agent in Mexico City was Dr. Arthur Gore, a Boston dentist. He was chosen for his understanding of business, his knowledge of Spanish, and his apparent interest in Christian benevolence. Upon arrival in Mexico City in July 1878, Gore rented a store on a main street in the city and began to sell Bibles. While his work got off to a good start, the Board of Managers grew concerned when it stopped receiving regular correspondence from him reporting sales and chronicling the work of colporteurs. It turns out that Gore was not doing much in Mexico City. Missionaries who were initially eager to work with Gore grew disappointed by his lack of zeal for the Bible Cause and began to complain to the ABS in New York about his ineptitude for the work at hand. Moreover, the ABS was losing money in Mexico on Gore's watch. The building he had rented to sell books was too expensive and in need of repair. The cost of rent was much higher than the monthly revenue he was taking in from sales. The building had a sign announcing the sale of Bibles, but the board was upset to learn that it nowhere mentioned the name of the American Bible Society. To make matters worse, Gore did not keep office hours and, according to one observer, was rarely ever seen at the building.[6]

In 1879, the ABS sent Rev. Edward Gilman, one of its corresponding secretaries and the brother of future ABS president and nationally known educator Daniel Coit Gilman, to Mexico to check on what was happening with the agency. Gilman spent six weeks in Mexico, traveling 4,500 miles throughout the countryside. He was joined by Augustus Taber, a New York importer of marble and a member of the Board of Managers. Gilman and Taber were faced with two tasks. First, they were to confirm the reports of Gore's incompetence, and, if what they had heard from missionaries was true, remove him from his post. This is exactly what happened. Gore was sent home. Second, Gilman and Taber were ordered to bring more efficiency to the ABS operation in Mexico.[7]

After Gore was fired, Gilman and Taber gathered a group of Protestant missionaries and local ministers affiliated with an organization called the Evangelical Alliance and discussed with them the prospects of continuing to staff a Bible depository and bookstore in Mexico City. These men gave the ABS officials their "most emphatic assurances" that they would do everything in their power to support the work of the Society. Despite the bad reputation Gore had brought to the Bible Cause, these men urged Gilman and Taber to keep the ABS building open for business. Gilman and Taber then appointed Rev. John W. Butler, a Methodist missionary in Mexico City, to serve as the interim agent of the ABS, and hired several colporteurs to work with him. Gilman and Taber also met with J. W. Foster, the US minister to Mexico and a Presbyterian layman. Foster expressed much interest in the work of the ABS and set up an appointment for them to meet with General Porfirio Díaz, the president of the Mexican Republic. Gilman presented Díaz with a Spanish

Bible and the president said that he looked forward to "the benefit which he expected to derive from it, and with the assurance that it should not lie unread."[8]

Gilman and Taber made suggestions about the most efficient way to put the Bible in the hands of the Mexican people. This required revisiting the old ABS debate over whether to sell Bibles or give them away. Some of the Protestant missionaries in Mexico advocated for the free distribution of Bibles because the people of the country were too poor to purchase copies. Gilman disagreed. As we have seen, the ABS believed that if a person purchased a Bible he or she would be more likely to read it and care for it. In addition, the ABS worried that if they gave away Bibles in a Catholic country like Mexico the recipients would be more likely to hand them over to priests who would eventually burn or destroy them. Moreover, the ABS needed the revenue gained from the sale of Bibles in order to reach other constituencies in the United States and around the globe. Gilman agreed that Bibles might be too expensive for ordinary Mexicans, so he recommended dropping the price of the ABS's cheapest New Testaments from sixteen cents to six cents and reduce the price of the Gospel portions from six cents to two cents.[9]

Following Gilman's and Taber's visit, the ABS chose Hiram Philetus Hamilton as its new agent in Mexico. At the time of his appointment he had finished graduate work at Union Theological Seminary and had just been ordained to the Presbyterian ministry at a church in Dutchess County, New York. He would spend the next twenty-six years as the ABS agent for Mexico. Hamilton wasted no time in expanding the Bible Cause among the people of Mexico. In his first year as agent he hired fifteen colporteurs. The ABS work in Mexico benefited from the relatively stable political conditions in the country under the leadership of Díaz, who served as president from 1876 to 1880 and again from 1884 to 1911. Díaz afforded religious liberty to all of those living in his country, but the Catholic Church still held a great deal of power in towns and villages. Hamilton and the missionaries he worked with in Mexico City, Guanajuato, Pachuca, Puebla, Guadalajara, and Zacatecas were confident that the Mexican government would not interfere with their work, but they were also convinced, as Hamilton put it, "that a very large number of people here consider religious liberty as the exclusive right of Rome."[10]

Catholic resistance to the Bible Cause in Mexico was strong. The liberal Mexican Constitution of 1857 refused to acknowledge the Catholic Church as the official religion of the state. Though Mexican conservatives made several efforts in the 1860s and 1870s to overturn the Constitution and restore economic, religious, and culture power to the Church, all of these efforts failed. When Díaz took office in 1876 he upheld the liberal Constitution and made sure that the Church would never have the kind of power it possessed during the time of Spanish colonization, but he also took a laissez-faire approach to enforcement, allowing the Church to regain some of its wealth and take matters of religious freedom (or lack thereof) into its own hands. Catholics were not interested in sharing Mexico with Protestants and Díaz did little to stop the persecution of Protestants at the local level.[11]

Hamilton noted that "while the more intelligent part of the priests take but little notice of us, the more ignorant continue to persecute us." When a colporteur named Lopez came to the town of San Juan Bautista to sell ABS Bibles, the priests issued a decree denouncing the Bible as "the book of the devil." Another Mexican colporteur was attacked on his way to Orizaba and was robbed of his books and money. The attackers may have been encouraged by a local priest. Catholic newspapers declared a desire to remove all Protestants from Mexico, while "liberal papers" refused to defend the rights of Protestants in the country because they did not want to lose readers. Hamilton believed that the people of Mexico wanted Bibles, but he also knew that they were unwilling to defy the orders of the village priests who threatened excommunication for anyone who read the Protestant scriptures. (As we saw in chapter 5, these priests were following orders from the papacy in Rome about the dangers of Bible societies.) If persecution was strong in a particular place, Hamilton instructed his colporteurs to simply pass through the town or village, "however fanatical," and at least leave a Scripture portion in a doorway or in the street. The new ABS agent believed that the Mexican people's irrational loyalty to "church powers" would eventually be undermined by missionaries, evangelical literature, and prayer from all those "who desire the extension of his kingdom on earth."[12]

The opposition to the work of the ABS was part of a much larger resistance to American involvement in Mexico. Díaz was intent on modernizing Mexico, and he relied on economic support from the United States to make that happen. During the so-called Pax Porfiriana, a time of relative peace and stability in the country, foreigners, especially businessmen seeking opportunities in oil, mines, and public utilities, were welcomed into Mexico. But while some Mexicans favored modernization, many were hesitant to embrace change and few benefited from these American capitalist ventures. The result was a strong anti-American sentiment in towns and villages across the country. The modernization of Mexico under Díaz was directly linked to his policies of religious freedom. The president did not only tolerate Protestantism, he encouraged its spread throughout the country. Díaz himself was a devout Catholic, but his efforts on this front were part of an attempt to win the confidence of American investors who associated Catholic countries with feudalism, superstition, and a general lack of commitment to progress. Opposition to Díaz's efforts to convince American businessmen to come to Mexico often played out in increasing hostility to Protestant missionaries, who were seen as part of a larger

American invasion that was threatening traditional ways of life and challenging the Catholic Church's longstanding hold on wealth and land in Mexico. Hamilton described this opposition as "open, public, and bold." Colporteurs were insulted (including chants of "Death to Protestants"), imprisoned, and, in a few cases, stoned. One colporteur spent six days in a Campeche prison "without just cause." In Oaxaca an antimissionary mob trapped a colporteur in his house and spent the night throwing stones at it as he "watched and prayed with his trembling wife and children."[13]

There was much to be overcome in Mexico. The people were poor. Hamilton said that there were many "who do not see a coin for months at a time." Others "exchange the mats they have woven for small quantities of beans and corn." The people subsisted on boiled beans wrapped by "small flat cakes of maize, called tortillas." They wore their clothing day and night until it dropped "to pieces." Women usually wore blue petticoats "falling in straight plaits before, the shoulders and waist being partially concealed by a long width of dark blue cotton cloth, having a hole in the middle, through which the head is thrust." Men wore "wide white cotton drawers, white cotton blouses," leather sandals and "broad-brimmed sombreros" to protect them from the sun. Their houses were made of adobe and usually included mats for beds, a charcoal furnace of clay, some earthen cooking utensils, and a stone to ground corn for tortillas. Hamilton, of course, described these conditions with the Bible Cause in mind: "It is strange that we often find a village in which there are but one or two people who can read." Those who could read, or merely wanted a Bible as a talisman, could seldom afford to pay for one. Though the Mexican agency under Hamilton rarely gave away Bibles for reasons first articulated by Gilman during his 1879 visit, many colporteurs were willing to make trades. An elderly man in Jalisco convinced a colporteur to take an old machete in exchange for a Bible. Others traded their rosary beads, cloth, and books for a copy of the word of God. Colporteurs, in turn, made some money on these items by selling them to tourists.[14]

But Hamilton believed that the Bible Cause would serve as an agent of progress in Mexico. The scriptures would help the country overcome its difficulties. When he spoke about progress, Hamilton was drawing upon the longstanding ABS belief that the Protestant Bible, wherever it was read, would always serve as a catalyst for greater freedom, education, and improvement. The "peace and prosperity" of Mexico, Hamilton believed, was directly related to the "gentle, restless influence of the Holy Bible in the homes of the people." If he and his colporteurs could "lift off the heavy hand of inquisitorial ecclesiasticism" in Mexico they could strengthen "the progressive element" in the country and pave the way for further improvement through the reading and application of God's word. When Díaz agreed in 1903 to attend a reception hosted by the

Young Men's Christian Association, Hamilton was thrilled. Díaz's vice president, Ramón Corral, a man who Hamilton described as an "enterprising and progressive citizen," even served as the chairman of a committee for the formation of a YMCA among the youth of Mexico City.

Hamilton's letters to the Bible House in New York are filled with stories of the difficulties faced by ABS colporteurs, but they also contain a sense of optimism about the future possibility of Protestant-style American civilization. In 1905, he reflected on the changes he had seen in Mexico since his arrival twenty-six years earlier. Public work projects were becoming a source of "civic pride and congratulations." Slums were getting cleaned and a new drainage system now made streets much more passable. Parks with fountains provided "pleasant breathing-places" for "poverty-stricken thousands." The temperance movement was making headway in parts of the country and the work of the Women's Christian Temperance Union was endorsed by President Díaz himself. Mexican railroads were facilitating commerce and rapidly breaking down local prejudices. By the end of the nineteenth century American economic, religious, and moral influence was so powerful in Mexico that it was virtually impossible for Díaz, the Catholic Church, or anyone else for that matter to stop it. Soon Mexico would be a "homogeneous nation" where the "spirit of intolerance will gladly disappear before the advance of enlightened civilization," and Hamilton wanted to make sure that the Bible was at the heart of such an advance. Indeed, a "brighter day" was on its way.[15]

In 1903, Hamilton began to grow ill. Over the course of nearly two years the ABS sent money to Mexico City to pay his medical bills, but treatment did not to help. He passed away on August 20, 1905, leaving the work of Bible distribution to his wife, Frances Snow Hamilton. During Hiram Hamilton's tenure the ABS distributed over 600,000 scriptures and had as many as thirty-seven colporteurs in the field.[16] In February 1906, Corresponding Secretary William Haven visited Mexico and recommended that Frances should remain head of the Agency "until further notice . . . while a permanent agent is being selected." But there was no one as qualified as Frances, and she would remain in "temporary" charge of the ABS work in Mexico for another nine years. In fact, the Bible Cause in Mexico became a family affair after Hiram Hamilton's death. When Frances took a short leave of absence to assist the ABS with an endowment campaign in New York, her son Edward continued the "steady progress" of the Mexico agency.[17] Frances Hamilton was the first female agent in the history of the American Bible Society. She was born in Rochester, New York in 1863, graduated with high honors from the Rochester Free Academy and Oswego Normal School, and arrived in Mexico to teach in a girls' school run by the Board of Foreign Missions of the Presbyterian Church. It was here that she met and eventually married Hiram. Frances developed a reputation as a committed worker for the Bible Cause in Mexico. She spoke Spanish well, was often used as a translator during negotiations with local Mexicans responsible for political or religious affairs, and understood the business end of the work. Upon her appointment as the ABS agent in Mexico she received the same salary and allowances that her husband had received. Like Hiram before her, Frances traveled throughout the country organizing distribution, securing buildings to serve as depositories, attending conventions of Protestant missionaries, and hiring colporteurs.[18]

One of the highlights of Frances's work with the ABS in Mexico was her attempt in 1910 to commemorate the centennial of Mexican independence. On the sixteenth of September, 1810, Miguel Hidalgo launched a call to arms beginning the rebellion that eventually led to Mexican independence. A century later, Díaz used the anniversary of this event to show visitors and the rest of the world how much progress Mexico had made under his leadership. His administration organized extravagant celebrations and constructed exhibits and monuments related to hygiene, medical care, and cosmopolitanism in urban life. National history was presented in a way that celebrated political liberty and portrayed the native population as uncivilized and degenerate. Díaz even had a monument of George Washington constructed.[19]

Frances had big plans for an ABS commemoration of the centennial and tried hard to find the most fitting way for Protestants in Mexico to celebrate the event. She concluded that the best way to commemorate this important political moment in the life of her adopted country was to announce a plan to convert 1 million "souls to Christ." She believed that there were "no truer patriots" in Mexico than the "evangelical Christians, known as 'Protestantes' [*sic*] throughout the country," and portrayed her vision for winning 1 million souls as a clear sign of such patriotism. For Frances, the work of the ABS was not merely about distribution. It was also about evangelization. Protestant conversions would go a long way toward making Mexico a civilized and Bible-believing place. The ABS in New York got on board with Francis's centennial vision by preparing a new edition of the four Gospels bound in red, white, and green, the colors of the Mexican flag, and Frances organized the distribution of these Bibles throughout the republic. The Centennial Edition of the Spanish Bible was sold at a very low price, but for such a special occasion as this the ABS broke with its normal policy in Mexico and decided to give away copies to anyone who could not afford one.[20]

The commemoration of independence from Spanish rule was a turning point in Mexican history. As the Porfirian elite used the anniversary to reflect on an era of liberal progress under Díaz, a revolution was already brewing that would eventually topple the president. Only two months following the centennial celebrations an insurgent group of Mexican peasants forced Díaz to resign. He would spend the rest of his life in exile. The leaders of the Mexican Revolution wanted access to land. The liberal policies of Díaz and his predecessors had been successful in confiscating land from the Church, but most of it was then sold to wealthy men interested in the president's plans for modernization. It was not, as many now supporting the Revolution had hoped, distributed among the landless. A growing number of radicals motivated by anarchism, socialism, and communism sought to defend the plight of the peasants and bring equality to Mexican society.[21]

The Revolution began in November 1910 when Díaz's troops attacked a group of political opponents in Puebla. The attack gave his adversaries a reason to organize an attempt to remove him from office. This initial phase of the Revolution, under the leadership of Francisco Madero, was successful. Díaz resigned in May 1911. In 1910 Díaz had put Madero in prison after the president defeated him in a national election that everyone in the country knew was fixed. Madero had the support of other Díaz opponents such as Pancho Villa, Ricardo Magón, and Emiliano Zapata, all representatives of Mexican farmers and laborers. He called for free elections and a more consistent application of the liberal 1857 Constitution. Frances Hamilton reported that when Madero entered Mexico City on June 7, 1911, "he received such an ovation as is seldom accorded to anyone in these prosaic days . . . the city went wild, receiving the hero with rapturous enthusiasm."[22]

On January 8, 1912, a group of Mexican pastors and Protestant missionaries joined Frances in presenting Madero with an ABS Bible. Dr. John Butler congratulated Madero on his election and reminded him that "from these sacred pages, we hope the Mexican people will learn the true democracy for which you had labored and sacrificed so much in these last years." He went on to quote the famed American orator Daniel Webster: "The best Christian will be always the best citizen." Madero thanked the delegation for the Bible, affirming the belief that its message was essential to the moral improvement of his people. He hoped that Mexicans, who in the past had "lacked Enlightenment," would soon be able to understand "the high principles" of the Bible and asked the Protestant delegation to join him in the "uplifting of the masses of the Mexican people." As Frances exited the meeting with Madero she paused on one of the palace's marble staircases and stared off into the light of the setting sun. She was impressed with the new Mexican president and could understand why the masses so adored him. She told the Board of Managers in New York that she was ready to join the people of Mexico in their cry of "VIVA MADERO!"[23]

But the rapturous enthusiasm would not last. Madero had made too many promises that he could not keep. The farmers who supported him were hoping for a broad distribution of land to the poor. Industrial workers sought shorter days and higher wages. Frances wrote that "hordes of bandits" were bringing chaos to all sectors of the republic. She could only conclude that Mexico, despite all of its improvements during the Díaz administration, still had a long way to go before it could "resume her place among the progressive nations of the earth." All Frances could offer were prayers for the people who were still destitute of the word of God.[24] Eventually a more radical fringe of the Revolution joined with some supporters of the old Díaz regime to overthrow Madero (with the support of the US government) and assassinate him. Following Madero's death, General Victoriano Huerta, a former Madero lieutenant, seized control. His leadership was recognized by Japan and Great Britain, but the United States, under the leadership of Woodrow Wilson, refused to support any government that came to power through violence rather than by the rule of law. Huerta did not last long either. An armed faction known as the Constitutionalists, with the support of the Mexican Church and the Wilson administration, removed Huerta from power and replaced him with Venustiano Carranza, an ardent Mexican nationalist. Though several other revolutionary groups, particularly one under the leadership of Villa, continued to threaten the Carranza government, by 1920 the Mexican Revolution had come to an end and a new constitution was put in place.[25]

In the midst of the upheaval the Board of Managers tried to convince Frances Hamilton to leave Mexico, for her own safety, and return to New York. She refused. Though she was thankful that the board was concerned about her welfare, she insisted on standing with "my work and my men," refusing to "abandon the poor fellows" in the midst of their "hard times." As the Revolution raged around her, Frances took out an insurance policy with Lloyds of London on the building in which the Mexican agency was housed so that the ABS's investment in the country would be protected in the event of looting or arson. If Mexico City came under "a siege," and her life was placed in danger, she was confident that she would receive help from American, British, and German officials who were also staying put. Though Frances continued to write to New York to describe the "anarchy and earthquake" that was tearing through the city, she was not deterred from her work on behalf of the Bible Cause. Though some of her colporteurs were targets for snipers, Frances continued to supervise Bible distribution and presided over the publication of the Gospel of John in Zapotec, the language of the native population on the Isthmus of Tehuantepec."[26]

By 1914, Frances claimed that she was living through "the darkest chapter of Mexico's history." Money was scarce, and railway tickets were being used as a form of currency. Few people could afford to purchase the Bible and since train travel was frequently interrupted by the political upheaval it was often impossible to supply the colporteurs in the field with books. Most of them were forced to stop the work of distribution. It was also in this year that Frances finally decided to leave Mexico. US troops had landed at Veracruz and ordered all Americans to exit the country before the army advanced on Mexico City. Frances and her fellow laborers obeyed the order with "heavy hearts." She left the work of the ABS in the hands of a German bookkeeper until the violence subsided and a successor was appointed. Hamilton returned to New York to work on some projects in the Bible House, but died only a month after her arrival. Her work in Mexico is best captured by a short introduction to a reprint of some of her letters in a 1912 issue of the *Bible Society Record*:

> It is certainly a remarkable thing that during a period of bloodshed, and when the fiercest passions are let loose, a woman's hand should have guided our ship so successfully. When public interest centers so much about woman and her relation to public affairs, it is worth while to note the power of this Christian woman, a model of gentleness and modesty, to direct the activity of thirty-two colporteurs, nearly all Mexicans, and in a Roman Catholic country at that.[27]

12

China

In the years following the Civil War, the United States passed Great Britain in the number of missionaries ministering around the world and the amount of money spent on their work. China illustrates this postwar missionary boom. In 1858 there were eighteen missionaries working in China. By 1905 that number had grown to 3,445.[1] The American Bible Society, as we have seen, was not a missionary agency per se. But all of its overseas distribution work in this period relied heavily on the effort of missionaries in the field. In this sense the ABS presence in China was no different than its gospel labors in the Levant or Mexico. Missionaries established Protestant churches, cultivated social connections with local people, and did the work of evangelization. One could find ABS agents doing all of these things as well, but their primary focus was on providing missionaries with Bibles or selling them directly to the people through colporteurs. Though Catholic missionaries had been present in China as early as the sixteenth century, the first Protestant missionary to reach the country was Robert Morrison of the London Missionary Society. He arrived in Canton in 1807. After seven years of work he baptized his first Chinese Protestant convert, but at the time of his death in 1834 the number of Protestants in the country stood at about ten. A decade after Morrison's death and the end of First Opium War (1839–1842) between China and Great Britain, the Qing Dynasty granted toleration to Christianity and gave missionaries the right to build hospitals and churches in five Chinese ports: Canton, Xiamen, Fuzhou, Ningbo, and Shanghai. By 1858, with the passage of the Treaty of Tientsin, which ended the opening phase of the Second Opium War (1856–1860), China had granted religious liberty to Christians and permitted missionaries to travel to inland regions without fear of persecution. But one hundred years after Morrison landed in Canton, indigenous Chinese Christian communities remained scarce.[2]

The earliest involvement of the ABS in China consisted of monetary donations to the work of missionaries. In 1833 the Society started to fund the publication, distribution, and translation needs of Christian workers affiliated with the American Board of Commissioners of Foreign Missions, the Dutch Reformed Church, and the Methodist Episcopal Church. This was the extent of its work until it established an agency of its own in China in 1875. Between 1860 and 1875 the ABS sent over $130,000 to support the Bible Cause in China and circulated just over 1 million Bibles and Testaments. Part of the ABS financial commitment was earmarked to support the work of Episcopalian missionary Samuel Schereschewsky, a Lithuanian Jewish convert to Christianity who was translating the Bible into Mandarin Chinese. Mandarin was a northern vernacular spoken by, or at least understood by, more than half of the Chinese people. Though the educated population of China frowned upon such a vernacular Bible, Schereschewsky and many of his fellow missionaries were motivated by the goal of making the scriptures available to all Chinese people, not just the elite. After his Mandarin Bible was completed in 1874, Schereschewsky became the Bishop of Shanghai and helped to found St. John's University in the city. He spent the last twenty years of his life revising his Mandarin Bible and producing a new translation of classical (Easy Wen-Li) Chinese that would be more suited for educated audiences and his students at St. John's. Schereschewsky's work is a story of suffering and perseverance. He was paralyzed by sunstroke in 1881 and was confined to a wheelchair, but he continued his translation work for twenty more years despite the fact that he could not speak or move from his chair. Schereschewsky was often seen typing with either one finger or a short stick. The ABS published his Wen-Li Bible, which the Chinese called "the one finger Bible," in 1900.[3]

The most difficult challenge that Bible translators in China had to face was how to render in Chinese a proper term for God. Schereschewsky was insistent that his Mandarin Bible be void of "ethnic characteristics" and "foreign traits" associated with the West that might prevent Chinese readers from understanding its message. But what language should be used to explain the Christian God in a translation designed for a people who did not have any concept of such a deity? The debate was over whether to use the word *Tianzhu* (Lord of Heaven) or *Shangdi* (Supreme Ruler). *Shangdi* represented the idea that God was "one," but it was associated in Chinese culture with a pantheistic concept of deity. And what about the Holy Spirit? Many Protestant missionaries wanted to translate the name of the third person of the Trinity with *Shen* (Spirit), but others thought that this word carried animistic connotations. *Shen* could also be used to describe a singular or plural god, or a deity that was female. Schereschewsky's favored *Tianzhu*, but he was also aware that this was the term that Roman Catholic missionaries in China were using. The last thing Protestant missionaries wanted was to have their message confused with Catholicism. In the end, this question of translation was never resolved. During the early part of the twentieth century Chinese Bibles were printed using all three words (*Tianzhu, Shangdi,* and *Shen*), and missionaries carried on spirited debates in their stations around China over which word provided the most accurate translation.[4]

Prior to 1875, missionaries distributed ABS Bibles in China. The BFBS, which also had a significant presence in China, sold Bibles using colporteurs. The BFBS believed that colporteurs would be more effective agents of Bible distribution because they were not as overt in their religious message as the missionaries, and would thus not meet with as much opposition. These differences led to a further debate among the advocates of the Bible Cause. Should the ABS and other Bible societies be doing the work of evangelism, or should they be content with merely translating the Bible into Chinese, selling it to the people, and leaving evangelism to the missionaries and the churches? Missionaries believed that the ABS needed to do more than just translate and distribute. Because the culture of China was so different from the West, Bible agents and colporteurs needed to develop a strategy for teaching the people how to *use* the Bible. For example, in 1863 Henry Blodget, a missionary of the ABCFM, asked whether it was more useful to circulate the scriptures among the "heathen people" of China before or after missionary work got underway. Blodget believed that because the Bible bore witness to the life, teachings, death, and resurrection of Jesus Christ, it could be easily understood without a teacher. His argument would have pleased many in the ABS who could reference story after story from the Society's history of the Bible "doing its work" in the world without a commentator or preacher. Those who embraced this view once proposed using balloons to drop 2,000 scripture portions over China—a plan that would allow the word of God to "fall literally like a refreshing shower over the incredulous 'Flowery Land.'" Those who disagreed with Blodget, such as Samuel Wells Williams, another missionary to China, argued that without a preacher to explain the Bible and introduce people to the God behind its words, the Chinese would never accept it as a holy book and probably use its pages for wrapping paper or for stuffing the soles of boots.[5]

Stories and reports from missionaries shed much light on how they balanced preaching the Gospel with the work of selling scriptures. Thomas Thompson, an ABCFM missionary stationed in the northern Chinese city of Kalgon, traveled with a team that consisted of a fellow missionary, a "native Christian helper," and a driver who was responsible for several Bible-carrying mules. Wherever the group traveled they preached, administered the sacraments, and sold Bibles. Thompson's account of his journey confirms the beliefs of other missionaries and Bible agents that the Chinese people were more prone to engage with the word of God when it was sold rather than given away without charge. In fact, Thompson noted they were even more interested in the Bible's content and message when it was sold at nondiscounted prices. While working in the town of Shan Si, Thompson helped his Chinese assistant make a more effective sales pitch to villagers who were reluctant to purchase Bibles. Rather than try to convince the people to purchase the Bibles because they were cheap, Thompson advised his assistant to raise his prices and focus his pitch on why the book was so expensive, a conversation that would naturally lead to discussion about the "contents and merits of the books."

Thompson and his group often preached to large crowds in the open air at market-day festivals. They were persecuted by local skeptics, but this did not stop them from challenging the prevailing culture of "superstition" in China. Thompson's sermons were frequently interrupted by Chinese people asking him questions about his foreign dress, eating habits, and other Western customs. His best customers were farmers and small tradesmen. Thompson wrote that they were more interested in the Bible than some of the literate Chinese. Many of these workers viewed the holy book as yet another text that could be used for divination, to cure diseases, or read and chanted "as a work of merit." He occasionally ran into Catholic priests and nuns who had established stations in northern China, and he told the ABS that he was often mistaken by townspeople for a Catholic missionary. Catholic missionaries, Thompson reported, were ultimately "hostile to our work," but he also realized that he had more in common with them than he did with the Chinese: "Their presence in the country seems to open the way for other foreigners and for a new religion."[6]

After the First Opium War opened up new opportunities for missionary activity in China, the ABS explored the idea of establishing its own agent in the country. Most of those discussions, however, were deferred since the ABS was spending large sums of money to bring Bibles to Civil War soldiers and the freedmen in the Reconstruction South and thus simply could not afford to make a permanent investment in China. But the idea continued to linger among some members of the Board of Managers. If the BFBS and the National Bible Society of Scotland (NBSS) had agencies in China, then why not the ABS? Missionaries wrote to the ABS about the "open door" in China, urging them to get involved in reaching 400 million people with the "Bread of Life." If the ABS hired an agent and entrusted him with a job similar to the labors performed by Isaac Bliss in the Levant or Hiram and Frances Hamilton in Mexico, he would need to be paid well enough to afford lodging in Shanghai or another city and have an expense account that would enable him to travel throughout China via river boats. Samuel Wells Williams advised any agent appointed by the ABS to have very low expectations. "China is not a Christian country," he reminded ABS General Secretary Joseph Holdich. Unlike the Muslims in the Levant, the people of China had never heard of the Bible and many were ignorant of its message. The obstacles were many.[7]

Blodget, on the other hand, was more optimistic. He acknowledged that China was a "difficult field" that required "long patience in those who would reap the harvest," but there were also aspects of Chinese life and culture that might aid the work of the Bible Cause. Blodget pointed to gatherings of "literary men" taking place in all of China's eighteen provinces. These men were often affiliated with schools and colleges. They could read, write, and exercise "mental discipline." And they were always looking for reading material. Blodget also believed that the ABS, with its extensive experience in the Bible-production business, would improve the quality of Chinese-language Bibles. Andew Happer, a Presbyterian missionary, also urged the ABS to come to China. Unlike Blodget, who thought the best hope for the Bible Cause in China was for the ABS to distribute Bibles among educated men of letters, Happer argued that the work of distribution should be focused on the country's female population. Only about 1 percent of Chinese women were literate. Since custom and tradition prevented them from becoming active in public life, few had been exposed to the Gospel. Happer hoped the ABS would consider coming to China to train a "class of women" to read the Bible who, in turn, would "gather the women of several adjacent houses into one house, and read to them the words of the inspired narrative."[8]

Missionaries knew that one of the best ways of selling China to the Board of Managers was through stories of changed lives. In an 1864 letter to Holdich, Blodget described an encounter between a British missionary and a Chinese soldier. The missionary was conducting a religious service when the soldier walked in, marched up the center aisle of the chapel, saluted the missionary, and sat down to listen to the sermon. At the end of the service the soldier told the missionary that he had just returned from two and a half years in the Shantung province, where he had been "driving out prowling banditti" who were terrorizing the people. When the missionary asked the soldier if he had ever been injured in the line of duty, he said that he had not and then credited his safety in battle to "the grace of the Lord Jesus Christ, in whom I have constantly trusted, and to whom have daily prayed for two years past." The missionary was "astonished" at the soldier's comment. Random encounters with Christian soldiers—or any Christian for that matter—were extremely rare in China. The missionary proceeded to ask the soldier to testify as to how he had come to "know anything of Christ and his salvation." The soldier then told a story about how three years earlier he was "walking the street without any definite object" and stumbled upon a "foreigner" from the United States "speaking of the love of God in sending his Son into the world to die for sinners." The missionary was Elijah Bridgman, one of the first missionaries to China. The soldier did not "receive any particular impression at the time from what he said," but Bridgman did ask him several questions, gave him a New Testament, and encouraged him to read it.

The rest of the story is the kind anecdotal material that the staff and Board of Managers of the ABS loved to hear. Several months later the soldier was lounging in his tent "at a loss how to spend my time" when he started to recall Bridgman's words. He then remembered the Testament that the missionary had given him and started to read it. The soldier said that the words of scripture were "mysterious to me at first," but soon his "curiosity was excited, and although I understood but little of what I read, I began to comprehend something of its teachings." It did not take him long before he began to "pray to God that I might be brought to the true knowledge of himself, and grow more & more in love with Jesus Christ." The soldier stopped attending the Buddhist temples where his fellow soldiers went "for idol worship" and he found a new "peace" in his "heart." The missionary, upon hearing this story, confirmed the soldier's salvation and warned him that to be a Christian in China might lead to hardships and trials. The soldier did not have to be told. Since his conversion many of his comrades "have often assailed me, and pronounced me foolish and mad in taking up with this new doctrine." Yet as this soldier's life was spared in battles in which many of his colleagues died in the fight, fellow soldiers asked him to "tell them something about this doctrine." Blodget concluded his letter to Holdich with a simple statement: "The most profitable investment of money will, in my judgment, be for the distribution of the Scriptures in the Mandarin Colloquial for the common people."[9]

The ABS must have found missionary letters like this one convincing because in 1875 the Board of Managers established an agency in China. Luther Gulick, a medical doctor and ABCFM missionary in Micronesia, was appointed to lead the agency of the American Bible Society for China and Japan (Japan became a separate agency in 1881). After ten years under Gulick's leadership, the ABS presence in China had grown exponentially. In 1885 Gulick presided over nine Western colporteurs and an additional forty-eight Chinese salesmen.[10] ABS colporteurs in China covered a massive amount of territory and had endless opportunities to sell the word of God. Much of their focus was on individual encounters with villagers who "know nothing of the Bible and its precious promises, but who might come to believe in its truths through the persistent calls of colporteurs." The work required door-to-door visits with women and children who would not naturally be in attendance at religious services. These colporteurs received a mixed response from the people whom they encountered along the way. Some of the Chinese people accepted them warmly and invited them to stay in their homes. Others demanded that they defend the doctrines of Christianity that did not match up well with local religious beliefs. One colporteur complained to the ABS about the abuse he received in some towns and villages: "My common appellation is 'foreign devil,' to which I am getting so accustomed that I fancy I shall mistake it for my own name." But through it all the ABS believed that the native Christians whom they hired as colporteurs "are the only persons who can do this work." The goal was to persuade the Chinese people that Jesus was more than "merely the sage of the western nations." He was not Confucius, he was the "Saviour of all men." As Henry Otis Dwight put it in his bicentennial history of the ABS, "every sale of a single Gospel in China might be deemed a step toward the conversion of the nation."[11]

The work of one of these colporteurs, John Thorne, became the stuff of legends. Gulick found Thorne while he was working as a missionary for the ABCFM in Nanking and eventually appointed him as a superintendent of native colporteurs in 1878. Thorne was an adventurer. In 1849 he traveled from New England to California in search of gold. He made a small fortune, then lost it, but managed to recover enough of it to travel back to New England. Thorne moved to China in the 1870s in the hopes of making some money dabbling in international trade. He was so successful in business that he was known by many as the "Merchant Prince of Shanghai." By 1877, after he had lost a lot of money through some bad business deals, he began to devote himself to the study of Chinese in preparation for missionary work. Thorne had a "striking and magnificent personal appearance" and a "kindly and affable manner" that endeared him to the Chinese people and made him a very successful colporteur. In one year he traveled over 3,000 miles by boat, 640 miles on foot, 140 miles in a chair, and 122 miles in a wheelbarrow as he delivered Bibles to the people in the nine different Chinese provinces. During a visit to some of the villages along the canal in the region of Tsingho, Thorne's tall frame and good looks drew such crowds that he created a traffic jam. In another village, after Thorne had sold all his books and was leaving, someone yelled at him "Oh, Foreign Devil; Foreign Devil! Please come back. More men are coming to get your books."[12]

Thorne was a popular lecturer on the Bible society circuit whenever he returned home to the United States. In 1884, in a speech before the Middletown, Connecticut Bible Society, he dazzled his audience with sensational details about his work as a colporteur. He described the feeling that colporteurs in China get when they arrive in a village that had never been visited by a foreigner: "Your blood curdles in your veins as you surmise it is possibly a sacrificial ceremony to which you are invited, and you yourself are the victim!" He continued:

> Your sixty or eighty books are held with a tight grip in the bend of the
> arm; you have, if the sun is out and hot, an umbrella raised over a pith

hat. A perspiring forehead; a limp collar; but it is hoped a firm thread, as if you were coming home from and receiving all the honours of vic- tory! You have left behind you the comfortable boat or roadside inn, at the bank of the river outside the gates, or in the suburbs of the city, and now you step out, amid the yells and derisive laughter, mockings and insults of a largely increasing crowd of all sorts and conditions of men. The ground whereon you tread was only a few moments ago . . . the abiding place of a couple of sleepy dogs; of the peanut man and his stall; and of the vendor of bean curd.

But Thorne did not stop there. He told his Connecticut audience about how local residents would send pigs between his legs while "hens and chickens which never flew before are now wildly darting through the air, striking you at all angles." He talked about being bombarded with peanuts and orange peel, and receiving punches in the back until he could escape the blows by ascend- ing atop a butcher's block above the crowd "to tell them about yourself and your mission." According to Thorne, these "are not isolated incidents in a col- porteur's or missionary life in China, but are happening every day in the battle with Satan's hosts." This was obviously not a job for the faint of heart.[13]

The persecution Thorne suffered as an ABS colporteur was part of a larger pattern of anti-Western sentiment in late nineteenth-century China. Much of this feeling was focused on American investors and businessmen, who saw unlimited opportunities in China for the sale of textiles and the building of railroads. In 1896, a group of New York capitalists formed the American China Development Company to promote trade and railroad investment in China. Meanwhile, other Western nations pushed the Chinese government to desig- nate certain ports and regions as "spheres of influence" where they would have exclusive trading and development rights. The United States was not happy about these spheres of influence, largely because it did not want American businessmen to be cut out of the action. Secretary of State John Hay wrote letters to the European nations with a vested interest in China asking them to open the ports within their spheres of influence to traders of all nations. Though none of the European countries endorsed the plan, neither did they oppose it. The response (or lack thereof) was enough for Hay to declare an "open door" for American business in China. Though Hay had the economic interests of the United States in mind, the Open Door Policy was supported by Christian missionaries who anticipated the support and protection of the US government.[14]

Many Chinese were appalled by the growing Western influence in their own backyard. Violent attacks against Catholic and Protestant missionar- ies sprung up all over China in the 1880s and 1890s, culminating with an uprising by an anti-Western society known as the Society of Righteous and Harmonious Fists (or "Boxers," as they were known in the West). The Boxers led a campaign to drive foreigners out of China along with any Chinese people who had been influenced by Western ideas. They had usually operated on the local level, using their martial arts skills and spiritual claims to invulnerability to protect villages from outsiders, but with the quiet but strong support of the anti-Western Empress Dowager Cixi, they were able to form a larger, more unified movement that quickly began to wreak havoc throughout northern China. The majority of the Boxers' wrath was targeted toward Chinese Christians and missionaries. Approximately 30,000 Chinese converts and 250 foreign missionaries were murdered. In June 1900 the Boxers occupied Beijing, the capital of China, and raided several foreign embassies, killing ambassadors from Japan and Germany in cold blood. Foreigners fled to their respective legations, where for two months they faced constant bombardment and starvation. Cixi declared war on all foreign nations with diplomatic connections to China. This was a big mistake. Cixi's decree prompted an international army, which included 2,500 US troops, to enter Beijing and squash the rebellion. After peace was restored, the European powers enforced the Boxer Protocol, giving them the right to retain a military presence in China. It also required the Chinese government to pay $333 million to cover the loss of life and property suffered during the uprising. From this point forward, the work of Christian missions in China would be conducted under the protective umbrella of Western soldiers.[15]

John Hykes, a Methodist missionary in China who replaced Gulick following the later's death, led the ABS through the horrors of the Boxer Rebellion. Hykes was convinced that Dowager Empress Cixi was using the Boxers to end the work of Christian benevolence in China. "The Boxer organization was," he wrote in the 1901 ABS *Annual Report*, "from its inception, intended to be not only an auxiliary to the Chinese army in the coming antiforeign crusade, but as a subterfuge to hide the real purposes of the government and, in the event of failure of the plot, to enable it to evade responsibility." He concluded that "the Boxer society was a child of the Chinese government, and that government is alone responsible for the outrages committed in its name." Hykes claimed that the Boxers were commanded by military officials appointed by Cixi, paid with government funds, armed with imperial weapons, and rewarded for "the very outrages for which the government would now disclaim responsibility."[16]

Though Hykes was willing to admit that a hatred of Christianity was one motivation for the uprising, he blamed most of it on the "political encroachments of foreign nations." China was being humiliated by outsiders exploiting its population, seaports, and land. Japan now possessed Formosa. German troops seized Kiao Chow Bay in retaliation for the murder of two Catholic priests in the Shangdon county of Jiya. Great Britain and France were also taking land in China. When news reached China of European attempts to divide the once-proud nation into spheres of influence, Hykes was not surprised that many Chinese were willing to "fight to the death" to prevent it. These interventions, he wrote, "exasperate China almost to the point of desperation." Hykes also argued that the missionary presence in China did not have the same negative effect on the people as that of American businessmen and politicians. In doing so he was also admitting that the missionary movement was not very successful in its attempts at influencing Chinese culture.[17]

Hykes's distinction between missionary work and Western economic interests in China fell on deaf ears. He was unable to convince anyone that Western missionaries were good for China. Missionaries continued to be perceived as social reformers and agents of progress who posed a serious threat to traditional Chinese culture. In June 1900, when Cixi declared war on foreign powers and tried to drive all Western influences from her country, Western consuls in China encouraged all of their people to leave the interior and head for the coast. Missionary stations, schools, hospitals, and chapels were either abandoned or closed and many were looted or burned by the Boxers. In some cases, in an attempt to make the extirpation of Westerners complete, the Boxers dug up the foundations of missionary buildings so that no trace of these material reminders of Western influence would remain. The ABS bookstore in Beijing was destroyed in June and books in other depositories across China were also damaged. Hykes estimated that the ABS lost 100,000 volumes, equivalent to about $10,000. Most of the ABS superintendents were forced to flee their homes. Frederick Gammon initially tried to defend his mission station during the siege of the city of Tientsin and, at one point, even staged "offensive operations against the besiegers." He supervised the construction of barricades and faced heavily artillery and rifle fire until he had no other alternative but to flee with his family. Frederick Mendenhall was assaulted in Lung Chow. His books were taken from him and thrown into the mud. He would have to be escorted to safety in Wuchow via gunboat.[18]

Though the Western ABS superintendents made it through the rebellion unharmed, this was not the case for the ABS's Chinese colporteurs. In Beijing, an entire staff of ABS colporteurs were killed. Some had their houses burned to the ground and their families murdered. Others heroically took scriptures to some of the most heated areas of the rebellion and died on behalf of the Bible Cause when they refused to recant their Christian beliefs. Some Chinese colporteurs were crucified on trees. "We shall probably never know how some of them obtained the martyr's crown," Hykes wrote, "but we are sure that they died 'witnessing a good confession,' and that they are accounted worthy of a place among those who were 'slain for the word of God, and for the testimony which they held.'" Those who were able to escape into the mountains managed to survive. Hykes believed that this "terrible baptism of fire" was necessary to the "upbuilding of a deeply spiritual Church" in China that would eventually "regenerate and reform this land." The blood of martyrs was the seed of both the church and the westernization of China.[19]

With the Boxer Rebellion quelled by Western military force, Hykes was ready to lead the China agency into the twentieth century. In 1907 Gammon was pleased to report the "remarkable receptivity of 'things foreign' by the people of China." Colporteurs moved through Chinese cities with "perfect freedom" and Bible sales were strong now that the "unpleasant experiences" of the rebellion were no longer serving as a hindrance. Indeed, Gammon proclaimed "the battle for toleration, against suspicion and dislike, was largely won. . . ." Bibles in Easy Wen-Li, Mandarin, and a host of Chinese dialects continued to be produced in conjunction with the British and Foreign Bible Society. Though the Protestant community in China only numbered around 100,000, the ABS was pleased with the ever-increasing demand for scriptures, even in this time of political chaos. In 1900, the ABS was selling fifty-four different Bibles, Testaments, and scripture portions in at least nine different languages, dialects, and translations and more were on the way.[20]

In the early decades of the twentieth century the work of Bible sales and distribution shifted from paid Western and Chinese colporteurs under the direction of American superintendents to a system of Chinese volunteers supervised by Chinese superintendents. By 1919, the ABS China agency could claim that they had no colporteurs on the payroll. Two years later, the ABS had 721 volunteers working in this capacity. Driven largely by a sense of Christian mission, these volunteers jumped at the chance to do God's work in their spare time.[21] This approach to distribution kept the Bible Cause going strong during times of political upsurge, such as the 1911 overthrow of the Qing Dynasty and the establishment of the Republic of China. Since the revolutionaries and the Protestant missionary community both wanted the Qing Dynasty out of power, Bible sales did not suffer. In fact, Bible circulation at the time of the Revolution was the largest in the history of the China agency. There were even times when the demand for Bibles—in both Chinese *and English*—was so great that the agency could not fill all the orders. The Revolution proved to be a boon for the ABS, opening up what Hykes called "a new era for Christian missions" in China supported by the republic's commitment to religious toleration. He was pleased to report that "the profession of Christianity is no longer a bar to official employment," and that native Christians were now occupying many important government positions. In 1913, an ABS colporteur was permitted to set up a Bible stand in the balcony of the Temple and Altar of Heaven on New Year's Day. His best explanation for such a boon was the toleration afforded to Christianity by the administration of president and Christian convert Sun Yat-sen.[22]

In spite of two world wars and an international economic depression, the work of the Bible Cause continued to grow in the decades following the Revolution of 1911. Between the establishment of the China agency in 1875 and the publication of Hykes's *The American Bible Society in China* in 1916, nearly 21 million scriptures had been distributed in the country. A local Bible society was established at Canton and in 1928 the ABS built a Bible House in Beijing, its first such building in China. By 1937, a constitution for a future Chinese Bible Society was written. It would be run by national Chinese Christians with the help of the ABS, the BFBS, and the NBSS, and would operate under the name Chinese Bible House. By 1951, these societies had withdrawn completely from the work of the Bible Cause and the China Bible Society was born.

But this is getting ahead of our story. Though the ABS and other national Bible societies experienced tremendous success in the wake of the 1911 Revolution, trouble was on the horizon. In 1921 the Communist Party in China was formed. One of its earliest efforts to spread its beliefs in the country took advantage of the growing popularity of Christianity. Members of the party regularly removed the pages from ABS Bibles and used the covers as binding for communist literature.[23] As we will see, communists were building a head of steam in China that would have long-term effects on the advancement of the Bible Cause in the country.

Figure 1 Elias Boudinot, first president of the American Bible Society, circa 1816.

THE BIBLE HOUSE AT CONSTANTINOPLE.

Figure 6 Constantinople Bible House. When the ABS would not pay for a Bible House in the Constantinople, Levant agent Isaac Bliss raised the funds and purchased the building himself.

Figure 1   Elias Boudinot, first president of the American Bible Society, circa 1816.

Figure 2 John Jay, second president of ABS from 1821 to 1828.

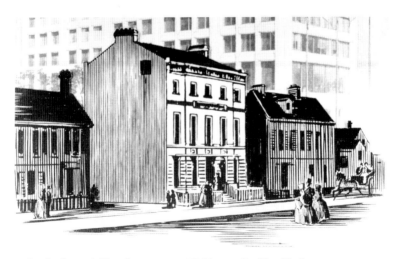

Figure 3 The first ABS headquarters on 72 Nassau St., New York.

Figure 4 Astor Place Bible House.

Figure 5 Women stitching in Astor Place Bible House. Women's labor was essential to the nineteenth-century production work of the ABS.

THE BIBLE HOUSE AT CONSTANTINOPLE.

Figure 6 Constantinople Bible House. When the ABS would not pay for a Bible House in the Constantinople, Levant agent Isaac Bliss raised the funds and purchased the building himself.

Figure 13 For most of the twentieth century the ABS measured success in the number of Bibles distributed, n.d.

Figure 14 Eugene Nida (right), head of ABS translation department and the man behind dynamic equivalence with Aruak translator and native helpers in Ethiopia, 1961.

Figure 15 Navaho woman using an ABS Finger-fono, 1959.

Figure 16 God's Word for a New Age was an ABS campaign in the 1960s to address the need for Bibles in an era of science and technology.

Figure 17 First meeting of the ABS's newly formed Department of Women's Activities, 1963.

Figure 18 *Good News for Modern Man*, the New Testament in Today's English Version, sold 5 million copies in its first year of publication, 1966.

Figure 19 Annie Vallotton provided the line-drawing illustrations for the Good News Bible.

Figure 20 ABS General Secretary Laton Holmgren (right) examines *Good News for Modern Man* with Father Johannes Willebrands, president of the Pontifical Council for Promoting Christian Unity, circa 1967–1969.

Figure 21 Robert Ross shares a copy of the scriptures with a construction worker during an ABS project to reach African Americans in Newark, New Jersey, 1969.

Figure 22 Alice Ball was the first female general secretary in ABS history and the champion of the Society's volunteer program.

Figure 23 Part of Alice Ball's work with women and volunteers was the creation of Scripture Courtesy Centers.

Figure 24 Eugene Habecker, the first president-CEO in ABS history, distributes Bibles at Ground Zero in the wake of the terrorist attacks of September 11, 2001.

13

African Americans
in the Wake of Reconstruction

As we saw in chapter 8, the American Bible Society did very little in the decades following Reconstruction to address the problem of race. As former slaves integrated into white society in the South, the ABS stayed true to its 1816 constitution. This meant that distribution to the African American population would be carried out by local auxiliaries. The problem, of course, was that many of the southern auxiliaries were led by former Confederates who were not willing to distribute Bibles to freedmen. In 1900, Henry Nelson Payne, a missionary and president of Mary Holmes Seminary in West Point, Mississippi, a school for black women, decided to break the silence in an article published in the *Bible Society Record* titled "The Bible Among the Negroes of the South." Payne's article was a scathing critique of the Society's negligence toward southern blacks and a clarion call for the ABS to meet the needs of those suffering under the poverty and discrimination of Jim Crow. Payne began by pointing out that 3 million (roughly one-third) of the African American population were members of Christian churches and "sincere disciples of Jesus Christ," but very few of them had "a knowledge of divine truth from a personal study of the Bible." As a result, "it is a sad and startling fact that irreligion, even infidelity, prevail among the younger and more intelligent class of negroes more than among the older ones." Payne estimated that "one colored home in twenty has in it a copy of the word of God."

The children of freedmen had not been taught to the read the Bible and had little or no money to purchase one. Payne pointed to one of his female students at Mary Holmes Seminary who claimed to have been a member of a church for four years, but had never read a chapter in the Bible before arriving at the school. In another example, Payne described his experience preaching in a 200-member "colored church" in which the pulpit Bible was falling apart and the pages with the verses from which he was planning to base his sermon were lost from among the loose leaves. The minister had to dash home in the middle of the service to locate the missing pages. Payne believed that such a lack of Bibles among the African American population was inexcusable in a "Christian nation." The United States, he added, makes great effort to bring foreigners "under Christian and saving influences" and affirms that Christianity is the "best antidote to socialism, anarchy, and crime." But they have largely forgotten "this other dark-hued people, born in our midst, speaking our language and inheriting our customs" who are "drifting out of the shoreless seas of doubt and unbelief because [they] are not anchored to the Rock of Ages, the immutable and immovable truth of God's word."[1]

Bringing the Bible to the black population involved certain challenges. Thomas Law, a southern Presbyterian clergymen and ABS agent, accepted the popular premise among whites that "the negro is often sadly deficient in moral stamina," and thus, while readily embracing the salvific teachings of God's word, "seem to make little effort or success in living up to them." Blacks relied too heavily on their preachers to explain the word of God to them. Many of these preachers, Law believed, were often more interested in promoting personal, political, and social agendas than in teaching the Bible to their people. Because of all these things, the African American community must remain "a great field for the present activity of the American Bible Society." Law rejected the belief, commonly held by the Board of Managers and ABS staff, that the "negroes of the South are as fully supplied with the Scriptures as any class of our country's population."[2]

Payne and Law must have struck a chord with the Board of Managers, for in July 1901 the ABS established the Agency Among the Colored People of the South. It would be based in Atlanta, Georgia. The Colored Agency, as it was called, was unlike any other ABS initiative to date. It was not an auxiliary society, but an effort to *directly* reach a specific class of the US population. For the first time in its history, the ABS recognized that they could only be effective in bringing Bibles to the black population of the South if they bypassed auxiliaries altogether. In the bigger picture, the Colored Agency reflected the ABS's general move away from auxiliaries and toward a more centralized approach to Bible distribution.

In 1890, the ABS Committee on Auxiliaries concluded that "whereas the auxiliaries of this Society were once an arm of power, we believe that, with honorable exceptions, they are today a serious drawback." The auxiliaries had become a "drawback" because many of them were no longer raising funds for the purchase of Bibles, practicing regular distribution, or consistently sending surplus funds to the Bible House. At the same time, more and more denominations were appealing to the ABS for Bibles. It made sense for the Society to alter its approach to distribution in order to work more freely and closely with these denominations. Auxiliaries would continue to function, and many would remain connected to the ABS well into the twentieth century, but they would no longer be counted upon as the primary means of distribution.[3]

Because the auxiliary was such a vital part of the organizational structure of the American Bible Society dating back to its founding in 1816, it would die a slow death. While the auxiliaries were always the subject of criticism from the Board of Managers and the staff of the Bible House, the first major critiques of the system did not occur until the 1880s. In 1885 Edward Gilman, a secretary of the ABS, argued before the Distribution Committee that the auxiliaries had once served an important purpose in advancing the Bible Cause in the United States, but were presently "moribund" and "past recovery." Gilman noted that in 1884 there were over 1,800 auxiliaries listed on the ABS rolls, but only 682 had made any kind of report or donation. Since many of these societies had small or inactive memberships, there was often no one to keep treasurers and other auxiliary leaders financially accountable.[4] It took two years before the ABS did anything in response to Gilman's speech. In 1886 the Distribution Committee recommended that inactive auxiliaries be dropped from the ABS rolls and endorsed a plan to change the way money was collected so that donors could designate whether they wanted their donation to support local work or the general work of the parent society in New York. In the meantime, the Committee continued to use ABS publications to remind the auxiliaries of the essential role that they had played in the history of the Society and urged them to follow through on their responsibility to sell Bibles and collect donations. While the ABS had been making such reminders for decades, the current Board of Managers and Bible House staff were now short on patience. It was time for reform. The ABS Board of Managers announced in 1888 that "if the Society is to rely upon auxiliaries in the future as it has done in the past, measures must be devised to make them more efficient."[5]

But few reforms actually took place. In 1889 the Board of Managers blamed the failure of the Fourth General Supply on the anemic state of its auxiliaries. In 1890 donations from auxiliaries saw a minor increase, but the money donated came from only slightly more than half of the auxiliaries on the ABS rolls. "It is safe to conclude," the Board of Managers stated, "that the majority of them have done little or nothing to promote the wider circulation of the Scriptures." As the economy began to pick up in the wake of the 1873 panic the ABS had the luxury of taking its time to restructure its distribution system, but as the nation again dipped into economic depression in the early 1890s the Board of Managers was forced to make more drastic and immediate changes to the auxiliary system. In 1891, the ABS decided to ignore auxiliaries that were ineffective and bypass the authority that they had to distribute Bibles locally. District superintendents across the country were permitted to offer ABS Bibles to booksellers in areas where auxiliaries were not active. A year later the

Society reported that its aggregate gifts from auxiliaries, churches, and individuals were less than what they were twenty-five years earlier. The ABS saw this as a "national calamity." There was a "famine in the land," but it was not a "famine of bread, nor a thirst for water, but of hearing the words of the Lord."[6]

As the nineteenth century came to a close, the ABS spent more resources cultivating relationships with churches and sending District Superintendents to meet regularly with ministers of local congregations. In 1899 the ABS invited its auxiliaries to attend a national conference to discuss the most productive methods to raise funds, the souring relationship between the auxiliaries and the ABS, and ways in which the auxiliary system might be saved. Out of 1,500 auxiliaries affiliated with the ABS, only fifty sent representatives to the conference, a clear sign of the weakness of this system of fundraising and distribution. At this meeting the ABS announced that it would remove its district superintendents from the field and require auxiliaries to work directly with the New York Bible House. In other words, the ABS would not be involved directly in the local supervision of Bible distribution. There would no longer be an ABS representative in the form of a district superintendent to hold their feet to the fire. The hope was to force the auxiliaries to reorganize and consolidate in order to be more financially efficient in their work. Though some auxiliaries reported changes in organization and new energies in the work of distribution, the age of auxiliaries was coming to an end. The future of the Bible Cause was local churches and Protestant denominations.[7]

The end would come in October 1900 at another conference on auxiliaries held at the Bible House in New York. The representatives of this meeting passed several resolves that they hoped would bring the organizational structure of the American Bible Society into the twentieth century. The conference concluded that the auxiliary system "has become unsuited" to the current purposes of the ABS, and that a new system needed to replace it. Auxiliaries would now be responsible for the sale and purchase of their own Bibles and would no longer receive boxes of bibles on credit. The ABS also reserved the right to raise funds for its work throughout the country, even in areas where an auxiliary already existed. The Society would work closely with churches on this front, sponsoring special services devoted to the Bible Cause in local congregations.[8] In May 1901, the Board of Managers endorsed the decisions of the conference and began the process of reorganization. In that year, the ABS established the Agency of the Colored People of the South as part of a new initiative of "home agencies" designed to reach people located within a given region of the country. Each of these home agencies would be governed by a field agent who would be responsible for bringing the domestic and international work of the ABS to the attention of churches, public gatherings, and denominational leaders. By the end of 1907, the ABS had established a Northwestern Agency (Illinois, Indiana, Michigan, Wisconsin, Iowa, Nebraska, and the Dakotas) in conjunction with the work of the Chicago Bible Society; a South Atlantic Agency (Virginia, West Virginia, North Carolina, South Carolina, Georgia, and Florida); a Central Agency (Missouri, Kansas, Colorado, Idaho, Montana, Utah, Wyoming, New Mexico, Arizona); a Pacific Agency (California, Nevada, Washington, and Oregon); a Southwestern Agency (Texas, Louisiana, Arkansas, and Oklahoma); and an Eastern Agency (New York and several surrounding states that did not have active local Bible societies). Within a few years, the Board of Managers was ready to call the home agencies system a success. Many auxiliaries admitted failure and turned their work over to their regional home agency. Colportage became more effective under this system as the Bible Cause became more centralized and the delicate balance between parent society and auxiliaries came to an end. While some auxiliaries, such as the Pennsylvania Bible Society and the New York Bible Society, continued to perform the work of distribution in their locales, it was clear that the ABS was willing to embrace the spirit of efficiency and centralized power that came to define the burgeoning Progressive movement in American political life.[9]

The Colored Agency of the South was created in the hope that African Americans would meet their own Bible distribution needs. This was the era of "separate but equal" as elucidated by the Supreme Court in *Plessy v. Ferguson* (1896). By creating a separate Colored Agency, the ABS was in essence endorsing this Supreme Court decision. Blacks would supply Bibles to blacks, and whites would supply Bibles to whites.[10] The goal was to help blacks reach their own neighborhoods with the Bible and "awaken the interest of the colored people themselves to their problem of reaching their families with the Holy Scriptures." The Colored Agency would tap those African Americans who possessed the "gift of leadership" and who could "better reach their own people than any other missionary workers." The goal was to distribute cheap Bibles to the impoverished African American population of the South. The "Negro problem," the ABS believed, "cannot be solved except on the basis of an open Bible."[11]

The catalyst behind the Colored Agency was ABS General Secretary William Ingraham Haven. He was the son of Gilbert Haven, a Methodist Episcopal Bishop who ministered to Union soldiers during the Civil War and continued his ministry to freedmen during Reconstruction. Haven's brother-in-law was the president of Gamon Seminary in Atlanta, a school dedicated to the training of African American ministers. Haven had spent a year teaching at Claffin University in Orangeburg, South Carolina, a black college founded by New England missionaries in 1869.[12] Haven chose John Percy Wragg to direct the Colored Agency. Wragg was a seminary-trained Atlanta pastor and a presiding elder in the Savannah and Atlanta Conferences of the Methodist Episcopal Church. He would lead this new agency for twenty-eight years.

Wragg focused initially on African Americans living and working in urban areas of the New South. Too many African Americans, he believed, had "drifted" into the cities, where they became "lost in the great sea of city sins." The message of salvation found in the scriptures was the only way of saving this generation. The ABS justified the opening of the Colored Agency by calling attention to the drastic rise in literacy among African Americans. At the time of its founding, the literacy rate among blacks in America had climbed to over 50 percent and by 1930 it had reached nearly 84 percent. The ABS wanted to bring Bibles to this newly literate sector of the black population in the hopes that the scriptures would inspire them to enter positions of leadership in the African American community. The ABS also touted the work of white denominations, especially the Methodist Episcopal Church, in supporting the Colored Agency in a spirit of "interracial cooperation and . . . interracial good will."[13]

Wragg immediately hired six African American colporteurs to serve in six states—Georgia, Alabama, Mississippi, Tennessee, Louisiana, and South Carolina. By 1920, he had expanded that number to sixteen colporteurs in thirteen different southern states. Wragg found it difficult to hire colporteurs because the agency could not afford to pay them more money than the hourly rate received by a common worker. He solved this problem by hiring women to work as colporteurs. Because of the scarcity of jobs available for colored women in the South, they were often willing to work for low wages. In 1911 Wragg hired Miss S. E. Evans, a student at Atlanta University, as his first female colporteur. Upon graduation from college, she moved to Mississippi and worked as a full-time, salaried Bible saleswoman for the ABS.[14]

Most of the colporteurs working for the Colored Agency traveled door-to-door selling Bibles and Wragg occasionally sent them to Sunday schools, church services, and various conferences, conventions, and denominational gatherings. In the countryside colporteurs had to travel long distances and often wait for people to come in from working the fields before making a sales pitch. Colporteurs reported much interest among the African American farmers they encountered. Many illiterate rural blacks asked colporteurs to read the Bible aloud or conduct Sunday worship services. One woman was so thrilled to see a colporteur from the Colored Agency that she invited him into her home with a round of clapping and singing, joyfully announcing: "I am so glad you came here to bring this Bible. No agents of the Gospel ever come here."[15]

Wragg was joined in the work of the Bible Cause by his wife, Jessie C. Wragg. The ABS was well aware of the success of Jessie's work among African

American women in the South. When Jessie wrote articles for the *Bible Society Record*, the editors prefaced them with glowing praise: "It is not often that we have been able to present to our readers an article from the pen of a colored woman." Jessie was a natural storyteller. One morning she was awakened at her and John's Atlanta home by a ringing doorbell. Concerned that her early visitor was experiencing some type of distress, Jessie rushed to door and found a "women thinly clad" with a piece of paper in her hand that read "American Bible Society, South Atlanta, GA." The woman was poor, but she had promised her daughter that she would buy her a Bible as a Christmas gift. Realizing that her mother could not afford a "fine Bible," the daughter had passed along the slip of paper that had been given to her several months earlier by a colporteur working for the Colored Agency. This colporteur had told the daughter that she could purchase a Bible from the ABS for a mere $1.20. Now the mother had stopped at the Wragg's house on her way to work in order to take that colporteur up on his offer. Jessie brought a Bible to the woman and encouraged her to read it with her daughter. The woman's eyes filled with tears. She did not know how to read, but assured Jessie that she would ask her daughter to read it to her every night before they went to bed.[16]

But not every day came with this kind of success. The Colored Agency had its share of difficulties in the first several decades of its existence. Many African Americans in the South were poor and could not afford to purchase Bibles from Wragg and his colporteurs. Some distributors in the rural parts of the South were willing to exchange Bibles for eggs and chickens in order to meet the spiritual needs of blacks "very anxious for the Word." In 1906, Wragg's Atlanta home was damaged by fire. After a distribution trip John arrived at the house to find Jessie in the street and the room where he stored ABS Bibles in flames. Wragg's library, which included many letters from the Colored Society colporteurs, was also consumed by the fire. Shortly after the Atlanta Race Riots of 1906, the Wraggs were driven from their home again—this time at gunpoint by police officers who thought that they were somehow involved in the riots.[17]

But most of the difficulties stemmed from the racial politics of the Jim Crow South. Black colporteurs working for the agency found it difficult to find places to spend the night during their travels. They were denied boarding rooms and occasionally slept on city streets. One colporteur wrote of sleeping "in the open air under the shelter of a tree in the summer, and of brushing the snow from about his bed on a winter morning!" It was common for these Bible distributors to be stopped by local officials and forced to purchase a license in order to continue their work. Since most colporteurs were just as poor as the people to whom they were selling Bibles, they would often have to rely on local African American ministers to help them pay these fees or intercede on their behalf. In 1943 a voluntary distributor, known only as "Aunt Sue," took

a bus from Charlotte to Winston-Salem, North Carolina, in the hopes of selling some Bibles along the way. When she attempted to board in Charlotte,
the driver explained to her that the bus was already full and "there was no
seat available for Negroes." Undeterred, and carrying Bibles, Aunt Sue stood
in the aisle and began to explain to the white riders that the book she had in
her hand will make "de white folks" love "de black folks, and vice-versa." She
distributed a Bible portion (John's Gospel) to everyone on the bus and later
one of the travelers who claimed that he was "converted by Aunt Sue on that
bus" bought two hundred additional scripture portions. The lesson that the
Colored Agency wanted its constituency, and the entire constituency of the
ABS, to learn from this story was that the Bible could break down racial barriers, even when preached by a "humble, unknown, and unlettered . . . Christian
Negro woman."[18]

Indeed, the ABS believed that the Colored Agency, through the distribution of the Bible, could provide an antidote to the growing racial problems
affecting American society. Wragg seemed to agree. The Bible could make
African Americans into better citizens. He often complained about the "dread-
ful crimes" and ignorance of blacks in the South and hoped that by placing the
word of God in their hands they would not only become "good Christians, but
good American citizens." Wragg probably agreed with Thomas Law, his white
colleague in the Bible Cause, who described blacks as "deficient in moral stamina" with a weak "sense of obligation" and a "defective" sense of obedience to
the law." These were his people, but they needed moral improvement. Wragg's
colporteurs addressed the problems of drunkenness in the African American
community by teaching young blacks what "the Book said about strong drink."
And when the Colored Agency noticed a dip in donations and Bible sales during World War I, Wragg did not fret. He encouraged his staff to wear buttons
displaying the American flag in order to "show their loyalty to their country."[19]

In the end, the ABS approach to race relations was generally a conservative
one. Wragg worked closely with African American children in public schools
and Sunday schools, teaching them the message of the Bible alongside a message of "thrift, industry, morality, and Christian thinking." By the 1930s, the
Colored Agency reported that the "American Negro is becoming more and
more race conscious" and defined by a "general sense of restlessness" brought
on by a combination of Jim Crow and the Great Depression. Because of this
restlessness blacks were easy prey for political and economic organizers fighting for the "advantages" that were "rightly due" to the African American community in the wake of slavery and segregation. While the agency did not deny
that the acquisition of these rights was important, its leaders also remained
concerned that those fighting for civil rights were "selfish and radical agitators"
who did not have the "highest interest" of the Negro "at heart." Of course, they

argued, it was the promoters of the Bible Cause, and the Christian church as a whole, that *did* have the "highest interest" of African Americans in the United States at heart. The churches, claimed the agency, did not neglect the battle over civil rights, but urged those engaged in the struggle to balance their activism with the "moral ideals and spiritual values" that came from the scriptures. For the ABS and its Colored Agency, these Christian ideals and values were meant to temper, rather than encourage, the quest for black rights in Jim Crow America.[20]

In its first two decades (1901–1920) the Colored Agency distributed 625,000 Bibles in the South, mostly through house canvassing and visitation to churches. But as more and more blacks migrated north in search of new jobs—a movement of African Americans often described by historians as the Great Migration—Wragg asked the ABS for permission to expand the Colored Agency to include the entire United States as its mission field. The ABS Board of Managers approved, and in 1920 it announced that the Colored Agency would now be called the Agency of the Colored People of the United States. Wragg was given authority to distribute Bibles to African Americans throughout the country as long as he was not interfering with the work of other ABS agents. He moved the headquarters of the Colored Agency to New York so that he could work more closely with the staff at the Bible House. This expansion enabled the agency to reach African Americans working in industrial plants and coal mines as well those in the cotton and tobacco fields. The newly revamped Colored Agency created five administrative centers in Atlanta, Charlotte, Cleveland, Houston, and Memphis. At the time of his retirement in 1929, Wragg had facilitated the distribution of over 1.7 million Bibles to African Americans. When he retired he requested that the agency be renamed the William Ingraham Haven Agency (eventually it was called simply "the Haven Agency") in honor of the late ABS General Secretary who championed the idea of a black agency. The Colored Agency lasted until 1959. After the Supreme Court issued its decision in *Brown v. Board of Education*, it no longer made sense for the ABS to have a "separate but equal" agency specifically designed for the distribution of Bibles to blacks.[21]

As we have seen, the failure of the ABS's auxiliary system coincided with the rise of a more centralized and top-down approach to the Bible Cause. The days in which the ABS needed to defer to auxiliaries in order to distribute Bibles to slaves, freedmen, and the postwar African American community were over. The Society was now able to focus attention on the Bible needs of African Americans in the South in ways that would have been impossible in the decades preceding and immediately following the Civil War. While it is tempting to argue that the problems the ABS faced in bringing the Bible to slaves, freedmen, and Jim Crow blacks in the nineteenth century was the motivating factor behind the Society's abandonment of the auxiliary system, it is more likely that the auxiliary system failed due to larger changes in the American economy and the long-term failure of federalism as a means of organizing a national benevolent society like the ABS. Whatever the reason for the shift from an auxiliary system to a system of home agencies, this organizational change meant that the ABS was now free from a constitutional mandate that prevented it from more aggressively bringing the Bible to the African American population. In the end, the Colored Agency represented an attempt by the ABS to *directly* reach the black population of the United States. But it also revealed its willingness to embrace the status quo of a "separate but equal" America.

14

The War to End All Wars

On June 28, 1914, Archduke Franz Ferdinand, the heir to the throne of the Austro-Hungarian Empire, was assassinated by a Serbian nationalist in Sarajevo, Bosnia. While the assassination of any royal successor would be big news, Ferdinand's death set off a chain reaction of alliances between European countries that had been in place since 1871. Austria-Hungary's closest ally was Germany, a new nation (since 1870) with a powerful army and a need to expand throughout the world. Germany urged Austria-Hungary to respond to the assassination by invading Serbia. The Serbs turned to Russia for help and in doing so triggered an alliance, known as the Triple Entente, between Russia, Great Britain, and France. By August, Germany, Austria-Hungary, and Italy, the third member of the so-called Central Powers, were at war with the Triple Entente. Germany invaded Belgium and began to move its army toward France. When the French army stopped the Germans at the River Marne in September, the war settled into a bloody stalemate along what would soon become known as the Western Front. Both sides hunkered down for nearly three years of trench warfare. Five million people would die as new military technology such as machine guns and tanks wreaked havoc in Europe.

As the United States mobilized for war, in New York the American Bible Society mobilized for distribution to the war front. The 1914 *Annual Report* put it best:

> The black shadow of war in its most dreadful phase overhangs the world. Almost without warning what has been so long dreaded, which men and nations dared to hope would never come, has befallen, and the great nations of Continental Europe are drawn one after another into the vortex. No one knows what will happen next or what the final outcome is to be . . . Christian nations in a death grapple! What a spectacle before the heathen!

The Bible Cause might suffer as a result of the war, but the ABS was prepared to do its part in bringing the word of God to the front. In fact, there were some in New York who saw the war as an opportunity to showcase the Bible as the "great channel of comfort and peace to the nations." As the war got underway, the ABS received a request from the Christian Tract Society, a Baptist benevolent organization in Kassel, Germany, who asked, "for Christ's sake," to send them Bibles in German, Russian, French, and Polish for distribution among the troops. This would be the first of many such requests the ABS received in the early months of the war. In 1914 the Society declared that it would only work "through our sister societies in Europe." It did not take sides.[1]

In order to meet the need in Europe, the ABS needed money. At the start of the war the Society was facing yet another season of financial difficulties. In the period between the first quarter of 1914 and the first quarter of 1915, donations to the ABS dropped by nearly $33,000, a total decrease in giving of 32 percent. Individual donations remained stable during this period, but giving by churches and legacies (always an unpredictable revenue source) had not reached projections. World War I presented another opportunity to appeal to donors who might help the ABS increase its distribution in this time of international crisis. In October 1915 it issued an emergency appeal to its constituency. With the ABS centennial approaching in 1916, the Society asked donors for $150,000 in "special gifts from churches and individuals or else they might be in danger of entering their centennial year with all of the Society's reserve funds exhausted" and be forced to endure a "calamitous retrenchment of all its work at home and abroad." Every field in which the ABS had an agency, with the exception of Turkey and Mexico, were in desperate need of funds.[2]

The ABS wanted to correct the impression that the Society was rich. "THIS IS NOT THE FACT," they emphatically told their donors in October 1915. In the previous decade the ABS had received a $500,000 gift from Olivia Sage, the widow of railroad magnate Russell Sage. The grant was matched by ABS donors, creating an endowment of 1 million dollars. But the interest on this money, which gave the ABS an annual yield of $75,000, would only cover expenses for a mere two months. Unrestricted legacy funds were held in reserve and used in times of urgent demand, but with new Bible needs popping up at home and abroad, perhaps now was the time to tap this fund. The ABS had opened nine new agencies in the United States in the decade prior to the outbreak of war. Each one of them cost the ABS about $100,000 a year to operate. When the ABS was faced with the choice of spending these legacy funds on distributing the Bible where it was needed, or keeping it in reserve, they almost always chose the former. It was time for all supporters of the Bible Cause to send money.[3]

While the Society was contributing to the Bible needs created by World War I, it also devoted a considerable amount of effort to the ongoing Mexican Revolution. As we have seen, the Wilson administration endorsed Venustiano Carranza, a constitutionalist and the current president of the Mexico who had just seized control of the government by overthrowing Victoriano Huerta. In supporting Carranza, Wilson was also withdrawing his initial and brief support of Francisco "Pancho" Villa, a former ally of Carranza who was now leading a rebel army in northern Mexico intent upon taking power from the man he once supported. Villa felt betrayed by Wilson's support of Carranza and began to retaliate by killing Americans. He murdered sixteen mining engineers who he pulled from a train in Mexico. He then crossed the border into the United States, burning the town of Columbus, New Mexico, and killing nineteen Americans in the process. He followed this with a raid into Texas. Wilson responded to Villa's killing spree by sending twelve thousand troops into Mexico, under the command of General John J. Pershing, to capture Villa "dead or alive." Pershing and his troops chased Villa through the Mexican countryside for close to a full year, but failed to find him. Meanwhile, President Carranza was not happy about the US invasion of Mexico and sent troops to put a stop to it. Mexico and the United States nearly went to war in June 1916, but Wilson put a halt to that possibility, realizing that a war with Mexico would distract the country's attention away from its increasing tensions with Germany.[4]

The newly formed ABS home agencies distributed Bibles to Pershing's troops stationed along the Mexican border. There was even an attempt to get a Bible to Pancho Villa. A Mexican Christian and friend of the ABS who knew the revolutionary promised to bring him a copy "with certain marked passages." The Southwestern Agency bore the brunt of the ABS burden in Mexico. J. J. Morgan, the secretary of the agency, purchased a "Bible car"—a Ford roadster equipped with a cabinet in the rear to store Bibles—to help with distribution. He then turned the keys over to S. Brooks McLane, a recent graduate of Austin College in Sherman, Texas. When McLane got behind the wheel of the Bible car in El Paso he knew nothing about military life. He described himself as a "walking question mark." There were 40,000 American soldiers in El Paso and McLane realized, through the help of chaplains and military officers, that soldiers could not afford to purchase Bibles. If the word of God was going to reach Pershing's soldiers it would need to be provided free of charge. After several weeks in El Paso, McLane and a small team tied cots and bedding on the running board of the car, found room for their groceries in one of the drawers of the Bible cabinet, attached two water bags, a lantern, and their suitcases to the side of the engine, and headed off across the Lone Star State.[5]

McLane, who was often called "the Bible Guy" by the troops, canvassed the Mexican-American border from El Paso to Brownsville delivering Bibles to American soldiers. Over the course of 1916 he distributed over 17,000 special khaki-covered Bibles to American troops. The work required patience. The Ford Roadster was constantly breaking down. While driving near Fort Hancock, McLane heard "something click" and was forced to pull into the town (which included only store and saloon) and wait thirty hours while a car part was sent from El Paso. McLane and the Bible Car often passed through unfinished roads covered in sand. At one point the Bible man was forced to rely upon the good will of a ranchman and his cow to pull his car out of the quagmire as the water boiled out of the radiator. Since his auto difficulties placed him so far behind schedule on this particular day, McLane decided to camp near a small canyon. It was dark, and he was unfamiliar with his surroundings, but his mind was put at ease when he heard the sound of someone nearby "whistling a good old gospel hymn."[6]

Though McLane claimed to know very little about everyday life in army camps, he was a quick learner. He often described the spiritual and psychological condition of the soldiers he met in Texas. They were far from home and the "temptations to evil" were "unusually strong." Unlike the ABS agents and chaplains in the Civil War who described soldiers scattered throughout the camps perusing their scriptures, McLane described a camp culture where it took courage to read the Bible in public. "The soldier needs the strength and grace which comes from God," in order to weather the "jests" of his fellow soldiers or the "finger of scorn" often "pointed at the Christian." But McLane was aware that even the scoffers had time to think and reflect on the possibility of death in battle. "It is in the quiet of the evening," he wrote, "just as the sun is going down on the Texas prairies," that "nature itself speaks to man of his God." It was in these moments of reflection, McLane believed, that the "silent missionary" in the form of a khaki Testament in a soldier's shirt pocket or locker "gets its chance."[7]

The ABS celebrated 100 years of Bible work in the midst of World War I. The planning for this gala event began in May 1914. Henry Otis Dwight, a former missionary in the Levant who had written several books on the history of that region, was relieved of his duties as the ABS recording secretary so he could write *The Centennial History of the American Bible Society.*[8] Dwight's 605-page tome was published by the internationally known trade publisher Macmillan and Company. The print run was 5,000 copies and the book sold for $1.00 in cloth and fifty cents in paperback. Dwight produced a sympathetic history of the ABS that began with the premise that God raised up the Society and its founders to carry forth the timeless message of the Gospel.[9] The centennial was advertised among ABS members and word of the event was passed along to public libraries, theological seminaries, universities and colleges, state superintendents of education, and political leaders. Advertisements calling attention to a "Universal Bible Sunday" on May 7 were placed in forty-one newspapers across the country and special inserts were created for church bulletins. ABS Corresponding Secretary William Haven took a world tour to prepare the various foreign agencies for the celebration.[10]

As the exact date of the centennial neared, the ABS sponsored a Pageant of the Bible Among the Nations in the Washington, DC, Convention Hall. Over twenty churches and Sunday schools from nearly every major Protestant denomination displayed tableaux representing the Bible's influence around the world. The ABS estimated that 10,000 people passed through the hall on May 6, 1915, to see the display. The following day, another eight to ten thousand people came to an ABS-sponsored meeting on the steps of the eastern front of the Capitol. US Vice President Thomas Marshall presided over the event. Speaker of the House of Representatives Champ Clark and US Senator from the state of Washington, Wesley Jones, delivered speeches. The celebration came to an end later that evening with a formal event at the Continental Memorial Hall of the Daughters of the American Revolution, with Woodrow Wilson as the guest of honor. In his words to 1,000 friends of the ABS who were gathered that evening, he reminded them that "in proportion as men yield themselves to the kindly light of the Gospel . . . they are bound together in bonds of mutual understanding and assured peace."[11] The connection between the ABS and the nation was on display everywhere.

After two days of Bible celebration in the nation's capital, the ABS and its friends returned to New York City, the place of its birth 100 years earlier. Several local city dignitaries and representatives from Bible societies around the world gathered at City Hall on May 9 in the same room that the ABS was founded on May 16, 1816. Prominent New York lawyer Frances Lynde Stetson used his speech to deplore various attempts by Roman Catholics and Jews to bar the teaching of the King James Version in public schools. "The State that denies to its children the opportunity of drinking from the deep wells of spiritual truth," he told the audience at City Hall, "leaves the soul of its people to die of thirst." Later that evening, a meeting was held at Carnegie Hall to highlight the international and missionary work of the society. Representatives of the British and Foreign Bible Society, the American Board of Commissioners of Foreign Missions, and the Bishop of the Methodist Episcopal Church delivered addresses.[12]

When Woodrow Wilson brought the United States into the war in April 1917, it raised the stakes for the ABS. In May the Society launched a major financial and promotional campaign to get a New Testament to every United States soldier and sailor who wanted one. Since the ABS was in a financial crisis

at the time that Congress declared war on Germany, it would need to once
again rely heavily upon local churches to support the effort. On the request of
the Federal Council of Churches, the ABS sent a committee of five representatives to Washington, DC, to discuss how best to organize a special distribution of scriptures to the US Army and Navy. The ABS would focus its efforts
on the free distribution of a special edition of Proverbs and scripture portions
of individual Gospels. It would raise money through what it called an "Army-
Navy Fund Campaign" and would involve the Home Agencies in the process
of getting this campaign underway.[13]

When the United States declared war on Germany, the ABS was aware that
many Christian and benevolent organizations would want to get involved in
the distribution of Bibles to the American troops at home and overseas. In
order to avoid duplication in efforts, the ABS worked with the Young Men's
Christian Association (YMCA) and the Army and Navy Chaplaincy Corps.
The YMCA was officially sanctioned by an executive order from President
Woodrow Wilson to serve the troops in the field. In September 1917 the War
Work Council of the YMCA requested that the ABS send them 1 million
khaki-bound Testaments free of charge. The Society agreed to the request, but
with its presses already running sixteen hours a day it could not fulfill the order
by itself, forcing the Board of Managers to hire three outside printing firms
to help produce the books. It was the largest single grant the ABS had ever
made.[14]

The ABS had hoped to print these YMCA Testaments with a high-grade
thin paper and strong bindings in anticipation of use in a war zone. The first
problem that they faced was a lack of quality paper. Fortunately, a Boston mill
was able to ship five 18-ton carloads to New York on short notice. The Schlueter
Printing Company, one of the firms that the ABS contracted with for this work,
ran four presses for twenty-four hours a day and six days a week from Labor
Day in September to St. Patrick's Day in March in order to complete the ABS's
order. Due to a coal shortage facing the country in the winter of 1917–1918,
much of the printing was done in very cold conditions. Workers claimed to
be too cold to work and frozen glue became a serious problem. Yet despite the
difficulties and the lack of quality, the Testaments were completed ahead of
schedule. Several state Bible societies pasted letters from local politicians into
the Bibles. The Maryland Bible Society included a letter from Woodrow Wilson
and the New York Bible Society added a letter from Theodore Roosevelt.[15]

As the war came to a close, the ABS and other advocates of the Bible Cause
reflected on the significant role that the Bible played during World War I.
The *Bible Society Record* featured testimonials by soldiers who found comfort and inspiration through their Khaki Testaments. One commentator was
thankful that the United States provided the troops with rifles, bayonets, and

ammunition, but "these alone," he added, "cannot win." The Bible provided the "spirit" necessary to defeat the Germans. "A soldier carrying a Testament in his pocket," he added, "knows that he is right [and] knows that God is with him . . . Who could ask for a more powerful ally?" The Bible was also touted as a source of morale among the troops. One American soldier was about to desert the army when a friend pointed to the Testament in his pocket and asked, "could you desert with this in your pocket?" After thinking for a moment, the soldier said, "I see what you mean, this book stands for loyalty." As might be expected, the young man "stuck to his post." Soldiers also testified to the role that the Bible played in helping them live "clean and upright lives." It offered comfort in "the darkest moments" of war, helped soldiers discover courage in the midst of the battle, and brought assurance of eternal life in the face of death. The message of the Bible was unique. It fulfilled the needs of American soldiers, the ABS claimed, in ways that other world religions—Islam, Buddhism, Zoroastrianism, Taoism, and Animism—could not.[16]

In April 1918 the *Bible Society Record* republished "The Militant Element of Christianity," a speech by famed navy admiral and historian Alfred T. Mahan delivered on the occasion of his presentation of Bibles to the cadets at the US Military Academy at West Point. Though the speech was delivered before the war, the ABS's decision to publish it in its flagship periodical speaks volumes to the way many in the Society understood the relationship between the Bible and war. Mahan wanted the cadets to be aware of the "masculine and militant side of religion as portrayed in the Bible." The "military calling," he added, is where "the religion of Christ finds its most vivid illustration." He described "practical Christianity" as a "call to battle, from him who came not to send peace, but a sword." Mahan described God as a "General" and Christ as a "Captain" who instilled in men the "martial virtues of patience, obedience, subordination, and self-sacrifice." Ignoring the fact that it was women, not men, who dominated the membership rolls of Christian churches, Mahan affirmed that such martial attributes are stronger in men than they are women because, ultimately, men were more religious. Mahan finished his speech by urging the cadets to live out the "soldiery" virtues of Christ. The Bible they received on that day would provide them with an example of a person in history who "faced death with courage, suffered pain and agony on the cross like a man, and ultimately subordinated himself to the will of his General." These future military officers belonged to the army of God and the army of the United States and, Mahan concluded, "the more faithfully you serve one, the more faithfully also you will serve the other."[17]

The ABS also promoted the Bible as an aid to nationalism in Europe. Those "ancient and honored nations long trodden under the heel of conqueror" were gaining hope in the possibility of self-determination and the realization of "national aspirations and revived independent national existence." For example, by providing the Bible to the people of the "Slavic races" in their own languages, the ABS believed that it was reconnecting these groups to their Christian roots and enabling them to forge a new national life around the teaching of the scriptures in their own language. If the Bible was at the center of American national life, the ABS implied, then it should also be an essential part of the construction of national identities in the postwar world. The Bible's role in the war was also a sign of the success of Western Civilization. While most cultural critics and pundits were pointing to World War I as evidence that Western Civilization was failing, the ABS saw signs of hope. The fact that "Western Christian nations" supplied the continent with 15 million volumes of scripture was a clear indicator that the Bible Cause was moving forward despite the bloodshed and ravages of war. Soldiers transformed by the Bible's teaching would return to their homes after the War and season the West with Christian "ideas and ideals" in such a way that would lead to the spread of democracy and the "worship of the one true God, and the sovereignty of Jesus Christ his Son and our Savior."[18]

The January 1919 edition of the *Bible Society Record* announced the ABS's plan for postwar distribution: "The Bible in Every Land." The war had opened a "new and unprecedented" demand for Bibles in the war-torn regions of Europe and the ABS was ready to answer the call. In 1919, the Society spent nearly three times as much money on this program as it did on its work at home. With the war over, the ABS promoted the Bible as a book of peace. Upon returning to the United States following his trip around the world to visit ABS agencies, William Haven stopped at a foreign missions conference in New Haven, Connecticut, where he delivered an address titled "The Contribution of the Bible and Christian Literature to the New Internationalism." Such internationalism was embodied in Woodrow Wilson's attempt to bring a more democratic order to the world in the wake of the war. In January 1918 Wilson unveiled before Congress his "Fourteen Points." Eight of these points dealt with his proposed territorial changes in postwar Europe, but the other six points captured the heart of Wilson's international vision. He called for unrestricted navigation, freer trade, a reduction in arms, and a League of Nations for the purpose of promoting peace and solving future disputes. As Wilson was in Paris trying to sell his vision to the leaders of the Allied Powers, Haven delivered his address.[19]

Haven began the address by making a case for the Bible as the source of the "Brotherhood" necessary to bring the world together in a spirit of peace. "The Bible is the one great international book," he suggested, because "it is found everywhere on the face of the earth." As he could testify in the wake of his trip around the world, the Bible was available to millions of people in over 100 different languages. For Haven, internationalism required "common thoughts" among the nations. The Bible, he believed, should serve as the source of those thoughts. He called it an "organizing Idealism." The Great War happened because people around the world neglected to read their Bibles and practice its teachings. If the United States and the West were going to be successful in creating a new international fellowship of nations, this neglect had to stop. It was time for a renewed emphasis on Bible distribution and translation, so that the world might be "saturated with Christian Idealism." The very fate of Western Civilization was at stake. The War was over, but political chaos still reigned. The threat of anarchy, atheism, and communism were all ready to fill the vacuums of power created throughout Europe. According to Haven, only the Bible had the power to provide a "Brotherhood" that was stronger than the kind of community promoted by the likes of Marx and Nietzsche. Haven's plea was for something much deeper than the restoration of new governments. "Leagues and Societies of Nations" were good as long as they were "leagues and societies of *holy* nations." Any kind of internationalism that fell short of this standard was as "valueless as the waters of a mirage upon the desert to satisfy the thirsty soul of humanity." Haven wanted a new world order that was Christian in character. The "only hope for the future" was a "regeneration of governments and nations through the power of Him whom the Bible reveals."[20]

Before Woodrow Wilson left for the peace conference at Versailles, the Board of Managers presented him with a specially made Bible that they hoped the president would bring to the negotiating table so that the "spirit and teachings of Christ" would be present in the room. The Bible was bound in white morocco with a gold cross on the cover and inscribed with the words "PEACE CONFERENCE: PRESENTED BY THE AMERICAN BIBLE SOCIETY." Wilson acknowledged receipt of the Bible and told the ABS that he would seek an opportunity to use it in France. Shortly after Wilson arrived in Paris, Haven and James Wood, the president of the Board of Managers, sent Wilson a telegram to endorse his commitment to worldwide freedom. The ABS reminded Wilson that there were parts of the world where Christian missionaries and Bible distributors could not do their work due to the lack of religious freedom, and they urged him to defend this fundamental human right at Versailles. Though the ABS believed that the Bible was the only foundation by which to build a society, they also respected the right of all religious groups around the world "to follow God's leadings in their comprehension of His Truth." After the cable was sent to Wilson it was published by the Associated Press, United Press International, and the New York News Association.

The ABS participated in a massive effort to bring the Bible to the troops fighting in Mexico and Europe during World War I. By the end of 1918,

the Society distributed a total of 4,558,871 Bibles, Testaments, and scripture portions. Most of these texts were small thin-paper Testaments that
fit comfortably inside the vest pocket. They were bound in Khaki with a
strong binding and a picture of an American flag and gold stars on the cover.
The number of Bibles distributed is staggering, especially when one considers that the United States mobilized 4,355,000 troops during the war.
Theoretically, every American soldier had access to an ABS text. (The ABS
also distributed over 1.6 million Bibles to "belligerent forces of other countries.") Between the three largest Bible societies in the world—the ABS, the
BFBS, and the NBSS—over 15 million Bibles were distributed in eighty-
one different languages.[21] While many believed that the war struck a major
blow to the cause of human progress, the ABS remained optimistic, and
even more confident, about its role in a different kind of progress—the
Christianization of the world.

15

The Bible in Times of Plenty and Want

As the United States and the world healed from the horrors of World War I, the American Bible Society went back to business as usual—working domestically and internationally to print, translate, and distribute the word of God. Keeping with its commitment to stay above divisive issues that might hinder its ability to bring the Bible to as many people as possible, the ABS did not take positions on some of the major cultural developments occurring in the United States during the decade. The ABS refused to make pronouncements on subjects such as Prohibition, the ever-changing youth culture, consumerism, immigration restriction, or the political corruption that American history textbooks tell us defined American life in the 1920s. The ABS was silent about the so-called Fundamentalist-Modernist controversy that divided Protestant denominations in this era. The 1926 *Annual Report* did make reference to the "famous Scopes Trial in Tennessee," but only to note that this nationally broadcast debate over the teaching of evolution in public schools had "produced no adverse effect on Bible distribution in the regions where it was held."[1] Though no one in the Bible House would deny that the scriptures spoke to contemporary issues, the Board of Managers and staff knew that Bible-believing Christians often differed on such matters. The Society was not in the business of interpreting the Bible and instructing people how it related to the spirit of the age. That was the work of the churches.

This, of course, does not mean that the ABS was immune from the changes taking place in American life during the 1920s and 1930s. Nor does it mean that these changes did not inform the Society's decisions about where to expend its resources and distribute Bibles. The ABS would work between the Great Wars to reach those groups in America—immigrants, Native Americans, the blind, the poor, the unemployed, African Americans, and the growing white middle class—who needed to be exposed to the message of God's word. It remained true to its mission—bringing people the good news of the Gospel and promoting the general principles of the Bible, without note or comment—as a means of Christianizing the larger culture.

Let's begin with immigration. The US policy toward immigration changed drastically in the 1920s. Between 1901 and 1920 roughly 14.5 million immigrants came to the United States. As we saw in chapter 9, most of them arrived via steamship from southern and eastern European destinations. Not everyone appreciated these newcomers. They were Catholic and Jewish and were darker skinned than the Irish and Germans who had come to the country in earlier waves of immigration. For those who favored immigration restriction, these newly arriving strangers seemed less willing to adapt to an American way of life. Organizations such as the Immigrant Restriction League used scientific arguments from the growing field of eugenics to show that they were racially different from the old immigrants and were thus, for the most part, incapable of assimilation. The champions of immigration restriction achieved a major victory in 1924 with the passage of the Johnson-Reed Immigration Act. The law reduced the number of immigrants to 164,000 per year and decided who got into the country and who did not based on quotas derived from the ethnic makeup of the United States in 1890.[2]

Though the number of immigrants would decline greatly due to the Immigration Act of 1924, the millions of new immigrants who arrived in the United States in the decades prior to this restriction law were still here. They needed Bibles. They needed to become American citizens. The ABS was there to help. In 1920 the Society echoed a now familiar refrain from the pages of the *Bible Society Record*. The assimilation of the "foreign elements into the body politic here in America" was a serious cultural issue deserving "the attention of the Christian public." This problem was not simply a matter of education, or providing the Bible to immigrants in the appropriate language, or even "implanting political ideas and ideals" in their heads. While all of these things were important, if not essential, to the work of assimilation, immigrants ultimately needed to be inculcated with "the spiritual truths contained in, and revealed by, the Word of God." Without the Bible, the ABS argued, "true assimilation cannot be accomplished." This "influx of foreigners" would eventually "threaten the very life of the republic." The Bible taught immigrants "character," and such character was intended to "form the backbone and the safeguard of our nation." Until the immigrant population learned these lessons, they would continue to be described by the ABS and others as a "problem." Once again, the ABS was not only offering a path to eternal life; it was "rendering a truly incalculable service to our country."[3]

Language was an important part of the assimilation process. The 1917 Immigration Act required a literacy test for entrance into the United States. Immigration inspectors at Ellis Island tested literacy by giving the new arrivals slips of paper containing thirty to forty words "in ordinary use, printed in plainly legible type in some one of the various languages or dialects of immigrants." After much consideration concerning what words should be placed on these slips of paper, the US Department of Labor, which handled immigration issues in 1917, turned to the ABS. Since the Society published Bibles in hundreds of languages, including those languages common among most of the immigrants arriving to American shores, it made sense to use the Bible to test the literacy of these new arrivals. The Department of Labor placed an order with the ABS and announced its decision in March, a month after the law was passed by Congress.[4]

Many anti-immigration groups complained that these strangers were unwilling to learn English. Though the ability to speak the English language did not prevent immigrants from gaining entry to the United States, after the passing of the Naturalization Act of 1906 the ability to speak in English was a requirement for citizenship.[5] Though the individual members of the ABS Board of Managers may have had differing positions on the immigration problem, and some of them no doubt believed that the ability to speak English was important to the assimilation process, the Society made no effort to promote the King James Bible as a textbook for teaching English to these strangers. As they tried to convert immigrants and make them good citizens of a Christian nation, they did so by using Protestant Bibles translated into their own languages.

Rather than follow the lead of the immigration restriction crowd by instilling fear in the American people about the inability of these outsiders to assimilate, the ABS usually accentuated the positive and reported stories in which ethnic populations, armed with Bibles, had made great strides in learning the American way of life. For example, General Secretary William Haven was impressed with the small community of Romanians who had recently settled in Akron, Ohio. This community collected $6,000 to pay for the initial expenses needed for a Romanian translation of the Bible. The Akron Romanians had expensive tastes. Haven was surprised by the "eagerness with which these men were determined to have the very best in paper and binding that could be produced." They did not want "the cheaper books or the cloth-bound books, but they wanted their Bibles and their New Testaments morocco bound, divinity circuit, and with their names on the cover in gold letters." According to Haven, price was no object. Haven was also impressed by a group of young men in the vestry of a Romanian Baptist Church singing "Onward Christian Soldiers" and "America" in preparation for what appears to have been a Fourth of July celebration. He was even more excited about the fact that this church was influential in "voting out Saloons" in Akron. His conclusion was that "Americanization and the Bible go hand in hand."[6]

S. H. Kirkbride, the superintendent of the Northwestern Agency, could not get his hands on enough Polish-language Bibles. Poles in Chicago and the surrounding area were "wild with desire" to have a Bible for their "comfort and salvation in this land" and to send to their relatives in Poland suffering in the aftermath of World War I. The Polish population in the Midwest, Kirkbride added, was "groping for spiritual light and life as eagerly as they are for political freedom." His experience working with this ethnic population led him to urge the ABS to become more involved in the reconstruction of postwar Europe. Nations in need of American food and money in the wake of the war also needed the kind of spiritual guidance that only the Bible could provide. Kirkbride was confident that the people of Europe "will be eager to take from our great republic the Bible, to be their inspiration and spiritual guide." In this regard, "America and the American Bible Society are practically synonymous."[7] Kirkbride also reminded the ABS of the need for the Bible in the "wilds" of northern Minnesota and Wisconsin, where immigrants on "the Range" were forming towns and cities. He estimated that 93 percent of the people living in this region were of foreign birth or the children of foreign-born parents. Kirkbride defended the human dignity of these immigrants, making sure that the ABS and its middle-class constituency knew that these people were more than just "Yaps," "Polaks," "Hunkies," and "Dagoes." Kirkland described them as a "heterogeneous mass" that had the potential to be "refined and transformed into educated, prosperous, useful, and Christian citizens."[8]

Unlike its decision in 1901 to open an agency for African Americans, the ABS did not do the same thing for Native Americans. But this does not mean that the Society ceased working among these groups after it moved to a system of home agencies and a more centralized organizational structure. The ABS continued to supply scriptures in various Indian languages to missionaries working with Native American communities. For example, in 1921 there were 65,751 Indians within the bounds of Kirkbride's Northwestern Agency, and several benevolent and missionary organizations working hard to bring them to Protestant faith. The ABS made efforts to supply all literate Indians in the United States with a Bible in their own language.

Translations into Indian languages also continued through the 1920s. Rev. Fred Mitchell led a team of scholars in Tolchaco, Arizona, that translated the Bible into Navajo so that the 32,500 members of this growing tribe (there were only about 8,000 Navajo at the end of the Civil War) could teach the Bible in their schools. The US Commissioner of Indian Affairs granted permission to teachers in government-funded Indian schools to read the Navajo translation "side by side with the English Bible." While the government believed that the ABS translation was useful as a stepping-stone toward teaching the Navajo how to speak English, the ABS saw this as an excellent way of lifting these people from the "dense darkness of heathenism."[9]

The ABS home agents had to be wise as serpents and innocent as doves when they worked with Indian schools. Many Indian young people were educated in reservation schools funded by the US government. None of these schools permitted religious instruction, but the Bureau of Indian Affairs did allow missionaries from nearby stations to minister on the reservations, provided that it was done without undue proselytizing. It also encouraged the ABS to provide Bibles for the purpose of teaching Indian children to read. As an official in the Bureau told Arthur Ragatz of the Society's Western Agency, "reading the Bible has never made a good Indian bad, but has gone a long way in helping make bad Indians good." The ABS hoped that missionaries, equipped with Bibles that were often distributed to children as graduation gifts, might bring "ever-increasing numbers of the Red race into the Protestant church."[10]

The ABS always had a special affinity for its work among the so-called Five Civilized Tribes. There were about 120,000 Cherokee, Chickasaw, Choctaw, Creek, and Seminole living in Oklahoma in 1920, and the ABS had translated the Bible into three of their languages (Choctaw, Cherokee, and Creek). In 1818 the Society was pleased to report that these Indians, living in their ancestral lands in the southeast, had "removed the appearance from the traditional Indian of paint and feathers" and become "nearly dressed men." After failed attempts at land ownership in the nineteenth century, following their removal to Indian Territory (present-day Oklahoma), and the influx of white settlers to Oklahoma during the first decade of the twentieth century, many of these tribes were living in poverty in white towns and rural communities. Christian missionaries made an effort to integrate them into white society by helping them with medical issues, teaching them English, and providing them with an education. From the perspective of the ABS's Southwestern Agency, the "red man of America" presented "the clearest call to missions which Christian America has to-day."[11]

As the ABS brought the Bible to immigrants and Native Americans, it also continued to connect the Bible with the larger story of the United States. On November 30, 1919, the ABS called for a "Universal Bible Sunday" across the nation. The Society encouraged ministers representing every Protestant denomination to arrange their morning services on this day in such a way that would emphasize "the priceless worth and marvelous power of the Christian Scriptures among all peoples of the world." The long-term plan was to make the last Sunday of November Universal Bible Sunday.[12] The second Universal Bible Sunday would be a special one. Ever aware of important moments in America's past where the Bible played a role, the ABS declared November 28, 1920, to be Mayflower Universal Bible Sunday in celebration of the landing of the Pilgrim Fathers at Plymouth three hundred years earlier. The ABS reminded its constituency that "the greatest gift brought by the Pilgrim Fathers to this country was the open Bible."

The Mayflower Universal Bible Sunday was a success. Several months following the November 1920 event, the *Bible Society Record* noted that "it did more, under God, to create a living interest in the tercentenary celebration of the Landing of the Pilgrims, and to emphasize the spiritual significance of the coming of the Pilgrims to America, than any other single plan." The ABS printed 100,000 copies of a historical booklet called "A Little Journey to Plymouth, Where the Mayflower Landed" and supplemented it with over 10,000 copies of two other booklets: "In the Name of God, Amen!" and "The Pilgrim and the Book," for adult readers. (This appears to be a rare case in which something other than Bibles, Testaments, or scripture portions came off the ABS presses.) These booklets emphasized "the indisputable fact that the Pilgrims were the folks they were because the Bible was the foundation of their religion, the keynote of their worship, the guide of their conduct, the strength of their character and the creator of a spiritual brotherhood, [and] the cornerstone of America's democratic institutions." The Mayflower Universal Bible Sunday was a smashing success. Ministers from around the country wrote to the Bible House in New York describing the popularity of the booklets and the large overflow crowds who showed up for worship on Sunday morning, November 28, 1920.[13]

In 1929 these warm feelings of patriotism gave way to an economic crisis. During the Great Depression the ABS had to balance its own financial difficulties with the high demand for the spiritual sustenance that the Bible could offer a suffering American population. In December 1934, the ABS used its annual Christmas greeting in the pages of the *Bible Society Record* to offer a clear diagnosis of the problem facing the country. The Society extolled the "courageous" efforts of the US government and ordinary Americans to relieve the burdens of the poor and offer "new ways of thinking" to help solve the country's economic woes, but also lamented the "personal and corporate selfishness" and the "unrealized degree to which competitive aggrandizement and social and racial class consciousness" was hurting American society. Even more damaging was the "separation of education and religion" and the failure of Christians to teach their children spiritual values at home. The Depression brought economic hardships that could have "eternal" implications for the lives of ordinary people unless something was done to meet the spiritual needs at the heart of the crisis. The game plan was a familiar one—distribute more Bibles, inform the churches of the role they might play in the process, educate the American public about the nation's historic relationship to the Bible in times of crisis, and work harder at obtaining the financial support needed to pull it all off.[14]

While this all sounded fine and good, the ABS was suffering economically just like everyone else. The number of ABS donors dropped from 21,000 in 1929 to 12,000 in 1934. The money the ABS took in from the sale of Bibles dropped from $305,081 in 1929 to $178,397 in 1932. Associate General Secretary Rome Betts connected this drop in donors and sales to families having to choose to put food on their tables or give to the work of benevolent societies. This was an understandable choice, but Betts also believed that the decline in giving to the ABS and other Christian organizations was representative of a decline in American values. "Have we as a people become so infatuated with the material and 'the number of things which a man possesseth,'" Betts fumed, "that we are increasingly forgetting our responsibilities toward those forces which truly help to create the abundant life of which Jesus spoke?" Betts estimated that the net taxable income of the American people in 1936 amounted to $19 billion. Of this number, nearly $3 billion could have been given to charity and claimed as an income tax exemption. Yet the American people donated less than $400 million to charity, a number that Betts pointed out was well below even the "Biblical tithe."[15]

ABS distribution during the 1930s was focused on special interest groups affected by the Depression. For example, in 1932 about 20,000 World War I veterans—known as the Bonus Army—arrived in Washington, DC, demanding the cash bonuses that the government had promised to every veteran of World War I. Bonus Army camps provided opportunities for ministry as Christian organizations and churches rushed to meet the spiritual needs of these men and their families. The National Capitol Agency, a federally sponsored organization responsible for the development of Washington, DC, landmarks, and the Washington City Bible Society requested 5,000 copies of the Gospel of John for distribution among the veterans. The ABS praised the members of the Bonus Army for their "fine attitude . . . toward the Bible, and their cordial reception of those who come to the camp in the name of our Lord Jesus Christ, to help them in their time of need."[16]

The Agency Among the Colored People of the United States was also active during the Great Depression. In 1932 the Atlanta Division reported "more than usual interest." There was a hunger for the "Bread of Life" among blacks in the South that was greater than the hunger in "many of the more favored places," but it was difficult to locate volunteer distributors due to the economic climate. "As the bread line lengthens," the agency reported, "and the number of those who cannot find work with which to purchase the bare necessities of life increase each day," it became considerably more difficult for African American colporteurs to "carry on." Those who were working on behalf of the agency reported that Bible sales were difficult among the African American communities due to their "embarrassing shortage of funds." In one instance, a colporteur received a shipment of 500 Bibles from the ABS designated for a "colored school" in Newnan, Georgia. There were enough Bibles in the delivery for every child in the school to receive one, but the colporteur needed to come up with some funds to underwrite the books because the parents could not afford to purchase them.[17]

The ABS also provided Bibles to the men employed in the Civilian Conservation Corps (CCC), a New Deal program that put young unmarried men to work thinning forests, building hiking trails and roads, and planting trees in rural areas. The Maryland Bible Society brought Bibles to workers who, according to Rev. Edgar Cordell Powers of the National Capital Society, maintained the kind of "healthy activity" and "strong bodies" that provided a "splendid foundation for alert mentality and power to grasp the spiritual verities of the Book." As of June 1933 the Society had distributed over 100,000 Bibles in CCC camps. In Vermont, a chaplain reported that the men were often seen resting in their bunks reading ABS Testaments. He added that "I have never seen a single New Testament go out by way of the waste basket." A West Virginia chaplain affirmed that some of the young men had started a Bible Class with their ABS Bibles. In Alabama, the Bibles were used for impromptu Sunday school classes, and in Iowa over five hundred workers began a "Chapter-a-Day Club." A Kansas CCC chaplain wrote that he distributed most of his Bibles after dark when men who were "timid and afraid to take a Testament in front of the company" during the day would stop by to pick one up.[18]

In 1935, in the midst of the Great Depression, the American Bible Society celebrated a century of service to the blind. Since it sold its first Bibles for the blind in 1835, the ABS had delivered over 100,000 embossed Bibles to individuals without sight in the United States and an additional 15,590 Bibles abroad. At the time of the anniversary the ABS had published embossed Bibles in several different reading systems and in twenty-five different languages. The Society commemorated its centennial of distributing to the blind with a service at Fifth Avenue Presbyterian Church in New York City. A choir from the New York Institute for the Education of the Blind performed several musical selections; a blind soloist, Rose Weinstein, and a blind organist and composer, Edwin Grasse, also performed. An Old Testament lesson was read from a Braille Bible and a New Testament lesson was recited by a talking book machine, a recent invention sponsored by the Library of Congress. These lessons were followed by addresses from Reverend L. B. Chamberlain, the ABS recording secretary, and J. Sutherland Bonnell, the pastor of the Fifth Avenue Presbyterian Church.[19] But the highlight of the event was a short speech from Helen Keller, the internationally known advocate for the deaf and blind. Keller expressed her "profound gratitude" to the ABS and praised the organization for its work in providing "new hope" to the disabled, for quickening "their wills to rebuild their broken lives," and for providing a "benefit" to the blind that was unmatched by any other organization. She concluded that the Bible "is a book to live with, to think from, and to die by."[20]

The ABS got involved in the production of Bibles for the blind when in April 1835 it began to support the work of Samuel Gridley Howe (the husband of Julia Ward Howe, the author of "The Battle Hymn of the Republic") in the development of a raised-letter printing system that allowed blind people to read independently. At the time Howe was the principal of the New England Institution for the Education of the Blind (later the Perkins School for the Blind) in Massachusetts, a school to teach blind children how to read, write, perform music, and gain useful skills in broom and mattress making. Howe developed a system of printing for the blind that featured raised letters of the common English alphabet (he was unaware of the work of Louis Braille, who was working on his system of raised points at roughly the same time). Unlike more cumbersome editions of the Bible with raised letters, Howe was able to produce books that were smaller and cheaper by using thinner paper and reduced type. His type became known at "Boston" or "Howe" type. The first book published in Boston type was *The Acts of the Apostles*, and, by 1835, an entire New Testament has been produced. A few years later Howe published the entire Old Testament in an eight-volume set, a work that was much less cumbersome and expensive when compared to the nineteen-volume work that had recently been done in Europe. This Bible was funded heavily by the ABS and sold by the Society at affordable prices. The original Boston-type Bible was published by Howe in Boston, but all subsequent editions, until 1922, were bound and embossed at the New York Bible House at Astor Place.[21]

In 1874, a new system of raised lettering for the blind known as "New York Point" was invented by W. B. Wait, a teacher in the New York Institute for the Education of the Blind. By 1894, the ABS was printing the entire Bible in the New York Point system, although this style fell quickly out of favor due to the cumbersome nature of the capital letters and a negative review from Helen Keller. By the second decade of the twentieth century, most of the ABS publishing efforts for the blind concentrated on what was commonly referred to as Revised Braille Grade 1½, a method of Braille taught to blind military personnel during World War I. These scriptures were sold throughout the country at prices well below cost thanks to ABS subsidies. In 1921, the Society experimented for the first time in its history with the publication of selected portions of scripture published in both New York Point and Revised Braille Grade 1½.[22]

In the 1930s the ABS partnered with the Library of Congress in the promotion of the "Talking Book." Phonographs and newly created reproducing machines, usually priced anywhere between thirty-five and sixty dollars, were used to play books recorded on special disks. The Four Gospels were published in 1934 by the American Foundation for the Blind. The Pratt-Smoot Act of 1931, which provided government funds to the Library of Congress to provide books for the blind, was amended to allow some of those funds to be used for talking books.[23] When the Library of Congress's Talking Book Service to the Blind was established with records that included the Gospels and the Psalms, the ABS described it as a "providential intervention." In 1938, with the help of the ABS, the Library of Congress had completed a sound recording of the entire New Testament and twelve books of the Old Testament on seventy-three separate disks, which were sold at twenty-five cents each. In 1944, one could to listen to the entire Bible on 169 disks in about eighty-four hours. The talking Bibles quickly outsold the traditional Braille Bibles. The response was so great that the ABS appointed its first full-time Secretary for the Blind.[24]

The two decades between the Great Wars brought mixed results to the work of the American Bible Society. The Society continued its distribution efforts to Indians, African Americans, immigrants, the poor, the blind, and the (largely) white middle class. It celebrated some important historical milestones in the life of the county, providing the Society with yet another chance to show the importance of the Bible to the democratic institutions of the United States. It also weathered the Great Depression and managed to balance its own financial needs with the spiritual needs of ordinary Americans suffering through the economic woes of the era.

In the midst of it all, the ABS decided to move out of the Bible House at Astor Place. The Board of Managers announced to the ABS constituency that the "grand old red-brick building had served its purposes." The magisterial Bible house that the ABS opened in 1853 was built as a manufacturing plant, but in 1935 it had been fourteen years (from 1922) since the ABS found that it was more profitable to have its books printed and bound by other, more modern, printing establishments. As a result, only about one-third of the structure was being used. The board also worried about the safety of the Astor Place Bible House. The ABS library of rare Bibles was growing, and many in the organization were afraid that the House was not fireproof. The new Bible House would be located at 450 Park Avenue, an uptown location where "the march of business" was moving. More importantly, in the midst of the Depression the Park Avenue Bible House was paid for completely through the sale of the Astor Place building. "Not one cent," the Managers wrote, "goes for its purchase from the funds given for the distribution of the Scriptures." The hope, of course, was that anyone who walked by this new building, located "at one of the prominent corners in the metropolis of the new world," would be reminded of the "need of the world today for the living Word of God."[25]

One of the speakers on the day in which the new Bible House was dedicated was President William Mather Lewis of Lafayette College. In his address titled "The Bible and Modern Problems" he decried the disastrous attempts to bring peace to the world through the "force" of politics. In a reference to the horror of World War I, he added, "we have tried international affairs and it has proved a ghastly failure." The only way to true peace, Lewis believed, was "to do justly, and to love mercy, and to walk humbly with thy God." This, indeed, was the primary way in which the message of the Bible might speak to the "problems" of the world.[26] Lewis was not a prophet, for another war was on the horizon—a war that made the so-called war to end all wars look tame by comparison. And if what Lewis said at the Bible House dedication about the true source of peace was correct, the ABS needed to be ready to face the greatest challenge of Bible distribution in its history.

16

Perfect Love Casteth Out Fear

At the time that Franklin Roosevelt delivered his State of the Union address in January 1941, the world was at war. Ten years earlier, the Japanese Army had seized control of Manchuria and withdrawn from the League of Nations. Adolf Hitler rose to power in Germany in 1933 and over the course of several years had remilitarized the Rhineland, annexed part of Czechoslovakia, rounded up and imprisoned Jews, invaded Poland, and bombed Great Britain. In 1935 Italy, under the leadership of Benito Mussolini, invaded Ethiopia. And in eleven months, the Japanese attack on Pearl Harbor would draw the United States into the conflict. Roosevelt's address before Congress is often referred to as his "Four Freedoms" speech. One of the freedoms he talked about was the "freedom from fear," which he believed could be accomplished through "a worldwide reduction of armaments to such a point and in such a thorough fashion that no nation will be in a position to commit an act of physical aggression against any neighbor—anywhere in the world."[1]

As Roosevelt pondered the potential of a world without fear, the American Bible Society was a bit more realistic about the war raging through Europe. "The world is sick with fear," stated the 1941 ABS *Annual Report*. Fear was the result of the epidemic-like spread of "ambition," "narrowness of loyalties," and "selfish desires" throughout the world. It plagued nations and "set countless thousands on the road to nowhere." Even in the United States, young men experienced fear as they prepared for the possibility of engaging in military conflict. In the midst of a world defined by fear, the ABS leadership turned to the familiar words of the Psalmist: "He sent his word, and healed them, and delivered them from their destructions." Driven by the healing promises of the scriptures, the ABS prepared itself for a worldwide distribution of the Bible. Indeed the world was full of fear, but the ABS would constantly remind its members that "perfect love casteth out fear."[2]

Since the ABS was one of the few Bible societies in the Western world that was untouched by war, General Secretary Eric North and his staff believed that it had a special responsibility to carry on the Bible Cause on behalf of its war-torn co-laborers in Europe. In 1940, the ABS Ways and Means Committee spearheaded a War Emergency Fund to meet the pressing needs for Bibles. The fund would exist outside of the ABS's regular budget and would rely heavily on contributions from churches and individual Americans. The goals of the fund were to aid Bible societies unable to do their work because of the war, provide scriptures to people suffering as a result of the conflict, and supply the US military with copies of the word of God. In order to accomplish the first and second goals, the ABS worked closely with the Ecumenical Commission for Chaplaincy Aid to War Prisoners under the leadership of Secretary Olivier Beguin in Geneva, Switzerland. The ABS eventually hired Beguin for the purpose of developing and coordinating its emergency work in Europe.[3]

Using its War Emergency Fund, the ABS tried to carry on the work of European Bible societies without interruption. For example, when the Netherlands Bible Society was unable to distribute scriptures to its Dutch colonies in the East Indies, the ABS picked up the load by sending money, printing paper, and gospel portions in the Javanese, Timorese, and T'ae languages. The ABS worked with the Ecumenical Office for Refugee Work and the YMCA to bring Bibles to Protestant churches in France. In October 1940, just as the devastating Battle of Britain was coming to an end, the BFBS asked the ABS to take over its work in the areas around the world where it was unable to operate. The ABS also provided the BFBS with money and printing supplies after much of its machinery was destroyed in the bombings. The Society supported the work of the BFBS in Poland, Italy, and Bulgaria. In its December 1940 Universal Bible Sunday literature, the ABS noted that it was indeed time that American Christians take "their rich heritage in the Bible, upon whose teachings the very foundation of our nation were laid," and share it in a "very positive, determined way with the family of nations."[4]

In the summer of 1940 North made a strong appeal to the American people to support the War Emergency Fund. His letter began with a sense of urgency that was apocalyptic in nature. North described a "staggering tornado of violent world war," the "disruption of human life," and the cries of "mothers of little children in lands far away" desperate for help. In the process he sought to reconcile the optimism of his Protestant liberalism with the destructive nature of war. "Are men destined to create civilizations," he asked, only to destroy them in a "whirlwind of hate and violence?" He wondered whether this, indeed, "was the last word for humanity." But North was also aware that the Bible could provide answers in times of despair. He encouraged the ABS faithful by reciting verses such as Psalm 24:1 ("the earth is the Lord's, and the fullness thereof; the world, and they that dwell therein"), John 14:16 ("I am the way, the truth, and the life, no man cometh unto the Father, but by me"), and John 16:33 ("in the world ye shall have tribulation; but be of good cheer, I have overcome the world"). North was to the Bible Cause during the war what Winston Churchill was to the English people—a constant source of optimism, encouragement, and inspiration.[5]

For North, God's work in these difficult times needed to be carried out through human effort. But how could such human effort be sustained when the ministry of most of the world's missionaries had been interrupted by war? North estimated that three-fourths of the world's Bible distribution came from the British, the Scottish, the Dutch, and the French. Many of these Bible societies were now unable to carry the load or had not been heard from since the war broke out. The only hope of "preventing this disaster," North concluded, "is an immediate, strong, and continued increase in the number and amount of the contributions our American people and churches make for this cause. There is no other way!" The War Emergency Fund brought Gospels and Testaments to over 5 million refugees in France, Belgium, the Netherlands, Spain, Czechoslovakia, Poland, Russia, Switzerland, Romania, and Hungary. This fund was also used to continue the work of the ABS and BFBS in India, China, Japan, Malaysia, Africa, and Latin America. North concluded his plea by urging ABS supporters to spread the word by writing for copies of a special War Emergency Fund leaflet, sharing copies of the *Bible Society Record* with friends and neighbors, taking special collections in church services, and sending the names of potential donors to the Park Avenue Bible House.[6]

In addition to direct appeals from the General Secretary, the ABS promoted the War Emergency Fund with the slogan "There Must Be No Blackout of the Bible." The slogan came from the common wartime practice, made popular during the Nazi Blitz of London in 1940, of reducing the glare of outdoor light in order to make it difficult for enemy bombers to see their targets. This motto was illustrated clearly on the cover of the September 1940 *Bible Society Record* through a picture of two forlorn-looking children placed over an image of a blacked-out cityscape. In October, Rome Betts, an ABS secretary and fundraiser who was tasked with traveling around the country to speak about the Society's response to the war effort, told supporters of the Bible Cause that they could prevent both literal and figurative blackouts, and the end of Western Civilization itself, by donating money that would enable the Bible to burst through the darkness with the light of Jesus Christ. Betts called for nothing short of a religious revival in wartime America. He urged people to read their Bibles, share the "light" of the Gospel with friends, and donate money to bring the Bible and its message to those living in overseas "missions lands." Though the "lights of Europe may be going out one by one," Betts was confident that Bible-loving Americans would keep them "burning steadily in our own hearts" and the "hearts of our fellow countrymen."[7]

American Protestants responded to the ABS's wartime needs. Donations were up, but a reading of *Annual Reports* and the *Bible Society Record* suggests that there was never enough money to meet the ever-growing need. ABS annuities, which the Society began calling Spiritual Defense Bonds, experienced unprecedented growth during the war years. In 1941 alone over one thousand new agreements were written, bringing over $850,000 into the ABS coffers. One annuitant made the direct connection between the purchase of war bonds and the purchase of ABS annuities: "A few days ago I bought a Defense bond—which is all right and what we Americans should do. But that was to buy guns and implements of war . . . Now I want to invest in a bond to buy Bibles, which, if they were used as freely as guns, there would be no need for the latter." He enclosed a check with his letter for $250.00.[8]

As war raged in Europe, the ABS and other supporters of the Bible Cause continued to bring the word of God to its stations in Asia. Such distribution, however, was becoming more difficult in imperial and expansionist Japan. In 1931–1932 Japanese troops invaded the Chinese province of Manchuria, followed by the initiation of a full-scale war with China in 1937. Japan's larger goal was to create a Greater East Asia Co-Prosperity Sphere, an empire that would include China, Southeast Asia, and much of the western Pacific Rim. The United States was not happy about Japan's imperial activities, especially since the State Department and the business community had grandiose plans for exporting American goods to China through its Open Door Policy. Since the Japanese invasion of China the United States had been boycotting Japanese silk and other products and had been outspoken opponents of Japanese aggression. After Japan signed the Tripartite Pact with Germany and Italy in September 1940, President Franklin Roosevelt stopped exporting steel and other metals to the island nation.

The ABS had been sending Bibles to Japan since 1861. In 1931, the year that the Japanese invaded Manchuria, the ABS distribution in the country had reached its height—69,292 Bibles and Testaments over a twelve-month period. In 1937, the nation's small Protestant community had formed the Japan Bible Society. Three years later the Japanese imperial government eliminated all foreign control of Christian churches.[9] It was in this context that the "Gospel blockade runner" made its way toward Japanese shores and provided for the ABS a sensational story of "international diplomacy, interdenominational fellowship, a shot fired across the bow, an air raid, a flood, and five tons of Bibles in a Bible-thirsty land."[10]

Carleton Lacy was a Methodist missionary in China until his denomination loaned him to the ABS in 1921 to serve as secretary of its China agency. One Sunday morning in late 1940 or early 1941, a friend of the Bible Cause approached Lacy after religious services somewhere in the United States and asked him how many Bibles he could send to Chekiang (Zhejiang), a south-eastern Chinese province located on the East China Sea. Lacy answered, "as many as there is any way to transport." He was aware that any Western shipment of Bibles to China via the Pacific needed to pass through a Japanese naval blockade. As a result, "it seemed almost a forlorn hope." When Lacy's friend asked him if the ABS could send up to three *tons* of Bibles, the agent thought his fellow churchman was playing a joke on him. But Lacy, ever enthusiastic about distributing the Bible where it was needed, took the question seriously. "Our stocks are pretty low, and freight rates are exorbitant," he answered, "but I surely would like to send in a good supply, and I think we could pack a ton or two in a couple of days." By the end of the week forty-four cases of Bibles were packed and ready to be loaded on a small trawler, the *Estelle L*, destined for the Oujiang River city of Wenchow (Wenzhou), Chekiang. The *Estelle L* had run the Japanese blockade of China several times in the past, carrying mostly gasoline, but the Japanese navy had recently stopped the ship and detained its crew for two weeks on a small island off the Chinese coast. The ship and its crew were eventually released after promising to stop blockade running in the future.

This trip, however, would be different. Western missionaries had successfully negotiated with both the Japanese Navy and Chinese government to allow ships to cross the blockade for humanitarian purposes. Ships carrying medical supplies for hospitals, food for benevolent workers, literature for churches, and other supplies necessary to keep mission stations opened and operating would be allowed to enter China without harassment. The *Estelle L* was chartered as one of these ships and the Japanese government promised the ABS safe passage through the blockade and a free landing in the port city of Wenchow. There were forty-one missionaries and relief workers on board the *Estelle L* from a variety of Christian traditions. There were Baptists, representatives of the China Inland Mission, Seventy-Day Adventists, Brethren, Roman Catholics, Methodists, and "one predestined Presbyterian." Lacy extolled the Society's commitment to ecumenical initiatives, claiming he, as an ABS Secretary, "more or less belong[ed] to them all." He joked that "Bible and blockade running seem to be the two points on which all denominations can and do get together."

As the *Estelle L* approached the mouth of the Oujiang River just before sunset, the crew saw the flashes of a Japanese warship blocking the way. The Chinese captain returned the signal, identifying that the vessel he was navigating was the American ship *Estelle L*, adding to the message that "clear passage has been promised." After it was allowed to pass and continue its journey into the mouth of the river, the crew was met with another flashing light, this time from a large Japanese destroyer. The captains of the boats conversed through megaphones until the *Estelle L* was once again allowed to proceed. Just as the boat filled with Bibles and missionaries was about the enter the river, a third Japanese ship flashed its light and the passengers of the *Estelle L* were awakened to a loud explosion that the crew quickly identified as a gun shot fired across its bow. The boat had not been hit, but Lacy and his peers were now frightened. Finally a Japanese officer approached the *Estelle L* and apologized: "Sorry I did not recognize you. Your safe passage has been arranged. Go ahead." The boat finally made it to Wenchow. The books were unloaded by Western missionaries and shipped to several neighboring Chinese provinces. Lacy claimed that they "sold like hot cakes."[11]

After the bombing of Pearl Harbor on December 7, 1941, and the US entrance into the war the following day, both the American military and the ABS began to mobilize. The Society was already sending millions of Bibles overseas to meet European needs, but it now had the additional responsibility of providing for America's own troops. Between 1940 and 1942 ABS distribution of Bibles increased by 42 percent (3,773,691 to 5,371,293). The large increase came with logistical headaches, especially in the first year of American involvement in the war. In New York, ABS General Secretary Frederick Copp requested leave to enter the service as an Army chaplain in 1942, creating a vacuum of leadership at the Bible House that was filled by three different people between the time of his departure and his return in late 1945. War-related postal delays made sending Bibles to the ABS's wartime distribution partners difficult. Chaplains in the war zone often did not receive ABS boxes because of restrictions on the number of packages that could be sent out of the United States to any one addressee per week. The ABS staff had constant meetings with organizations in need of wartime Bibles, including the American Merchant Marine Library Association, the Merchant Marine Training Schools, the National Association of Seamen's Welfare, and the American Seamen's Friend Society.[12]

The ABS worked closely with military chaplains, both at home and abroad. Though it was not always easy to obtain correct lists of chaplain assignments from the General Commission on Army and Navy Chaplains, the ABS was able to reach these war-time ministers during their training sessions through a promotional campaign that included posters, leaflets, and other forms of advertising. The Society established an arrangement with the Army Chaplains School at Harvard University and the Navy Chaplains School at Norfolk that allowed them to distribute packets of information about ABS Bible distribution at monthly graduation ceremonies. These packets included an ABS Testament, a copy of a poster that read "Ask Your Chaplain for a New Testament," a circular letter from General Secretary North addressed to the graduates, and a host of other miscellaneous leaflets and folders.[13]

The ABS quickly learned that it was cheaper and faster to publish Bibles in the United States and ship them overseas than it was to subsidize the printing of Bibles in Europe. The Bible House on Park Avenue became the worldwide center of Bible distribution during the war, with shipping and publishing costs amounting to over $350,000. The process of making so many Bibles had its own difficulties. In 1942 the ABS estimated that about 30 percent of the workers in the printing and binding industries had entered the armed forces and an additional 30 percent had gone to work for war-related industries. Paper from India was very difficult to obtain, forcing the ABS to conserve by publishing Bibles that were smaller in size and printed on lightweight and thinner bond. In 1943 alone, the ABS used over 900,000 pounds of paper to produce 1.2 million Bibles: a monumental achievement. Though the threat of German submarines was also a concern in shipping across the Atlantic, the ABS was proud to announce that not a single delivery of Bibles was lost to enemy action during 1943.[14]

Bible distribution to navy chaplains, and eventually seamen, always faced the risk that scriptures would become wet and thus unreadable. In 1943, the Society solved this problem by issuing Bibles in waterproof containers and envelopes for use on lifeboats, rafts, and planes. The ABS did not advertise this service until they learned, from a 1943 article in *Life* magazine, of the rescue of Eddie Rickenbacker. An American fighter ace during World War I with twenty-six aerial victories to his credit, Rickenbacker was a national celebrity and a prominent businessman (he owned Indianapolis Motor Speedway and ran Eastern Airlines) when World War II began. As a civilian supporter of the war, the fifty-two-year-old veteran made several tours to Europe and the Pacific to speak to the troops. During one of those trips Rickenbacker's plane strayed off course and began to malfunction, forcing the seven men on board to crash-land somewhere in a remote part of the South Pacific.

Rickenbacker and some members of the crew survived on two life rafts for twenty-one days before they were eventually rescued. They spent the days fishing (using a seagull that they captured for bait), talking of home, and burning in the hot Pacific sun. One of the crew members, a twenty-two-year-old Army Air Force pilot from Freehold, New Jersey named Johnny Bartek, had an ABS khaki-covered pocket New Testament. Another member of the crew, James Whitaker, would describe the Testament in his published account of the ordeal as having a "zipper arrangement that made it waterproof" and saved the book from the waves of the ocean slopping into the rafts. During their three weeks at sea the men, none of whom were particularly religious, held twice-daily prayer meetings and read from Bartek's Testament. Their favorite verses were Matthew 6:31–32: "Therefore take no thought saying, 'What shall eat?' Or 'What shall we drink?' Or 'Wherewithall shall we be clothed'; for your heavenly Father knoweth that ye have need of all these things; But seek ye first the kingdom of God, and his righteousness, and all these things shall be added unto you." Fortunately, from the ABS point of view at least, the page that contained this pertinent New Testament verse was dry and readable.[15]

Since its founding the ABS linked the message of the Christian scriptures with American democracy and patriotism, but World War II provided yet another opportunity for the Board of Managers and Bible House staff to make these connections. The 1941 Universal Bible Sunday, a day in which churches around the country devoted their services to the importance of the Bible in American life, happened to fall on December 8, the day following the Japanese attack on Pearl Harbor. As panic struck the country, and especially the West coast, the Don Lee Radio Network ran a special Universal Bible Sunday sermon from Karl Morgan Block, the Episcopal Bishop of California. The sermon was later published in the pages of the *Bible Society Record*. Block was aware of the gravity of this particular day. He noted "how fortuitous it was that the Sunday following the surprise attack of Japan that plunged us into this war has been dedicated to a recognition of the primary of the Holy Scriptures—Universal Bible Sunday." After all, Block added, "the Bible has been and must ever be the spiritual arsenal of our democracy." The scriptures would now be needed to undergird those "moral incentives that make a nation virile, brave, and secure." Block continued:

> The founding fathers of our republic discovered in the Good Book the ideals that gave birth to our nation. They conceived of democracy as the political expression of a central Christian affirmation—the dignity and eternal worth of the human soul. Upon this sovereign truth, they built our essential freedoms … We can trace in this Book of Books the ideas and ideals that undergird our democratic way of life. Behind this democratic process is the Jewish-Christian tradition. It has been given us as a sacred trust—a legacy we are now called upon to defend against the brutal ideologies of dictatorships. We have learned with travail of soul that the democratic privileges we enjoy are not socially inherited, and that eternal vigilance must ever be the price of liberty.[16]

For Block this would not only be a war for political freedom, but it was also, in essence, a holy war.

This kind of rhetoric filled the pages of ABS publications during the war. The 1945 *Annual Report* extolled the belief that "God is the 'Author of Liberty.' " If this war was about freedom, Americans needed to know that God had implanted such freedom in "man's breast" as a means of resisting the "chains of tyranny, of lying propaganda, [and] of fear." References to the

United States' founding fathers were prevalent in this literature, including a reminder that "our forefathers turned to the Bible (Leviticus 25:10) for the inscription on the Liberty Bell, 'Proclaim liberty throughout the land unto all the inhabitants thereof.'" The ABS provided supporters with accounts of German Protestants who used the teachings of the Bible to overthrow Hitler. They were also told that it was the biblical doctrine of sin that best explained the actions of the Axis Powers. The ABS was on a mission—to defeat tyranny and Christianize the West by "putting the Book that U.S. Grant called 'the sheet anchor of our liberties' into the hands of all the eager, struggling, needy people of the world."[17]

As had been the case with every American war in which the ABS supplied Bibles, the Board of Managers and staff were always eager to share stories about how the Bible was being used among the troops. In February 1942, the Society republished several reports from *Time* magazine written by popular correspondent Melville Jacoby, who was stationed with the troops in the Philippines during the Battle of Bataan. Jacoby described soldiers turning to God in the midst of the fighting. "More than one soldier," he wrote, "hearing bombs landing nearby . . . or having a bullet nick his helmet, admitted that he never believed in God before." Chaplains in Bataan noted a growing number of conversions. It was not unusual, they added, to see "a soldier sitting by a machine gun reading a Bible." Soldiers wrote short notes to their chaplain asking for copies of the Bible and at least 2,000 Testaments were distributed during Douglas MacArthur's occupation of the Philippine peninsula. Chaplains showed unusual courage in meeting the spiritual needs of soldiers at this intense battle by holding services in the jungles behind the battle lines and occasionally rushing to the front carrying Bibles as they waved their fist at the "Nip-fliers" dropping bombs above them.[18]

Though the ABS was the first to mobilize on behalf of the Bible Cause, the War Department also got involved in the scripture distribution business. In early 1942 Congress appropriated funds to provide over 1.2 million New Testaments for enlisted men. Over half of these Testaments were printed in the King James Version for the use of Protestant soldiers, but 450,000 "Selected Readings from the New Testaments" were published for Roman Catholic soldiers and 100,000 Old Testament selections for Jewish soldiers. When it learned about this initiative, the ABS offered to serve as the primary supplier of these texts, but their bid appears to have been turned down in favor of a government printer. It was agreed, however, that the text and spelling used in these special government editions of the Bible would be based on one of the Society's editions. All of these special editions were distributed to soldiers at the time of their enlistment in the army. The ABS did not seem to be bothered by the government's participation in Bible distribution, but did remind its readers that the Society was still the sole supplier of Bibles for the Navy and the Marine Corps.[19]

Much of the work of the ABS during World War II took place with soldiers in prison camps. In this regard, they worked closely with M. Olivier Beguin and the Ecumenical Commission for Chaplaincy. The Ecumenical Commission partnered with the International Red Cross, the YMCA, and the German Evangelical Aid Society for War Prisoners to obtain lists of European prison camps and then sent circular letters to the camps calling attention to the willingness of the Commission to provide Bibles for the prisoners. By March 1942 Beguin had identified 125 such camps. Since there was no guarantee that prison officials would distribute Bibles to their prisoners, the Commission only brought Bibles to camps that specifically requested them. In order to make the work efficient and orderly, prisoners who received a book were asked to fill out a card acknowledging the receipt of their package and send it back to the Commission headquarters in Geneva, Switzerland. In one instance, the ABS, through the efforts of Beguin and the Commission, provided 4,000 English Testaments to prisoners at Stalag VIII-B, a German prisoner of war camp near the town of Lamsdorf.[20]

Beguin's Geneva office was inundated with calls for Bibles, making the Swiss city the second most important Bible distribution center in the world during the war. He wrote letters to the ABS that included long lists of countries with prison camps in need Bibles. In 1944, for example, he sent 2,000 German Bibles to Christian missionaries working in Alsace, over 18,000 Italian Bibles and Testaments to Rome in the wake of the Allied invasion of Italy, and Polish, Serbian, and Czech Bibles to "evangelists" working with prisoners in these countries. The shortage of Bibles among the German prisoner camps was so great that Beguin's agents had to rummage through bookstores in order to "gather up even a few." In the immediate wake of the Allied invasion of Normandy in June 1944, Beguin fielded a "hurried call for Scriptures" from the Chaplain of the US Forces in Britain who needed Bibles for German prisoners captured in the battle. Five hundred Bibles, 5,000 Testaments, and 15,000 Gospel portions were on their way. A similar call for Bibles came from French prisoners in North Africa. Beguin was pleased to report that in many of these prison camps active Christian communities had emerged, providing "a spiritual home for church members" and exerting "a wholesome influence upon the camp as a whole."[21]

As the American Bible Society distributed Bibles throughout Europe during the war, it also continued its work at home. Many of the ABS home agencies worked hard at initiating and sustaining the kind of Bible-reading "revival" that Rome Betts had written about in September 1940. The renewed emphasis in bringing the word of God to the people of the United States was not unlike previous wars in which the ABS had urged Americans to live lives of virtue for the purpose of invoking God's favor on its political and military agenda. In May 1942, the Society rejoiced in the "growing interest in and hunger for God's word, which, in times like these, are found almost universally where the Bible is known." In Philadelphia, a ten-year-old girl bought ten dollars' worth of Bibles in memory of her brother who was killed at Pearl Harbor. A nurse found comfort from the Book of James while working in a crowded army hospital.[22]

The letters and testimonials poured into the Bible House in New York. A pastor in Tampa, Florida, reported unprecedented growth in his congregation since the Southern District began an intensive campaign of Bible distribution in the city. A radio revival in Dallas led to the sale of 54,000 scriptures. Representatives from the Rocky Mountain District traveled through the mining towns near the Grand Canyon and sold all of their stock to people who had never before seen a Bible salesman. In Alaska, the Pacific District was hard at work bringing Bibles to Indians, Eskimos, prospectors, fishermen, and airmen in the hopes of spreading the Gospel and "the American tradition." The Haven Memorial Agency Among the Colored People of the United States—now with four offices located in Atlanta, Charlotte, Cleveland, and Dallas—used Louisiana high school students to conduct surveys in order to be meet the needs of the destitute. And over 6,000 Bibles had been distributed among the blind in the form of embossed volumes and talking-book records.[23]

The ABS also met the needs of the more than 100,000 Japanese Americans who were relocated to internment camps throughout the American west. As was fitting with their policy to avoid commentary on political matters, the ABS did not make any formal statements about Franklin D. Roosevelt's Executive Order 9066, the decree that led to the deportation and incarceration of Japanese Americans. But a May 1943 article in the *Bible Society Record* written by Henry Ragatz, the agent of the ABS Rocky Mountain District, was hardly neutral in its coverage of Japanese internment. Ragatz believed that "Christian democracy" in the United States was facing a "severe test in the manner in which we handle the relocated." He wondered how a Christian nation could uproot tens of thousands of American citizens who were not guilty of any crimes. Ragatz decried the practice of dividing families during the process of relocation and complained about the primitive living conditions that the Japanese were forced to endure.[24]

After visiting the Amache relocation center in Granada, Colorado, and meeting with many detained Japanese Protestants, Ragatz pleaded with the ABS constituency to do what they could to help their "fellow Americans" and "brothers in Christ." Though the government had failed in its duty to handle the Japanese population in the West in a Christian manner, ABS volunteers, armed with hundreds of Bibles, could be a conduit of God's love to make life tolerable for these prisoners. A Japanese pastor at the Rivers, Arizona, relocation center wrote to the ABS with gratitude for providing his people with the "knowledge that Christian love is alive." The work of Bible distribution in the internment camps was a clear sign to Japanese children that not all Americans were supportive of the confinement of citizens in "concentration camps." Ragatz concluded that it was the Bible, not the race-based policies of the federal government, which truly "binds freedom-loving men together." Indeed, "Christian democracy is on the march" and the ABS was "lighting the path."[25]

As World War II drew to a close, the ABS leadership stopped to reflect on both the tragedy of the war and the opportunity the conflict provided for the Bible Cause in the world. The Society believed that the Bible was "put to the test" during the war. Would the promises of God's word meet the spiritual needs of people in a time of trouble? The answer, as might be expected, was "an aggressive yes." Hundreds of thousands of soldiers turned to the Bible before entering the fight or read scripture passages in foxholes and prisoner of war camps. The ABS was convinced that the Bible had helped Americans, and the rest of the world, "get through the war morally and spiritually whole." It had delivered "comfort and salvation."[26] But the work was not done. It was now time to use the Bible "as a mighty tool to create a better world order." The ABS plans for reconstructing Europe and the world in wake of this devastating conflict was just as ambitious as its plans for the Bible Cause in the war itself.

Bibles, Not Bombs

World War II came to an end in 1945, but the US involvement in world affairs was only beginning. The German surrender to the Allies in May, followed by the Japanese surrender three months later, brought a close to the deadliest war in human history. Fourteen million soldiers had lost their lives in the war, including 300,000 Americans. Another 25 million civilians had died. Much of Asia and Europe was left ruins. The United States came out of the war as the strongest nation in the world. The age of isolationism was over. A major shift in the global balance of power had taken place, as the United States would spend the next fifty years in a worldwide struggle to contain the Soviet Union and stop the spread of communism. Ever aware of these changes at home and abroad, the American Bible Society would do its part to bring spiritual relief to foreign nations and serve the needs of democracy abroad with a healthy dose of Biblical truth.

The ABS response to the postwar world mirrored the larger efforts of the US government. President Harry Truman devoted 12 percent of the federal budget ($17,000,000) to help the hungry and homeless in Europe through the Marshall Plan, while the ABS used a significant portion of its own resources to carry out a spiritual recovery plan through the distribution of Bibles. As the United States began to build international organizations such as the United Nations and the North Atlantic Treaty Organization (NATO) to stem the communist tide in Europe and promote world peace, the ABS, as we will see in subsequent chapters, worked closely with new international religious communities such as the World Council of Churches and the United Bible Societies to accomplish the same purposes. When Truman began to authorize massive defense spending resulting in what his successor Dwight Eisenhower would call the "Military Industrial Complex," ABS spending on Bible publication and distribution reached all-time highs. The ABS described its postwar efforts as "beyond any challenge it had ever faced in 130 years of service."[1] Whether it was the imposing power of aircraft carriers and missiles or the number of boxes of scriptures shipped, both the cold warriors in Washington, DC, and the defenders of the Bible Cause in New York measured success in the decades following World War II in terms of tonnage.

Truman, the nation's most famous Baptist, believed that Christianity was essential to the defeat of communism and the creation of a new world order based upon democracy and biblical morality. Sometimes the president sounded as if his road to the White House passed through the Bible House. For example, in 1947 he told Pope Pius XII that "I seek to encourage renewed faith in the dignity and worth of the human person in all lands, to the end that the individual's sacred rights, inherent in his relationship to God and his fellows, will be respected in every land." While such a statement, with its references to Catholic social teaching about the dignity of the human person, might be expected from any president when corresponding with a pope, Truman's words were not out of the ordinary. He truly believed that religion would play a significant role in the United States winning the Cold War. During his 1948 State of the Union Address, Truman reminded Americans that "the basic source of our strength is spiritual. For we are a people of faith. We believe in the dignity of man. We believe that he was created in the image of the Father of us all." He couched his foreign policy in providential terms: America was on a mission from God to spread its Judeo-Christian heritage abroad.[2] Though he would not work directly with the ABS until after he left office, the staff of the Bible House were confident that they were laboring side by side with Truman in the promotion of a Bible-centered postwar plan for peace.

The ABS's commitment to postwar peace and social reform also reflected its close relationship with ecumenical Protestantism. The Federal Council of Churches (FCC), the organization most responsible for promoting peace through Christian unity and social action, was a strong advocate for a post-war world defined by both democracy and Protestant Christianity. As World War II came to a close, nearly every major Protestant denomination in the United States, most of which were connected to the FCC, issued futuristic statements about the peacemaking role it would play in this so-called new world order. Most of these denominational plans supported the creation of the United Nations as a global peacekeeping force. The ABS proclamations about the nature of the postwar world were always generic in nature, focused more on the Bible's role in bringing order and peace than on the endorsement of a specific plan or organization. But like most mainline Protestants, the ABS approach was more akin to the vision of the FCC than those of the more con-servative, evangelical, or fundamentalist fellowships of churches such as the National Association of Evangelicals or the American Council of Christian Churches, organizations that were skeptical of FCC talk about a "one world-wide church" or the ecumenical movement's decision to focus more on social justice than evangelism. It was the mainline Protestants of the FCC, not the evangelicals and fundamentalists hidden away in their subcultural enclaves, who were shaping the national conversation about the relationship between Christianity and the future of the United States at home and abroad. And the ABS wanted to make sure that these Protestants had Bibles.

The ABS sought to bring a spiritual dimension to the postwar world. Its leadership prayed that God would bring a long season of peace in the world, but they were also aware that the encroaching nature of Soviet communism might make such peace difficult. Always optimistic about what God and their massive Bible distribution system could do, the Board of Managers held out hope that peace on earth and goodwill toward men was actually possible. A true "lasting peace," the *Bible Society Record* affirmed in February 1945, must be "founded upon moral law and Christian principles." If leaders neglected the teachings of the Bible in postwar planning, the entire process of reconstructing the free world would fall prey to the kinds of "fears" and "suspicions" that might return the world to war. The Bible was a "great international tool" that must be applied to our "moral, social, economic, political, and religious living." For the ABS, there was a certain eschatological flavor to all of this. If everyone—from international political leaders to ordinary people—would "practice the Bible," then the "ever-new Word would begin a redemptive process which could not end until the new heaven and the new earth became a reality among men."[3] High hopes indeed.

Two months after the Germans surrendered, the ABS rejoiced in the Allied victory but also sent a clear message to its membership about the need for dutiful contributions to a peaceful reconstruction of the world. The Society reiterated its longstanding belief that the biblical ideas of justice, righteousness, mercy, and love were "God's requirements for national morality and international peace." As the United States displayed its good will to the world it also needed to make sure that it was not permitting "conditions to exist anywhere that leaves masses of men so shut off from decent human rights, so enveloped in false propaganda, [and] so out of the fellowship of humanity that they either think of themselves a superior class or race, or feel so oppressed that they hate their fellow men." This kind of good will was "no Pollyanna emotion." The hatred that led to tyranny needed to be "eradicated." The American response to communism should be rooted in the Christian virtue of love, but such love, the ABS believed, was always "firm with the evildoer." This blend of good will and resistance to tyranny must define "national policy" in a time like this, but Americans would also need to remember that "national policy can only be the expression of national character, and national character is the sum of us all."[4] In the two decades following the end of the war, the ABS carried out this vision all over Europe, but most prominently in Germany and Russia.

When Adolf Hitler committed suicide in a Berlin military bunker on April 30, 1945, Germany was a wasteland occupied by American, British, French, and Soviet troops. Allied bombing campaigns in the last two years of the war eviscerated many once proud German cities such as Hamburg, Cologne, Dusseldorf, and Dresden. Civilians suffered the brunt of this assault. At the end of the war 20 million Germans were homeless. Transportation and communication networks had been destroyed. The German population was dealing with the psychological effects of losing about 4 million soldiers (one out of every fifteen people living in the country) during the war. Families were broken up by death and tens of thousands of children were orphaned. The occupation of the Soviet Red Army in eastern Germany came with much violence and rape. Food was scarce. In the American zone of German occupation, the daily ration for average citizens was under 900 calories a day. Thousands died of sickness and malnutrition. In 1945, in the British zone of occupation, one in four children died due to typhoid or diphtheria. In Berlin it was not unusual to find rotting corpses in the streets. There is little doubt that the devastation—in terms of life and property—led to a lot of spiritual searching in Germany, and the ABS and its European partners were ready to meet the need. The Society was confident that "no other place than America and no other people than Americans can provide the Book which the German churches, as the most hopeful constructive forces in Germany, can use to the greatest advantage at this time."[5]

The ABS believed that the opportunities for rebuilding Germany into a Christian nation again, at least in the zones occupied by the United States, France, and Great Britain, were "boundless." Indeed, most of the money the ABS raised through its War Emergency Fund went to support Bibles and Bible production in Germany. Olivier Beguin, the ABS's agent in Geneva, Switzerland who was active in the distribution of scriptures to prison camps during the war, described the need for Bibles in Germany as "colossal." The Nazi regime had discouraged the printing of Bibles. Newly married couples were no longer presented with a copy of the Bible, but with a copy of Hitler's *Mein Kampf*. Bibles were confiscated by Nazi officials during home raids for the purpose of gathering raw material for paper mills. Many German universities were unable to provide Bibles to theology students returning to classes in the summer of 1945. Following the war, ABS distribution efforts in Germany switched from soldiers and prisoners to civilians. Beguin estimated that 1.2 million German Protestants were without Bibles in 1946. The hunger for the word of God was evident. One Munich woman returned four times to a make-shift Bible distribution center, traveling fifteen miles on foot per visit.[6]

Between July 1945 and the end of 1947 the ABS had shipped over 2.2 million Bibles to Germany. Four million more were scheduled to be sent in 1948.

These Bibles were distributed free of charge to those suffering from war-related poverty and homelessness. They were also vended to bookstores and Bible societies who, in turn, would sell them at cost. The ABS aided German Bible societies and the evangelical churches (Protestant) by shipping hundreds of tons of cellulose, paper, machinery, and other raw materials for book publishing and binding. A representative of the evangelical churches informed the ABS that if it was too difficult to bring binding board, cloth, and thread (all were very bulky to ship) into the American and British occupied zones, it might be possible to make this material in Germany, assuming that the ABS could pay for ten tons of raw cotton, two tons of potato flour "for dressing," nine tons of board glue, nine tons of starch paste, hog bristles for brushes and 180 tons of used paper for "book binding pasteboards." The work in Germany was a massive undertaking of Christian philanthropy.[7]

Bibles were important in postwar Germany not only because the country was devastated by war and Protestants needed to replace Bibles that had been lost or destroyed, but the message of the Bible was an antidote to the lingering effects of Nazi Fascism. The ABS needed to reach people who "had previously been turned away from the message of the Bible . . . through Nazi propaganda." In Bavaria, Beguin gave special consideration to Bible requests from civilians who were Nazi sympathizers, "as this is the only way to lead them to a new conception of life." This also applied to Hitler's former ground troops, many of whom had been arrested and were incarcerated awaiting either trial or punishment. The ABS hoped that the long days and nights in prison might lead these former members of the Gestapo and Hitler's Secret Service to contemplate the state of their souls. A chaplain in the British zone thanked the ABS for providing Bibles, adding that he was ministering to these prisoners and praying that as they searched the word of God they might "find the way to our Lord and Savior." He shared testimonies of death-row conversions, including one Gestapo man who exchanged his "fanatical hate" for Christian love.[8]

During the 1950s, as the boundary between West Germany and East Germany became one of the many locations observers used to measure the political temperature of the Cold War, the ABS worked with East German Bible Societies in the hopes of reaching the communist country with God's word. Though the East German government refused to allow Bibles to pass across its borders, in the early 1950s it did begin to allow paper to come into the country that could, in turn, be used to manufacture Bibles. The ABS, in conjunction with the BFBS and the newly formed United Bible Societies (see chapter 20), established Bibelwerk, a small missionary agency created to meet the spiritual needs of East Germany. The sponsoring organizations paid for the salaries of two missionary-educators, provided them with cars, and commissioned them to provide Bibles for anyone on the other side of Germany's iron curtain who was in need. In addition to the traditional work of distribution, the Bibelwerk missionaries were required to "engage the church people in reading the Scriptures." The goal was to get people to know the Bible well enough to use its message as a source for revitalizing East German Protestantism and resisting persecution from the communist government. The ABS also prided itself in working with German Protestants to bring Bibles to refugees fleeing East German communism. All of this changed, however, with the construction of the Berlin Wall in 1961. For the next thirty years the ABS's work in Germany, which was mostly conducted under the auspices of the United Bible Societies, was conducted only in West Germany.[9]

In the late 1940s the ABS was very optimistic about the possibility of bringing the Bible to Russia, the larger Soviet Union, and the communist countries of Eastern Europe. A 1946 article in the *Bible Society Record* noted that "many fervent prayers have been offered that Russia in her postwar recovery might return to the Bible." The Russian Bible Society and the ABS were both founded in the second decade of the nineteenth century and had a long history of working together on behalf of the Bible Cause. But all of that changed after the Russian Revolution of 1917 when the new Soviet government closed the Russian Bible Society. If there was ever going to be a renewal of Bible distribution in Russia, the ABS believed that now was the time. The devastation brought to Russia by Hitler's invasion in 1940–1941, and the spiritual yearning among the Soviet people that the supporters of the Bible Cause hoped would follow in the wake of the bloodshed, might provide opportunities to bring the word of God to the Soviet people.[10]

In October 1945, the ABS Board of Managers met in New York with Alexei Sergeyev, the Russian Orthodox Archbishop of Yaroslavl and Rostove, during his tour of Orthodox Churches in the United States. General Secretary Eric North expressed the Society's interest in distributing Russian-language Bibles in the Soviet Union until the Russian Bible Society could once again resume operations. He reminded the Archbishop about the work the ABS had done in meeting the spiritual needs of Russian prisoners in Germany during the war and its capacity to produce large quantities of Russian-language Bibles. The conversations between Sergeyev and North resulted in a willingness on the part of the Soviet government to allow the ABS to send over 100,000 scriptures to Russian theological students and priests. But North warned the ABS constituency not to get too excited about this small triumph. One shipment of Bibles did not mean that "the door to Russia is now open." Over the next several years, ABS attempts to send Bibles to Russia were denied by Soviet officials. This included a 1948 Christmas donation of over 100,000 scriptures targeted for twenty different Russian seminaries. Until the doors to the Soviet Union were open, the ABS would wait patiently for another opportunity.

In anticipation of that day, North decided to increase the ABS stock of Russian-language Bibles so that it could act quickly whenever a telegram or phone call from the Orthodox Church arrived in New York requesting copies of the word of God. "We believe that no one is better prepared to enter Russia, as soon as the way is opened," North boasted, "than is the American Bible Society."[11]

As the ABS waited, Protestant fundamentalists responded to the Bible needs of Soviet Christians with a much greater sense of urgency. One of those fundamentalists was Carl McIntire, the crusading anticommunist Presbyterian preacher and founder of the American Council of Christian Churches, a small fellowship of denominations staunchly opposed to the theological liberalism, mainline Protestantism, and the ecumenical movement. In 1953 McIntire, along with the equally antiecumenical and anticommunist fundamentalist Billy James Hargis, developed a plan to use helium-filled balloons to airlift Russian-language Bibles into the Eastern European Soviet Bloc countries. When ABS General Secretary Robert Taylor saw McIntire promoting his balloon scheme on a late-evening television program sponsored by National City Bank, a New York bank that had provided lines of credit to the Society for several of its postwar distribution efforts, he wrote to his friends at the bank to warn them about McIntire and chide them for letting his "prepared publicity gag" appear on a news show that they had sponsored. Didn't the bank realize that McIntire "represents a small militant group" and was a "bitter enemy of the National Council of Churches which represented the great majority of American Protestants?" McIntire was also known, Taylor added, for his "scurrilous attacks" on what was presumably the ecumenical and mainline Protestant leanings of the ABS, particularly as it related to the ABS decision to sell the Revised Standard Version of the Bible (a story we will pick up later). The ABS represented mainstream American Christianity. McIntire was on the fringe.[12]

Taylor was especially worried because he believed that McIntire's plan had the potential of jeopardizing "Bible distribution now in progress" in the Soviet bloc. Protestants were working quietly to bring the Bible to Eastern Europe and it was essential that their work remain secret. If Bibles suddenly started dropping from the sky it might awaken the communist governments in these countries and perhaps prompt them to crack down on some of the underground distribution work that was already happening. On August 31, five days before McIntire and Hargis were scheduled to launch their Bible balloons across the Czechoslovakian border, Taylor, on behalf of the ABS, sent a telegram to President Dwight D. Eisenhower and John Foster Dulles, the secretary of state and a Presbyterian layperson, expressing his disapproval of the plan. He also relayed the disapproval of "Christians behind the Iron Curtain." The World Council of Churches also appealed to Washington, DC, to stop McIntire. If Dulles and Eisenhower responded to these complaints, we do not have the letters. But we do know that the anti-McIntire faction, at least at the outset, was successful. When Taylor's telegram arrived, the State Department had already decided to refuse McIntire permission to float his Bible balloons. What happened in the days that followed is unclear, but sometime in the first few days of September Eisenhower overruled Dulles. The Department of State eventually informed Taylor that "the US Government heartily and consistently welcomes the widest distribution of biblical and religious ideas and texts to people deprived of religious freedom." Though Eisenhower refused to official endorse McIntire's plan, he did conclude that the US government "considers the International Council of Churches project to send Bibles into Czechoslovakia via balloon from Western Germany a laudable private undertaking of the type not requiring specific US Government authorization." On September 4 McIntire sent thousands of balloons over the Iron Curtain with the unofficial blessing of the president of the United States. Taylor must have been furious.[13]

The ABS kept a close eye on religious developments (or lack thereof) in the Soviet Union. In the early 1960s, Taylor was concerned with a report that he mostly likely read in *Index Translationum*, the book translation database of the United Nations Scientific and Cultural Organization (UNESCO), that the Bible had lost its place as the world's most translated and published book. That distinction, the report noted, now belonged to the writings of Soviet leader Nikita Khrushchev and revolutionary Vladimir Lenin. In an ABS press released picked up by newspapers and magazines across the country through United Press International (UPI), the Society reported that the Soviet Union was in the midst of a "major governmental program for world distribution of anti-Christ propaganda." Taylor had learned that the USSR was spending $340 million to expand its printing and publishing activities. He was especially concerned about the widely circulated and translated "Textbook of Scientific Atheism" published by the Soviet Union to "give propagandists ready information on the best ways of criticizing religion-based morals and eradicating religious beliefs and superstitions wherever they exist."[14] Taylor was reacting to one of the strongest antireligion campaigns in the history of the Soviet Union. From 1958 to 1964 Khrushchev and the Soviet government sought to undermine the power of the Russian Orthodox Church by closing many of its churches, seminaries, monasteries, and convents and passing legislation that weakened its financial position. Though few in the West noticed this campaign, probably due to their desire to see Khrushchev as a political reformer, Taylor and the ABS could not miss it.[15]

In an article in the March 1962 *Bible Society Record*, Taylor claimed that the Soviets had distributed 100 million volumes of Khrushchev's and Lenin's writings in noncommunist countries around the world. What disturbed him most about this statistic was the fact that the ABS and its global partners in the United Bible Societies had only distributed, based on liberal estimates, about 55 million copies of the Bible. Taylor took these findings very seriously, but he also saw the report's publication as a wonderful opportunity to awaken potential ABS donors who feared the spread of godless communism. He called upon Protestant churches and denominations to "undergird the American Bible Society in its endeavor to distribute the Scriptures in every nation now being flooded with the red tide of Communist propaganda." Only the "the sword of the Spirit, which is the Word of God" had the power of defeating the "false ideologies" that the Soviets were spreading.[16]

Taylor believed that this new Soviet antireligious publication and distribution program should be of "grave concern" to American Christians. It was the first major government program devoted to the promotion and distribution of atheistic literature around the world. He lamented that the Soviets were doing a better job distributing antireligious propaganda than the Christian West was doing in defending the central tenets of the Christian faith. If anyone was aware of how effective a campaign to sell books at low prices could be, it was the general secretary of the American Bible Society. Taylor thus described the Soviet dissemination program as an "ironic tribute to the wisdom and efficiency of the methods used by the Bible Societies for generations in selling books in undeveloped lands at prices they could afford to pay." He had already received reports that a "well-printed" 272-page volume of Lenin's writings was selling in Beijing for three cents. The Soviet Union seemed to have unlimited resources at its disposal for the spread of anti-Christian propaganda while the American Bible Society had to "plead for adequate funds in order that millions of people may find in the Gospel the answer to their deepest needs." In order to counter the writings of Khrushchev and Lenin in the marketplace of ideas, Taylor announced the creation of a Cold War Emergency Fund (the natural successor to the War Emergency Fund) with the hopes of raising 2 million dollars to fight communism with the word of God.[17]

Another way that Taylor and the ABS responded to growing communist threat was through the creation of the Bible-a-Month Club. In order to compete with the supposed influx of Marxist literature around the world, employees of the ABS were encouraged to pledge two dollars a month, above and beyond their regular giving to the Society. The program was quickly extended to the entire ABS membership. For twenty-five dollars a year the ABS would send a gift Bible somewhere around the world on behalf of the person making the donation. Each month a different nation or region was featured. In the early years, the Bible-a-Month Club focused predominantly on Congo, India, Brazil, Korea, East Asia, Indonesia, the Philippines, Eastern Europe, and "Spanish America"—all areas where communism posed a legitimate danger to Western values. In India, the ABS sought to help Christians along the border with Red China, a region where Western missionaries had been driven out by communists. In May 1962, the money collected from the club was used to send nearly 800,000 volumes to Hong Kong in the hopes that these Bibles would eventually find their way through the bamboo curtain to Christians in Red China. The November and December contribution went toward funding the ABS's Worldwide Christmas Reading program and "special populations" (including immigrants and the impoverished) in the English-speaking world. Within a year, the Bible-a-Month Club had over 10,000 members.[18]

Fully aware that most of its donations came from women, the ABS turned to female executives of Protestant denominations to get behind the Bible-a-Month club and promote it among their congregations. A group of women leaders from twelve different denominations was convened in the spring of 1962 by Ruth Peale, the wife of the "power of positive thinking" guru Norman Vincent Peale, to discuss the best way of bringing the Bible-a-Month Club to their constituencies. These women may have had the spiritual interests of their denominations in mind when they arrived at the Bible House for this meeting, but they were also Cold Warriors. They discussed the essential role that the Bible must play in the "struggle for human freedom, equality, and independence." By promoting these virtues in the world, these women argued, they were also taking "an opportunity to claim it for Christ, for He had much to do with calling it forth." The Bible-a-Month was portrayed as just one weapon in the war "for the minds and souls of men" and a tool "to win the peoples from sinister and alien forces."[19]

Though the Western world entered the twentieth century with an oftentimes blind hope in human improvement, such utopian visions were shattered quickly by two world wars, a depression, and now the ever-present threat of atheistic communism. While the world tried to overcome these problems through international councils and organizations, relief agencies, mass movements for peace, and military might, ABS leadership believed that the West's problems were ultimately spiritual in nature. In this sense, the Society engaged the mid-twentieth century with its own understanding of progress, one that was bound with the advancement of the Kingdom of God as defined by the teachings of the Bible. The Bible was the only answer to the spiritual longings of the German civilian who lost his home after the bombing of Dresden or the Russian farmer suffering from the military effects of Hitler's invasion or the tyranny of a Soviet regime that made it difficult to eat and to worship.

But the Bible was also the best hope for the world as a whole in the sense that it provided answers to questions being asked about the best way to live as moral, political, and economic human beings. Europe needed to be reminded of these lessons in the decades following World War II, but there were other parts of the world, particularly in Asia, that needed to learn these Bible-based lessons for the first time.

18

Asia

The end of the war also brought renewed interest from the ABS in Asia. After the United States dropped atomic bombs on Hiroshima and Nagasaki, followed by the Japanese surrender on September 2, 1945, US occupation forces under the leadership of General Douglass MacArthur spent the next seven years transforming the island nation into something equivalent to a Western democratic state. When the occupation period ended in 1952, Japan was the United States' most important Asian ally and was on its way toward a thriving capitalist economy. The ABS praised the work of MacArthur in Westernizing Japan and gave credit to both the general's "wisdom" and the "home-like friendly character" of the American GIs stationed there. What particularly caught the attention of those at the Park Avenue Bible House was MacArthur's emphasis on religious freedom. The people of Japan were "freed of any patriotic necessity of believing in the divinity of the Emperor, or adhering to Shintoism as a national faith." They were now as ready as they had ever been to receive "the message of the Gospel." Japan was "one of the most promising missionary opportunities in the story of Christian progress," and the ABS "has surely never faced so thrilling an opportunity in its service to non-Christian people."[1]

MacArthur and the ABS painted a picture for Americans back home of a Japanese people who welcomed the occupation. The ABS rhetoric seemed to suggest that the arrival of MacArthur and the American forces triggered something akin to a national religious conversion. George Hixon, a chaplain with MacArthur's forces who worked closely with the ABS, wrote that "one day the Japanese army men were fighting like tigers . . . and then within twenty-four hours the men laid down their arms, and when the Americans came into Japan they found nothing but 'lambs.'" According to Hixon, it was as if the Japanese people were "arising from the dead." They had transitioned from the darkness of a tyrannical empire in which they were "misled," "deceived," and taught how to "hate" their enemies, to an "artistic and socially progressive people" who were now "kind and considerate, and generous to a fault."[2]

Christianity experienced significant growth as well. By 1949 the ABS reported that church attendance was doubling and tripling in major Japanese cities, and Christians were holding important political offices. MacArthur informed ABS Treasurer Gilbert Darlington that the demand for Bibles in Japan was "insatiable," and that millions of Japanese were becoming interested in Christianity. He urged the ABS to expand its work in Japan. General Secretary Eric North believed that the Christian faith provided a better foundation for "national and personal life" in Japan than the old religious system that was centered on the worship of the emperor. Japanese Christians were still too small in number and lacking in organization to exercise "a very great and intensive evangelistic impact" on their country, but North did think that the scriptures were capable of such an impact. "If we can intensify Scripture distribution," he told a representative of the BFBS working in Tokyo, and bring about "the permeation of Japanese life and thought with Christian ideals and Christian conceptions," there will be a "great many who will lay hold with conviction upon the heart of the Christian faith."[3]

The Japan Bible Society was formed in 1937 and was run largely by Protestant missionaries. Following the Allied victory in the Pacific, the Tokyo Bible House, the building in which the Japan Bible Society made its headquarters, was still standing, but about 80 percent of its publishing facilities had been destroyed by war. In 1946 and 1947 the ABS, through its War Emergency Fund, sent pencils, stationery, and over 105 tons of paper to the Tokyo Bible House. Kiyoshi Tanaka, the secretary of the Japan Bible Society, pleaded with the ABS for more paper, describing it as a "problem of life or death for the Bible work in Japan." The Society also provided the Japan Bible Society with 150,000 Japanese Bibles and over 1 million Testaments. These were the first Japanese Bibles published in America. Because of the size of the Japanese characters, the ABS Japanese Bible was 1,696 pages long, and each one weighed three pounds. The 440,000 pounds of paper used to produce this shipment was larger than what was needed to produce all of ABS English Bibles in any given year prior to World War II. These initial efforts seemed to pay off. By 1948 the Bible was the ninth bestselling book in Japan. And more Bibles were on the way. In the forty years following V-J Day the ABS shipped 3.5 million Bibles to Japan. This statistic was impressive in light of the fact that before the war the number of Bibles sent to Japan per year hovered around one hundred thousand.[4]

It was not until 1949, under the watchful eye of MacArthur and the forces of occupation, that the Japan Bible Society became an autonomous agency that operated independently of the ABS. As part of this transition Eric North flew to Tokyo to plan, with Tsunetaro Miyakoda, the first General Secretary of the Japan Bible Society, the most extensive program of scripture production and distribution ever undertaken in a non-Christian country. The Japan Bible

Society called this initiative "the Tanaka Plan." It was named after the long-time ABS agent and colporteur Kiyoshi Tanaka who was currently serving as the vice general secretary. The goal was to publish and distribute 10 million copies of the Bible in Japan in three years (1949–1951). During his visit North also met with MacArthur and helped the Japan Bible Society secure the general's approval of the Tanaka Plan. MacArthur must have thought the plan was not ambitious enough, because he urged North and the ABS to work with the Japan Bible Society to distribute over *30 million* copies of the Bible. He insisted on placing a Bible in every Japanese home. In fact, MacArthur believed that the distribution of Bibles in Japan constituted a historic moment in the history of Christianity: "There now exists an opportunity without counterpart since the birth of Christ for the spread of Christianity among the people of the Far East." "What Christian does not believe," he told North, "that every Japanese who reads the Scriptures sincerely will find there the One of whom he can joyfully say 'He restoreth by soul?'" The ABS agreed. In 1947 the *Bible Society Record* published an article by a YMCA missionary who wrote that "perhaps more than any other people [the Japanese] are seeking the meaning of Christianity and of democracy. Japan is passing through a period of history which may well determine the future of the Far East."[5]

The Tanaka Plan may have been a program designed and carried out by the Japan Bible Society, but the ABS was involved in almost every aspect of its execution. Though Miyakoda and his team published the Bibles in Tokyo, the paper and much of the funding for the project came from New York. MacArthur insisted that a representative from the ABS remain on the ground in Tokyo to help promote the Tanaka Plan. In April 1950 the ABS prepared a "giant presentation book," which it called "The Good Will Book," to be sent to the Japan Bible Society as an "expression of fellowship with the Japanese people and to express faith in Japan as a potential Christian community." The book included the signature of anyone who contributed at least one dollar to the ABS for the purpose of aiding the Bible Cause in Japan. The ABS publicity staff developed slogans to make the plan more enticing to potential donors. These included "Bibles for Japan!" and "Bibles instead of bombs, signatures instead of shots!" The ABS also turned to MacArthur for help in advertising this new fundraising endeavor. The promotion included a challenge from the general to reach "every village and hamlet" with a copy of the Bible. The Good Will Book campaign was a success. The two volumes of signatures were bound in blue morocco and together weighed 172 pounds. They contained 533 pages of autographs from people living in more than 14,000 US towns and cities. President Harry S. Truman signed the book. So did forty-one governors, and representatives from over thirty-one Protestant denominations. On December 26, 1950, over 1,500 people came to Hibya Hall in Tokyo to see Ivan Bennett,

the chief of chaplains of the Far East Command, present the Good Will Book
to the Japan Bible Society. MacArthur sent a note to Eric North apologizing
for not being able to attend ceremony.[6] Meanwhile, the ABS provided funds
for the Japan Bible Society to hire 150 colporteurs to travel by bicycle selling
New Testaments and Bibles in "every village and hamlet." Colporteurs were
equipped with a 35mm projector and promotional posters. Upon arrival in a
town or village, they usually asked local officials for permission to sell their
books. The average colporteur spent the day visiting homes and the evenings
showing a Bible-related film in a local meeting place. Only people who had
purchased a Bible during the day were permitted to enter the hall and watch
the movie. The purpose was to "hear more about the contents of the little book
he has just bought." Many of these films also included short public-service
announcements from the Japanese government.[7]

In the end, the Tanaka plan fell approximately 1.6 million Bibles short of its
projected goal of 10 million. With four General Supplies of the United States
under its belt, all of which did not meet their projective goals, the ABS had
experience with spinning the positive features of uncompleted Bible distribution programs. In this case, it described the distribution of over 8 million
Bibles in Japan as a "great achievement." But perhaps more importantly, the
work of Miyakoda, his staff, and his teams of colporteurs in executing the
Tanaka Plan was a clear sign to the ABS that the Japan Bible Society no longer
needed its direct support. In 1951 the ABS ended its administrative role in
Tokyo, although it continued to provide funds and resources to Japan through
the United Bible Societies. MacArthur left Japan in the same year and the US
occupation force was gone a year later.[8]

Things did not go as smoothly for the Bible Cause in China. In the decades
following the collapse of the Qing Dynasty in 1911, the success of ABS efforts
depended on the political stability of the country under the newly created
Republic of China. The Communist Party of China was growing stronger by
the year and was developing a profound influence on the ever-changing leadership of the fledgling republic. In 1925, Chiang Kai-Shek managed to bring
some stability to the country by seizing power after the death of Sun Yat-sen,
the first president of the republic. Chiang, as the leader of the Nationalist
Party, made every effort to drive the communists out of China, but he was
largely unsuccessful in winning the hearts and minds of the people in the
countryside who were longing for agrarian reforms. Meanwhile, the Japanese
invaded Manchuria (Northeast China) in 1931, resulting in the Second Sino-
Japanese War six years later. This meant that Chiang's government would need
to fight a war on two fronts, although Mao's Red Army did temporarily form a
United Front with the president's Nationalist government in order to defend

China from the Japanese aggressors. When the Japanese bombed Pearl Harbor in December 1941, the Chinese sided with the Allies. The war with Japan, which according to most historians ended in a stalemate, was a costly one for the Chinese. Despite the best efforts of Chiang and his army, the Japanese captured both Shanghai and the capital city of Nanking. The economic toll brought by that the war opened the door to a communist takeover. When the Allies defeated and eventually occupied Japan in 1945, the troubles in China continued. The United Front collapsed and the battle between Nationalists and the Chinese Communist Party for political power intensified.

On one level, the work of the ABS in China during the 1930s and 1940s seemed to move forward as if the political and military turmoil in the country did not exist. Between 1937 and 1939 the ABS sponsored open-air evangelistic campaigns, sold Bibles, and shared the Gospel on market and festival days in Chinese towns. Colporteurs encouraged Chinese children to bring Bibles to school and sell them to their friends. In the same year that Shanghai and Nanking were under Japanese attack, the ABS was sponsoring an exhibition of Chinese Bibles in Beijing. In Shanghai, New York, and London conversations continued about the creation of a Chinese Bible Society. Meanwhile colporteurs on China's western frontier traveled on the mountain trails along the Tibetan border selling Bibles and conducting services. Bible salesmen in Mongolia and Northern China often attached white flags with red crosses to their bicycles as they entered remote villages. Some sung hymns to the Chinese peasants they encountered working in the fields. Because many of the villages had limited accommodations for visitors, it was not unusual for colporteurs to spend their nights on the floor of Buddhist temples, in empty watchtowers, or in the open air, where they often feared attack from wolves "and other dangerous animals."[9]

On the other hand, the war taking place in China was all too real for ABS colporteurs and volunteers. For most of the war the Chinese Bible House in Shanghai was cut off from many of its missionary stations in the interior due to closed rail lines and high postage rates. Printing presses were destroyed—casualties of war. Suppliers of paper and other raw materials were unable to make deliveries. These difficulties forced the ABS to move its printing operations to Hong Kong. The ABS's Chinese agent, Carleton Lacy, was out of the country at the start of the war and was warned not to return until the military threat was over. Distribution was also difficult during the war, since the Japanese armies did not allow Bibles to be dispersed among its troops or in the hospitals that it established in the Chinese territories that they were occupying. In June 1940 the Japanese bombed the Bible House in Chongqing, and staff had to be evacuated as rainwater poured through a massive hole in the roof.[10]

In the same year a Chinese colporteur named Ko, working in Shansi, a region in which neither the Chinese nor the Japanese held military control, encountered a group of Chinese guerillas who stole his pass identifying him as a Bible salesman. Later, after he returned to Shanghai, a Japanese soldier demanded to see his credentials. When the colporteur could not produce the necessary documentation, he was accused of being a spy. Ko was wearing an armband of neutrality and was carrying Bibles, but this did not seem to matter. The solider forced Ko to his knees and was ready to execute him on the spot when another soldier who knew the colporteur intervened and saved his life. As it turns out, Ko had previously invited his rescuer into his home and had shown him Christian hospitality. From the perspective of the ABS, the lesson was clear: "A cup of cold water—in this instance it was a cup of hot tea— shall in no wise lose its reward." A sixty-five-year-old colporteur known only as "Mr. Lu" faced a similar situation. While visiting a new village in 1940, a local government official riding a bicycle asked him the nature of his profession. When Lu told him that he was a "preacher of the Gospel," six men carrying pistols accused him of being spy and took him away, sarcastically remarking that "you'll see your Lord pretty soon." As these soldiers debated as to whether to shoot Lu or bury him alive, as they had done to a previous man who they suspected to be Japanese spy, the village elders interceded on his behalf and convinced the men not to harm the bookseller. Others were not as fortunate as Ko and Lu. Colporteurs were regularly beaten, mugged, and in some cases murdered by Chinese and Japanese soldiers.[11]

While the ABS colporteurs were willing to provide Bibles to both the Nationalists and the Communists during the long civil war, many supporters of the Bible Cause in China (along with the US government, who had sent nearly $3 billion in aid to the Nationalist government between 1939 and 1945) were hoping that Chiang would remain in power. Communists had been interfering with the work of missionaries and ABS colporteurs since the 1920s. Chiang, on the other hand, was a Christian convert who claimed to be a "constant reader of the Bible." But as the war with Japan raged and the Nationalist government under Chiang continued to show its incompetence, especially in the years after World War II, promoters of the Bible Cause got a glimpse of the future and it did not look good.[12]

The final blow to missionary and Christian philanthropic work in China came when communist Mao Zedong, with overwhelming support from peasants and farmers in the Chinese countryside, overthrew Chiang Kai-shek and established the People's Republic of China in October 1949. Shortly after Mao took control, the ABS decided to establish an emergency office in Hong Kong. A complete set of plates and a copy of every Chinese-language scripture ever printed in China was shipped to this office in 1949. While the ABS and Western missionaries feared persecution, and many Chinese Christians fought against the communist takeover, not all Chinese Protestants opposed Mao and his popular revolution. In 1950 a "Christian Manifesto" supporting Mao's government was signed by thousands of China's leading Protestant churchmen. It called for Christians to cut ties with foreign missionaries and to promote "anti-imperialistic, anti-feudalistic, and anti-bureaucratic capitalistic education." Other Christians found the work of Western organizations committed to social justice and labor reform—such as the YMCA and YWCA—to be compatible with communism.[13]

In 1948 J. Leighton Stuart, the US ambassador to China and a former missionary who had been observing Mao and the Chinese Communist Party since the 1930s, was not willing to give up the fight to prevent China from going "red." In a telegram to the Bible House in New York, Stuart admitted that "thinking Chinese [people] are coming under the influence of dynamic new ideologies," but he was still confident that the word of God could penetrate the minds of these intellectuals and turn back the communist tide. He urged the ABS to distribute the Bible "on the most generous terms possible," implying that the Society should abandon its strict policy of selling the Bible instead of distributing it for free. But it was too late. In 1952, the ABS pulled out of China completely.[14]

While it is easy to suggest that the ABS left China because the Board of Managers feared persecution from Mao's government, the decision to leave, which coincided with the creation of the China Bible Society, the first Bible society in China to run without the cooperation of a Western society, had been in the planning stages for over thirty years. Many in the New York Bible House, in conversations with the BFBS and the NBSS, saw Mao's ascendancy as the right time to turn the work over to Chinese Protestants. The China Bible Society assumed the work of translation, printing, and distribution in seven Bible houses across China. The ABS hoped to stay connected with the Bible Cause in China through its emergency office in Hong Kong, but the Chinese Bible Society, perhaps feeling the pressure of Mao's policies, requested that the emergency office sever all connections with Shanghai.[15]

In the years immediately following the departure of the Western Bible societies, circulation in China fell rapidly. The word of God would not fare well in Red China, despite promises of religious freedom from the People's Republic. Mao's government took control of church schools and hospitals, closing that channel of distribution. Street-preaching and colportage were restricted throughout the country. Persecution of Chinese Christians continued. In 1951, the Western Bible societies had circulated over 1.1 million Bibles in China. By 1955, the number of Bibles distributed had dropped to just over fifty-three thousand. In 1959, the ABS learned that anyone who wanted to purchase a copy of the Bible in China had to register the intent behind his or her purchase. Sales dipped even further. The staff in New York also learned that the communist government had expelled the China Bible Society from the Shanghai Bible House, forcing it to work out of a room in a nearby church. It would be the last correspondence that the ABS would receive from Shanghai in several decades. From this point on it acquired news of the work of the Bible Cause in China through cryptic letters from friends who were still living there. It appeared, at least for now, that the ABS work in China had come to an end.[16]

In 1919 the ABS ceased its work in Korea as part of an agreement with the British and Foreign Bible Society that gave the British an exclusive right to promote the Bible Cause in Korea in exchange for ABS exclusivity in the Philippines. It was not until the outbreak of World War II that the ABS felt a moral obligation to return to Korea. The BFBS was still recovering from the war and could not meet the increasing demand for Bibles in the country. Until the BFBS was economically ready to continue its work with the fledgling Korean Bible Society, the ABS would finance the efforts there through its War Emergency Fund.[17]

The recent history of Korea had been intricately bound with Japanese imperialism. In 1876 the Meiji Dynasty in Japan forced the Koreans into a treaty which, for all intents and purposes, made the nation a part of the growing Japanese Empire. As Japan grew stronger in the Pacific, Korea's autonomy as a sovereign nation became weaker. By 1910 the Japanese had officially annexed Korea and it would remain a part of Japan until the end of World War II. After 1945, Korea was an independent nation. The Korean Bible Society was founded on September 19, 1940, but it closed later that day. On the evening of its opening Japanese imperial officials arrested E. T. Chung, the general secretary, for working too closely with foreigners from the West. (Bibles, hymn books, and Christian literature had been largely banned in Korea during the Japanese occupation.) During the seventy days Chung spent in prison the constitution was revised to make the Korean Bible Society a joint enterprise between Korea and Japan, thus excluding any foreign influence. It reopened on January 1, 1941, but when the Japanese attacked Pearl Harbor and entered World War II, it closed again and would not reopen until the American occupation started in September 1945. The ABS began sending Korean-language scriptures almost immediately.[18]

In the wake of World War II the Korean peninsula was temporarily divided at the thirty-eighth parallel for the purpose of military occupation by Soviet and US troops. It did not take long before governments were established in both regions with the Soviet-supported People's Democratic Republic in the North and the American-supported Republic of Korea in the South. President Harry Truman viewed the political division of Korea as part of his larger efforts to contain communism. When North Korea invaded South Korea, Truman worried that if the Soviet Union was able to gain a foothold in Korea communism might spread throughout Asia and eventually into the United States. With this in mind, he convinced the United Nations to approve the use of troops as a "police action" against Soviet aggression in Korea and appointed Douglas MacArthur to command UN forces made up almost entirely of United States and South Korean troops. Between the spring of 1950 and the spring of 1951, the UN troops and the North Koreans fought to a stalemate. The dividing line at the 38th parallel remained in place.

In 1948, the year that free elections took place creating the Republic of South Korea, the ABS announced that for the first time since the end of World War II Bibles were being published and printed in the capital city of Seoul. The number of Christians in Korea was small (about 2 to 3 percent of the population in 1945) but thriving, even after years of restrictions placed upon them by their Japanese colonizers. Many Christians welcomed the US occupation, assuming that since the United States was a Christian nation, and a successful one at that, then God must be on its side. The Korean Bible Society sold New Testaments, four different scripture portions, and the Gospels in Braille. These Bibles were supplemented by Korean Bibles and English Bibles donated by the ABS and BFBS for use among the troops. Chung thanked the ABS for a gift of 100,000 Korean Testaments and requested 1 million more to be distributed over a five-year period. He described them as "sweet rain after many years of continued drought." These books were distributed among school children and Korean Christians who had not had access to Bibles while the Korean Bible Society was closed during the war. They were not only needed for the spiritual benefit of their recipients, but they would also serve to counter the communist books coming into Seoul from "underground channels" originating in North Korea.[19]

Christianity did not fare very well in North Korea, despite the fact that the Christian church had always been more vibrant there. The communist North Korean government under Kim Il-sung initially preached a message of religious toleration, but it did not take long before Christianity was perceived as a belief system at odds with communism and associated with the United States. This perception was largely accurate. Most Christian leaders in North Korea opposed the communist government and saw the United States as a champion of religious toleration and democratic government. When Christians in North Korea refused to participate in official government celebrations they had their services disrupted, their churches desecrated, and their pastors publicly humiliated. By 1946, Christianity was under attack. The government ceased all Christian publications, religious education was no longer permitted in state-supported schools, and communist propaganda discredited Christianity as backward and unscientific. And it only got worse. By the time of the Korean War all churches were required to be members of a state-sponsored Christian association in which only communists were permitted to hold leadership positions. In 1950, those Christian leaders who had not yet fled the country were put in prison. North Korean churches were used as government offices.[20]

As the Korean War got underway, the Korean Bible Society made every effort to continue producing Bibles and the ABS continued its shipments to South Korea. The ABS reported that during the North Korean attacks during the summer of 1950 the troops went out of their way to target South Korean Christians. Bibles were destroyed, Christians were terrorized, and churches were pillaged. One Korean colporteur noted that the insurgents "mark the Christians especially, calling them by name and then exterminating them." He was also disturbed by the way in which some North Koreans tortured captured South Koreans by driving nails through their heads or burying them alive. Similar to what we have seen in China, the Korean Bible Society remained steadfast amidst the persecution and the Bible became a "rallying point for the anti-communist forces." J. C. F. Robertson, an ABS and BFBS agent in Seoul, spoke of the role of the Bible as a source of inspiration to democratic life on the peninsula: "Communism is not always the first in the field; the Holy Spirit too, has a strategy of preparing individuals and churches to enable them to stand." Robertson described an outbreak of Bible studies in the southern city of Pusan that was strengthening the faith and resistance of the South Korean people.[21]

South Korea would need this kind of spiritual strength when North Korean troops entered Seoul on June 28, 1950. Communist troops stormed churches and took Christian prisoners. Some were executed. Those who survived hid their Bibles. One woman wrapped up hers in old rags and hid it in a cabinet. Another concealed her Bible under the floorboards. Christians who fled Seoul feared for their lives as North Korean guards conducted searches on the roads leading out of the city. One pastor, fearful that he would be searched, hid his Bible in a bush. He passed through the checkpoint safely but experienced such shame and mortification that upon his return he felt the need to publicly repent for his actions before his congregation.[22] In September 1950, the Seoul Bible House was burned to the ground by communist troops as part a larger fire that North Korean troops had set in Seoul's business sector. Six members of the General Committee of the Korean Bible Society (the equivalent of the ABS's Board of Managers) were captured by the communists and executed. A member of the staff was killed by a bomb as she fled the Bible House, and others were conscripted into the North Korean Army. More than half a million volumes of bound scriptures were destroyed and tons of paper and unbound scriptures also went up in the flames.[23]

At the center of it all was Young Bin Im, a Korean graduate of Southern Methodist University and the Secretary of the Korea Bible Society. During the fire in the Seoul Bible House he managed to save the only manuscript of a Bible which was being revised in the ancient Korean alphabet of Hangul. The printing of the Bible had begun a few months earlier, and an additional 400 pages were typeset at the time of the fire, but the job was not yet complete. Im and his son carried the manuscript to his house in a large pickle jar, but when communist troops arrived to conduct a search of the house he quickly sent it into the countryside with a friend who was a farmer. As the troops searched his home, Im escaped by hiding in a woodpile in his backyard. After Seoul fell into communist hands again in November 1950, Im fled south to Pusan. He spent the last of his savings to get his family to the city via boat and managed to find passage himself in the luggage rack of a train boxcar with about 150 other riders. It was so cold that eight people froze to death during the journey. Upon arrival in Pusan, Im realized that all his luggage had been lost, but just before he climbed aboard the train he remembered to place the Hangul manuscript in a small suitcase that he still had with him. As Im told Eric North, "I cannot help but believe in miracles." He would spend the next months in Japan preparing the Hangul Bible for publication.[24]

Through it all, the sale of Bibles in Korea continued to grow. Im eventually returned from Japan where he reconstructed the four hundred typeset pages of the Hangul Bible that had been lost in the fire at the Bible House. The complete Bible in Hangul went on sale in October 1952. Im's reports to the ABS were cheerful and upbeat, but there was still work to be done in reconstructing South Korea and the Bible Cause following a war that, according to one estimation, ended the lives of 408 clergy and destroyed 1,373 churches. The Seoul Bible House needed rebuilding (it was reopened in 1957); displaced persons needed to be found or relocated; and the country was lacking food and other resources. Spiritual needs abounded among the injured soldiers, the refugee population, and the ever-growing numbers of orphans and widows.[25] But the Bible Cause would go on in Korea and the ABS continued its work there into the 1960s and beyond by distributing Bibles and money to keep the Korean Bible Society afloat.

When the American Bible Society pulled out of China in 1952 it was the end of its direct Bible work in the major nations of Asia. Though distribution and monetary support continued to flow to Japan and Korea through the United Bible Societies, the day of big foreign agencies working directly in these countries was over. In the wake of World War II the ABS offered spiritual support to Asian countries and spread the message of Christianity and Western ideals as an antidote to what many referred to as "Godless Communism." Because of the powerful presence of Douglas MacArthur's occupation force, Japan was never really a serious threat to turn toward communism. Today Japan is not a Christian nation, but the ABS did help Christianity gain a solid foothold in the country. In China, where political chaos reigned between 1937 and 1949, the ABS had little of chance of winning the country for Christ. The best they could do was to turn the work over to the China Bible Society and hope and pray for the best. In South Korea, the ABS contributed to a growing Christian church that was strengthened by the short war with the communists to the North. As the ABS worked to provide autonomy for the Japan Bible Society, the China Bible Society, and the Korea Bible Society, it was also engaged, as we will see in the next chapter, in an important enterprise that enabled it to continue having an impact on the Bible Cause around the world.

The Bible and One World

After two world wars and the conflict in Korea, many in the United States and the West wondered if a peaceful world would ever be possible. Up until this point, international cooperation for promoting global peace had largely failed. The most significant twentieth-century attempt along these lines, the League of Nations, founded in the wake of World War I, was unable to prevent a second world war. This, however, did not stop the victorious Allies from making another attempt at such an organization. In April 1945, 282 representatives from fifty-one countries gathered in San Francisco to create the United Nations, an organization designed to keep peace in the world by arbitrating disputes among rival nations and stopping those nations, by military force if necessary, that threatened peace. As we saw in the last chapter, the United Nations' role as a military peacekeeping force was first put to the test in a significant way in Korea, but its brightest moments stemmed from its commitment to humanitarian aid and its defense of human rights in the war-torn regions of Europe and Asia.

The creation of the United Nations was the culminating moment in a global conversation on internationalism that had been taking place among policy makers and intellectuals for most of the twentieth century. By the 1940s internationalism had grown popular in the United States as an alternative to the destructive nationalism that had led to two world wars. This philosophy, which was gaining adherents throughout Europe, Asia, and Africa as well, focused on individual human rights and a global understanding of the common good. It emphasized the ideas that united people, not the things that divided them. Some even argued that "world citizenship" should always trump individual loyalties to a particular nation.[1] This culture of internationalism was also fostered through organizations that were not connected to nation-states. On this front, religious institutions, especially those associated with liberal Protestant Christianity, led the way. A 1941 Gallup poll found that most Americans believed that a future war could only be avoided by the advancement of "reform based on toleration and Christian principles." Protestant defenders

of internationalism thought that the lack of cooperation among world powers was a spiritual problem that could only be solved through religious solutions.[2] Peace, equality, even democracy were ultimately grounded in Christian
principles, especially the belief in the inherent dignity of all human beings and
the social teachings of Jesus. This was the spirit, for example, behind the First
Assembly of the World Council of Churches held at Amsterdam in 1948.

In May 1947 the *Bible Society Record* began with an editorial titled "One
Book for One World." The title of the article echoed the bestselling travel-
ogue, *One World*, written by Wendell Wilkie, the Republican candidate for
president of the United States in 1940. ("One World" was also his campaign
slogan in that election. Following his defeat at the hands of Franklin Delano
Roosevelt, Wilkie was sent by the third-term president on a world tour to
spread a message of international cooperation.)[3] The ABS approach to worldwide collaboration shared many of the concerns of the World Council of
Churches, and even the United Nations, but it was focused more narrowly
on Bible distribution, translation, and publication as its contribution to this
new global order. Like many of the growing defenders of internationalism in
this era, the ABS began by noting that with the end of World War II, One
World was "not just something to be earnestly desired—it was an achievement speedily to be won if there were to be any world at all." In good ABS
fashion, the *Record* added that the notion of One World was not a new concept
to Christians. In fact, it was at the core of Jesus's teachings in the Garden
of Gethsemane (John 17) as he reflected on the meaning of his impending
death. The United Nations would bring much wisdom, study, and skill to
the pursuit of world unity. It could "analyze the project, chart a course, outline processes, point out pitfalls and prepare an architect's specifications for
the desired structure." But how could people who were so different in their
degrees of "culture and attainment" and "obsessed by blind provincial loyalties," and "steeped in ignorance and superstition and distrust," create a peaceful world? For the ABS, the answer lay in "the human heart." If all human
hearts could "beat in rhythm," a peaceful "world of nations" could be realized. And how might every heart beat as one? By applying the principles of
the Bible to every dimension of global life. The use of the Bible to cultivate a
world citizenry defined by love and compassion toward one another seemed
entirely logical to the ABS. The Bible, after all, was already the best-known
book in the world and had been in use longer than any other ancient text.
Thanks to the ABS, it was being translated into native languages that made it
easier to read and understand. For centuries it had "demonstrated its capacity
to mold the world's life wherever it has been taken seriously." Whatever good
existed in the world in terms of home life, education, law, social improvement,
or the arts stemmed ultimately from the principles contained in the Bible.[4]

As the United Nations, World Council of Churches, and other international organizations emerged following World War II, the ABS and the BFBS fulfilled a longstanding dream of creating their own international agency for the translation, publication, and distribution of the Bible. Several nations around the world now had their own Bible societies (many of which had been native extensions of Bible work begun by the foreign agencies of the ABS and the BFBS) and the time was right to bring them together in an international fellowship. In 1946, the United Bible Societies (UBS) was born out of this concern. Though the UBS did not have the kind of activist mission as the United Nations or World Council of Churches, it was a product of the culture of global cooperation sweeping the West and the world in the wake of World War II.

The original idea of an international organization to foster fellowship among the Bible societies of the world dates back to the end of the World War I. As Woodrow Wilson was busy selling his "Fourteen Points" and promoting the League of Nations, ABS Vice President Churchill Cutting proposed that a committee be formed to consider the subject of "some form of union for worldwide cooperation of all Bible Societies of the world." The committee proposed an Association of National Bible Societies that would make the ABS more efficient in its overseas work with other national Bible societies on matters related to translation and distribution. Such an international organization could be used as a platform to make "a joint appeal to the whole Christian world" on behalf of the Bible Cause. However, when the ABS took the lead on this project it ruffled the feathers of John Ritson, the general secretary of the BFBS. Ritson objected to the idea that the BFBS was in any way a national Bible society on par with other national Bible societies. "From its very inception," he told the ABS, the BFBS "has been a World Society." It already had an "international character," and did not need to be a part of such a federation in order to accomplish its global work.[5] The ABS knew that an international fellowship would be impossible without the support of the BFBS, so when Ritson would not budge the ABS decided to table the matter.[6]

In 1927, the ABS appointed Eric North as an associate general secretary. North came to New York after serving the Methodist Episcopal Church in several administrative capacities. Immediately before his arrival he had spent three years as the executive secretary of the China Union University, a Chinese institution of higher education sponsored by several Protestant denominations. In 1928 North ascended to the position of general secretary, which he would hold for the next twenty-eight years. North's support of the Protestant ecumenical movement and his commitment to cooperation and compromise made him the idea figure for bringing an international movement of Bible societies to fruition.[7] After Ritson retired, the leadership of the BFBS fell to two general secretaries who were more open to the idea of a worldwide fellowship of Bible societies: Arthur Wilkinson and John Temple. After Wilkinson sent a letter to North expressing his goodwill and prayers for the ABS, North asked his BFBS counterpart if he could fly to London to discuss the possibility of working together on joint Bible-related projects. Wilkinson asked North to deliver the keynote address at the BFBS annual meeting in May 1931, a gesture that solidified their relationship. North would later write that he knew within the "first half-hour" of their first conversation that they would "find cooperation a common objective." Temple and North became lifelong friends. Like North, Temple had also worked as a Methodist missionary in China. In the years subsequent to their first meeting in 1932 they spent a great deal of time traveling around the world together to monitor and supervise the work of national Bible societies. The historically chilly relationship between the ABS and the BFBS was finally beginning to thaw.[8]

During their 1931 visit in London, North and Wilkinson hammered out some ideas about how they might work together to advance the Bible Cause. They revisited old conversations between the ABS and BFBS about regulating Bible prices. They talked about the best way to cultivate stronger relationships with missionaries. And they discussed how these two Bible societies might cooperate more efficiently in those areas of the world where both societies were at work.[9] Negotiations continued in July 1932 when representatives from the two societies, along with delegates from the NBSS, met for the first time in history. North noted that everyone present at the London meeting shared a "common desire not simply to smooth out differences but to seek together the welfare of the whole work under God's guidance." The representatives dined together, shared communion, and even visited the home of retired BFBS General Secretary John Ritson. In preparation for the conference, Wilkinson provided the delegates with a white paper explaining the reasons for the gathering and the issues that he hoped might be addressed. The agenda focused on the best way to deal with "overlapping" fields of work and the general lack of communication between Bible societies around the world. Wilkinson lamented that little "deliberate thought" was ever given to these issues. Finally, Wilkinson raised the issue of "devolution," or the decision to entrust the work of the Bible Cause to the gifted and talented Christians from indigenous churches. Native churches, Wilkinson argued, have "passed the adolescent stage and have reached young manhood." It was now time to grant them "self-determination."[10] The conference got underway on July 26 with a speech by North on "The New Situation" in Bible work. He asked the delegates to lay aside past differences in order to more effectively carry out the work of the society. He announced the ABS was ready to "make even long-cherished principles subservient to the present necessity for co-operation." One of the primary matters of discussion was a plan for the three Bible societies to unite their efforts in China under the umbrella of the Shanghai Bible House, and it was decided to go forward with the formation of a China Bible Society. The ABS delegation left the meeting encouraged about the possibilities of continued cooperation.

The ABS now began to draft plans for a new fellowship of Bible societies. The ABS and the BFBS would play the most significant role in this fellowship and it would include national Bible societies, run by native Protestants, from around the world. Any Bible society would be invited to join this yet-to-be formed organization as long as it was founded on the "common basic principles of our societies," had "deep roots in the life of the Church and the Nation," was self-governing, was able to support itself financially, and was willing to be a participant "in the world-wide Bible work." North insisted that this be a "fellowship" of Bible societies. He did not want to give the society the power to dictate policy to the national societies that made up its membership. He concluded that the joint conference with the BFBS and the NBSS was "the greatest single advance in 150 years of Bible Society work."[11]

The next major step in the development of an international fellowship of Bible societies took place in 1939 at Woudschoten, Netherlands, on the occasion of the 125th anniversary of the Netherlands Bible Society (NBS). The meeting included delegates from the ABS, BFBS, NBSS, NBS, the Norwegian Bible Society, and the French Bible Society. North and John Mott, a vice president and a legend in the ecumenical movement, represented the ABS. The Woudschoten Conference brought the Bible societies firmly within the orbit of the growing ecumenical movement. Plans for the World Council of Churches were already underway and several of the delegates to the conference had been active in supporting this and other ecumenical endeavors. The NBS, for example, was represented by Hendrik Kraemer, one of the leading figures in the global ecumenical movement. Hendrik was a linguist who had just completed fifteen years of service to the NBS in Indonesia. At the time of the Woudschoten Conference he was teaching history and religion at Leiden University and had just published *The Christian Message in a Non-Christian World*, in which he defended the exclusive nature of "Biblical realism" against the truth-claims of non-Christian religions. His book offended many liberal Protestants, but Kraemer was adamant that ultimate truth could only be found in the message of the Bible. Kraemer was critical of American modernist Christianity for its compromises with relativism and pragmatism. He challenged the Bible societies present in Woudschoten to encourage not just the distribution and translation of the Bible, but the actual *use* of the Bible. He called for a "systematic and well-planned movement for teaching those who buy a Bible how to read and *use* it for private and family worship." For Kraemer, if the united and ecumenical fellowship of Bible societies was going to move forward it would need a plan for engaging with the text of the Bible. This had to be the "heart of the matter."[12]

During the Woudschoten Conference, H. C. Rutgers of the NBS put forth a detailed proposal for a Council of Bible Societies, but any attempt at creating such an organization was curtailed by the coming of World War II. In May 1946, Temple had convinced representatives from national Bible societies in Czechoslovakia, Denmark, Finland, France, Germany, England, Netherlands, Norway, Poland, Scotland, Sweden, Switzerland, and the United States, along with a delegation of visitors from the World Council of Churches, to attend a meeting an Elfinsward, the Conference Center of the Anglican Diocese of Chichester in Haywards Heath, England, to create an international fellowship of Bible societies. The ABS delegation included Eric North, General Secretary Rome Betts, and Associate Secretary Eugene Nida. A constitution was written and the United Bible Societies would become a reality as soon as six national societies approved it.[13]

Those attending the Haywards Heath meeting were some of the most important Protestant leaders in Europe. Hans Lilje, who was about a year away from becoming a bishop in the Evangelical Lutheran Church of Germany, had only recently been released from Nuremburg prison where he had been sent for his involvement with the Confessing Church movement. Lilje was almost executed on three different occasions by the Gestapo. During the conference he shared how his Christian faith carried him through the ordeal. Alexander Enholc, the representative of the Poland Bible Society, described a similar imprisonment at the hands of the Gestapo and the heroic work of his wife to keep the Bible society open while he was away. Eivind Berggrav, the Bishop of Norway, reminded the delegates that "the world cannot be remade through political remedies." Visser 't Hooft, the general secretary of the World Council of Churches, described the war and the years leading up to it as a time of renewed interest in the Bible in Europe. He hoped that the word of God would continue to hold a prominent place in the culture since the very success of the "ecumenical situation" depended on "whether this great gift God has given to His Church is going to be gratefully received and worked out by all the Churches together." Hooft proposed a "close fellowship" between the Bible Societies and the World Council of Churches, concluding that "the Bible Societies needed the Ecumenical Church, because it is "through the Church that the Bible remakes the world."[14]

The United Bible Societies would have three main goals. First, it would "stimulate effective Bible Society organization" in areas that would benefit from a "united rather than national position." Second, it would "secure information needed to enable the strong Societies to assist the weaker." And third, it would "serve as a clearinghouse for many kinds of useful data." In addition to these three stated objectives, the UBS would coordinate contributions made to national Bible societies in order to avoid the duplication of gifts, offer experience to national Bible societies in the areas of Bible production, distribution, and promotion, interpret the work of the Bible societies to local church and denominational leaders, and provide regular reports on editions of the Bible available in foreign languages. Though it was never stated, the ABS, BFBS, and a handful of other European Bible societies would carry much of the workload simply because these societies were operating from a relatively strong financial position.[15]

The following year in Amersfoort, Netherlands, the UBS Executive Committee approved the selection of John Temple as the first general secretary. The headquarters were established in London. M. Olivier Beguin would take care of day-to-day operations from his office in Geneva. A committee made up of Bishop Eivind Berggrav, Eric North, and Arthur Wilkinson would handle interim operations. A budget was adopted to cover expenses at the London and Geneva offices and the membership societies were encouraged to contribute 1 percent of their income to keep those offices up and running. The ABS donated more than half of these costs for the first year of operation. Other details, such as the use of the name United Bible Societies, the development of a UBS imprint, the cost of Bibles, qualifications for membership, and other areas of cooperation, were also ironed out.[16]

During the Amersfoort meeting the men who formed the UBS made it clear that they wanted their new organization to contribute to the evangelization of the world. Berggrav, who was chairing the meeting, took the members of the Executive Committee "into the heavenlies" with a devotional urging the UBS to be involved in much more than simply distribution. "When Bible Societies talk about millions in circulation," he said, "it was not just a book that was being offered, but as a Japanese colporteur once said, 'It is Jesus.'" North concurred. He bemoaned the fact that the Bible societies had given very little thought to how they might encourage people to use the Bible in their personal lives. North wanted to go beyond a mere conversation about how the Bible might be useful in evangelization and develop a systematic and practical approach to encourage its use. He was convinced that Bible societies around the world needed to do a better job of working with missionaries, colporteurs, pastors, schools, and colleges to "show how the Book could physically be brought into action . . . with effective results." In essence, North was echoing the call of Hendrik Kraemer at the 1939 meeting in Woudschoten.[17]

Not everyone agreed with North's plea. Temple argued that if Bible societies performed the kind of evangelistic training that North was suggesting, they "might attempt to do what was really the work of the Church." There were plenty of parachurch organizations committed to helping people use the Bible

effectively, but the task of the Bible societies, he argued, was to supply scriptures, not to teach the Bible. North pushed back. He insisted that the UBS
might have a powerful role to play in evangelism. If the churches were failing
in this area, he argued, the Bible societies had a responsibility to bring this to
their attention. After much debate, Arthur Wilkinson found a middle way. The
UBS would put together a booklet of testimonials from individuals who had
been converted from reading the Bible. Such stories, which filled the pages of
both ABS and BFBS publications, would show how the Holy Spirit used the
Bible to draw people to God. Such a booklet, Wilkinson believed, might be an
effective tool of evangelism. Though Wilkinson was unwilling to lay out any
hard and fast rules on the role of evangelism in the UBS, he did conclude that
it would be perfectly fine for the leaders of a national Bible society to "conceive
of their work as having a missionary element towards the people in their country." North seemed satisfied with the compromise and proposed that the UBS
issue a statement on evangelism along these lines to be read at the upcoming
meeting of the International Missionary Council to be held in Toronto.[18]

Finally, the UBS Executive Committee defined its relationship with the
World Council of Churches (WCC). Mark Boegner, representing the French
Bible Society, thought that the UBS should be allowed to send a delegation to
WCC events and encouraged those in attendance to pursue such a relationship. Beguin then suggested that the UBS take over Bible distribution for the
Bible Department of the WCC. North agreed. The WCC Bible Department
was created to bring Bibles to prisoners and civilians during the war at a time
when national Bible societies were weak. Now that the war was over it was time
for the department to "drop out of the picture and that there should be some
recognition of the relationship of the United Bible Societies to that work." The
United Bible Societies, as the ABS would later announce, was now ready to
take its "place among the ecumenical organizations of the Christian forces of
the world."[19]

Translation was another important part of the UBS mission. The scholarly
arm of the UBS was tasked with preparing Bibles in vernacular languages
that were accessible to ordinary readers. It was committed to empowering
local Christians to be responsible for such translations, though UBS translation teams would always be ready to serve as a scholarly resource. Before the
UBS was formed, most of the translation work outside of the United States
and Great Britain was done by missionaries who learned native languages and
translated the Bible into those tongues. Missionaries then submitted their
finished translations to the ABS or the BFBS for review. In order to perform
the work of checking and examining translations, the UBS created a translation subcommittee. With the aim of aiding native translators and discussing
recent trends in the process of translation, the UBS published an academic

journal called *The Bible Translator*. In the first issue, which appeared in 1950, Nida, who was appointed editor, said that *The Bible Translator* would serve as a means of aiding the "five or six hundred missionary translators throughout the world who are giving all or most of their time to the task of translating the Bible or Christian literature."[20]

The UBS also worked at developing a proper definition of what it meant to publish a Bible without note or comment. At Woudschoten the members in attendance discussed the use of readers' "helps," namely historical, geographical, or archaeological information (including illustrations and section headings) that might prove useful for understanding the cultural background of the biblical text. It was one thing for the UBS to produce *The Bible Translator* as a "help" for translators, but it was quite another thing to add such helps to the actual text. Yet by 1950 Nida and his teams of translators around the world were calling for the use of textual helps as a means of aiding indigenous populations, and even English-speaking audiences with limited biblical literacy, understand the text more fully. In 1958 Nida wrote a paper titled "Reader's Helps," in which he argued that it was possible to use marginal notes and other explanations within the scriptural text and still avoid the doctrinal interpretation of the text. Nida called for the use of section headings, parallel references, and notes that explained alternative readings.[21]

The UBS opposed communism. At the 1949 UBS Council Meeting in New York, W. J. Platt of the BFBS in New Zealand urged the Bible societies to work with distributors of Christian literature so that the word of God could be found in bookstores throughout the world as a means of competing with the "conflicting ideologies" found in communist literature. At the same conference Beguin, who replaced Temple as UBS general secretary after the latter's death in 1948, told a crowd of Bible society leaders assembled in New York's historic Christ Church that Europe was facing a spiritual crisis that was affecting "both sides of the iron curtain." Both East and West had traded a reliance upon God for a "belief in man's power, in man's wisdom, [and] in man's good will and goodness." Humanistic beliefs and materialism now defined everyday life throughout the continent with the only difference between East and West being that in Eastern Europe such a "materialistic ideology" was trying to "impose itself by force and power" whereas in the West it was trying to "hide itself hypocritically behind a spiritual curtain." Communism was "the logical and logically totalitarian outcome of man's actual denial of God's kingship over us and the world," but Western Christians needed to make sure that such an anti-Christian way of life did not define them as well.[22]

On the ecumenical front, Henry Pitney Van Dusen, the president of Union Theological Seminary in New York and one of the founders of the World

Council of Churches, made a passionate plea for world unity. Van Dusen drew a direct line between the interdenominational birth of the Bible society movement in the early nineteenth-century and the twentieth-century ecumenical movement, suggesting that the founding of the BFBS in 1804 and the ABS in 1816 marked "the modern movement for Christian unity." There was a certain logic to Van Dusen's argument. The Bible societies had always been in the business of translating, publishing, and distributing "identically the same Bible for all Communions and all traditions." As a result, they represented the "commonly confessed center," making "the compulsion to unity inescapable." Van Dusen next turned to the prospect of a distinctly "ecumenical theology." In a statement reflective of the ecumenical movement's reliance upon an understanding of Christianity that stemmed from the lowest common denominator, he rejected the idea that such a theology might be rooted in the Reformation or the doctrines of Thomas Aquinas, the teachings of St. Augustine, or even contemporary trends in theology. No; for Van Dusen, ecumenical theology needed to come directly from the Bible, since this is "whence all the diverse branches and traditions claim to have sprung and where each of them seeks its authority."[23] As was projected at the 1947 meeting of the Executive Council in Amersfoort, the UBS would maintain a close relationship with the World Council of Churches and the larger ecumenical movement. In 1960, Beguin reported that in recent years the UBS was represented at the World Council of Churches Conference on Evangelism, the Ecumenical Youth Conference in Lausanne, the World Student Christian Federation Conference in Strasbourg, and the World Council of Churches Working Committee and Central Committee Meetings. The UBS also opened an office in the WCC building in Geneva. The UBS (or the ABS) was never in the business of developing the kind of "ecumenical theology" that Van Dusen had proposed in 1949—that was not its mission. Rather, the UBS participated in what theologian Samuel Escobar would later call a "practical kind of ecumenism." The UBS was designed to "serve all churches, and in their service they try to obtain the cooperation of all churches."[24]

For nearly forty years most of the personnel associated with the administrative tasks of the UBS wore what former UBS General Secretary John Erickson called "two hats." They held salaried positions with the ABS, the BFBS or, in the case of Beguin, another agency or Bible society, but part of their work required them to promote the Bible Cause around the world among the national Bible societies who were part of the UBS fellowship. In other words, the UBS remained an umbrella fellowship for the continued international work of the ABS and the BFBS, although now they would extend their reach, when necessary, to help indigenous Bible societies around the world. In 1966 the ABS, BFBS, and six other Bible societies joined together to create a

"World Service Budget." This was done partly out of a need to distribute donations and income equally among all the national Bible societies and partly out
of resentment among the other UBS members of the dominant role played
by the ABS and the BFBS. All of the contributing societies agreed to place
their income into the World Service Budget and the UBS agreed to appropriate funds to cover Bible work that any given national Bible society could not
afford to finance through local sales and donations. This was the first attempt
by the UBS to coordinate a budget for the national Bible societies that were
part of the fellowship. The globe was divided up into four regions—Africa, the
Americas, Asia-Pacific, and Europe Middle East—with each region responsible for administering the amount of funds it received from the World Service
Budget.[25]

In 1988 the UBS decided to establish a permanent headquarters in
Reading, England, and elect a full-time general secretary who was not
employed by the ABS, the BFBS, or any other national Bible society. The
ABS, along with the BFBS, were the major players in early decades of the
UBS, and they would remain so well into the twenty-first century. The ABS
participated in UBS meetings and used its resources to help the fellowship
carry out its mission around the world. Every national Bible society in the
UBS received a copy of the *Bible Society Record* and the ABS shared other
resources from its library and archives with the national societies. The ABS
also reserved the right to take the lead in areas of the world where the Bible
Cause was struggling due to economic or political developments. As of
2015, the UBS works with societies in over 200 countries faithfully carrying out the work of the Bible Cause.[26]

20

The Bible Cause at Home
in a Postwar World

In 1959, several ABS district secretaries met in Chicago to evaluate the Society's organization structure. Out of that conference came a plan to replace eleven district offices with three new regional offices that would now take the lead in the distribution of scriptures in the United States. Each of the three regions—Eastern (Washington, DC), Central (Chicago), and Western (Los Angeles)—was led by a regional distribution secretary and concentrated its efforts on bringing the Bible to "special populations," planning interdenominational programs, and working with churches in evangelism and education programs. The ABS staff in New York was careful to remind its constituency that this was merely an organizational change—nothing about the mission of the Society had changed or would change as a result of it. The central purpose would remain "the missionary distribution of the Scriptures." Eric North, who was now working as an ABS consultant after twenty-eight years as general secretary, sent a memo to those in attendance at the conference listing twenty-one categories of "people in need" whom the ABS had an obligation to reach with the Bible. The list included prisoners, hospital patients, the aged, delinquent youth, the blind, migrants, inner-city dwellers, various ethnic groups, and Native Americans.[1]

Like the rest of the United States, the ABS entered the postwar world trying to catch its breath after the tumultuous decades of depression and international crisis. The years of War Emergency were over, and much of the ABS Bible work around the world was now in the hands of the national Bible societies that had come together under the umbrella of the United Bible Societies. The staff of the New York Bible House could now turn more fully to domestic matters. In the two decades prior to its 150th anniversary in 1966, the Society continued its domestic work with a renewed focus, firmed up its ecumenical credentials, and got caught up in an intense religious battle over a new translation of the Bible.

Between 1946 and 1959 the ABS distributed over 6.3 million complete Bibles (Old and New Testament), over 10.6 million New Testaments, and over 83.7 million scripture portions in the United States. The majority of these scriptures were either sold or donated by ABS districts across the country or granted to the US Armed Forces. The distribution of whole Bibles remained steady during this period, while Testaments and portions saw a significant rise. A small percentage of these scriptures were granted to churches and interdenominational Protestant agencies. The National Council of Churches (NCC, the successor to the Federal Council of Churches) received most of these grants. The ABS gave the NCC Bibles to support its work with Native Americans and migrant workers. Following closely behind the NCC in the number of scriptures granted (in order of the number of Bibles received) was the Home Mission Board of the Southern Baptist Convention, the American Sunday School Union, and federal prisons, penitentiaries, and correction facilities.[2] In 1956 ABS General Secretary Robert Taylor wrote, "the opportunities of the Society in public relations seem to be limited only by the staff time and the funds available. Each week brings some new interesting and acceptable idea for telling the Bible Society story."[3]

The *Bible Society Record* continued to serve as the main ABS publicity organ. It published its usual menu of stories, reports, and news items from the Bible Cause at home and around the world. The *Record* was sent to ABS "members," defined as donors who gave $1.00 or more per year. This flagship publication also experienced an astronomical rise in circulation. Between 1931 and 1966 the number of published copies of the *Record* jumped from 33,000 to 973,000. If a survey conducted by the ABS in 1957 is any indication, the prototypical reader of the *Record* was a fifty-five-year-old Methodist or Presbyterian housewife who lived in a town of under 2,000 people and was part of a congregation of two hundred. She taught Sunday school, read *Reader's Digest* and *Better Homes & Gardens*, enjoyed listening to Billy Graham and Charles Fuller on the radio, and usually contributed about $150 a year to "religious work." Indeed, the readership of the *Record*, as well as the overall constituency of the ABS, could not get more middle class. In 1955, the *Bible Society Record* published its 100th volume in its most current series. Words of congratulations rolled into the Bible House from dozens of periodical editors and publishers including DeWitt Wallace (*Reader's Digest*), Chet Shaw (*Newsweek*), Arthur Sulzberger (*New York Times*), John Oliver LaGorce (*National Geographic*), and Paul Hutchinson (*Christian Century*). Eleanor Roosevelt congratulated the ABS and encouraged them to keep encouraging people around the world to read their Bibles. The *Record* was considered by many as a piece of mainstream journalism, and the Board of Managers and staff liked it that way.[4]

The ABS also published hundreds of small leaflets, tracts, inserts, and circulars, usually anywhere from one to four pages, to promote its labors among churches and other organizations. Between 1946 and 1951 the Society distributed over 95 million of these publications. They included schedules to help families commit to regular Bible reading, Thanksgiving and Christmas messages, reminders to observe Universal Bible Sunday, posters announcing the theme of the annual Worldwide Bible Reading program, and bookmarks with scripture verses printed on them in every language in which the ABS distributed Bibles. The titles of the ABS's most popular pamphlets during the 1950s were "Where to Look in the Bible," "How to Read the Bible," "Getting More Out of Your Bible," "Worthwhile Ways of Reading the Bible," and "My Reading Record."[5] The ABS was not only in the business of distributing the Bible to the people who needed it, but it wanted to help them to understand and use the Bible in their everyday lives.

It was also in this period that the ABS began to promote itself in the religious and secular press. In 1948, National Family Opinion conducted a survey on behalf of the ABS to evaluate just how well the Society was known among the population of the United States. The survey concluded that over 55 percent of Americans were familiar with the ABS. More women than men knew of the Society and most of them had heard about it in church or through an advertisement in a religious periodical. We do not know exactly how the ABS responded to the results of the survey, but in 1950 the Society appears to have made a conscious effort to raise the number of people who knew of its work. Seven years later, General Secretary Taylor informed the ABS Advisory Council on how things were going: "For the past seven years the Society has given increased attention to publicity in daily and weekly newspapers and in magazines." He reported that ABS stories were pitched to national newspapers, local newspapers, wire services, and over 600 Christian periodicals.[6]

Another way that the ABS reached its audience with the message of God's word was through various forms of audio-visual materials. A Department of Visual Aids was established in 1945 to strengthen the ABS production of filmstrips, motion pictures, radio programming, and eventually television. In the late 1940s filmstrips replaced stereopticon slides as the primary way the Society communicated with its constituency in local churches. In 1961 Secretary James Nettinga wrote that filmstrips were "becoming one of the most important areas of audio-visual service to the churches," and encouraged the ABS to continue to produce one or two a year. By 1955 the ABS was also in the motion picture business. It was distributing close to 1,000 copies of seven films to churches, denominational publishing houses, and Armed Forces chaplains. During the Christmas season it circulated a popular seventeen-minute black and white film called "The Nativity," which could be rented for a twenty-four hour period at the low price of $7.50. These films were expensive to make and the ABS often had to rely on outside funding from businesses such as Westinghouse Electric or Allied Paper Corporation to get them completed. In 1959, between rentals, sales, and leases, these ABS films were shown about 15,000 times. The most popular film was an eighty-four-minute color documentary released for the first time in 1954 titled "The Bible: How It Came To Us." The film featured segments on the how the Bible was written, copied, translated, and printed in English.[7]

The ABS had been involved with the radio industry since the 1920s. It was common for the Society to petition several radio stations for free time so it could air short programs consisting of Bible reading and hymn singing. In 1945 the ABS sponsored "The Bible Quiz," a weekly program broadcast over WNEW in New York that tested listener's knowledge of the Bible. It was based on the very popular national program "Information Please Radio Quiz," which ran on NBC radio from 1938 to 1951. The show began with a song and the reading of a Bible passage. The role of quizmaster was performed by several different scholars and ministers over the years, including future ABS General Secretary Laton Holmgren. The contestants varied from adults to seminary students and children. In 1952 the show moved to television on New York's NBC affiliate. These Bible quiz shows were forerunners to the "The American Bible Society Challenge," an ABS-sponsored television program that began in 2012 and is hosted by popular comedian Jeff Foxworthy.[8]

The man behind the ABS commitment to radio was Francis Carr Stifler, the Secretary for Public Relations. Stifler came to the ABS in 1936 after pastoring churches in Illinois and New Jersey. He was the editor of the *Bible Society Record* and during the war years he hosted an ABS-sponsored program called "Democracy and the Bible" and followed that up with a daily program called "Gems for Thought." As the primary writer of ABS radio material, he prepared over 900 scripts for an ABS program on WFUO in St. Louis and was the primary writer for "The Bible Quiz" on WNEW. Stifler was also influential in negotiating contracts with hundreds of radio stations to promote the ABS annual Worldwide Bible Reading program. By 1950, Stifler was writing and producing "Timely Notes Bulletin," a one- to two-minute spot focused on news from the ABS or human interest stories related to the Bible Cause at home and abroad. Within seven years, "Timely Notes" was being heard over 600 stations around the country and reaching an estimated 90 million people.[9]

Radio, television, and print were not the only avenues by which the ABS brought the message of the Bible to the world. In the late 1950s the Society introduced the Finger-fono—a hand-turned phonograph originally designed by the Radio Corporation of America (RCA) and perfected by the ABS under the leadership of Treasurer Gilbert Darlington. The Finger-fono was about the size of a large dinner plate, cost a little over a dollar to make, and played eight-inch vinyl plastic recordings of a trained speaker reading passages from the Bible. It produced sound through an acoustic diaphragm and a needle located in the arm. The Finger-fono required no electrical power or mechanical device to operate, only a finger capable of fitting in the small finger-mold on the record and the strength to turn it. A newspaper in Lock Haven, Pennsylvania, described it as a machine that a child would love to play with or a "child-like person who could not read, but could listen." The purpose of this new piece of technology was to make the Bible available to the over 1 billion people around the world who could not read. Before bringing it to market, the ABS tested the device, with great success, in Liberia, Pakistan, India, and Mexico. Anyone with ten dollars could order three Finger-fonos and a supply of records and needles. The ABS sold them until the late 1960s when it was replaced by other forms of audio technology.[10]

The Finger-fono was particularly useful among the Navajo Indians of the American Southwest. The ABS tried out the device in 1956 at a Navajo missionary school in Farmington, New Mexico. Though the teachers in the school were skeptical at first, they agreed to accept an ABS gift of 1,000 Finger-fonos and Bible records in the Navajo language and distribute them among similar missionary schools in Gallup, New Mexico and Ganado and Flagstaff, Arizona. Some of the Navajo saw the Finger-fono as little more than another "gadget" with "little value." Many who were initially intrigued by the device eventually lost interest in it, but returned to it whenever new records of Bible passages arrived. The ABS had an easy explanation for this pattern. After listening to the same passages over and over again the users began to memorize them, a practice that warmed the hearts of the missionaries and the staff of the Society. By 1959, over 9,600 records in Navajo had been distributed among the schools to meet the growing demand. Records in Apache, Papago, and Hopi were on their way.[11]

As the ABS experimented with different ways to bring the Bible to the world and raise the necessary funds to do so, they also continued more traditional means of extending the Bible Cause at home. In several American cities, the Society held "Bible Reading Crusades." The largest and most influential of these crusades was conducted in 1946 by the Atlanta Division of the Agency Among the Colored People of the United States (now called the Haven Agency) among the African American coal miners and plant workers of Birmingham, Alabama. Daniel Stanton, the senior secretary of the Haven Agency, inspired the crusade. He wanted to meet the spiritual needs of the more than 100,000 African Americans living in the city. Stanton had spent most of his time in Birmingham gathering informally with these laborers, mostly on weekend afternoons on 4th Avenue North between 16th and 18th Streets, to share the Gospel and teach them the Bible. "These milling throngs," he wrote, "were 'making a living'; but the pace of the wheels of industry gave them little time to think of 'making a life.' "[12]

African American Christian businessmen in the city drafted A. G. Gaston to lead the crusade and serve as its primary organizer. Gaston was the grandson of a former slave, a World War I veteran, a layman in the African Methodist Episcopal Church, and a Birmingham businessman who made his money in insurance, banking, and the funeral services industry. He was the wealthiest African American in Birmingham and was known citywide for providing jobs for out-of-work blacks. He also built the A. G. Gaston Motel in 1954, an important civil rights landmark where Martin Luther King Jr., Ralph Abernathy, and other civil rights leaders stayed free of charge. As racial tensions broke out in Birmingham in the 1950s and 1960s Gaston became an advocate of working peacefully with the city's white businessmen, even at times disagreeing with the approach of King. It is not too much of a stretch to say that the significant role that Gaston played in Birmingham's civil rights movement had roots in his leadership of the city's Bible Reading Crusade in 1946. Gaston was the most influential African American businessman in the state of Alabama, but this was one of his first efforts to organize a citywide event of this scale.[13]

One of Gaston's first moves was to get the support of Birmingham's Negro Business League and African American ministers. He then set a goal of getting 50,000 people—roughly half of the African American population—to read the Bible together on May 12, 1946, the first day of the weeklong crusade. The black community of Birmingham responded in a way that far exceeded expectations. Stanton arranged for 40,000 copies of the Gospel of John to be distributed before the crusade so the city would be ready for the mass reading. The success of the first day reading prompted Gaston's committee to change its distribution goal to 75,000 readers. Gaston purchased 15,000 more copies of the Gospel of John from Stanton and created a subcommittee to provide one for every high school student in the city. Local businessmen turned their stores and offices into what the ABS described as "centers for stimulating an interest in the reading of the Book." Volunteer workers distributed Bibles in every industrial plant in Birmingham that employed African Americans. Others brought scripture portions into the "dark mines and into lives made still darker by sin." In the end, over 101,800 copies were distributed in the city during the week. The ABS granted 62,000 of those Bibles, its largest donation to an organization or denomination in the two decades following the end of World War II.[14]

In the late 1940s and 1950s the American Bible Society had to make some important decisions about how to respond to a new Bible translation that would soon rival the King James (KJV) in popularity and use. From the perspective of the ABS, the arrival of the Revised Standard Version (RSV) of the Bible raised both constitutional and publicity issues. First, how would a rival translation to the KJV be interpreted in light of Article I of the ABS Constitution? The original 1816 article read: "The only copies in the English language to be circulated by the Society, shall be the version now in common use." In 1904, the ABS amended this article in order to sell the English "Revised Version" of the KJV (a revision of the 1611 KJV) and the American Standard Version (an American edition of the Revised Version). The phrase "now in common use" in Article I was removed and replaced with a rather cumbersome statement that acknowledged the existence of the Revised Version and the American Standard Version.[15] But Article I still limited ABS circulation to one of these three versions of the KJV. How might this amendment apply to a completely different translation altogether? Second, if the ABS did somehow find a way to sell and distribute the RSV, backlash from friends and supporters who believed that the KJV to be the only accurate and inspired version of the word of God was inevitable.

The RSV was a product of the ecumenical movement. If Protestants were to come together in a unified fashion and work toward the building of one world church, then they would need a Bible to reflect such a movement. This translation drew upon the best available scholarship in Biblical studies, new archaeological finds that shed light on the Biblical text, and a new style that offered the word of God to readers without the trappings of seventeenth-century English. The proposal for such a Bible translation was authorized by the International Council of Religious Education (ICRE), an organization made up of representatives from forty different denominations committed to the Sunday school education of Protestant young people. The ICRE assembled an impressive team of thirty-two scholars that produced the RSV New Testament in 1946, followed by the entire Protestant Bible in 1952.[16]

The RSV was controversial. The scholars who produced it insisted on translating every passage—whether it be from the Greek, Hebrew, or Aramaic—with the ancient meaning of the text in mind. Such an approach conformed to scholarly practice, but at times it led to English translations that seemed to undermine, or at least raise questions about, cherished Christian doctrines found in the New Testament. The translation team, led by Luther A. Weigle, the Dean of Yale Divinity School, refused to allow New Testament theology to shape the meaning of the Old Testament text. Such an approach to the translation of ancient texts was behind what was easily the most popular criticism of the RSV—the translation of the Hebrew word *almah* in Isaiah 7:14. In this passage, which Christians had long understood as a prophecy of the virgin birth of Jesus Christ, the RSV committee translated *almah* as "young woman" rather than "virgin." The final text read: "Therefore the Lord himself will give you a sign. Behold, a *young woman* shall conceive and bear a son, and shall call his name Imman'uel" (italics mine). The committee's use of "young woman" was not chosen as a theological statement about the virgin birth of Christ, but rather as the most accurate rendering of *almah*. The English word "virgin" was best represented by another Hebrew word.[17] The translation of Isaiah 7:14 was one of many passages in the RSV that did not please conservative Protestants. For many evangelicals and fundamentalists the RSV seemed to deny the virgin birth of Christ. But the more astute conservative critics were quick to point out that the RSV was a product of the ecumenical movement—an attempt to create one church based on the teachings of liberal Protestant theologians. Should any of the Christian reading public be surprised that this committee produced such a sacrilegious version of the scriptures? The attacks only grew more strident when the International Council of Religious Education became a part of the National Council of Churches in 1950.[18]

Because of Article I of its Constitution the ABS could not sell the RSV, and it did not list it in its catalog. But this did not stop some ABS donors from asking the Society to state its official position on the new Bible. When the RSV New Testament appeared in 1946, the executive staff at the Bible House was prepared. They assigned the Secretary of the Versions Committee, Eugene Nida, to handle the flood of mail. Since the Isaiah 7:14 issue would not arise until the Old Testament appeared in 1952, most of the early criticism came from people who believed that the King James Version was the only translation that could be truly considered God's word. Nida responded to these letters with a general template that was polite and courteous. He sympathized with those who found the RSV an affront to their religious upbringings: "I have considerable sympathy for the viewpoint which you express. . . . For myself, I like very much to read the version on which I was brought up. I believe that that is true of many Christians." After connecting with the reader in his first paragraph, Nida got to the heart of the issue by pointing out the difficulties of King James English: There are "thousands and thousands of people who are not accustomed to the terminology of the King James Version, and they become confused and disinterested." If Nida was right, then the KJV was not "doing a real service" for these people. His letter concluded with a standard ABS declaration of neutrality: "The Bible Society has taken no action with regard to the new version. We prefer to wait and see the reactions of the Christian public."[19]

Not every ABS member was negative about the RSV. In 1946 a Lutheran army chaplain wanted the Society to use the new translation for its pocket-sized Testaments and asked for boxes to be sent within six months. A teacher in a Missouri Synod Lutheran School in Colorado wanted to use the RSV in his Bible classes. A Methodist pastor in Kansas City asked the ABS to start printing the RSV and selling it at the usual "moderate prices." As the positive mail continued to arrive at the Bible House, General Secretary Eric North thought it was time to change ABS policy. In a memo to the staff sent on September 26, 1949, North made it clear that the ABS would not be selling or advertising the new translation, although he did mention that the Society had "supplied" copies of the RSV, at the publisher's price (as opposed to the usual ABS discounted price) to "friends of the Society" who requested them "as a matter of service to our constituency." In the meantime, the ABS would continue to wait. If donors "should express widely the judgment that the Society should issue this version," then the Board of Managers would need to seriously consider another amendment to the Constitution.[20]

Over the next several months North remained in correspondence with John Trevor, the director of the Department of English Bible at the ICRE. Trevor urged the ABS to carry the RSV. He appealed to the general secretary's commitment to Bible work in Asia (where he had served as a missionary and educator before coming to the ABS) by noting that missionaries and native Christians in Japan had been asking for the RSV because the English in the translation was easier to read. Trevor's words, and the positive response the Bible House received from its members, seem to have convinced North. In November 1950 the general secretary wrote another memo to the ABS officers suggesting the possibility of altering the Constitution so that the Society could produce RSV Testaments for the armed forces, an inexpensive edition for missionary work, a Testament for general audiences, and a series of scripture portions. The response to his memo was overwhelmingly positive. North also received encouraging responses from the delegates in attendance at the first meeting of the National Council Churches held in Cleveland.[21] In early 1951, North and the Board of Managers felt that they could not let the ABS Constitution get in the way of the sale and distribution of the RSV. In May 1951 the board added the phrase "the New Testament of the Revised Standard Version first issued in 1946" to Article I of the Constitution. The decision to amend was strengthened when the BFBS announced that it wanted to make a similar amendment to its Constitution.[22]

But there was still work to do. North immediately sent a letter to the National Council of Churches (under whom the ICRE, and by extension Weigle's translation committee, was now housed) and Thomas Nelson & Sons, the publisher with exclusive rights to publish the RSV. Permissions needed to be granted before the ABS could add the RSV to its catalog. Roy Ross, the associate general secretary of the NCC, was happy to learn of the ABS's decision and gladly extended permission to publish the translation. The endorsement of a historic organization like the ABS would go a long way toward giving the RSV credibility. But gaining the permission of Thomas Nelson & Sons, a commercial publisher who hoped to make money on the RSV, would be more difficult.

Thomas Nelson & Sons CEO W. R. McCulley wrote to Ross to explain that North's letter "poses certain very definite problems for us." As the exclusive publisher of the RSV, Thomas Nelson & Sons had already spent a lot of money on promotion and planned on spending an additional $500,000 between June 1951 and the end of 1952 on more advertising. McCulley noted that if the ABS wanted to publish the RSV it would need to contribute to these advertising fees, but realizing that the Society was in the business of Christian benevolence, he added that such an arrangement, "of course," would be "unthinkable." McCulley was not happy. If the ABS got in the business of selling the RSV his publishing house would lose a lot of money. Yet he was willing to work with North. "I don't think there is anything in this world that cannot be settled by compromise and by intelligent discussion," McCulley wrote to Ross, "and I would appreciate very much having the opportunity to go over all these points with Dr. North and yourself to see just what can be arranged." In the end, McCulley was willing to consider manufacturing editions with the ABS imprint, but he would not "agree to having them undersell us."[23]

On June 11, 1951, ABS general secretaries North, Robert Taylor, and Frederick Copp met with Ross and McCulley to hammer out an agreement. McCulley agreed to sell a Thomas Nelson & Sons pocket Testament (for use in the Armed Forces) with an ABS imprint at the Thomas & Nelson list price. The same agreement would apply to the inexpensive New Testament, which North thought would be useful for missionaries. McCulley gave the ABS free reign to publish two- and five-cent scripture portions and diglot editions for work in foreign countries and among American Indians and Spanish-speaking Americans. Ross confirmed that the NCC did not expect any royalties from the ABS sales. A deal had been struck. From this point forward, the ABS would sell the RSV, although in limited formats. An announcement was made in the April 1952 issue of the *Bible Society Record*.[24]

As the RSV translation committee continued its work on the Old Testament, Eugene Nida kept in close contact with Luther Weigle, offering suggestions on how to improve early drafts of the text. Meanwhile, the NCC and the ABS worked together on potential ways to celebrate the arrival of the full RSV Bible. It was agreed that the 1952 ABS Worldwide Bible Reading Program would coincide with its release. The ABS was also in the process of producing twenty-four- and thirty-six-page New Testament scripture portions for sale and distribution in accordance with its agreement with Thomas Nelson & Sons. The Society continued to respond to negative mail from donors by affirming that its decision to sell the RSV did not mean that it was planning, either now or at some point in the future, to stop selling the 1611 KJV, the 1884 Revised Version, or the American Standard Version (1901). In a response to a letter from a concerned ABS member, Frederick Copp informed her that "the publishing of another version of the Bible does not in any sense constitute 'departing from the Faith once and for all delivered to the saints.' "[25]

One way in which the ABS dealt with the criticism about its decision to sell the RSV was to gather evidence proving that most American Protestants were very satisfied with the new translation. The society sent a questionnaire to twenty-nine different leaders of denominations asking them if they were using the RSV in Sunday school classes and whether or not they "regarded it favorably or unfavorably." Twenty-three of the denominations surveyed were using the new Bible translation and the rest were either "undecided" or not using it. The churches that gave a favorable response had a combined membership of over 34 million Christians. Yet the opposition continued. Fundamentalist gadfly Carl McIntire, whose American Council of Christian Churches represented the most conservative and separatist brand of Protestant fundamentalism, accused the ABS of altering its charter so that it could produce this "National Council Bible." He saw the decision to circulate the RSV, with all its "notes and remarks," as a violation of the ABS policy to print the Bible "without note or comment."[26]

In January 1952, the ABS issued a statement answering its critics and correcting some misconceptions that Christians had about the Society's decision to circulate the RSV. The statement insisted that most of those who wrote to the ABS in favor of the RSV had taken the time to read or examine the book, but "nearly 90%" of those who opposed the new translation, or are "anxious about the Society's relation to it," had not examined the text and had based their opinions of it largely on what they had read in pamphlets and magazine articles that "do not represent any very widespread opinion among the leadership of the Christian Churches nor among scholars." The ABS asserted strongly that the RSV did not reject the deity of Christ, the virgin birth, and other essential Christian doctrines. As to the criticism that the RSV's sponsoring agency, the National Council of Churches, was a communist organization intent upon creating a "superchurch" ready to milk ordinary people of their hard-earned money, the ABS simply responded: "This is utterly silly."[27]

With the proven success of the RSV Bible, the ABS anticipated making it a major catalog item once Thomas Nelson & Sons' ten-year lease was up in 1962. The ABS could not just continue to amend its Constitution to add every new version of the Bible that would appear from this point forward. After much consideration and study, the Board of Managers agreed to amend Article I in such a way that it would not need reamending in the near future. The final amendment, which was passed by the Board of Managers in January 1960, read "No version of the Holy Scriptures or any part thereof, whether in English or any other language, shall be published by the Society unless publication of such version has first been approved by the Board of Managers."[28]

The ABS learned a hard lesson during RSV controversy. The nineteenth-century evangelical Protestant world in which the ABS was founded had been deeply divided in the 1920s as so-called fundamentalists and modernists waged war for control of the major denominations. The landscape of American Protestantism would never be the same. As much as the moderate and liberal Christians of the Protestant mainline churches were seeking unity through the ecumenical movement, their understanding of unity did not always include the fundamentalists and evangelicals that were bounced from the denominations a generation earlier. The ABS made a good faith effort to work with "bodies outside the National Council," but at least for the next several decades this would be difficult. The National Council, with its commitment to building a Christian nation based on the principles of social justice and ecumenism, still held power in the culture at large. The ABS bond with the National Council was strong, but if it wanted to be a truly *national* Bible society it still had a lot of work to do to strengthen its ties with evangelicals and fundamentalists outside the NCC fold.

21

God's Word for a New Age

In May 1963, the Executive Council of the United Bible Societies proposed a five-year plan to promote the wider circulation of the Bible around the world. They called it "God's Word for a New Age." One of the goals of this new initiative was to address the Bible needs of non-Western countries, particularly those countries in Africa and Asia experiencing the end of European colonialism. UBS General Secretary Olivier Beguin estimated that of the 20 million Bibles the UBS distributed each year, nearly 40 percent of them went to the United States and 60 percent to the "Christian west." Beguin worried that historic Christian nations around the world were being threatened by communism, Islam, and Buddhism to such an extent that the teachings of the Bible might be soon be forbidden in these places. In addition to the needs of the non-Western world, God's Word for a New Age reaffirmed the belief that the distribution of the scriptures was an effective tool for evangelization. The members of the UBS standing committee who met in Eastbourne, England, to hatch this new plan (which included general secretaries Laton Holmgren and Charles Baas of the ABS) believed that the ultimate purpose of the Bible Cause was to win the world to Christ. Finally, the UBS urged Bible societies around the world to be more creative in presenting the Bible to its constituencies. It was, after all, a "new age."[1]

The God's Word for a New Age campaign required the resources of the ABS. In 1966, the Society funded about half of the UBS's World Service Budget.[2] American ingenuity and innovation was defining this new age, and it was the job of the ABS to make sure that the word of God was an influential part of it. The Society called attention to the campaign with a graphic of an open Bible superimposed on a globe with a satellite flying around it. The scientific and technological dimensions of this new age could not be missed. The September 1963 issue of the *Bible Society Record* featured a picture of ABS president Everett Smith and AT&T chairman Frederick Kappel standing in front of an actual size model of the Telstar satellite. In the caption Kappel celebrated the "new age of world-wide communications" that he hoped would "bring about better understanding among people everywhere." But the ABS Board of Managers knew that new ocean cable systems and satellite developments could not bring this kind of mutual understanding alone. Success would depend "largely on what people read."[3]

The world was changing. Progress was taking place at a faster rate than at any other point in human history. As Beguin said in Eastbourne, Western industry was moving into previously undeveloped areas of the world and atomic energy was "becoming a reality for peaceful, as well as destructive, purposes." Humans were not just "contemplating space," they were "exploring it." The ABS recalled the words of Tennyson: "The older changeth, yielding place to new." With technological changes came moral changes. Traditional religious and ethical beliefs were "being discarded" by young people in the United States and abroad. "Decadence" was threatening society. The atomic age had arrived and with it came even more suspicion, hatred, and prejudice, not to mention the threat of nuclear war. It was time to take the Bible "beyond the walls of our churches and homes into the streets and market places of our towns, and into the highways and byways of the world." The United States was exploring space, but only the Bible could "conquer the inner space of men's lives."[4]

The ABS membership had heard this story of decline many times before, and they knew how to right the ship. Donations were needed so that more Bibles could be sent. As was usually the case then the Society delivered such jeremiads, the need was now greater than ever. General Secretary Robert Taylor, always one of the more historically minded twentieth-century leaders of the ABS, reminded the membership how God had always been faithful to the Bible Cause in the United States of America. Since Elias Boudinot founded the Society in 1816 it had provided scriptures to the millions of immigrants arriving on American shores. The result, Taylor argued, "played a large part in making the United States a Biblically rooted nation." He challenged the supporters of the Bible Cause to look to our "forefathers" as an example for engaging yet another new age. The current situation was probably "more difficult" than the challenges that those nineteenth-century leaders of the Bible Cause had faced. The population of the United States was so much larger. The threat of communism was real. But there were still lessons to be learned from the past on how to stem the tide of moral decay and advance the Bible Cause into an uncertain future.[5]

Perhaps the most significant political and cultural issue that the ABS had to deal with in the early 1960s was the US Supreme Court's ruling in *Abington v. Schempp*, the decision that struck down the mandatory reading of the Bible in public schools. *Abington v. Schempp* followed on the heels of *Engel v. Vitale*, the verdict that made prayer in public schools unconstitutional. Both of these decisions drew heavy fire from American Christians. In August 1963, George Gallup concluded that 70 percent of Americans supported prayer and Bible reading in public schools. The debate over religion in public schools heightened over the course of the next several years as legislators, the most prominent being Illinois Republican Everett Dirksen, proposed a constitutional amendment that would allow prayer in public schools, essentially overturning the court's decision in *Engel v. Vitale*.[6] The so-called Dirksen Amendment, which fell nine vote short of the two-thirds minority needed for it to pass in the Senate, did not directly challenge *Abington v. Schempp*, but many ordinary Americans believed that if *Engel v. Vitale* could be overturned, so could *Abington v. Schempp*. Dirksen was their champion.

The American Bible Society did not make any formal statement about *Abington v. Schempp* (or *Engel v. Vitale* for that matter) until popular support for the Dirksen Amendment began to find its way into letters addressed to the Bible House. About one month before the amendment reached the Senate for a vote, Mary Peabody from Hancock, New Hampshire, wrote to the ABS to call attention to the "valiant effort" that Dirksen was making to bring the Bible back into public schools. (She obviously misunderstood that the Dirksen Amendment was about school prayer, not Bible reading.) Her letter was stapled to a postcard with an image of Jacob Duche, the chaplain to the First Continental Congress, praying in Christ Church, Philadelphia, with several of America's founding fathers on their knees surrounding him. Peabody had been present in Washington during hearings on the proposed amendment and was astonished to learn that the Methodist Church and the Seventh Day Adventists opposed it. As representatives from both of these Protestant denominations made their cases before the Senate, Peabody lamented that there was no one present to "oppose or answer their wicked arguments." Unless an organization like the ABS was committed to "rouse the nation" to protest against the "atheism" and "immorality" that *Engel v. Vitale* and *Abington v. Schempp* represented, the amendment would fail and "Freedom of Religion" would be lost. Another ABS donor from Rhode Island wrote to return a sheet of Bible seals sent to her by the Society because Congressman Peter Frelinghuysen, a vice president of the ABS (an honorary role), had voted against the Dirksen Amendment. She could no longer accept the seals "in good conscience."[7]

Many correspondents were angry with the ABS decision to use Chief Justice Earl Warren, who presided over the *Schempp* case (but did not write the majority opinion), in its publications. When General Secretary Laton Holmgren, in a small article that appeared in the September 1966 issue of the *Bible Society Record*, referenced Warren as a public figure who was committed to the teaching of the Bible as literature in public schools, a member from Reseda, California, sniffed it out. "In this . . . issue I found statements touching upon Earl Warren (NOT THE FIRST TIME) & church-related private schools," he wrote, "which only the un-informed could accept. Remove my name from your mailing list." On the other side of the country, a writer from Mountainside, New Jersey, had the same reaction to this issue. He wrote to Holmgren: "It seems to me [surprising] that a person responsible for eliminating prayer and bible reading in our schools would have that much effect on you to quote him." He gave Holmgren an ultimatum. If he found another reference to Earl Warren in the *Record* he would ask that the magazine no longer be sent to him. Another correspondent from Alexandria, Louisiana, noticed that the ABS had chosen Dwight D. Eisenhower as an honorary chairperson for its 150th anniversary commemoration. How could the ABS, she wondered, use Eisenhower for such a purpose when he was the president of the United States who appointed Earl Warren to the Supreme Court? She added that the ABS was so interested in "sending the Gospel to foreign countries" that it failed to see the atheists and Jews behind the Warren court who had removed prayer from public schools. None of these writers were privy to the fact that the ABS was considering presenting its newly conceived "American Bible Society Award" to Warren "for no other reason than having stirred up interest in the need for the Bible in modern-day life." Whoever ultimately rejected this idea probably made a wise decision.[8]

The ABS replied to nearly every letter that it received about *Abington v. Schempp* by putting a positive spin on the Supreme Court decision. Taylor's response to the writer from Reseda was typical: "The American Bible Society is . . . trying to get people to understand that the Supreme Court decision did not rule out the teaching of the Bible in the public schools." Taylor ripped into local school boards for giving people the opposite impression. In fact, as Secretary Homer Ogle wrote to another correspondent, "the Supreme Court is 100% behind the idea of teaching the Bible in the public schools," and the ABS was planning to launch a nationwide program to make sure that children would have access to the scriptures. The ABS answers to these letters must have been confusing to members who did not understand the complexities of the Supreme Court decision. Rather than seeing *Abington v. Schempp* as a blow to Bible reading, the ABS saw it as an opportunity.[9]

In January 1966 the *Record* ran a news report on a recent meeting of the ABS Advisory Council. The Society asked the members of the Council a simple question: "Should the Bible be included in a public school curriculum?" This, of course, was a very different kind of question than the one taken up by the Supreme Court in *Abington v. Schempp*. The issue for the ABS was not whether the Bible could be used in public schools for devotional purposes, but whether it could be a part of a school *curriculum*. The article quoted from Supreme Court Justice Tom Clark's majority opinion in the *Schempp* case:

> It might well be said that one's education is not complete without the study of comparative religion or the history of religion and its relationship to the advancement of civilization. It certainly may be said that the Bible is worthy of study for its religious and historic qualities. Nothing we have said here indicates that such study of the Bible or of religion, when presented objectively as part of a secular program of education, may not be effected consistent with the First Amendment.

With the use of the Bible in the curriculum as a very real option, the ABS was ready to embark on a program to bring Biblical literacy to public school children by providing schools with resources to help them teach the Bible as literature.[10] When it came to this issue, Taylor was a realist. He was willing to accept the fact that the days of devotional Bible reading in schools were over. The ABS would thus throw its resources behind the cause of Biblical literacy. In an interoffice memo titled "The Objective Teaching of the Bible in Public Schools," Taylor informed his staff that *Schempp* offered the ABS an "unusual opportunity." If any organization was equipped to advocate for the Bible in the school curriculum it was the ABS. He announced that a program of "research and experimentation" devoted to this issue was already under way in the state of Indiana, supported by the Lilly Endowment. Taylor was not willing to completely write off the possibility that the academic study of the Bible could lead to spiritual transformation among young readers. He ended his letter to one concerned ABS member by reminding him that "God works in mysterious ways . . . and it is quite possible for us to move from a rather perfunctory Bible reading and prayer period in schools to a vital study of the Holy Scriptures. If this is to occur, it demands the dedicated wisdom of many Christians."[11]

As part of its distribution of God's word in a "new age," the ABS was prepared to tackle the tumultuous changes brought to American society by the 1960s and the important role that young people played in shaping the culture. In 1965, 41 percent of Americans were under the age of twenty. Some of them would soon be packing their bags to serve their country in Vietnam. Others arrived on college campuses where they protested the very war that many of their childhood friends were fighting. Many turned to drugs, communes, sex, and other alternative lifestyles as a means of rejecting what they saw as the competitive, materialistic, and puritanical world of their parents. The civil rights movement of the 1950s and early 1960s took a radical turn, leading to urban riots and more militant forms of protest against American racism. And middle-class women began fighting for equal rights in a society where men held most, if not all, of the power. The ABS believed that it could bring "good news" in a country defined by belligerent rhetoric, violence, reform, and moral decay.

The Bible Cause had been present in Vietnam and Cambodia since 1892 when the BFBS began distributing scriptures in the region. The ABS joined the field in the early twentieth century, and by the time American troops first started arriving in significant numbers the two Bible societies had established a joint agency under the administration of the BFBS. The fighting between the French and the Vietnamese, followed by a civil war between the US-backed government of Ngo Dinh Diem and the communist armies of Ho Chi Minh, wreaked havoc on the 87,000 Vietnamese Christians and their congregations. Church buildings were destroyed, pastors were killed, and the distribution of Bibles became dangerous. The BFBS and ABS tried to meet the needs of thousands of refugees through colporteurs traveling in a Bible society Bookmobile.[12] Stories in ABS publications testified to the powerful role that the Bible played in bringing Vietnamese soldiers to Christ and undermining communism. In 1967, a group of Viet Cong (communist) troops emerged from the nearby mountains to rescue 1,300 of their fellow soldiers who were detained in a South Vietnam prison camp. What this group did not know was that the Bible society Bookmobile had been making regular stops at this prison. Gospel portions were distributed and 200 Vietcong soldiers converted to Christianity. The invading Vietcong forces drove off the guards, killed the commander of the prison, and broke the troops free, but they soon found that 350 of those inside refused to escape with them into the mountains. One of the men who was unwilling to leave was killed on the spot. This story was one of many that informed American audiences of the good work that the ABS was doing in Vietnam. "These men had been introduced to the truth," the 1968 *Annual Report* noted, "and for the first time in their lives knew what it meant to be 'really free.'"[13] The link between spiritual freedom and political freedom was unmistakable.

Throughout the 1960s, the ABS maintained its commitment to the US Armed Forces. In the years since World War I the Armed Forces received more ABS Bibles than any other organization. In 1968, two out of every three American soldiers were presented with a free copy of scripture. The ABS boasted that the 2.1 million Bibles it distributed that year represented an 80 percent increase over armed forces distribution in 1967. Special Bibles were designed for troops in Asia and other regions that featured photos "depicting the natural beauty" of their home states. The annual Easter and Christmas scripture selections were also popular among the troops.[14]

At home, the familiar ABS narrative about the decline of civilization continued. "The influence of Godlessness is manifest in every corner of the globe," the

Society told its supporters in 1968. Crime rates were on the rise. Americans were getting more divorces. Alcoholism had become commonplace again and pornography was making inroads into mainstream culture. Though the ABS never blamed these negative developments on American young people, its board and staff believed that the baby-boomer generation needed to be reached with the message of the Bible in order to quell the immorality. The ABS let its constituency know that it agreed with Dionne Warwick when she sang "What the world needs now is love, sweet love," but it made sure to also remind them that "God is Love." The Society made significant efforts in the late 1960s to connect with the counterculture. For example, when a "long haired-hippie" encountered an ABS display and asked for a book that would help him with his "thought life," he was offered a copy of the ABS's latest New Testament, *Good News for Modern Man*. Despite the man's "aloofness" and "lack of cooperation," he showed interest in the Testament, but decided instead to purchase a small RSV New Testament because it could more "effectively be hidden" in his pocket. The ABS passed out scriptures at rock festivals in the Pacific Northwest and designed Bible resources with the youth culture in mind because "the message of light and life should not be closeted in forbidding columns or regimented type and gloomy black covers."[15]

If the ABS was going to reach the youth culture with the message of the Bible, it would need to be active on college campuses. The Society estimated that college enrollment in the United States had increased 54 percent between 1960 and 1965. The good news was that more and more young people were pursuing higher education. The bad news was the moral depravity that seemed to define the college experience. "This jet-propelled evolution in learning," the ABS noted, "is leaving behind a vapor trail of impatience that causes students . . . to go on rampages of destroying property, stoning, rioting, picketing, striking and shooting." Only the Bible could put the future leaders of the United States back on the right track.[16] The Society tried to reach youth "where they are." In order to do so, it surveyed campus chaplains in 1965 to get a better sense of the Bible reading habits of American college and university students. Chaplains noted that only about 5 percent of students read the Bible. Those who did read the scriptures came from homes where devotional reading was practiced. The survey also revealed that college students wanted the Bible presented in "creative ways" so that it would "come alive" for them in their studies. As the 150th anniversary of the Society approached in 1966, ABS exhibits were scheduled to appear in 250 different college libraries. In 1967, more than 100,000 volumes of scripture, prepared in formats and designs "that would appeal to the 'now' generation," were distributed to college students on 890 campuses around the country.[17]

What is lacking in much of the ABS literature and records during this period is a sustained interaction with the civil rights movement. During the 1950s and 1960s, as the quest for equality and desegregation came to the American South, the *Annual*

Report and the *Bible Society Record* remained silent. As we have seen, for most of the first half of the twentieth century ABS distribution efforts were segregated. The sale of the Bible among African Americans was carried out by the Colored Agency (later named the Haven Agency). Such segregation in Bible work came to an end in 1959 when the ABS closed the Haven Agency, declaring that such "separate but equal" offices had become a "social anachronism." The agents of the Haven Agency worked among the African American population, but did not dabble, at least in their capacity as employees of the ABS, in political matters. This apolitical approach to Bible distribution had been in place for most of the Society's history.[18]

   Distribution in African–American communities, especially in areas where racial tension was high, continued after the closing of the Colored Agency. The ABS began projects in Atlanta, Buffalo, New York, Tampa, Richmond, Washington, DC, and Philadelphia that circulated over a million Bibles in poverty-stricken areas. These programs taught young African Americans that the answers to the problems of race and poverty were always found in the word of God: "The racial and personality conflicts already tearing apart the more densely populated cities of the world will soon strain all of mankind. . . . Either he can resort to attempted solutions of the past and continue to battle his neighbor for the food and land he needs or he can learn to share what is available with the teachings of Jesus Christ. The American Bible Society and the United Bible Societies are helping him make the right choice."[19] In 1969, in the wake of the race riots in Newark, New Jersey, in which twenty-five people were killed and over 10 million dollars of property was destroyed, the Society developed a project to distribute the Bible to people caught in urban poverty. In order to meet the needs of the people of Newark and other American cities during what was the highpoint of the Black Power Movement, the ABS set up a distribution center "in the heart of the ghetto" and circulated a special Gospel portion called "Real Power—Good News by a Man Named John." The Society hired a twenty-two-year-old unemployed Christian named Robert Ross (who the *Bible Society Record* described as being "with it") to lead the project. Ross and other ABS workers passed out Bibles in black Newark neighborhoods, met with city officials and community organizers, and designed programs in cooperation with churches, nonprofit organizations for promoting the arts, and federal-sponsored employment projects. The pilot program ended with an evangelistic crusade conducted by Brooklyn minister Tom Skinner in which the ABS provided copies of "Real Power" to those in attendance.[20]

   Women had always played a significant role in the ABS, working behind the scenes as volunteers and doing much of the labor to keep the nineteenth-century auxiliaries engaged in Bible work. Occasionally the ABS would note their contributions in its publications, but during the 1960s women began to play a much more organized role in the work of the Society. In 1962 the

ABS, aware of the untapped potential of female volunteers, established the Division of Women's Activities. The new division coordinated women's efforts to increase Bible reading at home and in hospitals, nursing homes, and prisons. The director of this new division was Inez Moser, a laywoman who had held several leadership positions in the Presbyterian Church–USA and the ecumenical movement before coming to the ABS. Moser created a Speaker Bureau to encourage women to get involved in grassroots Bible work by lecturing in churches and to civic groups on behalf of the Society and encouraging women to find new ways to distribute the scriptures. The requests for speakers, Moser claimed, "was more than I can handle alone." The Women's Speakers Bureau, which eventually was brought under the Circle of the Concerned, a larger women's group that was not exclusively focused on speaking, was a success. By 1970 the Speakers Bureau had over 163 speakers and the Circle of the Concerned had grown to over three thousand.[21]

1966 was a big year for the American Bible Society. In May, the Society commemorated its 150th year of labor on behalf of the Bible Cause. It was important to many associated with the ABS that the nation take notice of the contribution that the scriptures had made to American history and life. With this in mind, the ABS worked with lawmakers around the country to make 1966 "the Year of the Bible" in the United States. Also in this year the ABS moved into its fourth Bible House. It left the building on Park Avenue and 57th Street and occupied an impressive new twelve-story structure.

In 1963 Everett Smith, the president of the Board of Managers, announced that the ABS headquarters was relocating to the corner of Broadway and West 61st Street in the newly revitalized Lincoln Center area of New York City. The site had been purchased and plans for a new Bible House were in the works. Smith explained the move in terms of the rapid growth the ABS had experienced in recent years. At the time of the purchase of the land, the ABS had 299 employees, but only eighty of them were working at 450 Park Avenue. The rest were scattered in four different locations around the city. The new building would allow all ABS employees to work under one roof. The 1865 Broadway location provided more room for the Society's ever-expanding library that now included 22,000 copies of the Christian scriptures in over 1,000 languages. It was largest Bible library in the western hemisphere and attracted scholars from all over the world. The Board of Managers hoped that the new building would continue to serve as a tourist attraction much in the way that the Astor Place location and the Park Avenue building had appealed to New York City visitors. 1865 Broadway would also have plenty of space for exhibits. And with the "God's Word for a New Age" campaign still underway, and the Society's commitment to doubling its worldwide Bible distribution, the move made sense.[22]

In preparation for the May 1966 anniversary, the ABS planned to look back at 150 years of faithful service to the Bible Cause and look forward, under the auspices of "God's Word for a New Age," to what God had planned for the future. As part of the year's celebration, governors of all fifty states in the Union issued proclamations announcing 1966 as the Year of the Bible. Congress passed a similar resolution put forward by Senator Clairborne Pell and Representative Peter Frelinghuysen, both ABS vice presidents. In the fall of 1965, President Lyndon Johnson invited Americans to observe 1966 with "appropriate ceremonies and activities to the end that all our people may have a better knowledge and appreciation of the Holy Scriptures." The proclamation was important to the ABS for familiar reasons. Christianity was in a state of decline in America. Atheism in the form of communism was making inroads in the Western world. People around the globe were learning to read not from the Bible, but from the writings of Lenin and Stalin. "Let's face it," the editor of the *Bible Society Record* wrote, "this is not a Christian world." But it could be again. With "modern methods of distribution, creative ways may be found" to restore Christianity to its rightful place at the center of world culture. While the declaration of 1966 as the Year of the Bible may have been a mere ceremonial proclamation, for the Board of Managers and the staff ready to move into 1865 Broadway, the future of Christian civilization was at stake. The ABS could be comforted knowing that the president of the United States and the US Senate were joining in the fight to save it.[23]

There was also a 150th anniversary to plan. The ABS put together an impressive group of well-known businessmen and educators to serve on its 150th Anniversary Executive Committee. The members included former governor of New York and presidential candidate Thomas Dewey, editorial chairman of Time Inc., Henry Luce, the presidents of Princeton University and New York University, and the chairmen of US Steel, Chase Manhattan Bank, Chemical Bank, Mutual Life, AT&T, and IBM. James Oates Jr., the chairman of the Equitable Life Assurance Society of the United States, chaired the committee. Harry S. Truman and Dwight D. Eisenhower agreed to serve as honorary cochairmen, and Lyndon Johnson would be the honorary chairman of the committee.[24]

On the afternoon of April 3, 1966—Palm Sunday—the new Bible House was dedicated. A little more than a month later, on May 11, a 150th Anniversary Commemorative Service was held at City Hall, New York, the same building in which the ABS had been founded in 1816. Senator Claiborne Bell was the featured speaker. Fifteen descendants of the ABS founders (some wearing nineteenth-century garb) were recognized. Following the service a reception was held in historic St. Paul's Chapel where commemorative Bibles were presented to the official delegates of the BFBS to recognize the aid it had provided to the ABS at the time of its organization.

The following day a crowd of 3,000 people packed into New York's Philharmonic Hall for the 150th annual meeting of the ABS. Billy Graham was the speaker for the day. His speech was titled "Return to the Bible." He described the "distribution of the Scriptures" as the "greatest method of evangelism" and boldly declared that the ABS was "one the greatest evangelistic agencies in the history of the Christian Church." Graham did not neglect the "American" character of the ABS, stating that that "the Declaration of Independence and the Constitution are based on the precepts of this book. Without it there would have been no America!" Graham then moved into the familiar account of moral decline in the United States that was typical of all his sermons and not unlike the kind of rhetoric the ABS had been using as part of its God's Word for a New Age campaign. He listed the usual suspects (and some new ones): "beatniks," "rebellious youth," "price-rigging executives," "draft card burners," "professional bearded protestors," purveyors of "sexual immorality," and "dope addicts." America was on its way to becoming a "secular society." Only a "return to the Bible" would strengthen families, reverse the "terrifying crime statistics," "heal racial tensions," put "sex in the right perspective," and ultimately restore a "high sense of destiny to our nation."[25]

After Graham's message those in Philharmonic Hall formed a procession down Broadway to the new Bible House. Donald Coggan, the Archbishop of York and the president of the United Bible Societies, offered a prayer of blessing on the building. The next evening a dinner was held at the Waldorf Astoria Hotel, and then it was all over.[26] There was now work to be done. Scriptures needed to be distributed. Morality needed to be restored. And the United States needed to be returned to its Biblical heritage.

Catholics

Until the 1960s, the relationship between the ABS and the Roman Catholic Church was not a warm one. Though Catholics received a last-minute invitation to participate in the founding of the ABS in 1816, there was very little cooperation between the ABS and the Roman Catholic Church in the nineteenth century. In fact, it would be fair to say that Catholic–ABS relations were at times downright hostile.[1] The ABS distrust of Roman Catholics, and vice versa, continued well into the twentieth century. Yet as Catholic views of the Bible began to change as the century wore on, so did the relationship with the ABS. During the 1950s some liberal Catholic scholars called for a more accurate and "scientific" translation of the Bible that might draw from conversations with Protestants. Representatives from the ABS and UBS were saying positive things about the work of Catholic scholars. Though there was still resistance to the idea of cooperation with Protestants on matters related to the Bible, the papacy of John XXIII (1958–1963) put much of this opposition to rest and opened the door for unprecedented collaboration between the Catholic Church and Protestant denominations.[2]

John XXIII's papacy was short, but it was significant in terms of Catholic–Protestant relations. In 1960 he formed the Secretariat for Christian Unity in an attempt to get the Church engaged with the ecumenical movement. Then, in October 1962, he called for a Second Vatican Council (Vatican II). In November 1964 the Council issued *Unitatis Redintegratio* (Restoration of Unity), a decree that set forth the need for cooperation with the "separated Brethren" of the Protestant and Eastern Orthodox churches. It stressed that such unity was "one of the principal concerns" of the Council. Vatican II cast the blame for the Protestant Reformation on both the Catholic Church and the separated Brethren. It claimed that "all who have been justified by faith in Baptism are members of Christ's body and have a right to be called Christians." It even went as far to note that salvation might be found outside of the Catholic Church. In order to exercise this newfound call for unity, the conference asked for "dialogue between competent experts from different

Churches and Communities." Though the Council was clear about the fact that fundamental differences still existed between the theological beliefs of Catholics and Protestants, *Unitatis Redintegratio* made some historical concessions and opened several doors for conversation between the two forms of Christianity.[3]

One year later Paul VI, who continued the conference after John XXIII's death in June 1963, issued the "Dogmatic Constitution on Divine Revelation," a specific statement on the Catholic view of the Bible. While this document affirmed historic Catholic beliefs in the revelatory nature of the Bible, its inspiration and inerrancy, and the authoritative role of the teaching office of the Church in interpreting the Bible, it also taught that "easy access to the Sacred Scripture should be provided for all the Christian faithful." While the document acknowledged the Church's historic commitment to the Latin Vulgate, it also allowed, in the spirit of making the word of God "accessible at all times," the translation of the Bible into different languages from the "original texts of the sacred books." It added that these new translations from the original Greek and Hebrew (as opposed to the Latin Vulgate) could be "produced in cooperation with the separated brethren" so that "all Christians will be able to use them." The Dogmatic Constitution also encouraged the laity to read freely from the Bible: "All the Christian faithful . . . should gladly put themselves in touch with the sacred text itself, whether it be through the liturgy . . . or through devotional reading." In the end, the Council called "for a new stimulus for the life of the Spirit from a growing reverence for the word of God, which 'lasts forever.' "[4]

Even before the Second Vatican Council had issued these official statements on ecumenism and the Bible, the ABS and UBS were meeting to discuss what cooperation with Catholics in the Bible Cause might look like. In June 1964, twenty-five Bible society leaders and seventy-five church leaders gathered in Driebergen, Netherlands, to talk about the future of Bible work around the world in light of rising literacy rates and opportunities afforded by mass media. What is significant about this meeting was that two representatives of the Roman Catholic Church in the Netherlands were present. The delegates at Driebergen concluded that the Bible societies affiliated with UBS should encourage the "preparation, in collaboration with all Churches, including the Roman Catholic Church, of a common text in the original languages, to be the one source of translation for all Christians." The time was right. The word coming out of Vatican II was that the Catholics would be open to such an idea and Biblical scholarship had risen to such a level that such a common Bible was now a possibility. Laton Holmgren, who was part of the ABS delegation in Driebergen, informed his colleagues at the Bible House that "contacts with Roman Catholic circles should be pursued at all levels in order to produce a common text . . . to prepare common translations, and when circumstances permit, publish joint editions."⁵

Conversations continued within the UBS and ABS, both formally and informally, in the wake of the Driebergen conference. In October 1964, UBS General Secretary Oliver Beguin, who had just completed a short book on new trends in Roman Catholic attitudes toward the Bible, chronicled the early state of Protestant-Catholic discussions about a common Bible in the wake of what was happening in the Second Vatican Council. Catholic bishops in Pittsburgh, New Orleans, Washington, DC, and Columbus, Ohio, all made statements in support of a common Bible several years before Paul VI released the Dogmatic Constitution. They would find a Catholic ally in Cardinal Agostino Bea, the head of Paul VI's Secretariat on Christian Unity. In a series of lectures at Harvard University, Bea stressed the importance of the scriptures for "all Christians." Elsewhere in Boston, Cardinal Richard Cushing, who had recently endorsed a Catholic version of the Revised Standard Version for personal Bible study (but not liturgical use), also threw his support behind a common Bible as a means for promoting Christian unity. Beguin was pleased that Vatican II affirmed *Divino Afflante Spiritu* ("Inspired by the Holy Spirit"), Pius XII's 1943 encyclical allowing Catholic scholars to use modern critical techniques when interpreting the scriptures. Beguin was aware of at least thirty different cases between 1962 and 1964 in which Roman Catholics had sought cooperation with Protestant Bible societies. These included requests to publish Protestant texts with the inclusion of the Apocrypha, applications to publish Protestant Bibles with the addition of Catholic notes or slight textual changes, and consultations with Protestant translators in native settings around the world. Beguin was optimistic about such ecumenical cooperation, but he also warned the Bible societies of the UBS to proceed with caution and not be seduced by "blind optimism." There was still a lot that needed to happen including the convincing of "doubters," "fundamentalists," and "traditionalists"—before a truly common Bible could be brought to fruition.⁶

In the week following the festivities surrounding the 150th anniversary of the founding of the ABS, delegates from the UBS, many of them still in the country following the celebration, met in Bucks Hill Falls, Pennsylvania, to continue conversations concerning cooperation with Roman Catholics. Holmgren, who was spearheading these discussions from the ABS side, chaired the meeting. It got underway with an address from Walter M. Abbott, SJ, a forty-three-year-old Jesuit and the son of a Catholic convert from New England. Abbott was religion editor for the liberal Catholic magazine *America* and had gained a reputation as one of the nation's strongest advocates for cooperation among Catholics and Protestants in the creation of a common Bible. (Abbott called the day Paul VI released the Dogmatic Constitution "one of the greatest days of my life.") He told a room full of Protestants that the Catholic Church, through the decisions made at the Second Vatican Council, had "finally, fully, and formally joined the ecumenical movement" and, in essence, "had endorsed the idea of a common Bible." Abbott admitted that this was a "novel departure" for his Church, but he was willing to do what he could to make sure the decrees of the Vatican, particularly as they related to the scriptures, would be put into practice. He asked for help from the UBS and looked forward to more and more Catholics becoming familiar with the work of Bible societies around the world.[7]

On November 8, 1966, the Catholic Church finally made it official. Paul VI ordered Cardinal Bea of the Secretariat on Church Unity to move forward in the production and distribution of a common translation of the Bible in cooperation with the Protestants of the UBS. Abbott was appointed as a special assistant to Bea and charged with the task of directing the project. Eugene Nida, the director of ABS translations who had been following the work of Catholic biblical scholars for several decades, told the *New York Times* that this new development meant that "church politicians had caught up with the scholars." Nida knew that Catholic and Protestant scholars had agreed on the best Greek and Hebrew manuscripts for use in translation for "half a century," but it took Vatican II to make the possibility of such a common Bible a reality. Meanwhile, Abbott was on a plane from Rome to New York, where he would speak to the Advisory Council of the ABS, a group of delegates from seventy-five Protestant denominations in the United States. The speech took place on November 15 at the Park Sheraton Hotel. Abbott won over the crowd by describing this new joint effort in Bible translation as a "common witness to the non-Christian world." While he agreed with Nida that Protestant and Catholic biblical scholars had long been in agreement on the Greek and Hebrew texts needed to undertake such work, he was also realistic about the challenges ahead. If potential problems in this cooperative effort arose, they would no doubt stem from the appropriate translation of the Apocrypha and whether the Catholic Church would be willing to publish Bibles without note or comment.[8]

With the official approval of the Catholic Church, serious discussions could now begin on how to proceed with a common Bible that would be produced, translated, and distributed by both Catholics and Protestants. In January 1967 Beguin, Holmgren, Nida, John Watson of the BFBS, and several other national Bible societies affiliated with the UBS flew to the Vatican to get the conversations started. Cardinal Bea greeted them and introduced the thirteen Roman Catholic delegates who would be joining the discussions. Bea expressed "the hope that this meeting may clarify the possibilities of cooperation between the United Bible societies and the Catholic Church for a work that is basic and vital to the future of Christianity: translation and distribution of the Bible." Bea was confident that the "Holy Spirit is surely at work, drawing us together to the Bible." He called the meeting "one of the most important developments in contemporary Christian history." Holmgren's initial speech was filled with both optimism and realism. He "rejoiced" in the dialogue that was about to begin, but, like Abbott, he knew "there will be difficulties." He referenced

> the heritage of suspicion and hostility, the conservative resistance to change in both traditions, misinformation—or no information at all—regarding the policies and procedures of the other, the unequal size and strength of our constituencies in different parts of the world, and a whole cluster of practical problems involved in joint administration of such cooperative efforts as we are here to consider.

Holmgren ended by asking whether Jesus Christ's "command to preach the Gospel in all the World" will be defined by "shameful competition or joyful cooperation." He sensed the historic nature of this meeting: "What we do here may, indeed, hasten the day when we can triumphantly proclaim to a skeptical world that there is, indeed, one faith, one Gospel, one Lord of all."[9]

Abbott brought the consultation in Rome to a close with a presentation on the current state of the UBS-Catholic dialogue. Many of those in attendance on the UBS side were familiar with this history, but some of the representatives on the Catholic side would need to get up to speed on the purpose of the Bible Cause. The delegates continued to work on a document, originally composed at a meeting with UBS and Catholic representatives (and probably written by Nida) at Cret Berard, Switzerland, in November 1964, that set out rules for common translations. These discussions resulted in official papers that would be published over the course of the next several years.[10]

Following the conference in Rome, Holmgren headed to Argentina, Brazil, Uruguay, Paraguay, Bolivia, and Peru to inform the Bible societies in South America about the developments taking place in UBS–Catholic relations and to get a sense of how this heavily Catholic region of the world—a place where there was a history of animosity between Catholics and the Bible Cause—would react to such developments. Holmgren received little resistance to the idea of a common Bible, but South American Protestants urged the UBS to proceed with care. Later in the year he traveled to Venezuela, Colombia, and Ecuador. After his visits, Holmgren concluded that both Protestants and Catholics were willing to accept a common Bible. In fact, Catholic and Protestant Bible translators in several South American countries were already at work in translation efforts along these lines. Later in the year, the UBS received similar feedback from Catholic leaders in Burma, Thailand, Japan, and India.[11]

1968 proved to be a monumental year for the UBS–Catholic collaboration. In June, the long-awaited *Guiding Principles for Interconfessional Cooperation in Translating the Bible* was released jointly by the UBS and the Secretariat for Promoting Christian Unity. The document, which had been worked out in Cret Berard, included many of the same translation principles that the ABS and UBS had been using for decades, but certain accommodations were made to conform the principles to Catholic desires. The philosophy of translation put forth included: (1) the use of a critical edition of the Greek text prepared by a committee of scholars representing both the Protestant and Catholic faiths; (2) the use of the Masoretic Hebrew text of the Old Testament edited by Rudolph Kittel; (3) editions of the complete Bible bearing the imprimatur of the Catholic Church would contain the deuterocanonical text (which Protestants refer to as the Apocrypha), but would be published in a separate section before the New Testament; (4) the use of commentaries and other "critical studies" for translation would be jointly approved by a commission of Protestant and Catholic scholars; (5) Bibles could contain "helps" for readers, including alternative readings or renderings, explanations of proper names or plays on words, historical background information, maps, explanations of unfamiliar cultural terms, a cross-reference system, and sectional headings within the text; (6) translations would not include explanations in notes about differing Catholic and Protestant interpretations of a given passage; (7) translations could include an index, concordance, and illustrations; (8) prefaces should omit references to "ecclesiastical authority"; and (9) any edition prepared jointly by Protestants and Catholics would bear the imprint of the Bible society on the title page and the imprimatur of the "appropriate Catholic authority" on the back of the title page."[12]

Walter Abbott became a tireless promoter of the new guidelines among his fellow Catholics, writing several articles and pamphlets defending their purpose and lauding the collective efforts that went into making them. In a June article in the Jesuit magazine *La Civilita Cattolica*, which was later republished in pamphlet form with the title *The Shape of the Common Bible*, he offered commentary on the guidelines with the concerns of his fellow Catholics in mind. For example, he assured Catholics that the guidelines had been approved by the Pontifical Biblical Commission of the Roman Catholic Church. He explained the cooperation with Protestants as a direct result of Vatican II and the UBS's willingness to allow helps and nondoctrinal annotations that would satisfy Catholic requirements. On the latter point, canon law required that editions of the Bible must have notes, but it did not stipulate that such notes must be doctrinal or dogmatic in nature. For those Catholics who feared that these new common Bibles would be based on a Greek text that was edited by Protestants, Abbott was ready with an answer. Though the guidelines did mention a specific Greek text, Abbott added that there was already a general agreement on the use of the text edited by Kurt Aland, Matthew Black, Bruce Metzger, and Allen Wikgren. Since none of these editors were Catholic, it was agreed that Carlo Martini, SJ of the Pontifical Biblical Institute in Rome, would be added to the editorial team for the next edition, which was already under way. Abbott was also quick to note that the guidelines used the phrase "deuterocanonical books" and not the Protestant "Apocrypha" to describe the books for which there was disagreement over canonicity. He further explained that the new ordering of the books in the common Bibles (the moving of the deuterocanonical books into a separate section before the New Testament) was approved by Paul VI. The ordering of books was not considered a doctrinal matter.[13]

Abbott also clarified to his Catholic readers the procedure behind such joint translations. The guidelines noted that "procedures will differ radically" depending on whether the translation is a new translation or a revision. New translations, he argued, would be more conducive to ecumenical cooperation because they allowed for "freedom to adopt new forms of language and a more relevant style." The "psychological attitudes" of Catholics and Protestants toward one another in a given country would also need to be taken into consideration in all translation projects. Abbott was ready to admit, along with his UBS colleagues, that in some parts of the world the tensions between the two Christian bodies was too great for such translations to take place. He also knew that many conservative Protestant groups were opposed to working with Catholics. Where the religious "climate" of a given location was advantageous to a joint translation, the work was to be done by working committees of four to six translators equally divided between Catholic and Protestant constituencies. A review committee of eight to ten people "especially qualified in study of Bible texts, exegesis, and style," would evaluate all translations. Finally a consultative committee, made up of twenty-five to fifty Church leaders, would give final approval to translations. These committees would be chosen by natives who understood the religious landscape of their countries and regions. Outside consultants, who usually came from the ABS, BFBS, or the Catholic Church, could be used for the purpose of determining the qualifications of those involved. The procedure was not perfect—cooperation needed to be worked out in light of local circumstances and Abbott fully expected "pressures" to "build up"—but it was a start to the implementation of the ecumenical vision of both Vatican II and the UBS.[14]

Though the new relationship with Catholics was forged under the umbrella of the UBS, back home in the United States the ABS was responsible for making sure that all of its constituency was on board with the plan. Perhaps the greatest concern, which was expressed by many evangelical groups, was the decision to publish the Bible with the Apocrypha. This was a major point of discussion, for example, at the December 1968 meeting of the UBS Regional Conference of the America's in Oaxtepec, Mexico. Many in attendance were worried that Bible society representatives might be forced to distribute *only* Bibles containing the Apocrypha. In order to address these concerns, the ABS turned to Arnold T. Olson, the president of the Evangelical Free Church of America and the National Association of Evangelicals. Olson was also a member of the ABS Board of Managers and was in attendance at the Oaxtepec meeting. He was an ideal person to calm the fears of the evangelicals about Apocrypha. Olson's report from the meeting appeared in the April 1969 edition of the *Bible Society Record*. He recognized that the implementation of the Vatican II reforms concerning the Bible would take time, especially in Latin America where, as we have seen, Protestants suffered much persecution at the hands of local Catholics. Olson proved to be a good foot soldier in the ABS campaign to make this ecumenical experiment work. He explained that Father Walter Abbott had made it abundantly clear that he did not expect Protestants to accept the canonicity of the Apocrypha or even distribute Bibles that contained it. He only asked that the Bible societies provide Bibles containing the deuterocanonical books when Catholics asked for them. Olson reported that Protestants in Oaxtepec were willing to accept the fact that Catholics had made a major concession by allowing the deuterocanonical books to be segregated between the Old and New Testaments, but they also asked that an explanatory note be placed somewhere in the Bible explaining that Protestants and Catholics differed on the "value" attributed to these books. In addition, evangelicals requested that their contributions to the ABS would not go toward the printing of the Apocrypha.[15]

Some delegates at Oaxtepec were anxious about the ecumenical nature of this newfound cooperation between Protestants and Catholics. Olson handled this issue sympathetically: "A major fear was the Bible Societies might become tools in the hands of ecumenists to bring about an eventual organic union of all churches, Protestant and Catholic." This was a major concern among evangelicals in the United States, but it had more immediate relevance for Latin American Protestants. "Many who were at Oaxtepec," Olson wrote, "do not have to go as far back as the Reformation to know what takes place when one church exists. They have personally experienced life with a single church exercising ecclesiastical, education, economic, and political power over all the citizens of the state." To answer this concern, Olson called attention to the preamble of a document, probably prepared by the ABS, which had been distributed to all of the delegates in Oaxtepec. It was titled "Cooperation with the Roman Catholic Church." This paper made it clear that the UBS and ABS had enlisted the support of all Christian groups for the sole purpose of encouraging "the wider distribution of the Holy Scriptures throughout the land without doctrinal note or comment. It is no more their province to participate in the ecumenical dialogue than it is to legislate on the method of Christian baptism." The Bible society movement was not in the business of ecumenical dialogue for the sake of mere dialogue with other Christian bodies. Instead, its leaders were engaged with Catholics "in the most urgent task of our time—the proclamation of the good news of the Gospel in every land and in every tongue." Olson left the meeting with "his faith strengthened and his assurance renewed that the Holy Spirit still moves in the hearts, minds, and wills of men." And it was hard for any evangelical to argue with that.[16]

But there were still questions about such a reconciliation with Catholicism. Old prejudices die hard. As the ABS reported on the various conferences and consultations with the Catholic Church, it had to continuously explain what was happening to some of its disgruntled constituency. A donor from Michigan wrote in 1966: "We haven't sent in our Contributions [*sic*] ever since we heard that you are going to publish a Bible that agrees with both Catholics and Protestants. We cannot go along with this project as a bible like that will no longer be God's word." This writer's concerns were common among critics of this new ecumenical arrangement. Much of the opposition came down to the perceived differences between Protestant and Catholic views of salvation: "We say that a man is justified by faith without the deeds of the law. While others say a man is justified by faith and works." This critic chided the ABS for always trying to remain "relevant to our modern & liberal trends" when they should be "relevant to God's Word and ways." At the point the ABS received this letter, the relationship between the Bible societies and Catholics had not reached its full fruition. As a result, General Secretary Robert Taylor was able to answer his correspondent by saying "the Roman Catholic Church has made approaches to the Bible Societies and we have agreed to listen." But Taylor must have known that such an answer would only be viable for so long.[17]

Another ABS supporter, also from Michigan, had read in his local newspaper that "representations from 'Rome headquarters'" was coming to the Bible House in New York to promote a "Common Bible" for all. "I don't know what they mean by a Common Bible," he added, "but I fear tampering with God's Holy Word." This time Taylor took more time to respond. The newspaper reports, much to his chagrin, had left the impression that the ABS was trying to produce a common Bible in English when in fact it was actually just trying to reach an agreement on the Hebrew and Greek texts to be used in translating the Bible into "languages that thus far do not have the Scripture." Taylor realized that such cooperation had potential pitfalls, but he concluded his response by noting that "we are also aware that the present changes [in Catholic relations with the Bible Cause] may be the work of the Holy Spirit and we must try to find out."[18]

The new relationship between the Bible society movement and the Catholic Church was indeed a historic, and often forgotten, moment in the history of Catholic–Protestant relations. The détente between these two approaches to Christianity was a long time in coming. But there were still questions that needed to be answered. Should the ABS and other Bible societies invite Catholics to serve on their boards and committees or be employed as members of their staffs? Should ABS staff accept invitations to preach or present the Bible Cause in Roman Catholic churches and conferences? These questions would eventually be answered with an enthusiastic "yes," but for now they remained open-ended questions that would need to be worked out in the 1970s and 1980s. One effective means by which the ABS eased its transition toward this new relationship with Catholicism was through the publication, promotion, and distribution of a new, more contemporary, Bible translation that brought the "good news" to Christians and non-Christians alike in a way that was unprecedented in the 150 years of the Bible Cause.[19]

23

Good News

When Rick sees the cover of *Good News for Modern Man*, he experiences a flood of wonderful memories. In the late 1960s he was a member of a middle-school church youth group in California singing "Jesus folk-rock" under the guidance of older high school students with acoustic guitars. Rick's church "gave out copies of *Good News for Modern Man* like candy." As youth group started each week, he and his friends would "crowd in on the floor and some-body would start tossing—literally tossing—the Testament and a brown Youth for Christ songbook" to everyone in attendance that night. Like typi-cal adolescent boys, Rick and his friends would start getting rowdy, using the copies of *Good News* to beat one another over the head. Soon the youth pas-tor would manage to calm everyone down and the lesson would begin. As Rick looks back on his experience, he recalls that his favorite parts of *Good News for Modern Man* were the "simple line drawings" of Jesus that filled its pages. "That was my Jesus," Rick said. "Our parents' generation had that sort of whispy portrait of Jesus looking medicated," he added, "but we had the Jesus depicted in *Good News for Modern Man* . . . my Jesus was more intrigu-ing, sort-of-kindly and calm."[1]

Stan wasn't alive when *Good News for Modern Man* was released in 1966, but he remembers that there was a copy of the paperback New Testament at his grandmother's house. He was fascinated by the newspaper mastheads on the cover and as a native Georgian was thrilled that the *Atlanta Journal* had made the cut. Gene was a graduate student at Cornell University in the late 1960s. He has fond memories of receiving boxes of *Good News* portions and handing them out as part of a student evangelistic campaign on campus. Caryn, a Lutheran theologian, still has her copy of the *Good News Bible* given to her on November 11, 1979, by the women of the East Side Lutheran Church. Una read *Good News for Modern Man* in a class at her diocesan Catholic high school sometime in the mid-1970s. In 1972, Tom was a charismatic Catholic participating in an ecumenical "Jesus People" prayer meeting with Protestant Pentecostals. When they weren't laying on the ground speaking in tongues (which Tom called a "joyous Babble in the Spirit"), they were playing "Bible roulette" with their copies of *Good News for Modern Man*. Someone would randomly read a passage aloud and one or two people in the group would comment on how the particular passage was "intended for me." Everyone seems to have a story or memory about this Bible.[2]

When it was released in September 1966, *Good News for Modern Man* was a cultural phenomenon. It was one of the most successful religious publications in American history. *Good News* was the New Testament translation of the ABS-inspired Today's English Version (TEV). For the price of a quarter, the English-speaking public (and eventually the world) could read the Bible in language that the ABS said was "as fresh and immediate as the morning newspaper." While the Society had been translating, publishing, and distributing the King James Version and the Revised Standard Version for decades, Today's English Version was its first attempt at creating its own English-language translation of the Bible.[3]

Any discussion of the history of Today's English Version must begin with longtime ABS Director of Translations, Eugene Nida. Born into a Methodist family in Oklahoma City in 1914, Nida was raised in a Quaker meeting in Long Beach, California, embraced his wife's Baptist faith after they married, and later in life worshipped at a Presbyterian church in Darien, Connecticut. His spiritual journey represented the ecumenical flavor of the organization to which he would devote his life. Nida was a boy with a love for the Bible and a heart for the mission field. During the Great Depression he enrolled at UCLA to study ancient Greek in the hopes of becoming a Bible translator. He graduated in 1936 as the university's only Greek major and with one of the highest grade point averages in UCLA history. Nida then studied the Greek New Testament at nearby University of Southern California, and in 1943 received a PhD in linguistics and anthropology from the University of Michigan. In that year he married Althea Lucille Sprague, was ordained as an American Baptist Minister, and started working part-time for the ABS as a translator.[4] Nida's first contact with linguistics and Bible translation came following his graduation from UCLA when noted Bible translator and founder of Wycliffe Bible Translators William Cameron Townsend invited him to spend a session at Wycliffe's Summer Institute of Linguistics. He would eventually join the staff of the Summer Institute of Linguistics, where he helped train an entire generation of Bible translators. Nida spent the rest of his career providing leadership to the ABS translation efforts. He served as the academic and intellectual leader of the Society for more than fifty years. As executive secretary for translations he was constantly on the road, sometimes up to ten months a year. He consulted closely with missionaries and native translators, fixed translation problems and trained new translators to continue to carry on the work of the ABS and the UBS. At the time of his retirement in 1984 he had worked in eighty-five different countries.[5]

In the world of academic translation studies, Nida is known best for his theory of "dynamic equivalence." At the heart of this theory is the idea that a quality translation of a particular text—in this case the Bible—is proportionate to the "reader's unawareness that he is reading a translation at all." Nida was one of the first translation theorists to take the reader seriously. A good translation, he argued, will arouse a reader to have the same reaction to the text that the writer of the text hoped to produce in his "first and immediate" readers. For Nida, "the ultimate test" of a translation was how well the readers understood the message of the original text, the ease with which they could grasp this meaning, and the level of involvement with the text that they experienced as a result of reading the translation. On the latter point, Nida wrote, "perhaps no better compliment could come to a translator than to have someone say, 'I never knew before that God spoke my language.'" He was convinced that it was necessary every now and then to change the words of the Bible. Dynamic equivalence was less a "word for word" approach to translation, and more of a "meaning for meaning" or "thought for thought" method.[6]

Nida hoped that people would read the Bible, understand it, and be "transformed by its message." This meant that the Bible needed to be translated into a common language that all literate people—educated and uneducated—could understand. Nida was an academic with a passion for the church. As a young man he often wondered why the English edition of the Greek classics were so much easier to read than the popular English translations of the Bible. He became convinced that in order for the church to grasp the Bible's message, it had to stop focusing on words and concentrate more fully on message. Nida wanted people to start concentrating on the message of Scripture so that they could share its meaning with others. He argued that the church had become so familiar with the text of the King James Bible that it had lost all desire to think deeply about the message. New translations, especially those based on the principle of dynamic equivalence, had the potential to bring an end to complacency and force Christians to think about the meaning of scripture afresh and anew.[7]

The roots of the *Good News Bible* go back to the 1940s, when Nida and other translators working in Latin America were contemplating the production of a Bible in simple language that could be used by natives with only a limited understanding of Spanish and literate people who preferred a version that was easy to read. This Bible was eventually published in 1966 by the Bible Societies of Latin America as the "Version Popular." Portions of this Latin American translation had been so popular that Nida and the ABS began to think seriously about a common language translation in English. General Secretary

Laton Holmgren liked the idea and in 1961 gave Nida the approval to move forward with such a project, concluding his letter of support with the phrase "Let's go!"[8] Nida knew that there were other translators working on similar common Bibles. A Canadian Pentecostal translator and missionary named Annie Cressman approached the ABS for help in translating the Gospel of Mark for Christians in the Liberian district of Tchien. Nida assisted Cressman with her translation and it was published in 1959. Cressman's translation of the Gospel of Mark was so successful in Liberia that when she approached the ABS with a translation of the Gospel of John a few years later, Nida jumped at the opportunity to publish it. It appeared in 1962 under the title *He Gave His Only Son*. Meanwhile, when Cressman's Gospel of Mark translation continued to sell, the ABS adopted it as well, publishing it in the same year under the title *The True Servant*. Meanwhile, about two weeks before Holmgren approved a common translation in English, Nida received a letter from M. Wendell Belew, a secretary with the Home Mission Board of the Southern Baptist Convention. Belew asked Nida if he and the ABS would be willing to produce a "4th grade level" English Bible that could be used for readers whose first language was not English.

Nida would later deny that the Cressman translations and the Belew letter had anything to do with the decision to publish a common language Bible. He claimed that he and his translators had already established the "principles and procedures" for such a Bible in Latin America well before Cressman and Belew came along. But it is also hard to ignore the fact that Cressman's portions were a success. Similarly, Belew's letter signified that there were others in the United States who were interested in such a project. "With a Pentecostal in Africa and . . . a Southern Baptist," Nida wrote, "what better advice could you get on the matter of making a translation that everybody could read?" The ABS knew that translations of the Bible almost always bred controversy, but after their experience with the RSV in the 1950s, how could things get any worse?[9]

It was common for translation projects of this nature to start with the Gospel of Mark. The ABS encouraged Cressman to prepare a new translation of Mark that could be used by people living outside of West Africa. They also encouraged translator Robert Bratcher to prepare his own translation of Mark based on the principles being used in Latin America that would later be described as dynamic equivalence. The ABS translation committee made it clear that its interest in publishing a common language version of Mark was purely "experimental" in nature. The target audience was people for whom English was not their first language. After much debate over what to call this style of translation, the committee chose "Popular English" over "Plain English" and "Simple English," which they felt might come across as too derogatory.[10]

As a part-time member of the ABS translation staff, Bratcher was familiar with the kind of translation that Nida had in mind. His translation of Mark's Gospel included short and simple sentences each containing "one or two ideas or statements of fact" and he emphasized a style that he called "modern American vernacular." He warned the committee that such vernacular would require him to use contracted forms such as "don't" and "isn't" because, as he put it, "these forms are most natural in vernacular speech, and their studied avoidance sounds stilted and pedantic." Bratcher also strove for clarity in his translation of Mark. He did not use "archaic" terms such as "thee" or "thou." Terms that were unique to the first-century Jewish world were retained and explained in a glossary at the end of the text. Finally, Bratcher wanted his translation to be "precise." All ambiguity was to be avoided. If there were multiple ways to translate a particular Greek passage, Bratcher would choose one and simply disregard the others. There would be no alternative readings listed in footnotes. The Translation Committee was impressed with the creativity and accessibility of Bratcher and voted 40 to 0 to move ahead with a full New Testament under his supervision.[11]

Bratcher was the son of Southern Baptist missionaries in Brazil who attended Georgetown College, Kentucky, and was trained theologically at Southern Baptist Seminary in Louisville. He came to the ABS with experience as a Baptist pastor and US Navy chaplain during World War II. Bratcher taught at the Southern Baptist South Brazil Theological Seminary in Rio de Janeiro from 1949 to 1956 until he resigned from the Southern Baptist Foreign Mission Board over a dispute related to his teaching.[12] Bratcher and his team of translators worked in a Sunday school classroom at the Madison Avenue Baptist Church in New York. Nida would later remember the room: "It had a blackboard, chalk, copies of text, some commentaries, and a good supply of coffee."[13] After two and a half years of work, *Good News for Modern Man* was released in September 1966. It was 608 pages long and appeared with a gray paperback cover filled with black lines, giving it the look of a newspaper page. The title "Good News for Modern Man" was printed in bold red letters in the upper left corner protruding from what appears to be a tear or a hole in the newspaper cover. The phrase "The New Testament in Today's English Version" (the subtitle) was printed in smaller black letters within a similar jagged hole in the lower right. The image is one of "good news" breaking through the depressing stories that one reads in their daily newspaper. The message of Jesus Christ contained within the pages of this book was "breaking news" for mankind. Scattered throughout the cover—both the front and the back—were the mastheads of international newspapers, adding to the idea that the Gospel message was indeed "good news" to the world.[14]

The response was overwhelming. Large orders started to roll in. In its first year the ABS distributed over 5.5 million copies of the new translation and by the end of 1967 that number had reached over 8.5 million. A 1971 *New York Times* article noted that *Good News* was the bestselling paperback in the United States every year it had been in print, crushing competition such as *Valley of the Dolls, Rosemary's Baby, Airport,* and *Love Story.* In May 1971 it blew past Spock's *Baby and Child Care* (which had sold 25 million copies) as the all-time paperback bestseller, and by the end of 1971 it had already reached the 30 million mark. (James Nettinga, the ABS general secretary in charge of distribution, was not surprised *Good News* outsold Spock because *Good News for Modern Man* was a better and more effective "people's care book.") The sales created a new set of concerns in the Bible House. It struggled to maintain inventory. People ordered so many copies of the TEV at one time that the ABS estimated 25 percent of the orders fulfilled in 1967 required over $10.00 in postage. The Society had no other alternative but to start charging shipping and handling.[15]

Bratcher received his share of accolades for the TEV, but the wild success of his translation brought international attention to a fifty-year-old Swiss artist named Annie Vallotton, who was responsible for the illustrations. *Good News for Modern Man* included 378 artistic line drawings of Biblical stories. Vallotton called them "sparse" and "childishly naïve." The biblical scholar Raymond Brown, who was serving as president of the Catholic Biblical Association at the time the Testament was released, told the *New York Times* that he found the "little stick men . . . kind of catchy." The plain and simple style of her drawings was a perfect fit for a plain and simple translation. The ABS was quick to point out that the Vallotton's line drawings transcended nationality, language, and race. By omitting facial details, skin color, and other cultural indicators on her figures, she hoped that every reader would "see" their own Jesus, one that was "particularly right for him or her." The nature of these illustrations added to the ecumenical feel of *Good News for Modern Man.* "Her Bible illustrations . . . are quickly understood in almost any country," the *Bible Society Record* declared, "because they capture the essence of universal emotions and recognizable images." This was a Bible for all human beings. The presentation fit the ABS mission perfectly.[16] Nida defended Vallotton's illustrations against critics who felt that the inclusion of line drawings in a Bible "unduly popularizes it" or "lowers its sanctified character." For Nida, Vallotton's art had the potential of helping, even changing, the interpretation of the text for readers. He was overwhelmed by how much his artist was able to communicate so much in such a limited number of lines on a page. Vallotton's artwork made *Good News for Modern Man* appealing to children, "naïve people," and those with "little art background," but the American middle class, who preferred the illustrations they viewed each week in *Saturday Evening Post* or on their "picture cards," sometimes thought the drawings were too "lowbrow."[17]

Good News for Modern Man and Today's English Version got many positive reviews from the academic community. Once biblical scholars got over the fact that this was meant to be a translation for ordinary people rather than other scholars, they gave it glowing reviews. Lutheran New Testament scholar John Reumann, writing in the *Journal of Biblical Literature*, praised Bratcher's work and described the TEV as a "useful rendering" that can "fill a needed place in American Society." Another Lutheran, this one of the Missouri Synod variety, described the translation as "one of the best of the modern-speech versions." The Anglican journal the *Church Quarterly Review* noted that "any book which can sell eight million copies within a year of publication must have something special about it." The reviewer, biblical scholar Donald Ebor, admired the cover: "No more black and gloomy-get up, no funeral outside for the glad tidings! Thank heavens for that!" He also remarked on the "extraordinary skill" that Vallotton brought to the illustrations. Were her line drawings "crude? No; the adjective will not do. Simple? Yes; but amazingly eloquent."[18]

Meanwhile, the ABS was a wild success among everyday Christians seeking an accessible way of engaging with the word of God. Nida reported a conversation with a girl who read *Good News for Modern Man* and exclaimed, "Mommy, it must not be the Bible—I can understand it!" An Ivy League graduate and "rising tennis pro" suffering from mental illness in a psychiatric hospital was attracted to the cover of *Good News* and started reading. When he realized that this was not one of those "black-book Bibles," but rather a Bible he could understand, he discovered God's love. The encounter changed his life and he was dismissed from the hospital a few months later. An Australian pop singer who had dabbled in drugs, Eastern mysticism, and Hinduism and was "in hope of finding an answer to life's deepest questions" picked up *Good News for Modern Man* looking for a Jesus who was a "kind of Hinduized guru or teacher who had seen the light." When he had finished reading, he announced that "God had blown my mind." *Good News* was an inexpensive paperback that was meant to be used, marked, and scuffed up. Rick, who we met in the opening of this chapter, put it best: "*Good News for Modern Man* was never meant to look good on a bookshelf. It was at its best in disorderly stacks with its paperback cover bent and wrinkled."[19]

As Catholics began looking for readable translations following Vatican II (see chapter 22), many turned to *Good News for Modern Man*. Father Walter Abbott of the Vatican Secretariat for Christian Unity and, as we have seen, a staunch defender of Protestant–Catholic relations focusing on a shared Bible, called it "the best modern version for the people that I have yet seen." Warner Hutchinson, who was serving as Asia Consultant for the UBS, told the ABS in

May 1968 that *Good News* was being used in Catholic schools in New Guinea. Though it was not his area of supervision, he also reported that the Bishop of Chile had purchased 2,000 copies for distribution among his parishes. In March 1969, Cardinal Richard Cushing, Archbishop of Boston, approved the TEV for Catholic readers through an official imprimatur. The imprimatur edition was blue with a small Maltese cross on the spine and front. After a copy was shown to ABS officers, they requested that 250,000 be produced. General Secretary Laton Holmgren delivered Cushing's copy personally. Cushing predicted that this new Catholic edition would "be in great demand in the future."[20]

Others believed that the accessibility of *Good News for Modern Man* would make it an ideal tool for evangelism. Nida thought that it spoke directly to "those who have never become acquainted with the time-hallowed religious vocabulary and to those who have been alienated from established religious institutions." He thought that its use in evangelism was one of the reasons why *Good News* was so successful. Billy Graham informed Holmgren that he was now using the Testament in both his personal devotions and his evangelistic crusades. In 1968, the ABS produced 1.3 million copies of a special version of *Good News* (it did not appear in its catalog) for the Baptist General Convention of Texas as part of its participation in Crusade of the Americas, a massive Southern Baptist evangelistic campaign conducted throughout the western hemisphere. It was the largest request for Bibles the ABS had ever received and it took twenty-nine railroad cars, fifteen truck lines, and 29,000 cartons to deliver the "Texas-sized order." Inside the special Testament was published a list of "steps to becoming a Christian." It encouraged readers to acknowledge their need for God, recognize God's love, repent of their sins, accept Jesus Christ and his forgiveness as "the only way of encountering God," and commit to God's plan for their lives. The section ended with a prayer that readers could pray to receive salvation and there was a spot to write one's name and the date in which they accepted Jesus Christ as their personal savior and Lord.[21]

Not everyone, however, was so positive about *Good News for Modern Man*. Some scholars criticized it. The southern Episcopalian *St. Luke's Journal of Theology* panned Bratcher's interpretation of the Sermon on the Mount, especially his decision to use the word "happy" in the list of "Beatitudes" in the fifth chapter of Matthew's Gospel when the King James Version rendering of "blessed" better conveyed the "depth of meaning contained in the blessings pronounced." The reviewer also thought that Bratcher's use of language was too lowbrow. *Good News* "may well be the answer for younger teenagers, and for slum-dwellers who have not gone beyond sixth grade in school," but for others, including office workers, journalists, "professional people," executives, and "their wives," the translation did not represent "an expression of serious reality." The eminent Princeton textual critic Bruce Metzger, who had chaired the ABS Committee on Translation from 1964 to 1970, hoped that *Good News for Modern Man* would have a wide circulation, but thought the translation was limited by the restricted vocabulary Bratcher and his committee were forced to work with so that the Testament would be accessible to ordinary people. Evangelical scholars who were opposed to dynamic equivalence as an approach for translating the word of God were obviously upset with the TEV. In *Bibliotheca Sacra*, an academic journal associated with the conservative Dallas Theological Seminary, Zane Hodges chided the ABS translation for refusing to take seriously the verbal inspiration of the Bible: "A translator who intelligently honors the truth of inspiration must surely seek to represent the original text by the nearest semantic equivalents available in modern English. And this is precisely what *Today's English Version*, produced by the American Bible Society, has not done." Such a "loose paraphrasing translation," Hodges concluded, "is hardly deserving of the confidence of its readers or of much more than a cursory reading."[22]

One wave of popular criticism of the TEV translation of the New Testament stemmed from the ABS choice of a Gospel passage for its 1975 Christmas campaign. The flyer, which was distributed in September, included a painting of Mary, Joseph, and the baby Jesus in the manger situated above a rendering of the passage in the Gospel of Luke, chapter two, which tells the story of the birth of Jesus in Bethlehem. Most Christians were familiar with the King James Version of this story in which Mary is described as "being great with child." But the translators of *Good News for Modern Man*, in an attempt to be more contemporary, described Mary as being "pregnant." As it turned out, many Christians, perhaps of a certain age, were not ready yet to see the word "pregnant" in their Bibles and were definitely not comfortable with using it in a Christmas card to describe the virgin birth.

The letters began to pour into the Bible House. Most people returned the card, circled the word "pregnant," and wrote their negative remarks in the margins. One woman from Cheltenham, Pennsylvania thought that *Good News for Modern Man* was using language that was catering to the "sex issues in our media." A woman from Rittman, Oregon, wrote, "what kind of loose living was this? I read my Bible and know—but how about the person who doesn't?" A woman from Lyndon, Washington, complained that the passage did not explain how Mary became pregnant. "I could not send this version to my unsaved friends," she wrote. "They would take it up as today's immorality." A minister from Whitesburg, Georgia, told the ABS that the translation on the card made it sound as if Mary was a "prostitute." Another pastor from Newport, Indiana, lamented that he and his wife had to give "a public apology" to the youth in his church because he had given them copies of *Good News for*

Modern Man as a Christmas gift. Those who were more theologically informed were upset that the selection of this passage, coupled with the use of the word "pregnant," left out an important part of the Christmas story—the virgin birth of Christ. One pastor from Wyoming, Michigan returned his card with the words, written in pencil and capitalized, "WHAT ABOUT THE VIRGIN BIRTH? No Virgin Birth = No Son of God = No Salvation = No Heaven." There is no record of how the ABS responded to this backlash, but it is worth noting that a reprint of the card appearing in the October 1975 issue of the *Bible Society Record* printed the passage in the King James Version.[23]

Good News for Modern Man drew a host of other random complaints. One writer protested that the translators used the word "pervert" (which was used to describe people with a "homosexual inclination") in Revelation 22:15 in place of the KJV's "dog." He exchanged multiple letters with the ABS on this matter. Others did not appreciate that the Testament was receiving endorsements from individuals connected with the ecumenical National Council of Churches and the Roman Catholic Church. Rebecca Marchand from Fort Lauderdale, Florida, was bothered by the gender exclusive title. "Why was *Good News for Modern Man* ever called by that title? Especially in these days when women are trying to find equality." Marchand suggested a better title: "Good News for all People." She wanted the largely male leadership of the ABS to know that the "constant emphasis on 'MAN' really turns a lot of women off." As a follower of Jesus Christ, she knew that "every person is precious in His sight, and I think all people should be made to feel this truth." Arthur Whitney of the ABS responded by noting that the "Man" in the title, "as any dictionary will convey," was used as a "generic term" that does not "of necessity connote sex—male or female." But he did think that Marchand would be glad to know that when the entire TEV Bible became available it would be called "The Good News Bible."[24]

Some conservative opponents went further in their opposition. When Southern Baptists started distributing copies of *Good News for Modern Man* among churches in North Carolina, Rev. Lloyd Walters of Gordon Heights Baptist Church in Concord, North Carolina, held a ceremony in June 1970 in which copies were buried in the church graveyard under a sign that said "Life is in the 'Blood'—Here Lies T.E.V." In front of a group of congregants, reporters, and neighboring preachers from churches that, like Gordon Heights Baptist, had separated from the Southern Baptist Convention, Walters railed on the theological problems of the TEV for several hours, calling the new translation "a masterpiece of the devil" and a "stepping stone to a one-world church." In the same year, a blind man from Gulfport, Mississippi, who was passing out copies of *Good News for Modern Man* following Hurricane Camille received several threatening phone calls to stop "distributing the Testaments." Apparently unfazed by the calls, the man continued with his benevolent efforts until a man came to his front door one morning and stabbed him with a knife. The intruder broke the man's cane, tied his hands to his feet, and shoved a pillowcase over his head. He then proceeded to rob him of his money and use his knife to mutilate his copies of *Good News for Modern Man*. Upon leaving, the attacker offered a warning: "You were told not to give away any more!"[25]

Thanks to *Good News for Modern Man* the ABS entered the 1970s with a renewed sense of purpose. Bible distribution was at an all-time high and the "good news" of the Gospel seemed to be penetrating a culture in which Christianity had been struggling to maintain its historical foothold. Whatever criticism this paperback New Testament received was muted by the astronomical number of sales. Eugene Nida, Robert Bratcher, and Annie Vallotton would never become household names, but the same could not be said for their Bible translation. The next decades would bring a host of new challenges, including the publication of a complete *Good News Bible*.

24

More Good News

On September 13, 1967, work began on the translation of the Old Testament in Today's English Version (TEV). With the instant success of *Good News for Modern Man*, Eugene Nida opted to retain Robert Bratcher as the head translator. In 1973 Annie Vallotton was chosen once again to draw the illustrations after she received overwhelming support from ABS membership in a survey conducted in the *Bible Society Record*. Bratcher gathered a group of highly competent Old Testament scholars for the project. In putting his team together he deliberately avoided internationally known scholars with "advertised points of view" on certain sticky issues of translation. Bratcher did not want a team of egocentric academics who might make it appear as if the TEV represented the published views of any one member of the committee. By the end of the month a TEV translation of the book of Jonah was underway.[1]

In addition to Bratcher, the translation team included Barclay Newman, a Southern Baptist who had worked as a translator for the ABS and United Bible Societies in Asia; Keith Crim, a former faculty member at Taejon College in South Korea and a scholarly editor at John Knox Press; Heber Peacock, a seminary professor and an old acquaintance of Nida who had translation experience in Africa; Herbert G. Grether, a theological educator and translator with experience in Thailand; John A. Thompson, an ABS translator; and Roger Bullard, a professor at Atlantic Christian College in Wilson, North Carolina. Each book of the Old Testament was translated by an individual member of the committee and then reviewed and revised by the committee as a whole. Once an initial translation was established, it was sent to over 200 different translators around the world who sent back suggestions and comments. The translation was then sent to a panel of eight biblical scholars, linguists, and denominational leaders who offered opinion and advice. Finally, the text needed to be approved by the ABS Translations Committee. Most of the translation work was conducted at the Bible House in New York City, although during the summers the committee and their families would spend a couple of weeks at a YMCA camp in North Carolina.[2]

The *Good News Bible* translation team was a tight-knit group. Disagreements were settled quickly, and rarely would an issue need to be put to vote. Roger Bullard's account of his experience on the committee often sounds more like he was participating in a summer camp or a religious retreat than a serious translation project. He described his colleagues not only in terms of their scholarly expertise, but in terms of their sense of humor or personal habits as well. Bratcher liked to wear "conservative cut suits," read the *New York Times* each morning, and listen to a small AM radio throughout the course of the day. Newman's "humorously honed words" could "slice you into bits so quickly and cleanly that you did not at first realize what happened." Peacock was prone to do pushups in the middle of serious discussions about the text. They developed a slate of inside jokes, snacked on a large jar of peanuts ("members were especially prone to indulge when under pressure"), and competed against one another in badminton. Each meeting started with the reading of scripture and prayer. For many, it was the high point of their academic careers, a period of "deep involvement in rich friendships."[3]

The ABS knew that the translation of the Old Testament would provide certain challenges that might make the *Good News Bible* controversial among the Society's large evangelical constituency. As early drafts of the text appeared, five specific passages were identified as "difficult." The committee rendered Genesis 1:1 as "when God began to create the universe." The King James Version, however, translated the passage as "in the beginning, God created the heaven and the earth." The theological debate over this verse rested on whether God created the universe *ex nihilo*, from "nothing." By removing the phrase "in the beginning," the TEV translation seemed to open the door to a view that God might have created something else prior to the universe. The second difficult passage was Genesis 1:2. The TEV committee's original translation read "a wind from God" was moving over the water. Questions arose. Was this "wind" God himself, or was God working *through* the wind? And if God was working "through" the wind, was he involved in creation enough to satisfy the doctrinal sensibilities of some Christians?[4]

The third controversial passage was Genesis 3:15, the story of the temptation and fall of Adam and Eve in the Garden of Eden. The committee rendered it: "You and the woman will hate each other, her descendants and yours will always be enemies. They will crush your head, and you will bite their heels." The theological issue at stake here was whether this passage was a prediction of future problems between men and snakes, a forecast concerning the descendants (plural) of Eve and future forces of Satan or evil, or a prophecy of Jesus Christ, whose death and resurrection, according to Christian theology, would one day overcome evil once and for all. Should the noun be collective or singular? (The KJV and the RSV both used the word "he" rather than "descendants.")[5] Most evangelicals believed that the Christological interpretation ("he" or "it" shall "bruise your head") was not open to negotiation.

The fourth difficult passage was Deuteronomy 18:15, which the committee originally translated, "instead, he will send them prophets from among your people." The controversy centered around the committee's decision to use the English word "prophets" as opposed to the singular, "prophet." Was this a reference to any prophet, or was it a specific reference to Christ? The RSV used the singular: "The Lord your God will raise up for you a prophet." So did the KJV. The ABS expected that evangelicals would be angry about the failure to interpret this passage Christologically. The final difficult passage— Isaiah 7:14—was a verse which the translation team and the ABS were very familiar. As we have seen, the RSV received intense criticism for translating the Hebrew word *almah* with the phrase "young woman" instead of "virgin." The TEV committee believed that "young woman" was the correct translation and thus decided to follow the RSV translators on the matter.[6]

Before the *Good News Bible* ever made it to the shelves of bookstores, controversy over these difficult passages had emerged inside the walls of the New York Bible House. On June 13, 1974, Laton Holmgren, the general secretary of the ABS, and Oswald Hoffman, the voice of the popular and longstanding *Lutheran Hour* radio program and the chair of the ABS translations subcommittee, initiated a conversation with several members of the TEV translation team about the difficult passages. Hoffman said that he did not want to "dictate" anything to the team, but he was concerned about the hard stand that Bratcher's men had been taking on these passages. He specifically referenced the team's refusal to go with a Christological interpretation of Genesis 3:15. Hoffman, who knew his own Missouri Synod Lutheran Church's support of the inerrancy of the Bible, expressed concern over these decisions. In a letter to Nida summarizing the conversation, Bratcher quoted Hoffman as saying that if certain key passages "were not to the liking of a certain segment of our constituency," ABS would end up selling only "twenty-five" TEV Bibles. Hoffman urged the committee to change the interpretation of Genesis 3:15 so that it pointed more clearly and definitively toward the future work of Christ on the cross.[7]

Bratcher did not take kindly to Hoffman's remarks and grumbled to Nida in a phone conversation and a follow-up memo. He felt that Hoffman, with the support of Holmgren, was threatening him and his team. Though Hoffman and Holmgren never mentioned any penalties if the difficult passages were not changed, Bratcher felt that such consequences were definitely implicit in what he and his team were told. Bratcher thought that Hoffman and Holmgren were meddling in an area of scholarly expertise that they knew very little about. If the ABS administration forced his team to make

any changes to the translation in order to meet the theological sensibilities of "a certain segment" of the Society's constituency, then the "scholarly
integrity" of the TEV Old Testament would be compromised. Bratcher told
Nida that his team was "committed to translating the text of the Hebrew
Old Testament in terms of the meaning it had and the message it carried
at the time it was used as a document of faith by the Hebrews; we cannot
force upon it the interpretation . . . given by the Christian Church." A few
days later Robert Bullard whipped off a quick memo to Bratcher: "Had our
task been stated from the beginning as providing a translation which would
assuredly be pleasing to all constituencies, the work would have had to be
done on different lines, and I doubt very much that the present members of
the committee would have undertaken such an assignment." A showdown
was brewing. It pitted the academic reputation of Bratcher and his team
against the time-honored commitment of the ABS to distribute the word of
God to as many people as possible.[8]

Holmgren tried to bring peace. In essence, he agreed with Hoffman. If the
evangelical constituency was offended by the translation of these difficult passages and thus refused to buy the Bible, then what was the purpose of producing it in the first place? If there were "viable scholarly options" in the "few
highly sensitive passages under discussion," the ABS would want to "choose
the rendering which would be the least abusive to the majority of our supporting constituency." He thought that "optional readings" of the Hebrew text
could be placed in footnotes. This, Holmgren believed, was a "reasonable proposal, particularly if we are concerned about securing maximum readership
of the book." Holmgren wrote as a sincere Christian who wanted to reach as
many people as possible with the word of God, but he also wrote as the leader
of an organization that was in the Bible *business*. If the *Good News Bible* was a
flop, the ABS would need do deal with the financial fallout and the damage to
its reputation in the Christian world.[9]

It was now time for Heber Peacock, the primary translator of Genesis, to
take the offensive. In a memo to Bratcher he said that Holmgren and Hoffman
were asking the team to "violate every principle on which we have operated"
in order to satisfy "these demands for a wrong translation." For the tight-knit
translation team who had worked nearly eight years on this translation, this
was now becoming more a matter of "honesty" than "academic scholarship."
As Christians, every member of the translation team believed that they were
entrusted with a sacred trust—to make the word of God accessible to men and
women around the world. Heber alleged that the ABS was "willing to twist
the Scriptures, so that they will say what some people want to hear," while
the translation team was commissioned with the responsibility of pursuing
"truth" and of letting "the Word speak." If "traditionalists" disagreed with the

TEV translation, Peacock reminded Bratcher that they could still find the King James Version in the ABS catalog.[10]

As the ABS executive secretary for translations, and the man who hired Bratcher, Nida played a significant role in the controversy that had taken 1865 Broadway by storm. As a translator and an educator of translators, Nida was sympathetic to Bratcher' point of view, but he also had a much greater stake in the reputation and future of the ABS than anyone on the translation team. Though Nida could speak the language of Bratcher and his team, it was doubtful that he would throw his full support behind their dogmatic defense of their translation decisions on the difficult passages. Nida took a pragmatic approach. As much as professional Bible translators wanted to keep theology out of the translation process, the chances of it actually happening were slim to none. He told Bratcher that "2000 years of Christian theology cannot be changed and it will come to bear on the translation of these controversial passages." Nida was not happy about the way theology intruded into the translation process. He blamed seminaries for failing to educate pastors how to teach their congregations to understand Old Testament passages from the perspective of the original authors. Unfortunately, Nida implied, the church was not ready for such an intellectual engagement with the text of scriptures. They were the "weaker brother" which Paul wrote about in 1 Corinthian 8:13, and thus their collective conscience should not be offended. Nida also realized that the way these difficult passages were translated would create a significant public relations problem for the ABS and as a result, "we are faced with the problem not so much of what is the absolute truth as what is the truth which people can understand and are willing to accept as the truth." The real problem, according to Nida, was "an educational problem."[11]

As 1974 drew to a close, the translation issues concerning the difficult passages had still not been resolved. The ABS officers agreed that a final decision would be made at a meeting of the Board of Managers translations subcommittee meeting on February 14, 1975. Nida remained in contact with Bratcher and Peacock following the initial exchange of memos in the summer of 1974 and informed Holmgren that the two translators were unwilling to budge on their rendering of the passages at hand. Nida fully expected them to try to defend their positions during the February meeting of the translations subcommittee. Meanwhile, in a letter to Howard Clark Kee, a member of the Board of Managers who had worked with Bratcher on the TEV New Testament (*Good News for Modern Man*), Nida tried to explore the psychological reasons behind the stubborn stand that Bratcher and Peacock were taking. Nida sympathized with the past "emotional difficulties" that both men had to endure when their theological views were apparently criticized by conservatives in the Southern Baptist Church. Nida was not unfamiliar with the culture of

Protestant fundamentalism and evangelicalism. He had spent a year teaching at the fundamentalist Bible Institute of Los Angeles in the 1930s, and no doubt encountered many theologically conservative Christians during his work with Wycliffe Bible Translators. Yet Nida also knew that a fundamentalist mentality could also be found outside the boundaries of theologically conservative Protestantism: "Perhaps they are not fully aware as they should be of the fact that persons on the opposite end of the spectrum would be equally critical, though perhaps not as emotionally so."[12]

On February 14, Bratcher and Peacock faced a translations subcommittee made up three ministerial members of the ABS Board of Managers: Arnold T. Olson, the president of the Evangelical Free Church of America and the current vice president of the United Bible Societies; Bruce Metzger, the eminent scholar of the Greek New Testament who taught at Princeton Theological Seminary; and Bryant Kirkland, the pastor of New York's Fifth Avenue Presbyterian Church. Thomas Zimmerman, the general superintendent of the Assemblies of God, was also a member of the committee, but he was unable to attend the meeting. He did, however, send Holmgren his thoughts on the translation team's treatment of the difficult passages prior to the meeting. Zimmerman and his ministerial colleagues in the Assemblies of God, a rapidly growing evangelical Pentecostal denomination based in Springfield, Missouri, rejected Bratcher's and Peacock's translation of every one of the controversial verses. He told Holmgren that his denomination's negative assessment was made "not because we are conservatives," but because "our suggestions are based on sound exegesis." Zimmerman's comments were made available to Bratcher and Peacock before the meeting.[13]

Three days following the meeting, Bratcher wrote a summary of the proceedings to the members of his TEV Old Testament translation team. He was angry. The meeting began with a statement from Bratcher explaining the general principles the team had used to arrive at its translation decisions, although he claimed to be never asked for a statement "justifying or defending our translations of the passages in question." Olson spoke first with a strong defense of the positions Zimmerman had taken in his letter and wondered why Bratcher's team had been "so consistently one-sided" in its translation of these difficult passages. To Olson, it appeared that the translators had made a conscience effort to avoid rendering the Old Testament in such a way that the verses might be understood by readers in the "sense they were taken in the New Testament." Howard Clark Kee, who attended the meeting but did not have a vote, made it clear that the overwhelming success of *Good News for Modern Man* meant that the TEV was now considered a "major translation in this country." The *Good News Bible* would be perceived as an "authorized version," and as a result the ABS needed to be more sensitive to how the public might react to it.[14]

In the end, the three members of the committee decided to use the dependent, temporal clause in Genesis 1:1 so that the English text read "in the beginning, when God created the universe." In Genesis 1:2, the committee upheld the spirit of the team's translation and suggested the phrase "Spirit from God" be used. In Genesis 3:15, the committee replaced the plural "descendants" with the more ambiguous "offspring" in order to allow for the possibility of a Christological interpretation. All three members of the committee rejected the team's decision to use the plural "prophets" in Deuteronomy 18:15 instead of the singular, more Christological, "prophet." Finally, the committee agreed to use the phrase "young woman" (as opposed to "virgin") in Isaiah 7:14. Much of the controversy from a generation earlier surrounding the use of this phrase in the RSV rendition of this passage appears to have died down. Bratcher seemed less concerned with the specific decisions made by the committee and more upset with the fact that the members of the committee, men with no training in translation theory, were given the "right and authority to make any changes it wishes" in the text that he and his team had worked so hard on preparing. The following month the translators gathered in Wilson, North Carolina, presumably on the campus of Atlantic Christian College, to work on a plan to overturn the vote of the ABS's translation subcommittee.[15]

Warner Hutchinson, one of the three ABS general secretaries (along with Holmgren and Treasurer Charles Baas), was also present at the February 14 meeting and described the proceedings to John Dean of the BFBS as "irenic" and "responsible." But Hutchinson was distressed about the way Bratcher and Peacock behaved: "It seemed like they felt the meeting was 'stacked' against them and that there was no point in speaking." Hutchinson further noted that the translators seemed "tense" during the discussions and when the meeting was completed they left immediately "without a word to anyone." Hutchinson was aware that Bratcher had arranged a meeting for the purpose of planning a protest to the translation subcommittee's decision. He had even heard rumors that the translation team was either going to resign or make some kind of appeal "to the churches" to express its displeasure. Hutchinson approached this controversy from the perspective of an administrator. From his perspective, any translation team must remain accountable to the institution that employed it. The work of Bratcher's team was not "wholly independent of any authority." Rather, the team was hired to prepare a translation and submit it to "a responsible body" within the ABS who would render a final decision on its usefulness. Hutchinson concluded: "We have taken such extensive steps to protect translators and translation consultants from irresponsible Boards or highly conservative committees that it appears that they might have grandiose feelings regarding their own infallibility and unanswerability."[16]

On February 24, 1975, Holmgren told Nida that "we are apparently headed on a collision course." He insisted that the ABS, Nida, and Bratcher "work together to find a reasonable and responsible way out of our difficulty." Bratcher agreed with the always irenic Holmgren, and thus invited Nida and Hutchinson to his team's meeting at Atlantic Christian College on March 11. (It is unclear if they ever attended.) But Holmgren's attempt at reconciliation and Bratcher's gesture of hospitality probably came too late. On March 13, the ABS Board of Managers announced that it had officially approved the TEV Bible. One month later, Nida and Bratcher were sitting in an Atlanta Holiday Inn discussing the matter. Nida was correct in his assessment of Bratcher's emotional connection to the TEV project. Bratcher confessed that the ABS decision to change his translation reminded him of a moment in his career, perhaps when he was expelled as the dean of the Southern Baptist seminary in Brazil, when he was forbidden by the Southern Baptist Board of Missions from teaching "certain things about Genesis." When Nida asked Bratcher for the reason behind the Southern Baptist Board's decision, Bratcher told him that "it was a matter of a million dollars [in gifts and tithes]." Bratcher was ready to resign from the committee, although he was not sure that all of his team, especially Bullard and Newman, were willing to go that far.[17]

Things finally came to a head in November 1975. The translation subcommittee had rejected Bratcher's appeal and reaffirmed the decision on the difficult passages that it passed in February. Bratcher had had enough. He informed Nida that "the TEV Old Testament Committee has voted to renounce all further involvement in and responsibility for the TEV Old Testament translation." Bratcher signed the letter on behalf of the entire team. Two weeks later, Nida accepted the resignation. He thanked Bratcher and his team for their work and expressed his regret that they would not be carrying the translation through to publication. But he wanted to make one thing clear. The decision of the ABS translation subcommittee to change certain parts of Bratcher's translation was not "some new departure in Bible Society procedure." He reminded Bratcher that the Board of Managers always had the final power of veto on the TEV text. In this case, the ABS's desire to avoid controversy and produce a Bible that would reach the maximum number of its constituency trumped what the translation team saw as a matter of scholarly integrity.[18]

In May 1976 Laton Holmgren presented a copy of the entire *Good News Bible* in Today's English Version to the annual meeting of the ABS, and in October it was officially released to the general public. Over the next several years the ABS secured dozens of official endorsements for the *Good News Bible*. In the religious world, it received the support of evangelicals (Pat Robertson, Harold Ockenga, W. A. Criswell, and Billy Graham); mainline Protestants (Robert Schuller and

Paul Kaiser); and Roman Catholics (John Whealan, Archbishop of Hartford). From the world of politics endorsements came from John Glenn and Gerald Ford. In the world of sports, the ABS landed support from Bart Starr, Tom Landry, and Lou Holtz. The ABS officers obviously had the tremendous success of *Good News for Modern Man* in mind when they called for an initial press run of 1.2 million copies (as opposed to the 150,000 original copies of *Good News*), but all of those copies were sold before the end of the year. In September 1977 the ABS presented the 5 millionth copy of the complete *Good News Bible* to President Jimmy Carter, and in 1979 it released a version of the Bible with the deuterocanonical books (or the Apocrypha) for Catholic readers. A children's edition appeared in 1979, followed by a large-print version a year later.[19]

Response to the *Good News Bible* was mixed. Most scholars praised the translator's efforts to produce a Bible in simple language using the theory of dynamic equivalence. A reviewer in the *Scottish Journal of Theology* noted that the *Good News Bible* was "not only accurate and readable, but also a pleasure to use," though he lamented the loss of familiar terms. He noted that "leprosy" had been replaced by "a dreaded skin disease," the "Ark" was now "the Covenant Box," and "cubits and ephahs" had all been metricized. Other scholars criticized the gender-inclusive language. If the translators were trying to capture the cultural perspective of the Hebrews and bring the reader into the mindset of ancient Israel, the use of the term "person," devoid of "any connotations of gender," seemed to defeat such an overarching purpose. Dynamic equivalence meant that the translator had to "forsake his or her literary freedom and remain shackled to the idiom of the other's voice." The Catholic biblical scholar Michael Coogan, writing for the progressive Catholic magazine *America*, thought that the attempt to translate the Bible in the language of "bureaucrats, Presidential speechwriters and admen" undermined the literary quality of the text that he wanted his students to appreciate.[20]

The letters that the ABS received from its membership were largely negative, but there were a few donors who appreciated the *Good News Bible*'s clear and simple language. A writer from Escondido, California, wrote: "I read the Bible more since receiving this Good News Translation!" A woman from Marietta, Ohio, wrote that she appreciated the "rhythmical quality" of the King James Version, but "this version is *real*. It related; it belongs to me; it means business; it means what it says." A Catholic women in Minnesota was thankful that the *Good News Bible* was not only the first Bible she had ever owned, but it was also one that she could understand.[21]

But those who still preferred those rhythmic qualities of the King James Version were not happy with what the ABS had done to the language in their Bibles. A correspondent from St. Augustine, Florida, informed the ABS that she was praying that the King James Version would continue to be distributed by the Society "with as much vigor as the TEV." As she visited "non-Christian" bookstores she was disappointed to see very few copies of the Authorized Version, while the modern translations seemed to be in "super-abundance." The woman took the liberty to describe her conversion experience eighteen years earlier. Since then she had used many different Bibles, but finally came to the conviction that "the Holy Spirit speaks in a purer way to me in the King James Version." She was skeptical that people were receiving "a new-birth experience from the Holy Spirit" through the "modern versions." A man from Tekonsha, Michigan, stopped supporting the ABS because God specifically used certain (English) words to communicate his message and they were clearly missing from the *Good News Bible*. A syndicated newspaper cartoonist even offered a critique of the new style. In December 1976 a cartoon appeared in hundreds of newspapers across the country depicting a minister in a large cathedral reading an exaggerated version of the *Good News Bible* translation of Psalm 23:

> The Lord *is* my Shepherd; I don't need a thing.
> He gets me to flake out in green pastures;
> he leads me to a nice pond.
> He retreads my soul
> he wants me to be a straight arrow for his name's sake
> Even though I stroll through the valley of the shadow of
>   death, no sweat
> I'm not hassled 'cause your around with you're big stick, man.[22]

One of the more thoughtful criticisms of the new TEV style came in the form of a letter from seventy-seven-year-old K. E. Kroecker of Inman, Kansas. Kroecker's church had collected over $400 for the ABS in a special Christmas offering, and he prayed that the money would be used "for the Glory of God." Kroecker's wife was ill and the family's medical bills were high. He tried to do odd jobs around town to make ends meet. Yet despite his financial woes, Kroecker was committed to using a percentage of his money to support his church and a few organizations in the business of spreading the Gospel and feeding the hungry. The ABS was one of those organizations, but since the *Good News Bible* came into his town he had stopped donating to the Society. Kroecker did not believe that the *Good News Bible* was the "inspired word of God." He questioned the publication of such a book: "Why should we want to have the bible read like any ordinary book?" From his point of view, this new translation was causing nothing but problems in his small Kansas hometown. In one church, the local minister had to resign because he insisted on preaching from the *Good News Bible* when the rest of the congregation preferred the King James Version. In his own church, he claimed that "it is almost impossible to follow when the pastor uses the new translation." Kroecker and others of his generation had memorized the Bible using the King James Version. Children were coming home from Sunday school with Bible verses to memorize from the *Good News Bible*, and their parents and grandparents found it difficult to help them in their task. Some might see Kroecker's concerns as another example of an older gentleman unwilling to cope with changing times.[23] Perhaps this was the case. But his letter to the ABS also reveals the way that a modern translation like the *Good News Bible* had the power to shape the everyday experience of American Christianity.

Others opposed the theology contained in the *Good News Bible*. Harold Lindsell, the outgoing editor of the evangelical magazine *Christianity Today*, who was in the midst of writing a rather harsh defense of biblical inerrancy, wrote to the ABS to complain that the introductions to the *Good News Bible* were written "within the context of the higher critical methodology and essentially fit the theologically liberal context." Lindsell argued that such introductions undermined the ABS's rule to publish the Bible "without doctrinal note or comment." He ended his letter by noting that these introductory paragraphs were "very unacceptable to evangelicals," and warned the ABS that they would inevitably "harm" its work and "create problems for you."[24] In a series of internal memos, Nida admitted that Lindsell's evangelical critique created a "real problem" for the ABS. He understood why evangelicals were upset, but realized that this was just one of those cases where the ABS would be unable to please everyone in its constituency. "I am afraid we will simply have to ride out this wave of combative conservatism," he wrote, "and hope that more moderate evangelical seminaries, such as Fuller Theological Seminary, would begin to have a greater influence on these matters." But Nida could not let this matter pass without taking some shots at Lindsell. "Frankly," he wrote in one of his memos, "I don't see how [Lindsell] could possibly be satisfied with anything that we might put in an introduction which would be honest." He mentioned Lindsell's "radical position with regard to so-called 'inerrancy'" and said that the editor of *Christianity Today* was "hunting for bear." Nida believed that American evangelicals were moving away from extreme positions such as the inerrancy of the Bible and predicted that it would only be a matter of time before "more responsible groups within the Evangelical constituency" stopped taking Lindsell seriously.[25]

In 1974, retired ABS General Secretary Eric North wrote a letter to Laton Holmgren encouraging his successor to write the history of the American Bible Society for the years between 1966 and 1976. With the publication of *Good News for Modern Man* appearing at the start of this period, and the complete *Good News Bible* scheduled to appear at its end, North, who led the

ABS through the Great Depression and World War II, refused to underestimate the importance of this decade in the overall history of the Society. It is hard to argue with North's historical sensibility. In these years the ABS was responsible for one of the most popular books in the world. It had become a Bible-distributing superpower in a way that North could not have imagined when he became general secretary in 1928. In the next decade the ABS would pursue more innovative methods of distribution; foster a deeper engagement with popular culture, Roman Catholics, and evangelicals; and take advantage of even more celebratory opportunities to connect its mission with the story of Christian America.[26]

25

The Bible Cause in the Worst of Times

In 1979, a writer for *New West* magazine took stock of the decade that he had just lived through: "It was the worst of times, it was the worst of times." Indeed, there was a lot to forget about the 1970s. The United States suffered through its worst economic downturn since the Great Depression. The nation's dependence on foreign oil resulted in long lines to buy expensive gasoline. As prices skyrocketed, so did unemployment. High interest rates made it difficult for families to pursue the American dream through the purchase of a first home. The United States ended its involvement in Vietnam, but the nation was left to deal with millions of veterans who now needed to integrate back into society after fighting for their country in an unpopular and failed war. Richard Nixon resigned as president in the wake of the Watergate scandal, and America's trust in political authority would never been the same. A new revolution in the pursuit of civil rights was led by women, people with disabilities, and gays. Others viewed the 1970s as a time when individualism had run amuck. The white-suited writer Tom Wolfe saw selfishness all around him and labeled it the "Me Decade." At the same time, University of Rochester historian and cultural critic Christopher Lasch described a "culture of narcissism" pervading the United States. And in the middle of it all, perhaps serving as a temporary antidote to all the self-absorption, the United States celebrated its 200th birthday.[1]

The American Bible Society was not immune to these economic, religious, and cultural changes, but it weathered the storm well. With the continued success of *Good News for Modern Man* and the coming of the *Good News Bible*, scripture distribution was increasing much faster than the Society's budget. Between 1968 and 1973 distribution had more than doubled, but the budget had increased by only half. The recession meant that the Society's expenses were also increasing. A world paper shortage in the last months of 1973 led to skyrocketing prices and a worldwide demand for paper. The ABS failed to deliver Bibles on time and had to increase its prices. In January 1975, Treasurer Charles Baas wrote a special letter to the membership to ask for extra help in meeting a $750,000 deficit that the Society that had accrued over the course of the year. But despite these difficulties, the 1970s was a time of growth for the ABS. It was offering a product—the Bible—that promised to provide answers for troubled times. The ABS continued to rely on Bible sales and individual contributions through programs like the Bible-a-Month Club and its annual holiday appeals. In 1979 the Society distributed 108 million scriptures in the United States and another 150 million overseas. It was also still contributing roughly half of the United Bible Societies' World Service Budget.[2]

As the translation wing of the American Bible Society stayed busy with the *Good News Bible*, those responsible for distribution and fundraising worked on creative ways to get this new translation in the hands of as many people as possible. The ABS was now printing Bibles in a host of different colors and sizes to meet the needs of every generation of Americans. Its Bible cassettes were popular among the visually impaired, truck drivers, and New York City cabbies. It seemed like the ABS and its TEV Bibles were everywhere. For example, *Good News for Modern Man* was distributed at a summer festival in the Watts section of Los Angeles following the tragic race riots of the late 1960s. A California shopping mall displayed a Christmas tree decorated with ABS scripture portions. The troubled children at Boys Town in Omaha, Nebraska, each received a *Good News Bible* when they arrived for their stay. In 1981, ABS donated 30,000 scripture portions titled "Moving on Up" to Washington, DC, Catholic schools to commemorate Black History Month. Copies of *Good News for Modern Man* could be found at Frontier Days in Cheyenne, Wyoming, and in hundreds of Days Inn hotels. ABS Bibles were distributed at Mardis Gras in New Orleans, horse tracks, county fairs, trailer parks, rock music festivals, national parks, Yankee Stadium, Chicago's Cabrini Green housing project, the Dallas Cowboys' locker room, the Macy's Thanksgiving Day Parade, casinos in Atlantic City, the Newport Jazz Festival, and the Lake Tahoe Wedding Chapel. In 1977 the owner of surfboard shop in Canoga Park, California, bought 300 TEV New Testaments and then paid for an advertisement in *Surfing Magazine*, in which he offered a copy of the Testament to anyone who wrote to him requesting one.[3]

The ABS also continued to use media and new technology as a means of spreading its message. The November 21, 1971, episode of the CBS Sunday morning religion program *Look Up and Live* featured the work of the ABS. A year later, the ABS library displayed several of its Bibles related to colonial America on a Thanksgiving edition of NBC's *Today Show*. The ABS had dabbled in radio for several decades, but had never made a serious effort to use it for fundraising until they began to work with Lester Harmon of the Philadelphia Agency to produce the weekly "Around the World with the Bible." ABS Executive Secretary John Erickson hosted and produced the show and it starred retired Australian Bible Society executive and storyteller Herbert Arrowsmith. Every week between 1970 and 1974 Arrowsmith would entertain audiences listening on thirty-two different stations around the country with anecdotes from the work of the Bible Cause around the globe. Efforts were made to promote Bible reading and English literacy in mainland China through several radio partners. For example, the Far East Broadcasting Company sponsored the ABS/UBS show "The Most Popular English Book in China." It featured Bible readings in English and Chinese, with pauses to explain some of the more difficult English words.[4]

It was also during the 1970s that ABS introduced "Good News for New Readers." This Bible-based literacy program became one of the largest distribution and educational efforts in the Society's history. It was launched in 1973 to produce graded scripture portions for the millions of newly literate people in the world. Upon completion of all five levels, the user would have achieved sufficient reading skills to understand the *Good News Bible* in Today's English Version or a text of a similar reading level. Eugene Nida developed these scripture selections, using his expertise in Bible translation and linguistics to address the problems facing new readers. Each scripture selection included an illustration of a Bible scene with a few words from Today's English Version scattered on a folded 8.5 × 11 sheet.[5]

The primary purpose of Good News for New Readers was to the make the Bible more accessible to those who could not read it. "No one knows how many people might have discovered the way to eternal life," the ABS argued, "if they had been able to read 'For God loved the world so much that he gave His only Son, that everyone who believed in HIM may not die but have eternal life' (John 3:16, *Today's English Version*)." In the process, the ABS made a major contribution to the strengthening of global literacy. Working with current statistics from UNESCO, the ABS was aware that illiteracy rates around the world were experiencing a slight decline, producing more new readers. Good News for New Readers was thus less about teaching people how to read and more about providing reading material at achieved levels of efficiency. The ABS used the phrase "bridge materials" to describe these selections. This program was important because research suggested that new readers would return to a state of illiteracy unless they were provided with something suitable to read. And, of course, if they returned to a state of illiteracy they would possibly never again be able to read the word of God.[6]

The initial twelve-year proposal called for 75 million scripture selections appropriate for new readers to be distributed in 200 languages, but these targets needed to be raised very quickly due to the success of the program. (By 1980 New Reader scripture selections had been completed in 348 languages.) The UBS committed to raising $63 million to fund the project, with a significant part of this money provided by the ABS. In order to promote the program among churches and educational centers in the United States, the Society produced a film, *New Light, New Hope*, which appeared on hundreds of television stations throughout the country. The program was especially successful in places, such as Africa, where illiteracy was extremely high. Christian colporteurs in Tanzania sold a half-million scripture selections to rural schools and churches. When the Bible Society of Uganda began printing these selections, the Ministry of Education was so impressed with their quality and usefulness that it provided funds to triple the number purchased. Good News for New Readers was also used among Muslim literacy groups in Africa and even received an endorsement from the chief minister of India, a Hindu. The program was so successful in parts of Asia that the ABS and UBS could not keep up with the demand. In Brazil, Guatemala, Paraguay, Peru, and other parts of Latin America Good News for New Readers received endorsements from UNESCO, the Roman Catholic Church, and national ministries of education. In Bolivia, the national Bible society published New Reader selections in newspapers throughout the country.[7]

During the 1970s much of ABS's distribution in the United States was carried out through volunteers, mostly middle-class women. As we have seen, the ABS created a Women's Activities Department in 1962 to monitor and organize vast array of work that women were already doing to promote the Bible Cause in their local communities. In June 1973, due to the growing number of men interested in volunteering with the ABS, the name of this department was changed to Volunteer Activities. The number of volunteers working on behalf of the ABS in the United States grew astronomically during this period, from 7,000 in 1973 to nearly 70,000 at the department's height in 1987. The ABS liked to note that their volunteers "work in their own ways in their own time." Volunteers were asked to register with the Society, but there was no formal training program and no set of rules that needed to be followed.[8] The Volunteer Department allowed women to play an active part in the promotion of the Bible Cause while continuing to tend to their roles as wives and mothers. In this sense, middle-class women volunteers were contributing to spreading of the Gospel and the advancement of Christian America in much the same way that they had done throughout the entire history of the ABS and, for that matter, throughout American religious history generally. Their labors embodied the spirit of the Bible Cause as put forth by General Secretary Eric North in 1938: "The most important process which the Society carries on, is not at the Bible House in New York . . . The major work is done *where the man without the Scriptures is met by the man with the Scriptures.*"[9]

There were several avenues of Bible work open to volunteers. Many served as liaisons between their local churches and the ABS, making announcements and conducting meetings to keep their ministers and fellow congregants up to speed on new versions, editions, and portions. Some organized Good News Seminars—city- or townwide meetings where people could learn more about the work of the ABS, order copies of the scriptures, or sign up to join the ranks of the volunteers. Related to these seminars were informal meetings where volunteers gathered under the leadership of a volunteer coordinator to share tips and ideas about how to distribute Bibles more effectively. The distribution process varied from volunteer to volunteer. For example, an Avon saleslady handed out scriptures during visits with her customers. A school bus driver passed out portions to children on her bus. Another woman made sure that she and her husband left a scripture portion with their tip whenever they dined at a restaurant. Others passed out scriptures in airports, train depots, hair salons, and truck stops. When an ABS volunteer checked into a hotel and realized that there was not a Bible in the nightstand drawer she went outside to the trunk of her car, pulled out a box filled with copies of *Good News for Modern Man*, and convinced the clerk to put one in every room.[10]

The driving force behind the Volunteer Activities Department was Alice Ball, the first female general secretary of the ABS, a position she held from 1979 to her retirement in 1988. It was not easy for a woman to reach the highest administrative post in the ABS. Though women were contributing to work at the Bible House for much of the twentieth century, most of the major decisions related to finances, programs, fundraising, distribution, and promotion were made by an inner circle of white men from the Protestant mainline. The Board of Managers was also overwhelmingly male. Between 1920 and 1970, 221 men served on the ABS board, compared to nineteen women. Between 1970 and 1990, a time when women were gaining equality in the workplace at an ever-increasing rate, the ABS board was still 86 percent male. In 1970 retired General Secretary Robert Taylor told his senior staff that there should be no more than six females serving on the board at any one time. The ABS had never had a female president, and has had thirteen female honorary vice presidents in its 200-year history.[11]

Ball came to the ABS in 1955 after serving for ten years as a youth worker with the Salvation Army. She began as an administrative assistant in the Overseas Department where she supervised stenographers and secretaries, processed requests for Bibles, and answered correspondence with overseas agents. She eventually rose in the ranks and during most of the 1960s she had a leadership position in the ABS work in Latin America. In 1971, Ball was made an executive secretary of the ABS (one rank below general secretary) with the responsibility of running the newly created Department of Women's Activities. She remained in that post until 1979, when she was elected a general secretary with responsibility for all of the ABS work in the United States. Her new responsibilities included distribution, fundraising, the ABS library, and (at the time) over 35,000 volunteers.[12]

One of Ball's most innovative contributions to the work of Bible distribution in the United States was the creation of Scripture Courtesy Centers. Men and women interested in becoming an ABS Scripture Courtesy Center volunteer placed a prepaid order at regular catalog prices for the type of scriptures they wished to sell. In most cases they were provided with a cardboard display (known as a Good Newsstand), posters, and order forms to help them to make their Courtesy Center as attractive as possible. Most Scripture Courtesy Center volunteers publicized their Good Newsstands with flyers, announcements in local newspapers and church bulletins, and notices on library bulletin boards. At the height of this program, volunteers were running over 2,700 Courtesy Centers around the country. The familiar Good Newsstands could be found in living rooms, garages, laundromats, churches, bank lobbies, skating rinks, gift stores, restaurants, shopping centers, barbershops, and any other place where there was enough foot traffic to make the sale of ABS Bibles a worthwhile endeavor.[13]

Though volunteers had the freedom to choose which ABS scripture products they wanted to sell at their Courtesy Centers, and could set up their Good Newsstands in any location that they desired, Ball and her staff monitored the program closely. Volunteers received special account numbers for their Bible orders and Ball and her staff provided them with packets of forms and return envelopes to send the money made from sales to New York. A monthly newsletter called the "Volunteers Bulletin" offered tips and news about how to get the most out of a Scripture Courtesy Center. The ABS gave volunteers detailed instructions about how to set up their Good Newsstands. "The first thing to remember," the instructions noted, "is that it can be done." This was followed by a five-page memo with diagrams. Ball even sent staff members into the field to evaluate the work of the Scripture Courtesy Center Volunteers. The reports that these staff members filed provide a telling glimpse into the local world of ABS distribution.[14]

In May 1982, ABS staff member Ellen Cummiskey visited twelve volunteers who were running Scripture Courtesy Centers in Northern California. She began her trip with a visit to Connie Regener, who ran her Scripture Courtesy Center from the First Presbyterian Church of Richmond. Connie advertised her Courtesy Center with a poster on a kiosk in the middle of the "church patio" that included news about different church-related programs. Her Good Newsstand was positioned in the church's Fireside Room. According to Cummiskey, Connie was not using the cardboard stand provided by the ABS. Instead, she had a stand that was six feet wide and five feet high, with six shelves that Cummiskey estimated could hold about $200 worth of ABS

material. Connie found the stand sitting outside a local Newberry's 5&10, and
had her father-in-law swing by with his truck to pick it up and bring it to the
church. The stand had wheels, allowing Connie to roll it out to the patio just as
the congregation exited the sanctuary and headed for coffee hour.

Connie had heard about the ABS from her neighbor. One day while she was
visiting, a *Good News Bible* arrived in the mail. Connie was impressed with the
Bible and soon ordered a few copies of her own. She eventually signed up to
run a Courtesy Center. Most of her customers knew about the stand through
her announcement in the church bulletin, but she also sold Bibles during the
week to local pastors. Cummiskey reported that Connie's bestsellers were a
scripture portion called "God's Promises to You" and the gold-covered *Good
News Bible*. Her worst seller was the *Good News* illustrated children's Bible.
Occasionally Connie took her Courtesy Center on the road, selling Bibles to
senior citizens in a nearby retirement home. Cummiskey asked Connie if she
was willing to invite fifteen other Scripture Center volunteers to her home to
share ideas about the best way to sell Bibles.

Later in the week Cummiskey met Ruth Reader, who ran her Courtesy
Center out of little brown van she called "the Gingerbread House." Ruth drove
the van around town, inviting children to pray with her before providing them
with a scripture portion. Cummiskey also met with Joann Mizutani, a Japanese-
American in her twenties who owned a small gift shop. When the kids would
come by her shop to buy "potato chips or some other snack," Joann would put
a scripture portion "in the bag with their goodies." Mrs. Clark Benson had a
Courtesy Center in her living room with a "simple wood bookcase . . . with five
shelves." Gayle Wetzel regularly sold Bibles to international students at Stanford
University, while Sister Suzanne Hockel of St. Kevin's Roman Catholic Church
sold Spanish Bibles to San Francisco's Hispanic population. Cummiskey made
several other stops during her California trip. She took careful notes on each
Scripture Courtesy Center she visited and even reported on whether or not a
volunteer was suited for the work. This was the kind of attention to detail and
quality control that Alice Ball brought to her work at the ABS.[15]

As the 1970s progressed, the Today's English Version translation of the Bible
found its way into more and more Catholic parishes and organizations. As
we have seen, Vatican II brought about a renewed interest in the Bible among
the Catholic laity and put to rest many of the suspicions and prejudices about
Rome that had been harbored by American Protestants since before the time
of the American Revolution. In 1969, the Vatican passed a resolution recogniz-
ing the United Bible Societies as an agency "to which Roman Catholics could
turn for help in the implementations of the Second Vatican Council's concern
for easy access to Scripture for all men." The UBS responded by declaring that

it would "aim at giving the same recognition and providing the same services to Roman Catholics as to other confessions and denominations." In the same year Pope Paul VI provided $25,000 to the UBS to promote interconfessional projects between Protestant and Catholic scholars and presented a photocopy of the Codex B Vaticanus, an early fourth-century manuscript of the Bible housed in the Vatican library that was commonly known as the best Greek text of the New Testament, to the American Bible Society as a sign of his continuing interest in carrying out the mandates of the Second Vatican Council. By 1973, ABS/UBS and Roman Catholics translators were working together on translations of the New Testament in dozens of languages in Europe, Africa, Asia, and the Pacific Islands. Catholics around the world also became active in the work of Bible distribution. For example, in Southeast Asia, Catholics were responsible for 90 percent of scripture distribution in 1979.[16]

In the United States cooperation between Catholics and Protestants in the Bible Cause moved slowly, but progress was being made. One of the most famous Catholics in America, Fulton Sheen, announced in a 1972 speech before the Los Angeles Junior Chamber of Commerce that he personally distributed hundreds of ABS Testaments and portions each year. As the decade unfolded, copies of *Good News for Modern Man* and the *Good News Bible* were being used in diocesan and parish programs and Catholic schools in the Bronx, Philadelphia, Cleveland, Seattle, Wilmington, Los Angeles, Fresno, Newark, San Antonio, and Pittsburgh. A teacher at a Catholic high school in Pennsylvania placed an ad in the school newspaper suggesting that *Good News for Modern Man* would make an excellent Christmas gift. He sold twenty-five copies in three days. The Catholic diocese of Hartford promoted *Good News* on its radio and television programs. ABS displays and exhibits began showing up in new places, such as the Annual International Conference of the Roman Catholic Renewal Movement in South Bend, Indiana; the Los Angeles Archdiocese Meeting of Catholic Women; and the National Association of Roman Catholic Chaplains. The ABS Central Region sent complimentary copies of the Catholic imprimatur edition of *Good News* to every parish priest in the region (over 8,000 in total). Upon receiving his copy a priest in Minnesota bought 1,000 additional copies for his parishioners. In 1975, the ABS/UBS and the Vatican agreed to work together in the distribution of scriptures to pilgrims visiting the Vatican during the course of the Holy Year.[17]

Perhaps the most significant development in Catholic–Bible Cause relations was the decision to publish a version of the *Good News Bible* with the deuterocanonical books, or, as the Protestant liked to call them, the Apocrypha. The decision to include the Apocrypha in an ABS Bible reveals both the strides that had made in working with Catholics and the limits of such cooperation. A significant number of the ABS constituency still embraced serious concerns about cooperation with Catholics. The ABS was sensitive to the convictions of this part of its membership and thus approached the publication of the Apocrypha with caution. In the end, a compromise was reached. The ABS and UBS would fulfill the request of the Catholic Church for a *Good News Bible* containing the Apocrypha, but they would ask the Catholic Church (and eventually the Episcopalian Church, who also used the Apocrypha) to pay for the publication of these Bibles.

When work on the deuterocanonical books was announced in 1974, many Catholics became critical of the ABS/UBS refusal to fund these books. Father Walter Abbott, who had done so much in bringing a renewed spirit of cooperation with Protestants around the translation, publication, and distribution of the Bible, tried to calm these Catholic critics. In the same year he wrote an article for a publication of the World Catholic Federation for the Biblical Apostolate defending the ABS/UBS decision: "It must be evident that we have no right to criticize the decisions of the UBS in this matter. It is their right and duty to abide by the decision of their constituencies." The Catholic Church, he argued, had to start learning from the expertise of UBS translators and benefiting from their generosity. He concluded his article by reminding Catholics that the work with Protestant Bible societies was a direct implementation of the decrees of Vatican II. The *Good News Bible with Deuterocanonicals/Apocrypha* was published in 1979. The ABS made it clear to its membership that it was "normal policy . . . to publish the Scriptures *without* the Apocrypha," but from this point forward it would be willing to include these books in their Bibles whenever they were requested by a specific church community. In order to calm the fears of its Protestant constituency which was opposed to this decision, the ABS announced that the Apocrypha books would only be published in a special section located between the Old and New Testament. These editions would be paid for by the church community making the request for them to be included, and they would be published with a "clear explanatory note indicating the values attributed to these books by the different churches."[18]

As the nation struggled through an oil crisis, high interest rates, and stagflation, the American Bible Society was doing just fine. The TEV was a smashing success, and with an army of volunteers ready to bring it into new religious markets, the Society was able to make it through the decade without missing a beat. The 1970s also provided an opportunity for the ABS to reassert its historical connection to Christian nationalism and strengthen its relationship with the changing landscape of American Protestantism. It is to this story that we now turn.

26

God and Country

In 1970s and early 1980s American Protestantism went through some significant changes. The mainline churches experienced a precipitous decline after they had reached the height of their demographic and cultural power in the United States in the decades immediately following World War II. Meanwhile, evangelicalism began to surge. President Jimmy Carter described himself as a "born-again Christian," and *Newsweek* magazine, with the help of pollster George Gallup, proclaimed 1976 the Year of the Evangelical. With this rise in born-again religion, evangelicals and their more cantankerous fundamentalist brothers and sisters sought to "take back" an American society that they believed had been held hostage for too long by the cultural developments of the 1960s. Led by an outspoken Baptist minister from Lynchburg, Virginia, named Jerry Falwell, conservative Protestants and members of other religious groups sympathetic to his cause fought hard to bring prayer and Bible reading back to public schools, overturn the legalization of abortion in the wake of the Supreme Court decision *Roe v. Wade*, keep government from interfering in their segregated academies, and advance the idea that the United States needed to return to the Christian roots of its founding. Falwell and the other architects of the Christian Right would find sympathetic partners among the conservative wing of the Republican Party and its hero, Ronald Reagan.[1]

In July 1986, Alice Ball, general secretary in charge of the ABS National Division, did some long-range planning with her staff about how the Society might remain true its historic mission amidst this changing Protestant landscape. The planning team renewed its longstanding commitments to providing access to the Bible in a language that people could understand at a price that was affordable. They would continue to promote the word of God without doctrinal note or comment and without profit. The ABS would continue to cooperate with the UBS in providing scriptures to the world and it would not abandon its support to churches and anyone else "engaged in the use and distribution of the Scriptures throughout the United States." But this National Division planning committee also realized that the ABS would have to face some new challenges as it looked to the future. "In the past 10 years," the com-mittee noted, there had been a "turn toward a conservative point of view." This was no doubt a reference to the close connection between the growing preva-lence of evangelicalism and its relationship with the Republican Party. The committee also mentioned "gains in membership for Pentecostal and evangeli-cal churches" and the "fall off" among mainline churches.[2]

Ball's planning committee also wondered if it was time to stop measuring the success of the Bible Cause in terms of "dollars" (income and expenditures) and "numbers" (units of scriptures distributed, numbers of volunteers, etc.). While dollars and numbers were important, the committee concluded that "they are not enough," and "in some instances lead to 'doing more of the same' instead of generating a balance of maintaining service and developing new or better services." One way of breaking out of the rut was to focus more directly on evangelism. Only through concentrated efforts to "share the good news of Jesus Christ with men, women, and children everywhere" would the ABS be more effective in reaching "the unchurched who are very much in need of God's redemptive love." The committee acknowledged that the ABS had always been in the business of evangelism. In fact, it was "the central core of its ministry to the community." If the ABS was going to be effective in the shifting world of American Protestantism, it would need to develop scripture portions geared toward evangelism and connect more fully with evangelistic crusades and other models of personal evangelism such as Evangelism Explosion, the popu-lar program designed by Ft. Lauderdale clergyman D. James Kennedy. In fact, the committee resolved, it might even be necessary to consider the "promotion of ABS as an evangelism ministry." While it is hard to trace what became of the ideas floated in this long-term planning meeting, many of the issues and the questions raised would not go away.[3]

But this is all getting ahead of our story. Throughout the 1970s and early 1980s the ABS *did* make efforts to reach out to its evangelical constituency. At the same time, it continued to remind the nation that it was the *American* Bible Society through several programs and distribution efforts that connected the Bible Cause to the cause of American nationalism in a way that sounded a lot like their brothers and sisters on the Christian Right.

In order to grasp the ABS's work with evangelicals in this period we must go back to October 1968 and a joint meeting of the Evangelical Foreign Missions Association (EFMA) and the Interdenominational Foreign Missions Associ-ation (IFMA) held in Winona Lake, Indiana. These organizations repre-sented nearly every evangelical missionary agency ministering around the globe. Clyde Taylor, a former missionary in South America, the secretary of the EFMA, and the director of the National Association of Evangelicals,

invited the ABS to address the meeting on the subject of the Society's position on Catholicism. The evangelical missionaries were aware of the new spirit
of cooperation between the UBS and the Catholic Church on the translation
and distribution of the Bible and had some serious concerns. ABS General
Secretary Robert Taylor spoke to 200 evangelical missionaries who were skeptical—if not outright opposed—to cooperation with Catholics on Bible translation projects on the mission field. His address was titled "The Bible Societies
and the Catholic Church." After the talk Taylor answered questions so that
the missionaries present would be able to make an informed decision about
how the EFMA and IFMA should respond to the ABS–Catholic relationship.
While we don't know exactly what happened in the meeting, we do know that
it was a rough crowd. In a follow-up letter, Clyde Taylor apologized to Robert
Taylor for having to endure "all of the cross examination that you had." He
continued: "I had no idea . . . how bad a time they gave you in committee meeting. However, I imagined there were no holds barred."[4]

Clyde Taylor also wrote to inform Robert Taylor and the ABS about the
decisions these missionary organizations had reached during the Winona Lake
meeting. The missionaries of the EFMA and IFMA wished to inform the ABS
that it did not want to "enter into any relationship which would entail either
structural or formal relationship with the Roman Catholic Church as a church."
It also added that any EFMA or IFMA missionary who was involved in translation work with a member of the Catholic Church under the auspices of the UBS
would need to inform the Society that he was participating as an individual
and not as a representative of one of these evangelical agencies. Robert Taylor
expected these results and was pleased that the evangelical missionaries "did
not close the door" completely on cooperation with Catholics on the mission
field. For Taylor, it didn't matter whether they "act as individuals or a church,
the main idea is to get the Scriptures translated and distributed." He admitted
that he received some "pointed questions" in Winona Lake, and there was one
attendee who insisted on reading the conference "a great deal of Roman Catholic
law," but he felt he developed a "happy relationship" with the missionaries.[5]

After learning about what happened in Winona Lake, Laton Holmgren, the
ABS general secretary in charge of programming, wrote to Eugene Nida in
Switzerland to fill him in on the decisions made by the joint meeting of the
EFMA and IFMA. Holmgren wrote that the evangelical missionaries perceived the ABS to be an organization that promoted "ecumenical interests"
and thus did not want to be forced to participate with Catholics on ABS and
UBS translation projects. The missionaries asked the ABS to "curb the promotion of Ecumenism by its representatives." They referenced witnessing ABS
officers make speeches that promoted "ecumenical philosophy," and some
even tried to convince native church leaders who were evangelicals to support

ecumenical initiatives. The missionaries were also upset that the ABS had decided to enter into conversation with the Catholic Church "without consultation with conservative evangelicals." Finally, the joint missions committee of the EFMA and IFMA were opposed to the Catholic imprimatur on the *Good News Bible*. Nida understood their concerns. He would do his best to talk with as many of them as possible to try to calm their fears about the Catholic Church and the ecumenical movement.[6]

In an attempt to work through these difference, Holmgren invited the EFMA and IFMA Committee on Bible Society Matters to meet with him at Bible House in August 1969. Along with Clyde Taylor, one of the participants in that conversation was Francis Steele, an IFMA missionary and the director of North Africa Mission (later Arab World Ministries). At one point during the discussions, Steele handed Holmgren a document titled "Principles of Bible Translation." Upon reading it, Holmgren realized that the evangelical missionaries, in addition to concerns over Catholicism and ecumenism, also had serious problems with dynamic equivalence. As we have seen, much of the ABS's success in the late 1960s and 1970s rested on the achievement of Today's English Version (TEV), a "sense-for-sense" or "idea-for-idea" translation of the Bible. Steele was skeptical. He understood dynamic equivalence to be more interpretation than a faithful translation of the Bible. As he told Holmgren, "the translator will put down what he thinks was meant by the original author rather than simply translating the text before him." This gave the translator a great deal of latitude in handling of the word of God. On the other hand, Steele noted, those who subscribed to the "conservative doctrine of Biblical inspiration will take far fewer liberties in rendering the Biblical text into modern language." Conservatives working on evangelical translations believed that the words of the text were of "primary importance" because "God inspired not only the ideas but the words."[7]

Holmgren put Steele's memo into context. He latched on to Steele's use of the phrase "evangelical translations." Holmgren was aware that in evangelical circles this phrase was "more and more being set over against 'dynamic equivalent' translations." In fact, many evangelicals had already begun what they believed to be an accessible, yet more faithful, translation of the Bible that would appear in 1973 under the title New International Version (NIV). In fact, Steele was a member of the original NIV translation committee. The conversations taking place with these evangelical missionaries were about trying to keep the evangelical community in the ABS fold, but Holmgren was also aware that the NIV posed a possible threat to the success of the TEV. Ironically, the New International Version was funded by the New York Bible Society, a society that predated the ABS and had been influential in its creation. The New York Bible Society had been an ABS auxiliary until 1913. Also, unlike the ABS, it had landed firmly on the fundamentalist side of the so-called fundamentalist-modernist controversies of the 1920s. At the time that evangelical leaders approached the New York Bible Society about the possibility of publishing the NIV, it had been struggling financially and had recently moved out of New York to a new headquarters in New Jersey. It was the success of the NIV that pulled the New York Bible Society out of its economic difficulties. Eventually it changed its name to the International Bible Society, and left New Jersey in 1988 for the growing evangelical mecca of Colorado Springs, Colorado.[8]

Nida wrote a memo to Holmgren titled "Evangelical vs. Dynamic Equivalent Translations" in which he completely dismissed the notion that a dynamic equivalent translation could not also be an evangelical translation. "If 'evangelical' is to be understood in terms of greater faithfulness to the text of the Holy Scripture, a high view of divine inspiration, and an evangelistic concern for effective communication of the Word of God," he told Holmgren, "then a dynamic equivalent translation is certainly an evangelical one." He admitted that anyone who adhered to verbal inspiration would probably have problems with the TEV, but he defended *Good News for Modern Man* as being just as "meaningful to present-day people as they were to those who first received them." Ten years later, when the ABS was considering adding the NIV to its catalog, Oswald Hoffman, the Lutheran Missouri Synod host of the popular "Lutheran Hour" radio program, told Nida that the NIV was "a rather pedestrian version." Nida agreed with Hoffman, but also realized that "it no doubt will satisfy some of the people whom we hope to serve and help."[9]

Holmgren concurred with Nida's defense of the TEV, but he also knew that he did not want to lose the evangelicals over their concerns related to Catholicism, ecumenism, and dynamic equivalence. Since the EFMA and IFMA represented 10,000 missionaries throughout the world, Holmgren thought it was necessary to bring these concerns before the Executive Committee of the UBS, which was meeting in Canberra, Australia, in May 1970. Upon returning to Bible House after the meeting, he wrote "Evangelicals and the Bible Cause," a statement that made clear the ABS position on the various evangelical concerns. This was meant to be a conciliatory document that Holmgren and other ABS staff could use with evangelicals when such issues arose in the future. He began by affirming the Bible society movement's commitment to evangelism in words that would have clearly resonated with evangelicals.[10] "The Bible Societies have always believed that those engaged in this task must be zealously evangelistic in outlook and outreach," Holmgren wrote. He added that the ABS and the UBS believed that "every man on earth must be told of the Savior in his own tongue and given the opportunity to surrender his life to Him."

Holmgren went on to explain that the Bible societies had always been "fully interdenominational in character." The attempt of the ABS to have board and staff members from every denomination was not a "recent drift toward ecumenism," but a "fundamental tenet in the organizational structure from the beginning." The ABS was in the business, and had always been in the business, of bringing the Bible to the widest possible audience without doctrinal note or comment, and would thus work with any legitimate Christian body to achieve that goal—even Catholics and representatives of Protestant denominations that many evangelicals may have deemed to be liberal. On this point Holmgren was not being disingenuous—the ABS was an interdenominational organization from the beginning. But he failed to acknowledge that the Protestant landscape of America had changed drastically since 1816, a time when nearly all the Protestant denominations were largely evangelical in flavor. Holmgren knew that ecumenical efforts were underway to translate the Bible in several developing nations in a manner that was "earnestly and honestly" opposed by evangelicals "as a matter of deep Christian conviction," but he added that the ABS was not an extension of "institutional ecumenism" and welcomed the input of any and all Christian groups, including evangelicals.

While Holmgren defended the ABS commitment to dynamic equivalence, he also reminded evangelicals that the Society was involved in thousands of translation projects around the world using more standard versions. Finally, he tried to calm evangelical fears by reminding them that the ABS or UBS had no authority to force them to participate in joint translation projects with Catholics. On the other hand, it did not make sense to have two different translations of the Bible in any given language—one approved by evangelicals and another approved by the ABS. He affirmed the ABS commitment to never using the Society's funds to publish the Apocrypha and ended with a promise to consult with the leaders of the evangelical community on all future decisions related to publication, distribution, and translation. In the end, the ABS did not waver in its positions regarding the matters raised by evangelicals. Holmgren's statement showed a deep respect for evangelical anxieties and even managed to focus—through language and argument—on the ways in which the Bible Cause intersected with the traditional beliefs of American evangelicals. How would these evangelical missionaries that Taylor represented, and the evangelical community as a whole, respond to Holmgren's statement? Only time would tell.[11]

Another way that the ABS worked together with evangelicals was through "Key '73: Calling Our Continent to Christ," a year-long interdenominational event billed as "the first joint evangelistic effort ever undertaken by North America's leading churches." Evangelicals were the driving force behind Key '73.

Following the 1966 World Congress on Evangelism in Berlin, many evangelicals were inspired to reinvigorate evangelistic activity at home. In June 1967, an editorial by theologian Carl F. H. Henry in *Christianity Today* titled "Somehow, Let's Get Together," prompted evangelicals to search for partners from across the Christian spectrum to unite in a nationwide crusade to spread the Gospel in the United States. If evangelicals were going to promote Christian unity, they were going to do it on a playing field—the evangelistic crusade—on which they were most comfortable. The premise behind such an event was that there would be a "much bigger ingathering of souls, proportionately, if many, many Christians shared their faith at the same time, thereby reinforcing one another's witness." The name of the event came from five consultations between American church leaders that took place between 1967 and 1968 at a Marriott hotel near the Francis Scott Key Bridge in Rosslyn, Virginia. Several evangelical leaders embraced Key '73, but others became very concerned when Catholic bishops threw their support behind the event. The Key '73 committee was chaired by Thomas Zimmerman, superintendent of the Assemblies of God, and Theodore A. Raedeke, the former director of evangelism for the Lutheran Church Missouri Synod.[12] The year of evangelism began in late December with meetings for repentance, prayer, and Bible study. It included surveys of the spiritual needs of ordinary Americans, lay witnessing in local communities, traveling teams of Christian artists, television and other mass media programming, summer outreach to youth and visitors to state fairs, the dissemination of Christian literature, and the distribution of the Bible. The goal was to bring the Gospel to every person in the United States and Canada.[13]

The ABS threw its full support behind the Key '73. The 1973 *Annual Report* began with a reference to the event: "Two events made 1973 an outstanding year for the American Bible Society: the launching of the 'Good News for New Readers' program and the 'Key 73: evangelism emphasis.'" The ABS distributed more than 35 million portions of scripture designed specifically for this unique year of evangelism, including an edition of *Good News for Modern Man* with a Key '73 cover design. As churches and denominations planned their special evangelistic efforts, the ABS was there to provide support. The Georgia Baptist Convention, for example, ordered 1 million copies of "One Way," the *Good News* Gospel of John in newspaper format. In Santa Barbara, California, 600 Key '73 volunteers passed out 30,000 copies of an ABS portion called "Touched by Fire." The ABS also prepared one-minute public service radio spots to promote Key '73. In October, the Society sponsored a week-long, citywide festival in Wichita, Kansas, called "Good News Wichita." The plan was to choose a "typical American city for complete saturation of the community with the claims of the Bible Cause" through preaching, exhibits, displays, and media attention. Though "Good News Wichita" was an ABS event, the Society made several deliberate efforts to connect this Bible festival with the goals of Key '73.[14]

The ABS considered Key '73 a "tremendous success." The Key '73 special edition of *Good News for Modern Man* flew off the shelves so rapidly that the Society had to print an apology for its failure to meet orders in a timely manner. (The worldwide paper shortage mentioned in the previous chapter did not help matters.) Indeed, the event was a great moment in the modern history of evangelism if measured by the number of Bibles distributed, but most Christians involved in Key '73, and many who were not involved, viewed it as anything but a success. A September 1973 article in the *New York Times* declared it to be "a failure over-all." The continent-wide evangelistic campaign did not come anywhere close to confronting every person in the United States and Canada with the Gospel. The Key '73 committee was only able to raise one-quarter of its $2 million budget for national media efforts. Optimistic observers tried to focus on the bright side. The event was a step in the right direction for ecumenical relations in the United States. Though not everyone was reached with the saving message of the Gospel, many did experience a genuine conversation. Henry was disappointed that Key '73 "posed little basic challenge to the secular erosion of Christianity" in the United States.[15]

Many Protestant liberals took the opportunity to criticize American evangelicalism as a whole for trying to "claim the continent for Christ" and promote Christian nationalism. Senator Mark Hatfield, a progressive evangelical, indirectly chided the Key '73 organizers for trying to "Christianize the nation" and urged his fellow believers to stop efforts to integrate "politics and spirituality." Henry, upon reflection, wished that Key '73 had been focused on both the prevailing need "of new birth and new life" *and* a vision of public justice and political morality that had implications for the spiritual state of the country. Henry argued that the American founding fathers' believed that religion was directly connected to democratic government and national virtue. He expressed hope that future plans to renew evangelism efforts around the upcoming bicentennial would go a long way toward "Christianizing North America" and proving to the communists of the Soviet Union that religion was the driving force behind American values and ideals.[16] As far as these remarks were concerned, Henry could have been speaking as an employee of the American Bible Society. In the end, the Key '73 experience was a positive step for ABS–evangelical relations. Henry praised the Society for providing so many Bibles to the cause, and the ABS proved itself to be faithful partners in the work of national evangelism and the promotion of the United States as a civilization that was grounded in Biblical ideals.

Whatever efforts the ABS made to affirm evangelicals and work with them on joint projects such as Key '73 did not solve all their differences. In 1983, Billy

Melvin, a ministerial member of the ABS Board of Managers and the director of the National Association of Evangelicals, expressed concerns to Alice Ball, ABS general secretary, about some things he had been hearing in the evangelical community with respect to the Society. Ball planned a meeting at the Bible House. Melvin called together men who were serving or had served the National Association of Evangelicals in leadership roles. The purpose of the confidential meeting, as Melvin put it, was to "make a positive contribution to the work and ministry of the ABS and to strengthen their relationship with the evangelical community worldwide." The agenda revolved around the following questions: "What is the state of our relationship with ABS today?" "Do you sense a growing or declining relationship [between evangelicals and the ABS]?" "Does the ABS have strong ties to evangelical denominations?" "Does a public relations problem remain with the TEV?"[17]

Melvin attached to the agenda a list of denominations that gave money to the ABS in 1982. He underlined all of the denominations on the list that were affiliated with the National Association of Evangelicals (NAE). The ten largest contributors among the nonevangelical denominations had donated just over $952,000 to the ABS. This included, in order of contribution, the Southern Baptist Convention, Church of the Nazarene, United Methodist Church, Lutheran Church in America, American Lutheran Church, American Baptist Church, United Presbyterian Church, Mennonite Churches, Presbyterian Church in US, and United Churches of Christ. There were twenty-two NAE denominations that had given money to the ABS in 1982 and their total contribution came to $114,100, with 80 percent of the money coming from only two denominations: the Assemblies of God ($72,409) and the Wesleyan Church ($18,946). Granted, many of these evangelical denominations were small and did not have the resources of the longstanding mainline Protestant churches. On the other hand, Melvin was correct to notice a trend. Denominations connected with the NAE, with a few exceptions, did not support the ABS.[18]

The ABS did not dabble in politics, but if it had one thing in common with the Christian Right it was its belief that the moral health of the United States was directly proportional to the number of people reading the Bible and applying its principles to their lives and the life of the nation. The ABS, as we have seen, never passed up an opportunity to connect its mission to the success of the American experiment. Consider the Society's response to the death of Dwight D. Eisenhower. Sometime around March 1969, ABS officers John Erickson and Paul Wright were having lunch in New York with Rome Betts, a former ABS officer who was now the president of the American Heart Association. Betts asked Erickson and Wright, who were both working as ABS fundraisers, what the Society planned to do to commemorate Eisenhower's recent death, especially since the former president had such a deep and abiding love for the Bible. Intrigued by the possibility of doing something special for the family of the deceased former president, but unsure how to go about it, Erickson mentioned his dilemma to Edward Mayer, the Philadelphia Agency direct marketer who had been helping the ABS with its fundraising needs. Mayer happened to know Dwight's son John Eisenhower and after much discussion about the nature of such a commemorative gesture, it was decided, with the blessing of Mamie and her children, that the ABS would produce a special Eisenhower Memorial Edition of *Good News for Modern Man*.[19]

The paperback New Testament was titled: *Good News for Modern Man: Dwight D. Eisenhower Memorial Edition*. There was photo of Ike on the back cover and a quote of his that read "the Bible is endorsed by the ages. Our civilization is built upon its words. In no other book is there such a collection of inspired wisdom, reality and hope." Erickson wrote the fundraising appeal: "In appreciation of your gift of five dollars or more we would like to share with you a special copy of the Dwight D. Eisenhower Memorial Edition of the TEV New Testament." Those who purchased a copy of the Eisenhower edition would have their name entered in a memorial volume deposited at the Eisenhower Presidential Library in Abilene, Kansas. The appeal to ABS membership was sent sometime in mid- to late 1969, and then Erickson and the rest of the staff sat back and watched the responses pour in to 1865 Broadway. As of February 1970, over 104,000 people had purchased a copy of the Eisenhower New Testament. Erickson and his wife Nancy visited Mamie at the Eisenhower farm in Gettysburg, Pennsylvania, and presented her with a copy of the book. In 1971 he traveled to Abilene to deposit eight bound volumes containing the names of all those who donated to the ABS in Ike's name. The Eisenhower campaign generation tens of thousands of letters. Most of them included words of appreciation for Ike, memories of his role in World War II and as president, and moving testimonials about what this Bible-believing president had meant to them as Christians and as Americans. Erickson read through most of the letters and was often moved to tears when he realized the way people's lives were strengthened, moved, and protected by Ike. The Eisenhower Memorial Bible Fund resulted in over 100,000 new donors to the ABS.[20]

On one level, the decision to produce a special New Testament to commemorate Eisenhower was a radical departure from common ABS practice. The ABS promoted the Bible, not individual people. It took Erickson a lot of effort to convince Edward Wagner, the president of the ABS, to support the project because it seemed to be making the person on the back cover more important than the message inside the book. But on another level, the Eisenhower Memorial New Testament made perfect sense for the ABS. It was yet another way of connecting the Bible Cause to American ideals. Though the gushing letters remembering Ike have been lost, it is not too far of a stretch to suggest that those who wrote these emotional epistles connected Ike's love of the Bible to American civil religion. Indeed, Ike was not only an American hero, but he made no bones about connecting his love of the United States to his love of God and the Bible. Eisenhower believed that religion played a public role in American life. He regularly connected piety and patriotism, and suggested that "without God there could be no American form of Government, nor an American way of life." In 1953, on the urging of the National Association of Evangelicals, Eisenhower was the first to sign a statement that declared that the United States was founded on the teaching of the Bible. Ike and the American Bible Society were a perfect fit.[21]

Just as the excitement surrounding the Eisenhower Bible began to wane, the ABS starting preparations for the American bicentennial celebration in 1976. The planning began with "Good News, America!," a ten-year campaign to place a portion of scripture in the hands of every literate man, woman, and child in the United States. The goal was to "call Americans, especially those who do not regularly attend church, to personal faith and to renewed commitment." The Good News, America! campaign was a grassroots effort that would rely upon local churches and the growing army of ABS volunteers. The first phase of the program was designed to relate the scriptures to America's bicentennial and in the process meet the large number of requests for scripture portions that could be used in patriotic celebrations and study groups.[22]

In 1975, the bicentennial publications began to roll off of the ABS presses. In November a special portion called "Faith, Justice, and Repentance" was published. It was pitched as a Bible-based "Call to the Nation." Bicentennial editions of the Old Testament and New Testament were prepared to meet requests from Southern Baptists and Pentecostals. The ABS also repurposed some previously published scripture portions, including the popular "One Nation Under God," a meditation on Psalm 33:6–22 ("happy is the nation whose God is the Lord") that connected the Bible to the Pledge of Allegiance; "Sing a New Song" (Psalms 95 through 100), a reminder of the role of the Bible in the culture of Puritan New England; and "Plead My Cause, O Lord" (Psalm 35), a portion designed to draw attention to the psalm and prayer that Rev. Jacob Duche prayed at the opening of the First Continental Congress in Philadelphia in September 1774. In the years leading up to the bicentennial, ABS volunteers served a dual purpose as agents of the Bible Cause and American nationalism. And if anyone happened to miss the connections between the Bible and the American Founding, they could climb on board the American Freedom Train that was traveling around the country displaying various artifacts and documents related to the America's past. The ABS loaned the group responsible for the train an original copy of printer Robert Aitken's 1782 Bible, the first English Bible printed in the United States.[23]

1976 was another busy year for the ABS. The year-long bicentennial celebration was in full-swing across the nation, and the *Good News Bible* was released. Laton Holmgren described its publication as the Society's "gift to America on its 200th anniversary." More bicentennial scripture portions were published, including a portion from Isaiah 61:1–4 titled "Proclaim Liberty Throughout All the Land." The portion was printed in the shape of a bell and showed a photographic likeness of the Liberty Bell on the cover. ABS volunteers, in conjunction with the Pennsylvania Bible Society, distributed over 60,000 of these portions at Independence National Historical Park during the month of July. This was a time to draw "national attention to the Biblical heritage that so richly influenced the founding of this nation." The ABS encouraged its membership to celebrate the bicentennial by "affording God's word the position of prominence and leadership it has maintained not only over the past 200 years but since that wintry day in 1620 when a small band of pilgrims established a permanent colony in what is now Plymouth, Mass." An article in the *Bible Society Record* described the Mayflower Compact as "our country's first 'Constitution' and noted that liberty stemmed from the 'Laws of Nature and Nature's God.'"[24] It was a grand celebration of both God and country.

Following a crushing defeat in the Fundamentalist–Modernist controversies of the 1920s, American evangelicals abandoned public life and created a subculture where they could lick their wounds and focus on what they did they best—evangelism and the pursuit of personal piety.[25] For the next fifty years it would be liberal Protestants, not fundamentalists and evangelicals, who would be in a position of power to shape American culture. The ABS latched on to the Protestant mainline because its ecumenical approach to Christianity provided opportunities to distribute Bibles to as many people as possible and its position at the center of American religious life meant that mainliners provided an ideal partner for the Society in the project of nation-building. But times were changing. During the late 1970s and early 1980s the American evangelical slumber had come to an end. Evangelicals began making more demands on the ABS to meet their particular Bible needs, while others left the Bible Cause altogether, preferring to align themselves with other Bible organizations, such as the International Bible Society. Some evangelicals made strong connections between their Christian mission and what they perceived to be the Christian origins of the United States. As we will see in the next chapter, this evangelical presence, both outside and inside the Bible House, only grew stronger as the ABS entered the 1990s.

Engaging the Age of Evangelicalism

What happens to the American Bible Society when Americans stop buying Bibles? On October 28, 1996, an article in the business section of the *New York Times* reported that the $200 million market for Bibles "is as flat as a leather Bible cover." A director for marketing at Oxford University Press suggested that the American market for the holy book had reached a saturation point. The standard wisdom in the publishing world was that Bibles were immune to economic ups and downs. During times of prosperity, people could afford to spend their extra money on Bibles as gifts. During times of economic crisis, people were willing to spend whatever they had for a book that would provide them with comfort and support. Most experts blamed the glut in the market on the rise of the so-called big box stores: Barnes & Noble, Walmart, and Sam's Club, that also sold Bibles. The competition was fierce. Many Christian bookstores went out of business, while others, such as the Family Bookstore chain, returned hundreds of thousands of dollars' worth of Bibles that it could not sell. According to the *Times* article, the latest ABS translation to hit the market, the Contemporary English Version (CEV), had only captured 1 percent of the Bible market for its publisher Thomas Nelson.[1]

One reader who was disturbed by the *Times* article was Eugene Habecker, the president and CEO of the ABS. Habecker penned a letter to the editor that was published a few days later. He did not dispute the fact that Bibles sales were going through a "sluggish season," but he did note that the recently released CEV was doing quite well—much better than the *Times* seemed to suggest. What bothered Habecker the most about the article was the fact that so many Americans owned a Bible (he estimated that there was one in at least 90 percent of homes), but few had any idea what was in it or how to engage with its content. "The people who have Bibles . . . don't use them enough," Habecker wrote, "or when they do, they don't remember what they have read."[2] Though the new chief executive of the ABS had only been at 1865 Broadway for a little over a year, he had already concluded that the Society, despite its impressive distribution numbers, was not doing enough to teach people how to "use" the

Bible. This problem needed to be addressed. He would address it, and it would become the most important legacy of his presidency.

When Eugene Habecker arrived in New York in the summer of 1991 he was assuming an administrative position—president and chief executive officer—that was brand new. The Society had an organizational structure that, with a few small changes here and there, had been in place since its founding in 1816. The president of the ABS under this structure was essentially the president of the Board of Managers. He operated as the public face of the Society, but played very little role in day-to-day operations at the Bible House. Elias Boudinot was the first president of the ABS, and twenty-two men had succeeded him in this position. The ABS had always been run by general secretaries, each with a particular responsibility for the work of the organization. As Robert Taylor, the general secretary who presided over fundraising and promotions during the 1950s and 1960s, liked to say, "there is no way that any one person should be 'mister or misses ABS.' "[3] There were many who believed that the structure of general secretaries had been working just fine, but others on the Board of Managers wanted a change. Those pushing for a chief executive model—especially the vice president of the board, Ruth Peale—were convinced that the general secretary system was too confusing to the ABS's overseas partners. The secretaries of the national Bible societies around the world that held membership in the UBS often complained that they never knew which member of the ABS leadership to contact when conducting the business of the Bible Cause.[4]

Things came to a head in 1988 when James Wood, the president of the ABS Board, and Ruth Peale called together the leaders of the national Bible societies attending the meeting of UBS Executive Council in Budapest, Hungary. The purpose of the meeting was to discuss the ABS leadership structure. When they returned to New York, Wood and Peale recommended to the Board of Managers that the organization of the ABS be changed in order to allow for a single executive. The board approved the recommendation and a search committee was formed. After much deliberation and debate, it was decided that the ABS would look for its new leader outside of the Bible House. While they searched for the right candidate, Bryant Kirkland, the retired pastor of the Fifth Avenue Presbyterian Church in New York City, would serve as the interim president and CEO.

Habecker was one of the earlier frontrunners for the position. He was currently serving as the president of Huntington College, an evangelical school in Indiana affiliated with the United Church of the Brethren. Habecker was born on a dairy farm in Hershey, Pennsylvania; attended college at the evangelical Taylor University in Upland, Indiana; earned a law degree at Temple University and a PhD in business administration from the University of Michigan; and had experience as an administrator at several Christian colleges. The résumé was impressive. Peale, Wood, and the search committee wanted him, but Habecker was not yet ready to leave Huntington. He did, however, leave the door open. Two years later, when the ABS search committee contacted him again, he accepted the post.[5] Habecker had the business acumen and the background in administration to run the ABS. The search committee and the Board of Managers believed that he was the right person to lead the Society through this organizational transition. Habecker also identified himself as an evangelical Christian. He made it clear to the Board of Managers that he was not a "narrow evangelical" or a "Jerry Falwell-type evangelical," but he did wonder whether an organization that had had its disagreements with evangelicals in the past, and was run largely—both at the board level and the administrative staff level—by mainline Protestants, would be interested in an evangelical as its first permanent CEO. Ruth Peale and the other members of the search committee calmed his fears.[6]

Habecker's first major challenge was to put the ABS's new administrative structure in place. He worked hard to break down the administrative silos that had characterized the work of the Society in the days when it was run by three general secretaries. He called for a deeper sense of unity and common purpose among the staff at Bible House. Habecker also set out to make the ABS more accountable to its donors, especially those who gave money for overseas projects carried out under the auspices of the UBS. As we have seen, the UBS funded national Bible societies around the world through a World Service Budget. The wealthier societies, or the "contributing" Bible societies as they were known, provided the money for the budget through yearly grants, while the Bible societies around the world with fewer resources received financial support from the World Service Budget to carry out its work. Since the early 1970s, when the World Service Budget model was put in place, the ABS usually donated roughly 50 percent of the entire budget.[7] The problem for Habecker was that the monetary grant the ABS set aside each year for the UBS World Service Budget was unrestricted. The ABS would provide a lump sum and the UBS would decide how it would be distributed and spent. Donors did not know how their money was being used, and some of them threatened to stop giving until they had a clearer sense of the projects that their contributions were supporting. Eventually, through the help of Robert Briggs, one of Habecker's vice presidents, Global Scripture Impact (GSI) was created. The purpose of GSI was to monitor and evaluate Bible-related projects around the world, particularly where donor funds were being used, and provide a detailed report to the donors complete with images, a colorful design, statistics, and a narrative about whether the project was performing according to plan.[8]

Perhaps Habecker's greatest challenge on the organizational front was to reorder the ABS Board, which would now be called the Board of Trustees. Habecker moved the ABS from a membership-controlled board to a self-perpetuating board. Prior to his arrival, ABS Board members were elected by the Society's membership. A member of the society was anyone who donated five dollars to the ABS over the course of any given year. Those who sat on the board were chosen during the annual meeting which, according to Habecker, was often attended by less than one hundred ABS members, mostly Bible House staff. He worried that if an outside group wanted to take over the ABS, all they had to do was pay five dollars and vote their own people onto the board. Moreover, the current process, he believed, gave ABS staff too much power in electing the board. Under a self-perpetuating board, the board itself would take responsibility for the recruitment of its new members and a governance committee was established to oversee the process. Habecker also thought that board was too large, making it unwieldy and difficult to conduct business. Under his watch it was gradually reduced from seventy-two members to twenty-one members.[9]

Habecker's concerns over the glut in Bible production, coupled with what he believed about the lack of biblical literacy in the culture and the general lack of Bible *use* in America, led him to pursue a slightly different course from those who came immediately before him. For most of the twentieth century, the ABS understood itself as a service organization. It published Bibles, produced translations informed by the best and most innovative scholarship, and distributed those Bibles through sales and grants to as wide of an audience as possible. The ABS leadership—both the Board of Managers and the Bible House staff—drew careful boundaries around what the Bible Society did, and what it did not do. For example, the ABS wanted people around the world to be confronted with the saving and life-transforming message of Jesus Christ, but it did not engage in evangelism. The ABS sold Bibles, Testaments, and scripture portions to churches and denominations, but it did not make suggestions about how those groups should teach, interpret, or use the Bible. The ABS was willing to work with any Protestant organization—and later any Catholic or Orthodox communion—that asked for its help. The ultimate goal was to deliver a quality product and, as the nineteenth-century ABS agents in the field used to say, "let the Bible do its work." The ABS was part of the larger work of building the Kingdom of God, but it had a narrow and limited role in such efforts.[10]

Throughout ABS history there were people affiliated with the Bible Cause who pushed these boundaries. Agents, volunteers, auxiliary societies, and colporteurs—both at home and abroad—regularly showed people how to use the Bible as a means of knowing God and strengthening their spiritual lives.

ABS distributors often preached to the people in the churches that they visited. As we have seen, in 1939 Dutch theologian Hendrik Kraemer urged the representatives of the major Bible societies meeting in Woudschoten to teach people who bought the Bible how to read it, interpret it, and apply its message. ABS General Secretary Eric North, who was also at that meeting, complained that people around the world were receiving scriptures that were not being used. He wanted to do everything in his power to remedy this problem. In 1986 the ABS National Division proposed the idea of measuring success qualitatively, rather than quantitatively (in terms of the numbers of Bibles distributed). But until the 1990s, the belief that the ABS should not get involved in work that belonged to the churches remained the dominant way of understanding the Society's mission and purpose.[11]

As a former college president, Habecker maintained an abiding concern for the future of the Bible Cause among young people. Not only did he want the youth of America to experience God through the Bible, but he also realized that without the next generation the financial future of the ABS was in doubt. High distribution numbers were not enough. Perhaps the goal was less about trying to win a large share of the ever-competitive Bible market and more about teaching people how to use and understand the Bible that they already owned. While many of Habecker's critics saw this as a new direction, he believed that he was returning to the original vision of the ABS, a vision that somehow got lost over the course of the previous century. The work of in-house ABS historian Peter Wosh had shown him that at some point in its nineteenth-century history the Society had narrowed its vision from missionary work to the business of merely "producing the Scriptures and coordinating their distribution." According to Wosh, this transition occurred around the time that the ABS moved into the Astor Place Bible House in 1853 and was illustrated best in the work of Isaac Bliss in Constantinople. Though Habecker did not put it exactly in these terms, it was clear that his vision was to somehow restore the ABS to its pre-1853 function as a missionary organization with a practical, ministry-oriented purpose.[12]

When it came to moving the ABS in this direction, Habecker had a strong ally in Lamar Vest, a member of the Board of Trustees. Vest was a leader in the Church of God, a Pentecostal denomination headquartered in Cleveland, Tennessee, and also served as the chairman of the board of the National Association of Evangelicals. After sitting through his first several ABS Board meetings, Vest grew frustrated with the proceedings and told Habecker that he was going to resign. "It seemed to me," Vest would later say, "that our number one discussion on the Board is how much money we have in the bank and how many Bibles we distributed, and so we are judging our successes by our bank account and judging our ministry in tonnage." ("Tonnage" would become a buzzword for Habecker, Vest, and their supporters to describe their belief that the ABS was measuring success based on the number of Bibles distributed.) How could the ABS pat itself on the back for shipping out "three more tons of Bibles this year than last year" when, according to Vest, Bible knowledge and literacy was on the decline? Was the ABS in the business of putting a "ninth Bible on the shelf of the people who already had eight Bibles that they weren't reading?" Habecker agreed, and he asked the Pentecostal from Tennessee to help him change things.[13]

Habecker eventually appointed Vest to chair a new "mission and vision" task force. Vest's committee included Char Binkley, an evangelical radio executive; Richard Jeske, a Lutheran pastor active in Lutheran-Episcopalian dialogue; and Dennis Dickerson, an African American historian who taught at Vanderbilt University. Habecker and Sally Robinson, a Canon in the Episcopal Church who was the first female chair of the ABS Board, served as ex officio members of the committee. The new vision statement that the task force submitted to the Board of Trustees in 2001 set the American Bible Society on a new course. Prior to 2001, the ABS statement of purpose read:

> The purpose of the American Bible Society is to provide the Holy Scriptures to every man, woman, and child in a language and form each can readily understand, and at a price each can easily afford. This purpose, undertaken without doctrinal note or comment, and without profit, is a cause which all Christians and all churches are urged to support.

Vest's committee changed the statement of purpose to a mission statement that read: "The mission of the American Bible Society is to make the Bible available to every person in a language and format each can understand and afford so that all may experience its life-changing message."[14]

The new statement came with two significant changes. First, it eliminated the phrase "without doctrinal note or comment." Second, it added the clause "so that all may experience its life-changing message." By eliminating the first phrase, the ABS appeared to be suggesting that it could now participate in the practice of teaching and interpretation. It could publish Bibles with notes that were specific to a particular faith tradition. This new departure enabled the ABS to work more closely with churches and denominations and provide "helps" that reflected the beliefs of a specific religious tradition. Shortly after this, the ABS began to use the word "ministry" to define its programs. For example, the current ABS website describes the Society as a "Christian ministry that has been engaging people with the life-changing message of God's word for nearly 200 years." The ABS was no longer a service organization, a publisher, or a Bible distributor; it was now directly working to make sure that people's lives were changed through their encounters with the word of God. This was further confirmed by adding the clause at the end of the mission statement. In doing so, Vest claimed to be answering what he called the "so what?" question—the reason why he and others should be advancing the Bible Cause. This also added an additional responsibility to the work of the Society. Success would now be measured in changed lives—a result that a previous generation had always believed was the work of the church.[15]

The "Mission and Vision Statement for the Third Millennium," as it was officially called, did not end there. Vest, like Habecker, was a former college president who was worried about the future of the Bible Cause. His committee's statement had a heavy emphasis on reaching young people. "The fundamental standard by which we are to judge our success," the document stated, "will be found not in the number of volumes we produce and circulate but in how we influence a new generation." The statement also introduced the term "engagement." This word had been bandied about the Bible House ever since Habecker arrived, but Vest and his committee gave it center stage in their document. Lives would be changed by an "engagement with Scripture." The ABS needed to increase "circulation and engagement." From this point forward, "engagement" would become the word the ABS would use to describe the core of what it was all about.

Scriptural engagement could be carried out in locations that existed beyond the walls of the church. While the ABS did not neglect the traditional ways in which Christians engaged with the Bible—sermons, Bible study, devotional reading, and so on—it also understood engagement "through creative interaction with the wider culture." This could be accomplished through media, entertainment, and the arts. Under Habecker's watch the first floor of 1865 Broadway went through a major renovation. A glass façade, complete with video screens and images, was created in the hopes that millions of people who passed the building each year would look inside or even enter the Bible House to browse ABS Bibles or grab a cup of coffee. Habecker and his wife Mary Lou championed the creation of an art gallery that would eventually become the Museum of Biblical Art (MOBIA). Visitors to MOBIA, which was located on the second floor of Bible House, could see major exhibits of Bible-related art. Over the years there were exhibits on stained glass, holy art from imperial Russia, folk art from Peru, children's depictions of Bible stories, Ukrainian sacred images, and the history of the King James Version. Each piece of artwork was accompanied by a description of the work, a brief biography of the artist, and, most importantly, an explanation of the meaning of the Bible passage portrayed in the given work.

Another example of this kind of scripture engagement was the production of music videos. A team of Bible scholars and translators, led by a former Missouri State University religion professor named Robert Hodgson, created seven performance videos based on popular stories from the Bible. The target audience for these videos was young men and women who would not necessarily pick up a Bible, but might be interested in issues related to faith and values. They were modeled after the music videos that teenagers watched every day on Music Television (MTV). Each video was produced with the full scholarly integrity of Hodgson and his team behind it, much in the same way that ABS translators vetted the Society's Bibles. The producers took the words of the CEV and gave them to professional musicians who wrote them into a song and performed it. Some of the musicians that participated in the project were Women of Calabash, Rory Block, and Sweet Honey in the Rock. Several years before he starred as Jesus in *The Passion of the Christ*, Jim Caviezel was playing the Son of God in an ABS music video on the resurrection.[16]

In 1999, the ABS made an effort to get more African Americans to engage with the scriptures through the publication of *The African American Jubilee Edition* of the Contemporary English Version. The Bible claimed to help African Americans "see how they are inextricably connected to the ancient world of the Bible," and allowed them to "fully understand the inter-relatedness of the biblical stories and their own rich heritage by critically examining the elements of place, people, culture, and story." The ABS reminded its readers that the Bible had a lot to say about issues related to race, gender, oppression, and prejudice. The idea for an *African American Jubilee Bible* came from Charles H. Smith, the assistant director of heritage markets at the ABS. Smith and the ABS gathered a remarkable list of authors—either members of the African American Christian community or academics studying the African American experience—to write introductory essays. Virgil Wood, a Baptist minister and a former executive board member of Martin Luther King Jr.'s Southern Christian Leadership Conference, framed the new edition around "Jubilee," a biblical and theological concept that had a profound influence on how the African American community had always understood justice and freedom. The finished product was filled with colorful maps and photos that told the story of the black experience in America alongside the story and message of the Old and New Testament.[17]

The move toward scripture engagement had its naysayers. Some believed that by focusing on engagement, or anything beyond service to churches and denominations, Habecker was taking the ABS down the wrong path. Some of the opposition, as we will see, came from members of the Board of Trustees, but ABS translators also had their criticisms of scripture engagement. Historically, translators were the guardians of ABS neutrality as embodied in its commitment to publish the Bible without doctrinal note or comment. Eugene Nida believed that Bible scholars were central to what the ABS was all about. Translators reviewed ABS Bibles and other materials for balance and fairness. They made sure that the Bibles the Society produced could be used comfortably by readers of all denominations. They also made sure that all ABS publications fell within the parameters of mainstream Biblical scholarship as defined by professional organizations such as the Society of Biblical Literature. As the ABS began to focus on engagement or ministry, and started to shed its identity as a Bible publisher, academic quality control was no longer as important as it used to be. Academic vetting took too much time, the Society was not planning any new translations, and the need to publish materials without doctrinal note or comment was no longer a priority. Many of those committed to this scholarly function of the ABS felt marginalized. The spirit of innovation and ingenuity that defined a previous era—an era perhaps best characterized by the short-lived Center for Scripture and Media based out of Springfield, Missouri (which produced the MTV-style music videos mentioned above)—was being stifled. The ABS continued to innovate, but such experimentation did not usually pass through the rigorous academic standards that characterized previous attempts to deliver the Bible in new and creative ways.[18]

When it became clear that the principle of no doctrinal note or comment would no longer serve as the penultimate test for Bible society publications, some members of the Translation Department, including its head, David Burke, dug in their heels. In 2002, aware that the ABS commitment to this principle was eroding, Burke, a Johns Hopkins trained scholar of Near-Eastern Studies who had been a leader in Lutheran-Catholic dialogue in the United States before coming to the Society in 1987, presented a paper on this issue at a meeting of UBS translators in Malaga, Spain. The sense of urgency expressed in the paper struck a nerve with those worried that the principle of "no doctrinal note or comment" was being threatened. Burke asked his audience (and eventual readers) to consider what might happen if those "who lead and serve the Bible Society were to abandon its historical posture" on this front and begin to embrace "doctrinal positioning under one banner or another" in the form of "Application Bibles" or a "range of Bible-based resources of a prescriptive, homiletic or theological nature?" Burke's paper was a tour de force. He offered a comprehensive history of the phrase "no doctrinal note of comment," distinguished the difference between a Bible "help" and a "doctrinal note," defended the belief that the Bible societies were not churches and thus were not in the business of interpreting the Bible, and called the Bible societies to remain true to this principle.[19] It is unclear what kind of impact Burke's essay had on the global Bible society community, but he probably published it too late. Vest's mission statement had already been approved by the Board of Trustees, and the phrase "no doctrinal note or comment" was nowhere to be found on its pages.

In 2003, in the wake of an article in *Forbes* magazine calling attention to several "bad business deals" that had cost the ABS millions of dollars, Habecker decided that it was time to rethink the Society's business model.[20] Budget cuts were made in most ABS departments and staff members were laid off—eighty-five total employees by one estimate. Burke's team of translators and scholars, now operating under a new ABS initiative called the Nida Institute for Biblical Scholarship, was hit especially hard. Over a dozen of Burke's staff were let go and many of the Nida Institute's experimental projects linking scholarship with new forms of media were deprioritized. The staff of the archives and the ABS library was severely reduced, making research difficult. Burke resigned in protest. Today the Nida Institute remains the intellectual arm of the ABS. Under the leadership of Philip Towner, the former director of translation services of the UBS, it does most of its work training Bible translators through seminars held around the world and at San Pellegrino University in Italy. Towner also helps the ABS and international Bible societies to think more historically and theologically about the ministry of scripture engagement. In 2011 the Institute began the publication of *Translation*, an international and interdisciplinary journal on the relationship between translation studies and culture that attempts to bring the academic world of Bible translation into conversation with the larger scholarly of world of translation studies.[21]

Habecker's presidency also led to some changes in the religious identity of the American Bible Society. These changes had an effect on the makeup of the Board of Trustees, the culture of the Bible House, and the partners that the Society was willing to work with. When Habecker arrived at the ABS in 1991, the Board of Managers (later Board of Trustees) was largely made up of men and women with ties to the historic mainline Protestant churches. As he worked to shrink the board, Habecker also sought to change its religious identity by adding more Roman Catholics and evangelical Christians. The critics of this move believed that Habecker was trying to orchestrate an "evangelical takeover." Habecker admitted that he was trying to reduce the number of board members connected to mainline Protestantism, but he was motivated less by some kind of evangelical takeover and more by the historic ABS commitment to embracing Christians of all persuasions. Habecker believed that the large number of mainline Protestants on the board did not represent the demographic makeup of American Christians. Mainline churches were in decline. Evangelicalism was thriving. Catholicism remained the largest religious body in the United States. At one point Habecker entertained the idea of allotting seats on the board by religious identity in accordance with the percentage of Americans affiliated with the four major Christian traditions: mainline Protestant, evangelical Protestant, Roman Catholic, and Orthodox.[22]

Habecker was fond of using the term "interconfessional," rather than "ecumenical," to describe the religious makeup of the ABS Board. "Ecumenical" carried too much baggage. For some, it was a worn-out term left over from midcentury attempts by organizations like the National Council of Churches or the World Council of Churches to create one, unified communion of Christians. As we have seen, it was a term that raised red flags for evangelicals. Habecker's decision to diversify the board emphasized both unity and difference. He hoped that every member might bear testimony to the belief that "Jesus Christ is Lord," but in the process they would also keep strong ties to their specific ways of living out or practicing such a credo.[23] While his use of the term "interconfessional" represented such a conviction, it was also a means by which Habecker was able to disconnect the ABS from its twentieth-century links to the Protestant Ecumenical Movement.

Habecker was very sensitive to the fact that those associated with the Bible Cause spoke a variety of religious languages. People expressed their faith (or in some cases did not express their faith) in different ways. Yet anyone connected with life in the Bible House in this era could see that the culture of day-to-day ABS operations had taken on a decidedly different tone under the new CEO, a tone that might best be described as evangelical. Many welcomed this change. Others did not. Habecker drew criticism for trying to create a culture in which members of the staff prayed for one another. Meetings were opened in prayer at a much higher rate than they had been before. Habecker and his staff brought a greater devotional flavor to the Monday morning voluntary meeting Moments for the Word. One regular attendee of these meetings—a Catholic—noted that each session usually ended with a very strong message about accepting Jesus Christ as one's savior. And when during a presentation at a staff meeting one of Habecker's vice presidents described the kind of person who the ABS was trying to reach with the Bible as a "passionate Christ-follower," he was reprimanded by a staff member who thought that such language was exclusive in nature and shouldn't be used in the Bible House or in ABS literature.[24]

Outside the Bible House, the ABS began working more closely with evangelical groups. In the past, the ABS had partnered most extensively with Protestant denominations (and eventually Catholic dioceses). The denominations would purchase Bibles, Testaments, and scripture portions from the ABS for congregational use or special events and programs. Most of the larger mainline Protestant denominations also donated money to the continuing work of the Society. Each year the ABS would grant millions of dollars to the UBS to support the Bible Cause around the world. Not all of the societies who received this money had evangelical leanings. But under Habecker, a new

trend developed in the ABS grant-making practices. By 2005, the final year of
his presidency, the ABS was making large grants to ministries such as Campus
Crusade for Christ, an evangelical ministry on college campuses with a program for distributing Bibles to military personnel; Faith Comes By Hearing,
an evangelical ministry that produces audio Bibles; and Scripture Union,
an evangelism and discipleship ministry for youth and families. Habecker
started a trend in this regard. For example, in 2013 and 2014, the ABS made
grants to evangelical organizations such as Liberty University, Willow Creek
Association, Child Evangelism Fellowship, Trans-World Radio, WorldServe
Ministries, the Lausanne Committee for World Evangelism, Scripture Union,
the Seed Company, and Campus Crusade for Christ. In addition to these new
partners, in 2011 the ABS became a member of the Evangelical Council for
Financial Accountability, an organization that keeps evangelical ministries
and churches financially accountable to their constituencies.[25]

The Habekcer years had its share of highlights. One of them was a new Bible
translation. The Contemporary English Version (CEV) of the Bible was the
brainchild of Barclay Newman, a veteran of Robert Bratcher's *Good News
Bible* translation team. Like Today's English Version, the CEV was translated using the theory of dynamic equivalence. Since Newman's target was
younger readers and uneducated adults, the English in the CEV was designed
for a lower reading level than the TEV. Newman spent considerable time with
children and studied forms of media—newspapers, magazines, movies, and
television—that appealed to ordinary English speakers. Work began on the
CEV in 1984. The New Testament was published in 1991, and the entire Bible
appeared four years later from Thomas Nelson. While much of the work on the
Bible had taken place prior to Habecker's arrival, he enthusiastically traveled
around the country to promote it.[26]

One of the highpoints of the ABS engagement with its home in New York
City occurred following the September 11, 2001, terrorist attacks on the
towers of the World Trade Center. In the wake of the tragedy the staff of
the Society went to work distributing Bibles, providing words of encouragement and comfort to those in need, and sharing the good news of Jesus
Christ. The ABS quickly put together a booklet of scripture portions titled
"God Is Our Shelter and Strength." Two days after the attacks a New York
City police vehicle pulled up in front of the 1865 Broadway to pick up ten
cases of scripture booklets for distribution at Ground Zero. Police officers
asked Habecker to help them make the delivery, and Habecker and Richard
Sterns (the president of World Vision, who happened to be visiting that day)
jumped in the car and headed downtown. In the days that followed the ABS
took out ads in *USA Today*, the *Wall Street Journal*, and the *New York Times*

offering consolation from the scriptures. Similarly, over 5,300 public service announcements were sent to English-language and Spanish-language
radio stations around the country. The ABS website received an unprecedented number of visits. A distribution station was set up outside the Bible
House. On September 23 at the "Prayer for America" at Yankee Stadium,
more than twenty ABS volunteers handed out over 30,000 copies of "God
is Our Shelter and Strength." New York City needed spiritual support in a
time of crisis and the ABS responded.[27]

After about eleven years as president and CEO, the tasks of leading the ABS
through a new organizational structure, bringing more religious balance to the
Board of Trustees, and implementing a new mission statement, were taking
their toll on Habecker. The opposition to his presidency, which was related in
one way or another to all these initiatives, had not gone away. In 2002, concerned that opposition from the board was hurting the general work of the
Bible Society and causing anxiety for his staff, Habecker submitted his resignation. Lamar Vest, who was now chairman of the board, refused to accept it.
After a long night of soul searching and prayer, Habecker returned the next
day and asked the board to openly declare itself. Did they support the direction that Habecker was taking the Society? If the answer was "yes," Habecker
would stay. If the answer was "no," he would follow through on his letter of
resignation. It was a dramatic moment in the history of the ABS. Habecker,
and especially Vest, see it as a historic moment as well. Roughly 80 percent
of the board gave Habecker a vote of confidence. The ABS president had his
mandate. Those who voted against him gradually resigned and Habecker
was finally able to move the Society, without opposition, in the direction he
had been trying to go for over a decade. In his May 2003 report to the board
Habecker proclaimed: "We are shifting *from* a distribution-only mindset *to* a
Scripture-engagement mindset." The change was complete. From this point
forward, the days in which the ABS measured success based on tonnage were
over. The ABS would now be a ministry devoted to Scripture engagement.[28]

Epilogue

The Bible Cause in the Twenty-First Century

The Board of Trustees' declaration of support for Eugene Habecker was a significant moment in the history of the American Bible Society. On one level, nothing had changed. The ABS would continue to be in the business of publishing, translating, and distributing the word of God in order to meet the spiritual needs of individuals. It would continue to try to build a Christian culture informed by the Bible's moral and religious teachings. On another level, everything changed. The ABS transitioned from a service organization entrusted with providing Bibles for Christian churches and denominations, to a ministry devoted to teaching people how to use or engage the Bible in their daily lives.

Moreover, the ABS, as a *national* Bible society, would continue to try to position itself at the center of American culture. In the nineteenth century, the ABS was an evangelical benevolent society in an evangelical culture. For most of the twentieth century, the ABS gravitated to the cultural power of the historic Protestant mainline. Today, in a much more heterogeneous American society where there is no one manifestation of Christianity with the power to shape the culture in the way that evangelicals did in the nineteenth century and the Protestant mainline did in the twentieth century, the ABS has decided to work most closely with institutions, organizations, and communities that have strong evangelical sympathies. The ABS continues to celebrate its interconfessionality, or its willingness and desire to work with all varieties of global Christianity, but it tends to finds its strongest partners, as Vice President Geof Morin likes to say, among the "evangelical expressions" of such Christian communities. Eugene Habecker may not have led an "evangelical takeover" of the ABS, but it is hard to spend a significant amount of time studying this organization without coming to the conclusion that in the last twenty years it has taken an evangelical turn. To the extent that evangelicalism is still a potent force in American public and religious life, and is spreading like wildfire around the world in a host of different denominational forms, the ABS seems to have chosen well.[1]

After Habecker left the ABS to become president of Taylor University in 2005, some of the old guard who were not in favor of the Society's move toward scriptural engagement hoped that things might return to the way things were before his arrival in 1991. Habecker's replacement, Paul Irwin, was an ordained United Methodist clergyman who prior to taking the helm of the ABS served as the president of the Humane Society. He came to the Bible House with a strong reputation as a fundraiser. Irwin hired people who knew how to raise money, but rarely wore their religion on their sleeves. Lamar Vest, who had moved from his position on the board to a staff position as executive vice president in charge of Global Scripture Ministries, did his best to keep Irwin focused on the principles of scripture engagement as found in the 2001 Vision Statement. In the end, whatever hopes people had about Irwin turning back the clock were dashed when the *New York Times* published in May 2008 an article titled "An E-Commerce Empire, From Porn to Puppies." The story revealed that Irwin had paid $5 million to an Internet design company without realizing that its owner had ties to the pornography industry. Irwin resigned. Vest replaced him.[2]

Vest spent four years as the ABS president (2009–2013) before he returned to Cleveland, Tennessee, and another position of leadership in the Church of God. He was replaced by Douglas Birdsall, an evangelical scholar of world missions who was a leader in the Lausanne Movement, an international program to promote global evangelism. Birdsall did not last long. Disagreements with the board over the future of the Society led him and the ABS to part ways before he was even inaugurated as president. In February 2014, Roy Peterson, the president and CEO of the Seed Company, an evangelical Bible translation ministry affiliated with Wycliffe Bible Translators, succeeded Birdsall as ABS president.[3]

Under Peterson's leadership, the American Bible Society continues its historic commitment to meeting the spiritual needs of people around the world and building a Christian civilization at home and abroad through scripture engagement. If he has learned one thing from the history of the ABS, it is how to get people excited about the Bible Cause through grand vision statements. By 2025, Peterson wants to see 100 million Americans engaged with the Bible, scriptures available in every world language, and the expansion of the ABS endowment to $1 billion. It's an ambitious goal, and that is why he has Executive Vice President of Ministry Mobilization Geof Morin, who has been at the ABS since 2007, to help him. Morin represents the future of the Bible Cause. He has worked in global advertising, sung at the Metropolitan Opera, and is an ordained priest in the Episcopal Diocese of Philadelphia. He oversees ABS marketing, communications, and Bible technology, and runs Mission U.S., Mission Global, the title given to the Society's domestic and international ministries. He is passionate about scripture engagement and the role it can play in the universal Christian church—Protestant, Catholic, and Orthodox.[4]

In its 2025 "Strategic Vision" statement the ABS defines scripture engagement as "encountering God through the Bible to become faithful followers of Jesus Christ." Through the help of the Nida Institute for Biblical Scholarship, the ABS has developed a theoretical and theological framework for how such engagements with scripture should take place. At the core of this idea of scriptural engagement is the belief that people can encounter—and have encountered—the claims of the Bible in diverse ways and by multiple means, including public hearings, performances, reading, worship, art, and music, to name a few. Such encounters involve the full range of human faculties: emotions, the intellect, the imagination, and the soul. Inherent within this view of scripture engagement is the belief that God, by entering into human culture through the person of Jesus Christ, has invested this world with meaning and has created human beings for community. To put it simply, the Bible has the potential, through the power of the Holy Spirit, to transform lives when it is experienced with other people and through various forms of culture. While the American Bible Society has always relied upon the Spirit to enlighten the scriptures for those who receive it, prior to the twenty-first century any attempt at offering a theological explanation for the ways in which such spiritual enlightenment takes place would have been perceived as violating the Society's commitment to producing the Bible "without doctrinal note or comment."[5]

One of the criticisms of the so-called tonnage approach to the Bible Cause was that it was impossible to gauge the spiritual impact of the scriptures on people's lives apart from the anecdotes and stories told through the correspondence of agents, colporteurs, and Bible recipients themselves. It was one thing to spend millions of dollars producing and distributing Bibles, Testaments, and scripture portions, and quite another thing to know if those scriptures were simply placed on a shelf, treated like a family talisman, or actually read. While the ABS has always accepted this as a valid critique of its organization, there was never any serious attempt to try to respond to it apart from something akin to the common mantra of "letting the Bible do its work." The idea of scripture engagement offers an answer to this historic problem. But if the success of the Bible Cause will now be measured by the number of people who have an encounter with Jesus Christ through the scriptures, and not by how many boxes of Bibles were sent to this or that location, then the ABS must come up with metrics that can be used to measure spiritual growth, an experience that is often personal, intimate, and private. How do you measure life change?

It is a question that the current ABS administration has pondered for a long time. While Lamar Vest was president, the success of the Bible Cause around the world was measured through what became known as Global Scripture Impact reports. These reports, as we saw in the last chapter, stemmed less from the ABS desire to measure the quality of scripture engagement and more from the need to show donors how their money was being used. While Global Scripture Impact remains an important part of the ABS mission, especially in its ongoing relationship with the United Bible Societies, Morin and colleagues have gone even further in the process of developing metrics to measure the impact of scripture engagement. These include monitoring, through surveys and other sociological methods, changes in Bible reading, spiritual practices, and ways of behaving; value shifts in the larger culture; giving to charitable organizations; participation in ministries related to justice, mercy, and reconciliation; and an individual's expression of solidarity with the oppressed. Such a social scientific approach to analyzing whether or not scripture engagement is working requires measurements of spiritual health to be taken both before scripture engagement happens and after it occurs.[6]

The ABS has entrusted this work of measuring the success of scripture engagement to the Barna Group, a Christian research organization known for its work in observing the state of American Christianity and offering "spiritual indicators" about where the United States is moving on matters of faith and culture. With the help of Barna-created surveys specifically designed for this purpose, Peterson is convinced that by 2025 the ABS will have "defensible numbers" to show that 100 million people in the United States are actively using the scriptures. The ABS also relies upon Barna for its annual State of the Bible Survey. Morin, who spearheads this project, likes to call it a "Bible thermometer." The State of the Bible report is more than just a fun way for the ABS to let the country know who it is and what it does. Rather, the success of Peterson's 2025 vision is directed related to its findings. The ABS is just getting to the point where it has enough data to be able to see some trends about what Americans think about the Bible. The evidence suggests that there is still a lot of work to do. At the moment, the ABS and Barna estimate that roughly 47 million Americans are actively engaging with the Bible. This number will need to be more than doubled in the next decade in order to meet Peterson's projections.[7]

With a theoretical framework and a system for measuring success in place, the ABS hopes to achieve its 2025 goals in the following ways: First, it will work with other translation agencies and organizations, such as UBS, Wycliffe Bible Translators, and the Seed Company, to translate (and in some cases retranslate) the Bible into the 1,800 languages that still lack a copy of the word of God. Second, it will reach its goal of 100 million people engaged with the scriptures through programs focused on metro areas around the country, the creation of a Bible Discovery Center at its new Philadelphia headquarters, and a program—which Morin calls Project Magellan—to influence America's perception of the Bible by working closely with churches, media, businesses, government, education, arts, entertainment, and the social sector. As part of Project Magellan the ABS has already been involved as consultants—or what Morin calls "scripture engagement experts"—in Hollywood films such as *Exodus* and *Noah* and television projects such as *A.D.*, the mini-series produced by Mark Burnett and Roma Downey. (Morin notes that during the period when *Noah* was in theaters, the readership of Genesis 9 and 10 on the ABS digital channels skyrocketed.) Similarly, the ABS has over 11 million people engaging with the Bible on a host of different Facebook pages.[8]

Third, through a project that it calls Scripture 911, the ABS is working with several partners to provide scripture engagement tools for victims of trauma around the world. This part of the plan includes a Biblical Trauma Healing Institute. Fourth, the ABS plans to increase annual revenue and build the endowment to $1 billion by moving away from its "overdependence on revenue from community giving" (small gifts up to $5.00) to "funding primarily from major gift financial partners" (over $10,000). Apparently the days of the Bible-A-Month Club and five dollar memberships are over. Fifth, and finally, the ABS hopes to reach its 2025 goals through its already established ministries such as Global Scripture Impact and Bibles.com.

Morin dreams big about the potential of scripture engagement to transform people's lives. He imagines, for example, a Digital Bible Library where the ABS would work with the UBS to create an online collection of every translation of the Bible ever made. And then there is his idea for a "wearable Bible." He describes such a Bible in terms of what he sees as the natural progression "from desktop to mobile to body." This Bible would be a screen on a watchband that would measure the spiritual health of the wearer much in the same way that similar bands measure heart rates and offer other kinds of medical reporting. According to Morin, "it's a very small step from the biometric to the spiritual." He admits that this all sounds a little "freaky right now," but confirms that ABS is moving in this direction. For example, someday in the near future, Morin projects, a Bible will be able to predict someone's anxiety levels and immediately offer them a scripture verse—perhaps Philippians 4:6 ("be anxious for nothing")—that will provide comfort and spiritual strength. Discussions with technology firms are already underway. ABS innovation continues. Why buy a Finger-fono when you can you have a wearable Bible?[9]

As it has done since the days of Elias Boudinot and John Jay, the ABS continues to take seriously its role in creating a more moral and Christian nation. While the current leadership team is not interested in going back to the days of its founding, it does believe, like Boudinot did 200 years ago, that American culture is ailing and the only prescription for this moral sickness is a healthy dose of God's word. Like Boudinot, who feared that the Age of Revelation was about to give way to Thomas Paine's Age of Reason, the ABS looks at the depressing data on the state of the Bible in America life and responds by coming up with creative ways to bring the Bible to bear on the practice of American democracy. Something needs to be done, and the ABS has the resources and the talent to do it.[10]

This brings us to the recent ABS decision to leave New York City after 199 years and move the organization to Philadelphia, where it now occupies two floors in the Wells Fargo Building on 401 Market Street, just steps from Independence Hall. The move was driven by financial concerns. The 1865 Broadway Bible House needed 25 to 50 million dollars' worth of repairs in order to meet the city building code. The ABS owned both the twelve-story building and thirty-seven additional stories of New York City airspace. For Peterson, the decision to sell the building and move to another location was a matter of Christian stewardship. He imagines what the ABS will be able to do with the money from the sale in terms of promoting its agenda of scripture engagement. The ABS moved in summer 2015.

Peterson has also managed to do some revisionist history to help justify the transition to Philadelphia. He suggests that despite the ABS's 199-year presence in the city, New York was never the Society's true identity. On one level, Peterson is correct. The ABS was founded in New York because of the hospitality of the New York Bible Society, which supported Boudinot's plan for a national Bible society and agreed to host the meeting that established it. While it was certainly possible that the ABS might have ended up in another city, the fact remains that it *did* end up in New York and it remained there for two centuries. It is hard to dismiss two centuries of history. If, as Peterson notes, the ABS "inadvertently" made New York its identity when "it was never supposed to be our identity," the fact remains that between 1816 and 2015 the American Bible Society was a New York City institution.[11]

Peterson is quick to note that Philadelphia was Elias Boudinot's hometown. According to his will (a copy of which Peterson, at least at the time he was interviewed, had sitting on his desk), Boudinot had left land to the city. The new ABS president is not willing to go any farther with this argument other than to note that an ABS move to Philadelphia, at least as history is concerned, may not be as random as some would like to make it out to be. Peterson, however, is more certain about how the transition to Philadelphia will allow the ABS to connect itself once again to the story of the United States. What better place for the ABS to celebrate its bicentennial in May 2016 than the place where America was born? This was a place where God and country came together in 1776, and with the ABS only a stone's throw away from the Liberty Bell and Independence Hall, Peterson is hoping that the Society can help middle-class Americans remember that fact.

Peterson wants the ABS, with a soon-to-be constructed Bible Discovery Center highlighting the history of the Bible in the United States, to become a Philadelphia tourist attraction. He estimates that after three years in Philadelphia over 250,000 people will come to the Bible Discovery Center to "hear the story of the Bible." Peterson wants the "best of the best" to help him in the construction of this Discovery Center, and that is why he has turned to the Green family, the owners of the retail craft store Hobby Lobby. The Greens made national headlines in 2014 when the Supreme Court ruled that they did not have to violate their conscience by conforming to a part of the Affordable Care Act that would have forced them to provide certain contraceptives to Hobby Lobby employees. In the last several years, the Greens have been active in a host of philanthropic activities on behalf of the evangelical community and are currently a major ABS donor. Peterson is excited that the Greens have been willing to help the ABS Bible Discovery Center gets off the ground by sharing some of the intellectual property it has gathered in the process of building their soon-to-be-opened Museum of the Bible in Washington, DC.

As the Bible Cause in America enters its third century the future looks bright, but the challenges ahead are great. As the American Bible Society pauses to look back, in search of a useable past to help it move forward, it will find that a lot has changed over the years. The commitment to bringing the Bible to people who need it and, in turn, building a society that better reflects the teachings of the scriptures, however, remains the same.

NOTES

Introduction

1. John Erickson, interview by John Fea, Crawford, Nebraska, March 17–18, 2015; Roy Peterson, interview by John Fea, American Bible Society, New York, NY, March 23, 2015.
2. Laton Holmgren, "Evangelicals and the Bible Cause," Laton Holmgren Papers, RG 18.08, Box 1, Folder 3, ABS Archives, New York; *Bible Society Record* 49:3 (March 1904), 33.
3. Chris Thyberg e-mail to author, December 13, 2013.
4. Henry Otis Dwight, *The Centennial History of the American Bible Society* (New York: Macmillan, 1916); Creighton Lacy to Laton Holmgren, September 1, 1974; Robert Taylor to Arthur Whitney, September 21, 1970; Robert Taylor to Laton Holmgren, September 25, 1974, Laton Holmgren Papers, RG 18.08, Box 15, Folder 1, ABS Archives, New York.
5. Robert Taylor to Laton Holmgren, September 25, 1974.

Chapter 1

1. On Boudinot see George Adams Boyd, *Elias Boudinot: Patriot and Statesman, 1740–1821* (Princeton, NJ: Princeton University Press, 1952).
2. On the Princeton Circle see Mark A. Noll, *Princeton and the Republic, 1768–1822: The Search for a Christian Enlightenment in the Era of Samuel Stanhope Smith* (Princeton, NJ: Princeton University Press, 1989).
3. Elias Boudinot, *The Age of Revelation or The Age of Reason Shewn to be an Age of Infidelity* (Philadelphia: Asbury Dickins, 1801), xvii.
4. Paul C. Gutjahr, *An American Bible: A History of the Good Book in the United States, 1777–1880* (Redwood City, CA: Stanford University Press, 1999), 10–11. Gutjahr estimates that *The Age of Revelation* sold fewer than 2,000 copies.
5. Boyd, *Elias Boudinot*, 253–254; Elias Boudinot, *A Star in the West* (Trenton, NJ: D. Fenton, 1816), 27.
6. *The Panoplist and Missionary Magazine* Ser. II Vol. 5 (June 1810), 35–36; Ser. II Vol. 4 (1811–1812), 376; David Paul Nord, *Faith in Reading: Religious Publishing and the Birth of Mass Media in America* (New York: Oxford University Press, 2004), 42–56.
7. Rebecca Bromley, "The Spread of the Bible Societies, 1810–1816," ABS Historical Essay 8, 1963, ABS Archives, New York, 1–10.
8. Gutjahr, *An American Bible*, 13.
9. Nord, *Faith in Reading*, 46–47; Bible Society of Baltimore, *An Address to the public by the Board of Managers of the Bible Society of Baltimore* ... (Baltimore: Benjamin Edes, 1815), 13; Daniel Walker Howe, *What Hath God Wrought: The Transformation of America, 1815–1848* (New York: Oxford University Press, 2007), 212.
10. Bromley, "The Spread of the Bible Societies, 1810–1816," 10–15.

11. Nord, *Faith in Reading*, 4–5.
12. Eric M. North and Rebecca Bromley, "The Pressure Toward a National Bible Society 1808–1816." ABS Historical Essay 9, 1963, ABS Archives, New York, 8–41.
13. Elias Boudinot, "To the Board of Managers of the New-Jersey Bible Society," August 30, 1814, cited in North and Bromley, "The Pressure Toward a National Bible Society," 41–42.
14. North and Bromley, "The Pressure Toward a National Bible Society," 46–47.
15. Elias Boudinot to Elisha Boudinot, March 31, 1815, cited in Boyd, *Elias Boudinot*, 285.
16. "A Clergyman," *Some questions and answers of the subject of the American Bible Society* (New York: Van Winkle & Wiley, 1816), 6, 12.
17. Elias Boudinot, *An Answer to the objections of the managers of the Philadelphia Bible Society . . .* (Burlington, NJ: David Allinson, 1815).
18. North and Bromley, "The Pressure Toward a National Bible Society."
19. Elias Boudinot to Alexander Proudfit, June 9, 1815, Boudinot Correspondence, ABS Archives, New York.
20. Ibid.
21. Ibid.
22. Mills and Smith Report, cited in North and Bromley, "The Pressure Toward a National Bible Society," 80–95.
23. John Caldwell to Elias Boudinot, September 22, 1815, Boudinot File, ABS Archives, New York.
24. *The Panoplist and Missionary Magazine* 12 (1816), 90–92; North and Bromley, "The Pressure Toward a National Bible Society," 102–104.
25. North and Bromley, "The Pressure Toward a National Bible Society," 112. Of course other Episcopalians, most notably William White, the Bishop of Pennsylvania, were strong supporters of the Bible societies.
26. William Jay to Elias Boudinot, March 25, 1816, in Eric North, ed., "The Correspondence of Elias Boudinot with the American Bible Society," ABS Historical Essay 201, ABS Archives, New York.
27. William Jay, *A Memoir On the Subject of a General Bible Society for the United States of America By a Citizen of the State of New York* (Burlington, NJ: n.p., 1816); Eric M. North, "The Formation of the American Bible Society, 1816," ABS Historical Essay 11, 1963, ABS Archives, New York; Elias Boudinot to William Jay, April 4, 1816, Boudinot File, ABS Archives, New York.
28. Elias Boudinot to John Caldwell, April 25, 1816, Boudinot File ABS Archives, New York.
29. The Bible Society of Baltimore would also refuse to join the ABS for similar reasons to that of the Philadelphia Bible Society. See *The sixth annual report of the Bible Society of Baltimore . . . September, 1816*, 7–8.
30. Elias Boudinot to Joshua M. Wallace, May 3, 1816.

Chapter 2

1. Henry Otis Dwight, *The Centennial History of the Americn Bible Society* (New York: Macmillan, 1916), 22–24; Creighton Lacy, *The Word Carrying Giant: The Growth of the American Bible Society* (Pasadena, CA: William Carey Library, 1977), 2.
2. Minutes of the ABS Annual Meeting, May 8, 1816; Eric M. North, "The Formation of the American Bible Society, 1816," ABS Historical Essay 11, 1963, ABS Archives, New York, 54–55.
3. Samuel Bayard to Elias Boudinot, May 11, 1816, Boudinot File, ABS Archives, New York; Elisha Boudinot to Elias Boudinot, May 11, 1816; Dwight, *The Centennial History of the American Bible Society*, 24.
4. Joshua M. Wallace to Tace Wallace, May 11, 1816, Boudinot File, ABS Archives, New York; Gardiner Spring, *Memoirs of the Late Samuel J. Mills* (New York: New York Evangelical Missionary Society, 1820), 99.
5. Ivan Nothdurft, "The Founders of the American Bible Society," ABS Historical Essay 12, Part VI, 1980, ABS Archives, New York, n.p.; Margaret T. Hills and Elizabeth Eisenhart,

"The Founders of the American Bible Society," ABS Historical Essay 12, 1963, ABS Archives, New York, n.p.

6. On these British connections see Peter Wosh, *Spreading the Word: The Bible Business in Nineteenth-Century America* (Ithaca, NY: Cornell University Press, 1994), 39–43.

7. *Constitution of the ABS*, 16; *Proceedings of a Meeting of the Citizens of New York and Others* (1816), 10.

8. *Annual Report of the ABS* (New York: ABS, 1817), 19.

9. *The Second Annual report of the Board of Managers of the Kentucky Bible Society,* (Lexington, 1818), 4; *Annual Report of the ABS* (New York: ABS, 1819). The relationship with the Kentucky Bible Society did not last long due to the lack of skilled workers and the publication of inferior Bibles. See David Paul Nord, *Faith in Reading: Religious Publishing and the Birth of Mass Media* (New York: Oxford University Press, 2004), 67–68.

10. *Annual Report of the ABS* (New York: ABS, 1817).

11. James Madison, Seventh Annual Message to Congress, December 5, 1815, www.presidency.ucsb.edu/ws/?pid=29457, accessed July 25, 2014; Daniel Walker Howe, *What Hath God Wrought: The Transformation of America, 1815–1848* (New York: Oxford University Press, 2007), 80–84.

12. *Constitution of the ABS.*

13. *ABS Quarterly Extracts* 2 (November 1818), 42.

14. *ABS Quarterly Extracts* 5 (January 1820), 166.

15. *ABS Quarterly Extracts* 10 (October 1820).

16. *Annual Report of the ABS* (New York: ABS, 1818), 21–22.

17. Samuel Bayard, *Memorial of the board of managers of the American Bible Society, soliciting from Congress an exemption from the charge of postage and from duty on paper for printing Bibles . . . January 1818.* The House of Representatives was presented with the petition on January 16, 1817. The Senate received the petition on December 23, 1817. On January 25, 1817, the petition was read before the House and it was "ordered to lie on the table." On April 4, 1818, the Senate decided that the petition should be "discharged from the further consideration thereof respectively." See "A Century of Lawmaking for a New Nation: U.S. Congressional Documents and Debates, 1774–1875," Library of Congress, http://memory.loc.gov/ammem/hlawquery.html, accessed August 6, 2014.

18. *Extracts from the Correspondence of the ABS* 47 (August 1826), 2–3.

19. *Extracts from the Correspondence of the ABS* 11 (May 1822), 32–35.

20. *Extracts from the Correspondence of the ABS* 45 (May 1825), 8–9.

21. *ABS Quarterly Extracts* 2 (November 1818), 43.

22. *Proceedings of a Meeting of the Citizens of New-York and Others Convened in the City Hall on the 13th of May, 1816* . . . (New York: J. Seymour, 1816), 8.

23. *Extracts from the Correspondence of the ABS* 46 (June 1825), 23.

24. *Proceedings of a Meeting of the Citizens of New-York and Others Convened in the City-Hall on the 13th of May, 1816,* 15.

25. William Jay, *The Life of John Jay,* Vol. 1 (New York: J. & J. Harper, 1833), 501.

26. Elias Boudinot, *An Address Delivered before the New Jersey Bible Society* (1811), n.p.

27. Elias Boudinot, *The Second Advent* (Trenton, NJ: Fenton Hutchinson, 1815), 513–515, 528–552.

28. Thomas Jefferson to Dr Thomas Cooper, November 2, 1822, www.beliefnet.com/resourcelib/docs/54/Letter_from_Thomas_Jefferson_to_Dr_Thomas_Cooper_1.html, accessed August 6, 2014.

29. Elias Boudinot, *The Age of Revelation or The Age of Reason Shewn to be an Age of Infidelity* (Philadelphia: Asbury Dickins, 1801), xii, xv, xvii, xxi.

30. *Extracts from the Correspondence of the ABS* 35 (May 1824), 10.

31. *ABS Quarterly Extracts* 8 (October 1820), 239; *ABS Quarterly Extracts* 10 (April 1822), 75; *Extracts from the Correspondence of the ABS* 35 (May 1824), 5–6.

32. Joshua M. Wallace to Tace Wallace, May 13, 1816, Boudinot File, ABS Archives, New York; *Proceedings of a Meeting of the Citizens of New-York and Others.*

33. North, "Formation of the ABS," 68–69.

34. Boudinot would attend Annual Meetings in 1818, 1819, 1820, and 1821.
35. ABS Annual Meeting, May 1822.

Chapter 3

1. *New York Mirror*, September 4, 1830.
2. Eric North, "The Society's Places of Meeting and Houses, 1816–1820," ABS Historical Essay 21, 1963–1964, 1–27; Margaret T. Hills, "The Production and Supply of Scriptures, 1821–1830," ABS Historical Essay 18, Part II, 1964, 9–21; Henry Otis Dwight, *The Centennial History of the American Bible Society* (New York: Macmillan, 1916), 84; David Paul Nord, *Faith in Reading: Religious Publishing and the Birth of Mass Media in America* (New York: Oxford University Press, 2004), 68.
3. Hills, "The Production and Supply of Scriptures," 21.
4. On the relationship between the parent society and its auxiliaries see *Bible Society Record* 32:2 (February 1849), 6.
5. *Extracts from the Correspondence of the ABS* (hereafter *Extracts*) 8 (October 1820), 243–244.
6. *Extracts* 7 (November 1827), 110; 8 (October 1820), 239, 252.
7. *Bible Society Record* 1:26 (August 1851), 102.
8. *Bible Society Record* 1:27 (September 1851), 106; Paul C. Gutjahr, *An American Bible: A History of the Good Book in the United States, 1777–1880* (Redwood City, CA: Stanford University Press, 1999), 35–37.
9. *Extracts* 6 (April 1820), 192; 7 (January 1822), 50; 39 & 40 (September and October, 1824), 49.
10. *Extracts* 11 (July 1828), 173; 7 (January 1837), 51.
11. *Extracts* 7 (January 1837), 51.
12. *Extracts* 41 and 42 (November and December, 1824), 61–62.
13. *Bible Society Record* 30:10 (September 1848), 391; 31:11 (October 1849), 14.
14. *Extracts* 34 (March 1840), 39–40.
15. *Bible Society Record* 5:9 (September 1860), 134–135.
16. *Extracts* 4 (October 1821), 25; 12 (April 1835), 107.
17. *Extracts* 50 (November 1842), 599–600.
18. *Bible Society Record* 29:7 (July 1848), 373–374.
19. *Extracts* 45 (May 1825), 14;
20. Creighton Lacy, *The Word Carrying Giant: The Growth of the American Bible Society* (Pasadena, CA: William Carey Library, 1977), 61–82. *Bible Society Record* 1:8 (February 1850), 30; 1:25 (July 1851), 99; 1:9 (March 1850), 31.
21. Lacy, *The Word Carrying Giant*, 82.
22. Peter Wosh, *Spreading the Word: The Bible Business in Nineteenth-Century America* (Ithaca, NY: Cornell University Press, 1994), 89–104.
23. *Extracts* 9 (March 1822), 65–66.
24. *Extracts* 38 (November 1840), 412.
25. *Extracts* 5 (January 1820), 162–164; 42 (July 1841), 472.

Chapter 4

1. *Annual Report of the ABS* (New York: ABS, 1829), 77–78.
2. Margaret T. Hills and Elizabeth J. Eisenhart, "The Founders of the American Bible Society," ABS Historical Essay 12, 1963, ABS Archives, New York, 43–44.
3. *Extracts from the Correspondence of the ABS* (hereafter *Extracts*) 46 (1825), 57–58.
4. *Extracts* 46 (June 1825), 39–40; Eric North, "Distribution in the United States: Part II, 1821–1830," ABS Historical Essay 14:2, 1964, ABS Archives, New York, 83.
5. Minutes of the Board of Managers, April 2, 23, 30, 1829 in "Minutes of the Board of Managers, May 1816–January 1840," RG 4 Box 15, ABS Archives, New York; *Extracts* 17 (May 1829), 238.

6. *Extracts* 17 (May 1829), 234.
7. Minutes of the Board of Managers, June 18, 1829, "Minutes of the Board of Managers, May 1816–January 1840."
8. *Extracts* 17 (May 1829), 236–242.
9. *Extracts* 22 (April 1823), 170–171.
10. *Extracts* 17 (May 1829), 238–239.
11. *Extracts* 19 (August 1829), 262–263.
12. *Extracts* 25 (February 1830), 317.
13. *Extracts* 20 (September 1829), 269.
14. Minutes of the Board of Managers of the American Bible Society, October 1, 1829, November 5, 1829, December 3, 1829, January 7, 1830, "Minutes of the Board of Managers, May 1816–January 1840."
15. *Extracts* 18 (July 1829), 252; 18 (August 1829), 264; 27 (April 1830), 336; 26 (March 1830), 331; 26 (August 1830), 379.
16. Mississippi Bible Society to John Brigham, October 19, 1829, ABS Corresponding Secretary Papers, RG 17, Box 1, Folder 12, ABS Archives, New York.
17. ABS Secretary for Domestic Correspondence Papers, 1826–1833, RG 16, Box 10, ABS Archives, New York.
18. William Arnian to ABS, June 30, 1829, ABS Corresponding Secretary Papers, RG 17, Box 12, Folder 6, ABS Archives, New York.
19. Herbert C. Thompson to John Brigham, July 29, 1829, ABS Secretary for Domestic Correspondence Papers, 1826–1833, RG 15, Box 10, ABS Archives, New York.
20. John Mason Peck to John Brigham, July 2, 1829, Secretary for Domestic Correspondence Papers, 1826–1833, RG 15, Box 9, Folder: "Correspondence, Agents, John Mason Peck: 1826–1831," ABS Archives, New York.
21. Margaret Townsend, "The Headquarters Officers of the American Bible Society, 1816–1966," ABS Historical Essay 102-D, 1968, ABS Archives, New York, n.p.
22. *Extracts* 36 (January 1831), 421; *Extracts* 32 (September 1830), 381.
23. Minutes of the Board of Managers, March 4, 1830, RG 4, Box 15, ABS Archives, New York.
24. *Extracts* 26 (March 1830), 325–326.
25. Sumner Mandeville to John Brigham, February 23, 1831, ABS Secretary for Domestic Correspondence Papers, 1826–1833, RG 15, Box 9, Folder: "Correspondence, Agents, Sumner Mandeville, 1829–1833," ABS Archives, New York.
26. Solomon Hardy to John Brigham, February 17, 1831; Solomon Hardy to John Brigham, May 4, 1831, ABS Secretary for Domestic Correspondence Papers, 1826–1833, RG 15, Box 9, Folder: "Correspondence—Agents, Solomon Hardy, 1831," ABS Archives, New York.
27. *Extracts* 31 (August 1830), 374; 27 (April 1830), 338; 37 (January 1831), 425.
28. *Extracts* 34 (November 1830), 401. By early 1831 an ABS agent was assigned to Alabama.
29. *Extracts* 40 (May 1831), 457.
30. George Sheldon to John Brigham, April 22, 1831, ABS Secretary for Domestic Correspondence Papers, 1826–1833, Folder: "Correspondence—Agents, 1829–1833, George Sheldon," ABS Archives, New York.
31. Sumner Mandeville to John Brigham, March 18, 1831, ABS Secretary for Domestic Correspondence Papers, 1826–1833, Folder: "Correspondence—Agents, 1829–1833, Sumner Mandeville," ABS Archives, New York.
32. Reuben Taylor to John Brigham, January 21, 1831, ABS Secretary for Domestic Correspondence Papers, 1826–1833, Folder: "Correspondence—Agents, 1830–32, Reuben Taylor," ABS Archives, New York.
33. *Extracts* 40 (May 1831), 455–456.
34. *Extracts* 50 (May 1832), 570.
35. *Extracts* 57 (June 1833), 664.

Chapter 5

1. David Sehat, *The Myth of American Religious Freedom* (New York: Oxford University Press, 2011), 52–59.

2. *Bible Society Record* 33:3 (March 1855), 129; *Extracts from the Correspondence of the ABS* 40 (May 1831), 458–459.

3. Richard Carwardine, *Evangelicals and Politics in Antebellum America* (New Haven, CT: Yale University Press, 1993), 44; Charles I. Foster, *An Errand of Mercy: The Evangelical United Front, 1790–1837* (Chapel Hill: University of North Carolina Press, 1960), 121, 275–279; Lyman Beecher, *The Remedy for Dueling* (1807), cited in Robert A. Abzug, *Cosmos Crumbling: American Reform and the Religious Imagination* (New York: Oxford University Press, 1994), 45.

4. Steven Mintz, *Moralists & Modernizers: America's Pre-Civil War Reformers* (Baltimore: Johns Hopkins University Press, 1995), 23–43; Nathan Hatch, *The Democratization of American Christianity* (New Haven, CT: Yale University Press, 1991).

5. *Extracts from the Correspondence of the ABS* 42 (July 1831), 480; *Bible Society Record* 14:1 (January 146), 213–214.

6. *Extracts from the Correspondence of the ABS* 5 (September 30, 1834), 50; 55 (March 1833), 50.

7. See Mintz, *Moralists & Modernizers*; Ronald Walters, *American Reformers, 1815–1860* (New York: Hill & Wang, 1978).

8. Anne Boylan, *Sunday School: The Formation of An American Institution, 1790–1880* (New Haven, CT: Yale University Press, 1988), 6, 10, 13, 22–23, 43–44, 60–100.

9. *Annual Report of the ABS* (New York: ABS, 1829), 11.

10. Eric North, "Distribution of Scriptures in the U.S., 1831–1840," ABS Historical Essay 14, Part III, 1964, 142, ABS Archives, New York; Eric North and Dorothy Compagno, "Distribution of Scriptures in the U.S., 1851–1860," ABS Historical Essay 14, Part V, 1964, 61, *Extracts from the Correspondence of the ABS* 41 (June 1831), 470.

11. *Bible Society Record* 22:3 (March 1847), 240–241; (February 1855), 127–128.

12. This section is drawn from several works, including Abzug, *Cosmos Crumbling*, 79–104; Mintz, *Moralists and Modernizers*, 72–76; W. J. Rorabaugh, *The Alcoholic Republic: An American Tradition* (New York: Oxford University Press, 1981).

13. Abzug, *Cosmos Crumbling*, 86–89.

14. *Extracts from Correspondence of the ABS* 8 (October 1820), 246.

15. *Extracts from Correspondence of the ABS* 40 (November 1840), 406–407; 55 (March 1833), 644.

16. *ABS Quarterly Extracts* 1 (August 1818), 8; Anne M. Boylan, *The Origins of Women's Activism: New York and Boston, 1797–1840* (Chapel Hill: University of North Carolina Press, 2002), 237–241.

17. Boylan, *Origins of Women's Activism*, 28–29.

18. *ABS Quarterly Extracts* 1 (August 1818).

19. *Monthly Abstracts from the Correspondence of the ABS*, 10 (April 1822), 77–78; Lori Ginzberg, *Women and the Work of Benevolence: Morality, Politics, and Class in the Nineteenth-Century United States* (New Haven, CT: Yale University Press, 1990), 11–14.

20. *Extracts from the Correspondence of the ABS* 8 (October 1820), 239; 23 (April 1838), 172.

21. Mary F. Cordato, "Women's Involvement in the Bible Cause: 1816 to Present," ABS Historical Working Paper Series, 1993-1, ABS Archives, New York, NY, 12–16.

22. Cordato, "Women's Involvement in the Bible Cause," 18–20; *Bible Society Record* 7:5 (May 1862), 70.

23. *Extracts from the Correspondence of the ABS* 8 (January 1828), 118; 48 (July 1842), 563; 19 and 20 (January 1838), 149.

24. *Bible Society Record* 1:12 (June 1850), 48; *Extracts from the Correspondence of the ABS* 8 (January 1828), 118.

25. Brooks Holifield, *Theology in America: Christian Thought from the Age of the Puritans to the Civil War* (New Haven, CT: Yale University Press, 2003), 286; Cecil Lambert, "Rise of the Anti-Mission Baptists: Sources and Leaders, 1800–1840," *Church History* 27:1

(March 1858), 70; Richard Lyle Power, "A Crusade to End Yankee Culture, 1820–1865," *New England Quarterly* 13:4 (December 1940), 638–639.

26. Quoted in Power, "Crusade to End Yankee Culture," 638.

27. Holifield, *Theology in America*, 287; Bruce Dorsey, "Friends Becoming Enemies: Philadelphia Benevolence and the Neglected Era of American Quaker History," *Journal of the Early Republic* 18:3 (Autumn 1998), 408–410.

28. *The Reformer* 7 (January 1826), 23; 8 (April 1827), 56; 5 (1824), 155.

29. *The Reformer* 7 (February 1826), 19; 5 (1824), 3–6.

Chapter 6

1. *Extracts from the Correspondence of the ABS* 25 (February 1830), 319.

2. *Bible Society Record* (hereafter *BSR*) 36:6 (June 1852), 11–12; George Marsden, "Everyone One's Own Interpreter?: The Bible, Science, and Authority in Mid-Nineteenth-Century America," in Nathan Hatch and Mark Noll, ed., *The Bible in America: Essays in Cultural History* (New York: Oxford University Press, 1982), 79–100.

3. *Extracts from the Correspondence of the ABS* 35 (May 1824), 5.

4. *Extracts from the Correspondence of the ABS* 45 (May 1825), 5.

5. *BSR* 1:5 (May 1856), 95.

6. *BSR* 1:34 (April 1852), 135.

7. *Extracts from the Correspondence of the ABS* 39 (January 1841), 423.

8. *BSR* 34:4 (April 1855), 133.

9. *BSR* 2:4 (October 1852), 15.

10. *BSR* 16:5 (May 1846), 168.

11. The BFBS argued that if there was not a translation of the Greek word *baptizo* that did not favor one denomination over the other, then the word should simply be transliterated in the translated text. Creighton Lacy, *The Word Carrying Giant: The Growth of the American Bible Society* (Pasadena, CA: William Carey Library, 1977), 88; Margaret T. Hills, "Text and Translation: Principles and Problems, 1831–1860," ABS Historical Essay 16, Part III, 1967, ABS Archives, New York, 12.

12. Lacy, *The Word Carrying Giant*, 90, 92; *Annual Report of the ABS* (New York: ABS, 1836), 26–27. In the 1850s Cone eventually left the American and Foreign Bible Society to form the American Bible Union. The purpose of this organization was to publish a distinctly "Baptist Bible."

13. *Extracts from the Correspondence of the ABS* 34 (December 1830), 417–418.

14. Ivan Nothdurft, "The American Bible Society and Roman Catholicism, 1816–1979," ABS Historical Essay 23, Part VII, Vol. I, n.d., ABS Archives, New York. As Protestants, the ABS leadership believed that the Apocryphal books, which were part of the Roman Catholic canon, were not inspired by God. *BSR* 5:3 (March 1865), 37–38.

15. Patrick Carey, *Catholics in America: A History* (Lanham, MD: Rowman & Littlefield, 2004), 30; Jay Dolan, *The American Catholic Experience: A History from Colonial Times to the Present* (Notre Dame, IN: University of Notre Dame Press, 1992), 128.

16. *BSR* 24:9 (September 1847), 292.

17. *Extracts from the Correspondence of the ABS* 50 (November 1842), 593; *BSR* 9:3 (March 1845), 133; 22:5 (May 1847), 267.

18. *Extracts from the Correspondence of the ABS* 55 (November 1843), 4; *BSR* 1:3 (September 1849), 9.

19. *Extracts from the Correspondence of the ABS* 55 (November 1843), 4; John T. McGreevy, *Catholicism and American Freedom: A History* (New York: Norton, 2003), 25–37.

20. Gerald P. Fogarty, "The Quest for a Catholic Vernacular Bible in America," in Hatch and Noll, ed. *The Bible in America*, 163, 166.

21. *BSR* 17:7 (July 1846), 178–179; 28:5 (May 1848), 362.

22. *BSR* 1:6 (December 1849), 21–22; 1:10 (April 1850), 37.

23. *BSR* 5:7 (July 1844), 75–76; 1:18 (December 1850), 71.

24. For a history of the Mexican-American War see Robert W. Johannsen, *To The Halls of the Montezumas: The Mexican War in the American Imagination* (New York: Oxford University Press, 1985).

25. *Extracts from the Correspondence of the ABS* 41 (May 1841), 460–461; *BSR* 5:7 (July 1844). On the Mexican-American War as a religious war see John C. Pinheiro, *Missionaries of Republicanism: A Religious History of the Mexican-American War* (New York: Oxford University Press, 2014).

26. *BSR* 25:11 (November 1847), 310.

27. Eric M. North and Dorothy U. Compagno, "Distribution of Scriptures in the U.S., 1841–1850," ABS Historical Essay 14, Part IV, ABS Archives, New York, 125–128.

Chapter 7

1. *Annual Report of the ABS* (New York: ABS, 1854), 297–304. Peter Wosh, *Spreading the Word: The Bible Business in Nineteenth-Century America* (Ithaca, NY: Cornell University Press, 1994), 9–34.

2. Robert L. Cvornyek, "The Bible in Slavery and Freedom: The American Bible Society and the Afro-American Community, 1816–1960," ABS Historical Working Paper Series, 1990, ABS Archives, New York, 3–6.

3. *First Annual Report of the American Anti-Slavery Society . . . May 6, 1834* (New York: Dorr & Butterfield, 1834), 29–33.

4. *American Anti-Slavery Reporter* 1:6 (June 1834), 81–82.

5. Cvornyek, "The Bible in Slavery and Freedom," 7–8; "Report of a Committee of the ABS on the Subject of Distributing the Scriptures Among the Slaves, June 30, 1847" and "Slaves Should Have the Bible, January 23, 1847, signed by a group of abolitionists," ABS Corresponding Secretary Papers, RG 17, Box 29, Folder 1, ABS Archives, New York.

6. *Annual Report of the American and Foreign Anti-Mission Society* (New York: American and Foreign Anti-Slavery Society, 1849–1853), 6–9, 63.

7. Ibid., 127.

8. W. Stetson to J. Holdrick, July 13, 1858, ABS Corresponding Secretary Papers, RG 17, Box 29, Folder 1, ABS Archives, New York.

9. Wosh, *Spreading the* Word, 214–215.

10. *Bible Society Record* (hereafter *BSR*) 6:5 (May 1861), 68–69; 6:3 (March 1861), 29, 40.

11. *BSR* 6:5 (May 1860), 70; 6:2 (February 1861), 25; 6:6 (June 1861), 85–86.

12. *BSR* 6:6 (June 1861), 85.

13. ABS Distribution Records, 1816–2012, ABS Archives, New York.

14. *BSR* 6:6 (June 1861), 84; 7:4 (April 1862), 52.

15. *BSR* 6:7 (July 1861), 101; 6:6 (June 1861), 84; 6:8 (August 1861), 116; 6:12 (December 1861), 180; 10:4 (April 1865), 54; 7:11 (November 1862), 164. On the raising of prices compare *Annual Report of the ABS* (New York: ABS, 1862), 14–16 with the *Annual Report of the ABS* (New York: ABS, 1863), 14–16.

16. *BSR* 8:11 (November 1863), 163; "Supply of the Army of the United States With the Holy Scriptures," ABS Corresponding Secretary Papers, RG 17, Box 29, File 5, ABS Archives, New York.

17. Lemuel Moss, *Annals of the United States Christian Commission* (Philadelphia: J. B. Lippincott, 1868); Steven E. Woodworth, *While God Is Marching On: The Religious World of Civil War Soldiers* (Lawrence: University Press of Kansas, 2001), 167–174; *BSR* 8:4 (April 1863), 53.

18. Willie Lee Rose, *Rehearsal for Reconstruction: The Port Royal Experiment* (Athens: University of Georgia Press, 1999); *BSR* 8:5 (May 1863), 67–68; 9:1 (January 1864), 4–5.

19. Dorothy Compagno, "Distribution of the Scriptures in the U.S.A.: The Civil War," ABS Historical Essay 14, Part VI-A, ABS Archives, New York, 3; *BSR* 8:1 (January 1863), 10; McNeill to Washington City Bible Society, May 20, 1861, cited in Compagno, "Distribution of the Scriptures in the U.S.A.: The Civil War," 2; Wosh, *Spreading the Word*, 212.

20. *BSR* 6:9 (September 1861), 133; Woodworth, *While God Is Marching On*, 70, 166; George Rable, *God's Almost Chosen Peoples: A Religious History of the American Civil War* (Chapel Hill: University of North Carolina Press, 2010), 130.
21. Compagno, "Distribution of the Scriptures in the U.S.A.: The Civil War," 5.
22. Ibid., 5–6.
23. Thomas Quinan to William Taylor, January 23, 1863; Thomas Queenan to William Taylor, December 5, 1863; and Thomas Queenan to William Taylor, January 30, 1863, ABS Corresponding Secretary Papers, RG 17, Folder 3, ABS Archives, New York.
24. *BSR* 8:7 (July 1863), 101; ABS Board of Managers Minutes, December 1863, RG 4, Box 16, Folder: "Board of Managers Minutes, January 1862 to October 1868," ABS Archives, New York; Ethel Porter to William Taylor, April, n.d., 1864, ABS Corresponding Secretary Papers, Folder 9.
25. *BSR* 8:10 (October 1863), 155.
26. Ethel Porter to ABS, February 6, 1865; Assistant Secretary of the Navy to the ABS, October 20, 1864, Porter to William Taylor, July 13, 1864; RG 17, Folder 9, ABS Archives, New York.
27. Woodworth, *While God Is Marching On*, 41; *BSR* 6:9 (September 1861), 132–133; 7:3 (March 1861), 40; 7:3 (March 1861), 41; 9:9 (September 1864), 138.
28. *BSR* 7:7 (July 1862), 102–103.
29. Woodworth, *While God Is Marching On*, 193, 197, 214, 226.
30. *BSR* 10:4 (April 1865), 55; 7:9 (September 1862), 138.
31. *BSR* 8:2 (February 1863); 8:8 (August 1863), 116–117.
32. *BSR* 8:9 (September 1863), 137; Woodworth, *While God Is Marching On*, 71.
33. *BSR* 6:6 (June 1862), 87; 7:2 (February 1863), 26; Woodworth, *While God Is Marching On*, 72.
34. *BSR* 6:11 (November 1861), 164; 7:9 (September 1863), 137–138; 9:6 (June 1864).

Chapter 8

1. *Bible Society Record* (hereafter *BSR*), 10:10 (October 1865), 145; *Annual Report of the ABS* (New York: ABS, 1865), 20; John Knox Witherspoon to ABS, October 1, 1867, ABS Corresponding Secretary Papers, RG 17, Box 29, Folder 3, ABS Archives, New York; Daniel Stowell, *Rebuilding Zion: The Religious Reconstruction of the South, 1863–1877* (New York: Oxford University Press, 1998), 130–145.
2. *BSR* 10:6 (June 1865), 89; *Annual Report of the ABS* (New York: ABS, 1865), 19.
3. *BSR* 10:7 (July 1865), 105; Stowell, *Rebuilding Zion*, 162–178.
4. *BSR* 10:7 (July 1865), 98.
5. Edward J. Blum, *Reforming the White Republic: Race, Religion, and American Nationalism, 1865–1898* (Baton Rouge: Lousiana State University Press, 2005), 34.
6. *Annual Report of the ABS* (New York: ABS, 1866), 38, 60–61; Robert L. Cvornyek, "The Bible in Slavery and Freedom: The American Bible Society and the Afro-American Community, 1816–1960," ABS Historical Working Papers Series, 1990, ABS Archives, New York, 28; *BSR* 10:8 (August 1865), 122.
7. *Annual Report of the ABS* (New York: ABS, 1868), 40–43; (1869), 56–59, 44–45, 43; (1870).
8. *Annual Report of the ABS* (New York: ABS, 1869), 42; (1870), 35; (1871), 30–31.
9. The best overview of the Reconstruction period remains Eric Foner, *Reconstruction: America's Unfinished Revolution, 1863–1877* (New York: Harper-Collins, 1988).
10. "Memo from John Holdrich, n.d.," ABS Corresponding Secretary Papers, RG 17, Box 29, Folder 3, ABS Archives, New York.
11. This approach to reunion—an approach that celebrated the reconciliation of southern and northern whites—is chronicled most fully in David W. Blight, *Race and Reunion: The Civil War in American Memory* (Cambridge, MA: Harvard University Press, 2001).
12. *Annual Report of the ABS* (New York: ABS, 1867), 41; Wosh, *Spreading the Word*, 224–226; *Annual Report of the ABS* (New York: ABS, 1865), 12. Wosh writes: "Bible Society

326   NOTES

administrators wanted the freedmen to receive the Scriptures, but they preferred to fun-
nel Bibles through the hands of white southerners."

13. *Annual Meeting of the ABS* (New York: ABS, 1866), 41; (1867), 41–42, 39; *BSR* 10:9
(September 1865), 134; Cvornyek, "The Bible in Slavery and Freedom," 29; *BSR* 10:9
(September 1865), 136.

14. *BSR* 11:4 (April 1866), 54; *BSR* 12:3 (March 1867), 38–39; *BSR* 12:10 (October 1867),
153; *Annual Report of the ABS* (New York: ABS, 1869), 93.

15. Cvornyek, "The Bible in Slavery and Freedom," 30–32; *BSR* 10:9 (September 1865), 136;
W. S. Miller to William Taylor, December 16, 1866; Thomas Quinan to William Taylor,
August 19, 1865; William Taylor to ABS, July 10, 1865, ABS Corresponding Secretary
Papers, RG 17, Box 29, Folder 3, ABS Archives, New York.

16. Wosh, *Spreading the Word*, 221–224; Cvornyek, "The Bible in Slavery and Freedom,"
23–25; *Annual Report of the ABS* (New York: ABS, 1866), 40; (1867), 35, Appendix B: 10;
BSR 11:2 (February 1866), 22–23.

17. *BSR* 10:11 (November 1865), 165.

18. Wosh, *Spreading the Word*, 225, 226; *Annual Report of the ABS* (New York: ABS, 1876), 55;
(1877), 48–49.

19. Stowell, *Rebuilding Zion*, 68–70, 73–75, 80–99; Paul Harvey, *Redeeming the South: Religious
Cultures and Racial Identities Among Southern Baptists* (Chapel Hill: University of North
Carolina Press, 1997), 45–74.

20. Stowell, *Rebuilding Zion*, 77; *BSR* 11:8 (August 1866), 121–122; *BSR* 12:10 (October
1867), 152–153.

21. *Annual Report of the ABS* (New York: ABS, 1874), 58–59, 85, 86.

22. Mary F. Cordato, "The Bible on Display: The American Bible Society's Participation at
World's Fairs, 1867-1982," Working Paper 1990-4, ABS Archives, New York.

23. On the relationship between race, religion, and Reconstruction, see Blum, *Reforging the
White Republic*.

Chapter 9

1. *Bible Society Record* (hereafter *BSR*) 27:5 (May 1882), 73; Dorothy U. Compagno,
"Distribution of the Scriptures in the U.S.A., 1861–1900," ABS Archives, New York, 3;
Annual Report of the ABS (New York: ABS, 1882), 139–140.

2. *Annual Report of the ABS* (New York: ABS, 1882), 146–147.

3. *Annual Report of the ABS* (New York: ABS, 1889), 44, 45.

4. *Annual Report of the ABS* (New York: ABS, 1890), 45, 46, 48; Creighton Lacy, *The Word
Carrying Giant: The Growth of the American Bible Society* (Pasadena, CA: William Carey
Library, 1977), 110–111.

5. *Annual Report of the ABS* (New York: ABS, 1895), 49, 53; 55–56; 61–62.

6. *Annual Report of the ABS* (New York: ABS, 1897), 43, 44–45; (1906), 23.

7. *Annual Report of the ABS* (New York: ABS, 1892), 47–48; (1909), 52–53.

8. *Annual Report of the ABS* (New York: ABS, 1894), 43–44; (1910), 60–61.

9. *Annual Report of the ABS* (New York: ABS, 1879), 69–70; (1882), 46; (1892), 81; (1893), 47.

10. *Annual Report of the ABS* (New York: ABS, 1881), 74; (1891), 53–54; (1895), 44.

11. *Annual Report of the ABS* (New York: ABS, 1909), 75–76.

12. *Annual Report of the ABS* (New York: ABS, 1909), 52–54, 55–56.

13. Frederick Jackson Turner, "The Significance of the Frontier in American History," 1893,
http://xroads.virginia.edu/~Hyper/TURNER/chapter1.html#foot1, accessed April 15,
2015.

14. *Annual Report of the ABS* (New York: ABS, 1873), 18.

15. Richard White, *Railroaded: The Transcontinentals and the Making of Modern America*
(New York: Norton, 2011), xxi, 203, 211.

16. *BSR* 18:6 (June 1873), 90; *BSR* 19:7 (July 1874), 108–109.

17. Creighton Lacy, *The Word Carrying Giant*, 101; *BSR* 1:12 (June 1850), 47.

18. *BSR* 4:9 (September 1859), 137; 5:9 (September 1860), 136.

19. *Annual Report of the ABS* (New York: ABS, 1871), 36–37; *BSR* 1:12 (June 1850), 47; *Extracts from the Correspondence of the ABS* 19 (January 1838), 145; *BSR* 1:36 (June 1852), 10.
20. *BSR* 1:17 (November, 1850), 68.
21. *Annual Report of the ABS* (New York: ABS, 1871), 37, 38, 39.
22. *Annual Report of the ABS* (New York: ABS, 1872), 41; (1874), 43.
23. *BSR* 10:3 (March 1865), 39.
24. *Annual Report of the ABS* (New York: ABS, 1867), 10. On late nineteenth-century Indian history see Frederick E. Hoxie, *A Final Promise: The Campaign to Assimilate the Indians, 1880–1920* (Lincoln: University of Nebraska Press, 1984); Robert M. Utley, *The Indian Frontier of the American West, 1846–1890* (Albuquerque: University of New Mexico Press, 1984), and Robert V. Hine and John Mack Faragher, *The American West: A New Interpretive History* (New Haven, CT: Yale University Press, 2000).
25. *Annual Report of the ABS* (New York: ABS, 1870), 132; (1871), 111–112; (1873), 116; (1878), 108; (1881), 130.
26. Hoxie, *A Final Promise*, 29–38, 42; Philip Weeks, *Farewell, My Nation: The American Indian and the United States, 1820–1890* (Arlington Heights, IL: Harlan Davidson, 1990), 229–230.
27. *Annual Report of the ABS* (New York: ABS, 1873), 116; *BSR* 18:2 (February 1873), 21–22.
28. "Report of the Commissioner of Indian Affairs, September 21, 1887," in *The Executive Documents of the House of Representatives for the First Session of the Fiftieth Congress, 1887–1888* (Washington, DC: Government Printing Office, 1889), Vol. 2, 19, 20.
29. *BSR* 28:2 (February 15, 1883), 25–26; *BSR* 32:10 (October 20, 1887), 145–146.
30. *BSR* 32:10 (October 1887), 147–149.
31. *BSR* 32:12 (December 1887), 178.
32. *BSR* 33:2 (February 1888), 17–18; William T. Hagan, "United States Indian Policies, 1860–1900," in *Handbook of North American Indians*, William C. Sturtevant, General Editor, Vol 2: *History of Indian-White Relations*, ed. Wilcomb E. Washburn, (Washington, DC: Smithsonian Institution, 1988), 58–59.

Chapter 10

1. Creighton Lacy, *The Word Carrying Giant: The Growth of the American Bible Society* (Pasadena, CA: William Carey Library, 1977), 65, 68, 69, 72.
2. *Annual Report of the ABS* (New York: ABS, 1865), 43.
3. *Bible Society Record* 42:2 (February 1897), 22; Joseph Grabill, *Protestant Diplomacy and the Near East: Missionary Influence on American Policy, 1810–1927* (Minneapolis: University of Minnesota Press, 1971), 5, 34; Hans-Lukas Kieser, *Nearest East: American Millennialism and Mission to the Middle East* (Philadelphia: Temple University Press, 2010), 17, 32; Samir Khalaf, *Protestant Missionaries in the Levant: Ungodly Puritans, 1820–1860* (London: Routledge, 2012), xiv.
4. Peter Wosh, *Spreading the Word: The Bible Business in Nineteenth-Century America* (Ithaca, NY: Cornell University Press, 1994), 151–161.
5. Grabill, *Protestant Diplomacy and the Near East*, 5; Rebecca Bromley, "Distribution Abroad, 1831–1840," ABS Historical Essay 15, Part III, ABS Archives, New York, D-20, D-27-28, 32.
6. Bromley, "Distribution Abroad, 1831–1840," D-37, D-38.
7. Ibid., D-38.
8. Ibid., D-7.
9. Thomas Kidd, *American Christians and Islam: Evangelical Culture and Muslims from the Colonial Period to the Age of Terrorism* (Princeton, NJ: Princeton University Press, 2009), 38; Hans-Lukas Keiser, *Nearest East: American Millennialism and Mission to the Middle East* (Philadelphia: Temple University Press, 2010), 35; Bromley, "Distribution Abroad, 1831–1840," D-45; D-38.
10. Bromley, "Distribution Abroad, 1831–1840," D-41, D-42; *Annual Report of the ABS* (New York: ABS, 1839), 102–105; Wosh, *Spreading the Word*, 168–174.

11. Bromley, "Distribution Abroad, 1831–1840," D-22, D-23.
12. Richard Clogg, "Enlightening 'A Poor, Oppressed, and Darkened Nation': Some Early Activities of the BFBS in the Levant," in Stephen Batalden, Kathleen Cann, and John Dean, ed. *Sowing the Word: The Cultural Impact of the British and Foreign Bible Society, 1804–2004* (Sheffield: Sheffield Phoenix Press, 2004), 234–250.
13. Bromley, "Distribution Abroad, 1841–1860," D-26.
14. Ibid., D-34, D-35.
15. Ibid., D-33.
16. Ibid., D-37.
17. Ibid., D-38, D-39.
18. Ibid., D-51, D-52
19. Ibid., D-112, D-113.
20. Ibid., D-114; *Annual Report of the ABS* (New York: ABS, 1868), 98.
21. Rebecca Bromley, "Distribution Abroad: The Levant, 1861–1900," ABS Historical Essay 15, Part V, 1966, D-115, D-116; Wosh, *Spreading the Word*, 244.
22. Bromley, "Distribution Abroad: The Levant, 1861–1900," D-52–57.
23. Ibid., D-57–58.
24. Grabill, *Protestant Diplomacy and the Near East*, 35; Bromley, "Distribution Abroad: The Levant, 1861–1900," D-58, D-59.
25. Bromley, "Distribution Abroad: The Levant, 1901–1930," Historical Essay 15, Part VI, March 1966, ABS Archives, New York, 1–3. On the Young Turk Revolution see Bedross Der Matossian, *Shattered Dreams of Revolution: From Liberty to Violence in the Late Ottoman Empire* (Redwood City, CA: Stanford University Press, 2014).
26. *Annual Report of the ABS* (New York: ABS, 1909), 197–198; Bromley "Distribution Abroad: The Levant, 1901–1930," 35–36.

Chapter 11

1. Peter Wosh, *Spreading the Word: The Bible Business in Nineteenth-Century America* (Ithaca, NY: Cornell University Press, 1994), 239.
2. *Annual Report of the ABS* (New York: ABS, 1847), 56; Rebecca Bromley, "Distribution Abroad, 1841–1860," ABS Historical Essay 15, Part IV, ABS Archives, New York, C-2–4.
3. *Annual Report of the ABS* (New York: ABS, 1872), 91–92.
4. Dorothy U. Compagno, "Distribution in Latin America," Appendix, 1–2.
5. Ibid., 17–18, 26–27.
6. Ibid., 18, 21–27.
7. Ibid.
8. Ibid.
9. Ibid.
10. Ibid., 27; Paul Garner, *Porfirio Díaz: Profiles in Power* (Edinburgh: Pearson Education, 2001), 121.
11. John Frederick Schwaller, *The History of the Catholic Church in Latin America: From Conquest to Revolution and Beyond* (New York: New York University Press, 2011), 146–148, 174–175.
12. *Annual Report of the ABS* (New York: ABS, 1884), 89–90, 80; (1885), 92; (1882), 87–89.
13. Garner, *Porfirio Díaz*, 121; John H. Coatsworth, "Obstacles to Economic Growth in Nineteenth-Century Mexico," *American Historical Review* 83:1 (February 1978), 90; *Annual Report of the ABS* (New York: ABS, 1884), 80–82; (1886), 90; (1887), 92; Compagno, "Distribution in Latin America," 28.
14. *Annual Report of the ABS* (New York: ABS, 1891), 102–103; *Bible Society Record* 43:8 (August 1898), 115–116.
15. *Annual Report of the ABS* (New York: ABS, 1892), 101–102; (1898), 92; Garner, *Porfirio Díaz*, 141; *Annual Report of the ABS* (New York: ABS, 1905), 57–58.
16. Compagno, "Distribution in Latin America, 1861–1900," 46, 44.
17. Dorothy Compagno. "Distribution Abroad: Mexico, 1901–1930," ABS Historical Essay 15, Part VI-C-1, ABS Archives, New York, 9, 10.
18. *Bible Society Record* 53:10 (October 1908), 153–154.

19. Mauricio Tenorio Trillo, "1910 Mexico City: Space and Nation in the City of the *Centenario*," *Journal of Latin American Studies* 28:1 (February 1996), 75–104; Garner, *Porfirio Díaz*, 158–159.

20. *Annual Report of the ABS* (New York: ABS, 1910), 223; (1911), 234–236.

21. Schwaller, *The History of the Catholic Church in Latin America*, 190–191.

22. *Annual Report of the ABS* (New York: ABS, 1912), 231–232.

23. Compagno, "Distribution Abroad: Mexico, 1901–1930," 19.

24. *Annual Report of the ABS* (New York: ABS, 1912), 231–232; Schwaller, *The History of the Catholic Church in Latin America*, 190–191.

25. Schwaller, *The History of the Catholic Church in Latin America*, 192–194; Compagno, "Distribution Abroad: Mexico, 1901–1930," 19.

26. Compagno, "Distribution Abroad: Mexico, 1901–1930"; *Annual Report of the ABS* (New York: ABS, 1913), 258–260.

27. *Annual Report of the ABS* (New York: ABS, 1914), 274; Compagno, "Distribution Abroad: Mexico, 1901–1930," 26; *Bible Society Record* 57:9 (September 1912), 133–134.

Chapter 12

1. William R. Hutchison, *Errand to the World: American Protestant Thought and Foreign Missions* (Chicago: University of Chicago Press, 1987), 91, 93; Creighton Lacy, *The Word Carrying Giant: The Growth of the American Bible Society* (Pasadena, CA: William Carey Library, 1977), 141.

2. Xi Lian, *Redeemed by Fire: The Rise of Popular Christianity in Modern China* (New Haven, CT: Yale University Press, 2010), 17–26, 31.

3. Eric North, "Distribution Abroad, 1861–1900: China," ABS Historical Essay 15, Part V-F-2, 1965, ABS Archives, New York, 1A–1B. On Schereschewsky, see Irene Eber, "Translating the Ancestors: S. I. J. Schereschewsky's 1875 Chinese Version of Genesis," *Bulletin of the School of Oriental and African Studies, University of London* 56:2 (1993), 219–233.

4. Eber, "Translating the Ancestors," 222–227; Lacy, *The Word Carrying Giant*, 143; North, "Distribution Abroad, 1861–1900: China," 7.

5. North, "Distribution Abroad, 1861–1900: China," 1D; Lacy, *The Word Carrying Giant*, 141–142.

6. *Bible Society Record* 56:4 (April 1871), 49–50.

7. North, "Distribution Abroad, 1861–1900: China," 3–7.

8. Ibid., 7–12.

9. Ibid., 15–19.

10. Henry Otis Dwight, *The Centennial History of the American Bible Society* (New York: Macmillan, 1916), 401, 409; Lacy, *The Word Carrying Giant*, 142.

11. *Annual Report of the ABS* (New York: ABS, 1879), 110–111; Dwight, *The Centennial History of the American Bible Society*, 407; *Annual Report of the ABS* (New York: ABS, 1883), 128.

12. John Hykes, *The American Bible Society in China* (New York: American Bible Society, 1916); Dwight, *The Centennial History of the American Bible Society*, 405–406.

13. *Bible Society Record* 29:2 (February 1884), 23–25.

14. Andrew Preston, *Sword of the Spirit, Shield of Faith: Religion in American War and Diplomacy* (New York: Anchor, 2012), 194.

15. Paul A. Cohen, *History in Three Keys: The Boxers as Event, Experience, and Myth* (New York: Columbia University Press, 1998).

16. *Annual Report of the ABS* (New York: ABS, 1901), 95–96.

17. Ibid., 98–99.

18. Ibid., 113–117; Preston, *Sword of the Spirit*, 195.

19. Ibid., 100–102; Lian, *Redeemed by Fire*, 32.

20. Ibid., 104–109; *Annual Report of the ABS* (New York: ABS, 1907), 163.

21. Janice Pearson, "Distribution Abroad, 1901–1930: China," ABS Historical Essay 15, Part VI-F-2, 1967, ABS Archives, New York, 16–21.

22. Ibid., 37–42; *Annual Report of the ABS* (New York: ABS, 1912), 325–326; Hykes, *The American Bible Society in China*, 46.
23. Lacy, *The Word Carrying Giant*, 232; Janice Pearson, "Distribution Abroad, 1931–1966: China," ABS Historical Essay 15, Part VII-F-2, 1968, ABS Archives, New York, 90–147, 178–182.

Chapter 13

1. *Bible Society Record* (hereafter *BSR*) 45:1 (January 1900), 13–14.
2. *BSR* 45:2 (February 1900), 23–24.
3. *Annual Report of the ABS* (New York: ABS, 1902), 154; Robert L. Cvornyek, "The Bible in Slavery and Freedom: The American Bible Society and the Afro-American Community, 1816–1960," ABS Historical Working Papers Series, 1990, ABS Archives, New York, 35; Mary Cordato, "The Relationship of the American Bible Society to its Auxiliaries: A Historical Timeline Study," ABS Historical Working Paper Series, 1991, ABS Archives, New York, 1–2.
4. Eric M. North and Rebecca Bromley, "Distribution of the Scriptures in the USA, 1861–1900: The Auxiliary System and the Record," ABS Historical Essay 14, Part VI, 1965, ABS Archives, New York, B-117.
5. North and Bromley, "Distribution of the Scriptures in the USA, 1861–1900," B-118; *Annual Report of the ABS* (New York: ABS, 1887), 39–42, 38–39.
6. *Annual Report of the ABS* (New York: ABS, 1889), 40; (1890), 41–42; (1891), 48–49; (1892), 46.
7. Cordato, "The Relationship of the American Bible Society to its Auxiliaries," 1–2; North and Bromley, "Distribution of the Scriptures in the USA, 1861–1900," B-126–127, B-121, B-123; *Annual Report of the ABS* (New York: ABS, 1899), 32.
8. *Annual Report of the ABS* (New York: ABS, 1902), 172–174.
9. *Annual Report of the ABS* (New York: ABS, 1902), 158; (1907), 220–221; (1909), 91–93, 97–98, 109–111, 117, 128–130; (1910), 24; John H. Zimmerman, "Distribution in the USA, 1901–1930," ABS Historical Essay 14, Part VII, 1967, ABS Archives, New York, 88–89, 44. On January 1, 1935, the ABS reorganized again, changing the name of the "Agencies" to "Districts" and creating six Bible depositories throughout the country. See Ivan Nothdurft, "Distribution in the U.S.A., 1961–1966," ABS Historical Essay 14, Part VIII, 1973, ABS Archives, New York, 34.
10. *BSR* 59:1 (January 1914), 11–12.
11. *BSR* 46:6 (June 1901), 82–83; *Annual Meeting of the ABS* (New York: ABS, 1906), 31.
12. Cvornyek, "The Bible in Slavery and Freedom," 36.
13. Cvornyek, "The Bible in Slavery and Freedom," 36–39; *BSR* 86:2 (February 1941), 23–25.
14. Cvornyek, "The Bible in Slavery and Freedom," 36–39.
15. *BSR* 47:8 (August 1902), 124; Cvornyek, "The Bible in Slavery and Freedom," 43.
16. *BSR* 53:11 (November 1908), 175–176.
17. *Annual Report of the ABS* (New York: ABS, 1904), 197, 215–216, 219.
18. *BSR* 54:5 (May 1909), 73–74; 66:3 (March 1921), 50; *Annual Report of the ABS* (New York: ABS, 1943), 61–62.
19. *BSR* 54:5 (May 1909), 73–74; 54:5 (July 1909), 111–113; 45:2 (February 1900), 23–24; *Annual Report of the ABS* (New York: ABS, 1905), 212; *BSR* 64:5 (May 1918), 89–90.
20. *BSR* 73:5 (May 1928), 74.
21. Cvornyek, "The Bible in Slavery and Freedom," 46–49, 58–59; *BSR* 66:3 (March 1921), 51.

Chapter 14

1. *Bible Society Record* (hereafter *BSR*) 59:9 (September 1914), 137, 136.
2. *BSR* 60:6 (June 1915), 88; *BSR* 60:10 (October 1915), n.p.
3. *BSR* 60:10 (October 1915), n.p.

4. For an overview of Mexican-US relations in this period see P. Edward Haley, *Revolution and Intervention: The Diplomacy of Taft and Wilson with Mexico, 1910–1917* (Cambridge, MA: MIT Press, 1970).

5. John H. Zimmerman, "Distribution in the USA, 1901–1930," ABS Historical Essay 14, Part VII, 1967, ABS Archives, New York, 245; *Annual Report of the ABS* (New York: ABS, 1917), 176–185.

6. *Annual Report of the ABS* (New York: ABS, 1917), 31–32, 94, 103, 151; Zimmerman, "Distribution in the USA, 1901–1930," 236–237; *BSR* 63:1 (January 1917), 10; *Annual Report of the ABS* (New York: ABS, 1917), 176–185.

7. *Annual Report of the ABS* (New York: ABS, 1917), 176–185.

8. Ibid., 14–15; Henry Otis Dwight, *The Centennial History of the American Bible Society* (New York: Macmillan, 1916).

9. *Annual Report of the ABS* (New York: ABS, 1917), 17–18.

10. *Annual Report of the ABS* (New York: ABS, 1917), 18–19.

11. Ibid., 19–20; *New York Times*, May 8, 1916, 11.

12. *Annual Report of the ABS* (New York: ABS, 1917), 19–20; *New York Times*, May 10, 1916, 7.

13. Zimmerman, "Distribution in the USA, 1901–1930," 245, 246, 247.

14. Ibid., 247–248; *Annual Report of the ABS* (New York: ABS, 1918), 108; *BSR* 62:9 (September 1917), 162.

15. *BSR* 63:4 (April 1918), 73–75; Creighton Lacy, *The Word Carrying Giant: The Growth of the American Bible Society* (Pasadena, CA: William Carey Library, 1977), 162.

16. *BSR* 63:4 (April 1918), 63–66.

17. Ibid., 67–69.

18. Ibid., 60.

19. *BSR* 64:1 (January 1919), 1, 9–13.

20. Ibid., 9–13.

21. *Annual Report of the ABS* (New York: ABS, 1918), 36; *BSR* 64:2 (February 1919), 30.

Chapter 15

1. *Annual Report of the ABS* (New York: ABS, 1926), 22.

2. Desmond King, *Making Americans: Immigration, Race, and the Origins of the Diverse Democracy* (Cambridge, MA: Harvard University Press, 2000), 199–228.

3. *Bible Society Record* (hereafter *BSR*) 64:4 (April 1920), 49–52.

4. "An Act to Regulate the Immigration of Aliens to, and the Residence of Aliens in, the United States, February 5, 1917," http://library.uwb.edu/guides/usimmigration/39%20 stat%20874.pdf, accessed May 5, 2015; *BSR* 62:4 (April 1917), 76.

5. Donna Gabaccia, *Immigration and American Diversity: A Social and Cultural History* (Malden, MA: Blackwell, 2002), 124–125.

6. *BSR* 64:7 (July 1919), 109–110.

7. *Annual Report of the ABS* (New York: ABS, 1919), 61–62.

8. *BSR* 66:6 (June 1921), 104.

9. John H. Zimmerman, "Distribution in the USA, 1901–1930," ABS Historical Essay 14, Part VII, 1967, ABS Archives, New York, 349; *BSR* 63:2 (February 1918), 17–18.

10. *BSR* 75:12 (December 1930), 200–202.

11. *Annual Report of the ABS* (New York: ABS, 1920), 146; *BSR* 82:6 (July 1937), 105–106.

12. *BSR* 64:9 (September 1919), 137; 64:10 (October/November/December 1920), 155–156.

13. *BSR* 66:3 (March 1921), 54–56.

14. *BSR* 79:9 (December 1934), 135.

15. Creighton Lacy, *The Word Carrying Giant: The Growth of the American Bible Society* (Pasadena, CA: William Carey Library, 1977), 164; *BSR* 83:9 (November 1938), 144–146.

16. *BSR* 77:8 (August 1932), 134–135.

17. *BSR* 77:11 (November 1932), 188–189.

18. *BSR* 79:7 (September 1934), 95; 80:7 (September 1935).

19. *Annual Report of the ABS* (New York: ABS, 1935), 19–20; (1936), 22–23.

20. *BSR* 80:10 (December 1936), 151, 163.

21. Harold Schwartz, *Samuel Gridley Howe: Social Reformer* (Cambridge, MA: Harvard University Press, 1956), 59–60; *BSR* 80:10 (December 1935), 155–157.

22. Lacy, *The Word Carrying Giant*, 170–171.

23. Edward M. Peterson, "The Talking Book," *Bulletin of the American Library Association* 25:5 (May 1934), 243–244; National Library Service, "That All May Read," www.loc.gov/nls/about_history.html, accessed May 12, 2015.

24. Lacy, *The Word Carrying Giant*, 171–172; *Annual Report of the ABS* (New York: ABS, 1938), 22–23.

25. *BSR* 80:6 (July 1935), 87; 82:1 (January 1937), 3–5.

26. *BSR* 80:6 (July 1935), 87; 82:1 (January 1937), 6.

Chapter 16

1. Franklin Delano Roosevelt, 1941 State of the Union Address, January 6, 1941, http://voicesofdemocracy.umd.edu/fdr-the-four-freedoms-speech-text/, accessed May 12, 2015.

2. *Annual Report of the ABS* (New York: ABS, 1941), 9–10.

3. Edwin H. Robertson, *Taking the Word to the World: 50 Years of the United Bible Societies* (Nashville, TN: Thomas Nelson, 1996), 12; Marjorie L. Miller, "War Service of the ABS, 1940–1948," ABS Historical Essay 15, Part VII-B, 1969, ABS Archives, New York, 1.

4. Miller, "War Service of the ABS, 1940–1948," 2–4; *Bible Society Record* (hereafter *BSR*) 85:9 (November 1940), 149.

5. *BSR*, 85:6 (July 1940), 92–94.

6. Ibid.

7. *BSR* 85:9 (November 1940), 139–140.

8. *BSR* 84:7 (April 1942), 57.

9. Henry Otis Dwight, *The Centennial History of the American Bible Society* (New York: Macmillan, 1916), 313–314; Creighton Lacy, *The Word Carrying Giant: The Growth of the American Bible Society* (Pasadena, CA: William Carey Library, 1977), 239–240.

10. *BSR* 86:2 (February 1941), 31–32.

11. Ibid.

12. Ivan Nothdurft, "Distribution in the U.S.A., 1931–1966," ABS Historical Essay 14, Part VIII, 1973, ABS Archives, New York, 152–154.

13. Ibid., 155.

14. Miller, "War Service of the ABS, 1940–1948," 5; *Annual Report of the ABS* (New York: ABS, 1943), 35–36; (1944), 34–37.

15. For Rickenbacker's account of the ordeal see "Pacific Mission," *Life Magazine*, January 25, 1943, 19–24, 90, 92–96, 99–100. For Whitaker's account see James Whitaker, *We Thought We Heard the Angels Sing* (New York: E. P. Dutton, 1943), especially 50. Nothdurft, "Distribution in the U.S.A., 1931–1966," 156–157; *Annual Report of the ABS* (New York: ABS, 1944), 13.

16. *BSR* 82:2 (February 1942), 26–27.

17. *Annual Report of the ABS* (New York: ABS, 1945), 9–12.

18. *BSR* 87:4 (April 1942), 52.

19. *BSR* 87:4 (April 1942), 52, 53.

20. *BSR* (March 1942), 36–37.

21. *BSR* 89:8 (October 1944), 116–118; 88:1 (January 1943), 2–12.

22. *BSR* 87:5 (May 1942), 70–74.

23. Ibid.

24. *BSR* 88:5 (May 1943), 75–76.

25. Ibid.

26. *BSR* 90:2 (February 1945), 19–20.

Chapter 17

1. *Annual Report of the ABS* (New York: ABS, 1946), 11–13.
2. "Harry Truman to Pius XII," August 6, 1947, quoted in Andrew Preston, *Sword of the Spirit, Shield of Faith: Religion in American War and Diplomacy* (New York: Anchor, 2012), 412–413. This paragraph and the one after it rely heavily on Preston, 384, 399, 412, 413, 419–420.
3. *Bible Society Record* (hereafter *BSR*) 90:2 (February 1945), 19–20.
4. *BSR* 90:6 (July 1945), 83.
5. Tony Judt, *Postwar: A History of Europe Since 1945* (New York: Penguin, 2005), 16–22; Marjorie L. Miller, "War Service of the ABS, 1940–1948," ABS Historical Essay 15, Part VII-B, 1969, ABS Archives, New York, 13–14.
6. *Annual Report of the ABS* (New York: ABS, 1946), 11–13; *BSR* 93:1 (January 1948), 4–6; Miller, "War Service of the ABS, 1940–1948," 13–14.
7. Miller, "War Service of the ABS, 1940–1948," 9; Michael Flood, "Production and Supply, 1931–1966," ABS Historical Essay 18, Part VI-A, 1968, ABS Archives, New York, 98; *Annual Report of the ABS* (New York: ABS, 1948), 11–12; (1959), 234.
8. *BSR* 92:3 (March 1947), 34; *Annual Report of the ABS* (New York: ABS, 1957), 214, 215; (1946), 11–13.
9. *Annual Report of the ABS* (New York: ABS, 1957), 214, 215; (1946), 11–13; *BSR* 104:4 (April 1959), 52.
10. *BSR* 91:1 (January 1946), 10.
11. Ibid.; *Annual Report of the* ABS (New York: ABS, 1951), 310–311; *BSR* 92:6 (July 1947), 88.
12. Richard Jordan, *The Second Coming of Paisley: Militant Fundamentalism and Ulster Politics* (Syracuse, NY: Syracuse University Press, 2013), 67–68; Robert Taylor to Gilbert Darlington, January 14, 1953, RG 18.07, Box 3, Folder 20, ABS Archives, New York; Robert Taylor to Howard Sheperd, January 14, 1953, ibid. On McIntire see John Fea, "Carl McIntire: From Fundamentalist Presbyterian to Presbyterian Fundamentalist," *American Presbyterian* 72:2 (Winter 1994), 253–268.
13. Robert Taylor to John Foster Dulles, August 31, 1953, and Henry J. Kellerman to Robert Taylor, RG 18.07, Box 3, Folder 20, ABS Archives, New York; *New York Times*, August 31, 1953, 6.
14. ABS Press Release: "Bible Loses to Khrushchev," January 23, 1962, RG 18.07, Box 2, Folder 17, ABS Archives, New York. *Life* magazine did not do a story on the ABS press release, but it did cover the *Index Translationum* report. See *Life* 50:23, June 9, 1961, 50.
15. On Khrushchev's antireligion campaign see Dimitry Pospielovsky, *A History of Marxist-Leninist Atheism and Soviet Anti-Religious Policies* (New York: St. Martin's, 1987), 82–95, and Pospielovsky, *Soviet Anti-Religious Campaigns and Persecutions* (New York: St. Martin's, 1988), 98–99. In 1962, Gilbert Darlington appears to have questioned the UNESCO findings and prepared a memo to the General Secretary of the United Bible Societies to stop giving the impression that these communist works were being printed in more languages than the Bible. Ivan Nothdurft, "The American Bible Society and Its Relationship to the Other National Bible Societies," ABS Historical Essay 24, Part VII, 1980, ABS Archives, New York, 166.
16. *BSR* 107:2 (March 1962), 42–43.
17. *BSR* 107:3 (March 1962), 42–43.
18. *BSR* 107:3 (March 1962), 43; 107:6 (June 1962), 77; 108:2 (February 1963), 21.
19. *BSR* 107:6 (July–August 1962), 92–93.

Chapter 18

1. Marjorie L. Miller, "War Service of the ABS, 1940–1948," 1969, ABS Historical Essay 15, Part VII-B, 1969, ABS Archives, New York, Appendix I, 13–14; *Annual Meeting of the ABS* (New York: ABS, 1947), 14–15.
2. *Bible Society Record* (hereafter *BSR*) 92:1 (January 1947), 4–5.

3. *BSR* 94:9 (September 1949), 108; Doris Hall, "Distribution Abroad: Japan, 1931–1966," ABS Historical Essay 15, Part VIII-F, 1968, ABS Archives, New York, 128, 157.

4. Creighton Lacy, *The Word Carrying Giant: The Growth of the American Bible Society* (Pasadena, CA: William Carey Library, 1977), 240–241; Hall, "Distribution Abroad: Japan, 1931–1966,"130; *BSR* 92:12 (December 1947), 1.

5. Hall, "Distribution Abroad: Japan, 1931–1966," 147; *Annual Report of the ABS* (New York: ABS, 1949), 267; (1950), 27–30; Lacy, *The Word Carrying Giant*, 241; *BSR* 92:6 (July 1947), 83–84.

6. *BSR* 95:4 (April 1950), 50; Hall, "Distribution Abroad: Japan, 1931–1966," 165–177.

7. *BSR* 95:7 (September 1950), 104–105; *Annual Record of the ABS* (New York: ABS, 1950), 287.

8. *Annual Report of the ABS* (New York: ABS, 1952), 31; Hall, "Distribution Abroad: Japan, 1931–1966," 180–186.

9. *Annual Report of the ABS* (New York: ABS, 1937), 221–222; (1939), 215; Janice Pearson, "Distribution Abroad, 1931–1966: China," ABS Historical Essay 15, Part VII-F-2, 1968, ABS Archives, New York, 61; *Annual Report of the ABS* (New York: ABS, 1941), 232–237.

10. Pearson, "Distribution Abroad, 1931–1966: China," 150–151, 153, 157; *BSR* 85:9 (September 1940), 111–113.

11. *Annual Report of the ABS* (New York: ABS, 1940), 226–227.

12. *Annual Report of the ABS* (New York: ABS, 1938), 205; Pearson, "Distribution Abroad, 1931–1966: China," 176.

13. Vincent Goossaert and David A. Palmer, *The Religious Question in Modern China* (Chicago: University of Chicago Press, 2011), 147; Lian Xi, *Redeemed by Fire: The Rise of Popular Christianity in Modern China* (New Haven, CT: Yale University Press, 2010), 197; Pearson, "Distribution Abroad, 1931–1966: China," 176, 179; *Annual Report of the ABS* (New York: ABS, 1951), 271; Emily Honig, "Christianity, Feminism, and Communism: The Life and Times of Deng Yuzhi," in Daniel H. Bays, ed., *Christianity in China: From the Eighteenth Century to the Present* (Redwood City, CA: Stanford University Press, 1996), 243–262.

14. *Annual Report of the ABS* (New York: ABS, 1949), 17.

15. Pearson, "Distribution Abroad, 1931–1966: China," 180–182; *Annual Report of the ABS* (New York: ABS, 1951), 271; (1952), 285–286.

16. Pearson, "Distribution Abroad, 1931–1966: China," 176, 179; *Annual Report of the ABS* (New York: ABS, 1958), 278–279.

17. *Annual Report of the ABS* (New York: ABS, 1936), 233; Doris Catherine Hall, "Distribution Abroad: The American Bible Society's Service to Korea, 1931–1966," ABS Historical Essay 15, Part VII-F-6, 1967, ABS Archives, New York, 2–3.

18. *Annual Report of the ABS* (New York: ABS, 1949), 262–265. On the history of Korea in this period see Ki-baik Lee, *A New History of Korea* (Cambridge, MA: Harvard University Press, 1984), 306–390.

19. *Annual Report of the ABS* (New York: ABS, 1949), 262–265; Sebastian Kim and Kirsteen Kim, *A History of Korean Christianity* (New York: Cambridge University Press, 2015), 157, 168; *BSR* 95:8 (October 1950), 115–116; (March 1948), 38.

20. This paragraph relies heavily on Kim and Kim, *A History of Korean Christianity*, 162–168.

21. *Annual Report of the ABS* (New York: ABS, 1950), 282; *BSR* 95:9 (November 1950), 130.

22. *Annual Report of the ABS* (New York: ABS, 1951), 302.

23. *Annual Report of the ABS* (1951) 300–301, 299; (1952), 299, 301; *BSR* 95:12 (December 1950), 148–149.

24. *BSR* 95:12 (December 1950), 74–75; 98:1 (January 1953), 5–6.

25. Yi Mahn-yol, "Korean Protestants and the Reunification Movement," in Robert E. Buswell Jr. and Timothy S. Lee, ed., *Christianity in Korea* (Honolulu: University of Hawaiʻi Press), 239; Kim and Kim, *A History of Korean Christianity*, 182.

Chapter 19

1. Glenda Sluga, *Internationalism in the Age of Nationalism* (Philadelphia: University of Pennsylvania Press, 2013), 47–66, 87–88.
2. Daniel Gorman, "Ecumenical Internationalism: Willoughby Dickinson, the League of Nations and the World Alliance for Promoting International Friendship Through Churches," *Journal of Contemporary History* 45 (January 2010), 51–73; Andrew Preston, *Sword of the Spirit, Shield of Faith: Religion in American War and Diplomacy* (New York: Anchor, 2012), 408.
3. Sluga, *Internationalism in the Age of Nationalism*, 84–85.
4. *Bible Society Record* 92:5 (May 1947), 67, 76.
5. ABS, "ABS History: The ABS and Other Societies Abroad," ABS Historical Essay 24, Part II, 1970, ABS Archives, New York, 64; Edwin H. Robertson, *Taking the Word to the World: 50 Years of the United Bible Societies* (Nashville, TN: Thomas Nelson, 1996), 4.
6. ABS, "ABS History: The ABS and Other Societies Abroad," 67–69.
7. Robertson, *Taking the Word to the World*, 4–5; Laton Holmgren to Eric North, November 3, 1976, RG 18.00, Box 8, Folder 7, ABS Archives, New York.
8. Robertson, *Taking the Word to the World*, 152, 5; Eric North, "The Bible Society Conferences of 1932," ABS Historical Essay 24, Part III, 1969, ABS Archives, New York, 2.
9. North, "The Bible Society Conferences of 1932," 3–7.
10. Ibid. 31–34.
11. Ibid, 41–52; Eugene Nida, interview by Peter Wosh, Kennett Square, PA, July 28, 1989, Oral History Collection, ABS Archives, New York.
12. Robertson, *Taking the Word to the World*, 9–10. On Kraemer see Tim S. Perry, *Radical Difference: A Defence of Hendrik Kraemer's Theology of Religions* (Waterloo, ON: Wilfred Laurier University Press, 2001), 35–45.
13. Eric North, "The United Bible Societies," *UBS Bulletin* 1st Quarter (1950), 3–5; Ivan Nothdurft, "The Emerging United Bible Societies, 1946–1949," ABS Historical Essay 24, Part V, 1970, ABS Archives, New York, 12; Robertson, *Taking the Word to the World*, 17.
14. Nothdurft, "The Emerging United Bible Societies, 1946–1949," 30–38.
15. Robertson, *Taking the Word to the World*, 25–26; Nothdurft, "The Emerging United Bible Societies," 33.
16. Nothdurft, "The Emerging United Bible Societies, 1946–1949," 22; *Bible Society Record* 92:10 (October 1947), 115.
17. Nothdurft, "The Emerging United Bible Societies, 1946–1949," 58–59.
18. Ibid., 58–60.
19. Ibid., 68; *Bible Society Record* 92:10 (October 1947), 115.
20. Robertson, *Taking the Word to the World*, 59–65.
21. David Burke, "Text and Context: The Relevance and Viability of the Bible Society Movement's Fundamental Principle—'Without Doctrinal Note and Comment'—Past, Present and Future," *UBS Bulletin* 194/195 (2002), 305–307; Robertson, *Taking the Word to the World*, 64–66.
22. M. Olivier Beguin, "The Bible in the European Crisis," in *The Bible in the Church and the World Today: Being Addresses Delivered During the Meeting in New York of the Council of the United Bible Societies, June 1949* (New York: ABS, 1949), 1–5.
23. Henry Pitney Van Dusen, "The Bible and Christian Unity," in *The Bible in the Church and the World Today*, 13–17.
24. Ivan Nothdurft, "The American Bible Society and Its Relationship to the Other National Bible Societies," ABS Historical Essay 25, Part VII, 1980, ABS Archives, New York, 60–61; Nothdurft, "The ABS and Its Relationship with Other National Bible Societies," ABS Historical Essay 24, Part VI, 1980, ABS Archives, New York, 327; Samuel Escobar, "The United Bible Societies and World Mission," *International Bulletin of Missionary Research* 30:2 (April 2006), 80.
25. Robertson, *Taking the Word to the World*, 133; Edwin S. Cutler, "Financial Administration, 1901–1966," ABS Historical Essay 20, Parts IV–V, 1969, ABS Archives, New York, 69–70.

26. Nothdurft, "The ABS and Its Relationship with Other National Bible Societies," ABS Historical Essay 24, Part VI, 61–62, 65, 66, 74, 296, 330; Nothdurft, "The ABS and Its Relationship with Other National Bible Societies," Essay 24, Part VII, 67; John Erickson, interview by John Fea, March 17, 2015, Crawford, Nebraska; website of the United Bible Societies, www.biblesociety.org, accessed June 1, 2015.

Chapter 20

1. Janice Pearson, "Recent Trends in ABS Work: 1956–1966," ABS Historical Essay 103, 1970, ABS Archives, New York, 10.
2. These statistics are drawn from ABS Distribution Records, 1816–2012, ABS Archives, New York; Ivan Nothdurft, "Distribution in the USA, 1931–1966," ABS Historical Essay 14, Part VIII, 1973, ABS Archives, New York, 186, 189, 194, 212, 214, 218, 223, 227, 231.
3. John Zimmerman, "Public Relations: Promotion and Publicity, 1931–1966," ABS Historical Essay 17, Part VI–I, 1968, ABS Archives, New York, 4.
4. Zimmerman, "Public Relations: Promotion and Publicity, 1931–1966," 4, 10, 22, 26–27, 40–45; *Bible Society Record* (hereafter *BSR*) 92:12 (December 1947), 157; 100:1 (January 1955), 14–15.
5. *Annual Report of the ABS* (New York: ABS, 1952), 34–36; Zimmerman, "Public Relations: Promotion and Publicity, 1931–1966," 53–59.
6. Zimmerman, "Public Relations: Promotion and Publicity, 1931–1966," 81–83.
7. Zimmerman, "Public Relations: Promotion and Publicity, 1931–1966," 86–87, 93; *BSR* 100:1 (January 1955), 25; *Annual Report of the ABS* (New York: ABS, 1960), 36; *BSR* 101:12 (December 1956), 154.
8. Zimmerman, "Public Relations: Promotion and Publicity, 1931–1966," 110–115.
9. Ibid., 104–105; *BSR* 100:2 (February 1955), 34.
10. *BSR* 102:8 (October 1957), 117; *The Lock Haven (PA) Express*, December 19, 1959, 7.
11. *BSR* 103:7 (September 1958), 134; 104:1 (January 1959), 5.
12. *BSR* 91:12 (December 1946), 149–150.
13. *Annual Record of the ABS* (New York: ABS, 1947), 58–59; *BSR* 91:12 (December 1946), 149–150. On Gaston see Suzanne E. Smith, *Funeral Directors and the African American Way of Death* (Cambridge, MA: Harvard University Press, 2010), 109, 142–153; Fred H. Downs, "A. G. Gaston: A Story of Philosophy, Perseverance, and Philanthropy," in Marybeth Gasman and Katherine Sedgwick, ed., *Uplifting a People: African American Philanthropy and Education* (New York: Peter Lang, 2005), 119–133.
14. *Annual Record of the ABS* (New York: ABS, 1947), 58–59; Ivan Nothdurft, "Distribution in the USA, 1931–1966," ABS Historical Essay 14, Part VIII, 1973, ABS Archives, New York, 186.
15. Eric North, "A History of the Constitution of the American Bible Society, 1816–1900," ABS Historical Essay 13, Part I, 1963, 30, and Part II, 1966, 11–14, ABS Archives, New York.
16. Peter J. Thuesen, *In Discordance with the Scriptures: American Protestant Battles Over Translating the Bible* (New York: Oxford University Press, 1999), 68–78.
17. Thuesen, *In Discordance with the Scriptures*, 82–83, 96.
18. Ibid., 87–88, 94–119.
19. Ivan Nothdurft, "Text and Translation: English Versions, The ABS and the Revised Standard Version, 1946–1977," ABS Historical Essay 16, Part VII-B-1, 1980, ABS Archives, New York, 2.
20. Ibid., 3–6.
21. Ibid., 6–11.
22. Ibid., 13–14; *BSR* 97:4 (April 1952), 65.
23. Nothdurft, "Text and Translation," 15–20.
24. Ibid., 20–24; *BSR* 97:4 (April 1952), 65.
25. Nothdurft, "Text and Translation," 30–39, 46.
26. Ibid., 64–66, 70; Carl McIntire, *The New Bible (Revised Standard Version): Why Christians Should Not Accept It* (Collingswood, NJ: Christian Beacon Press, 1952), www.carlmcintire.

org/booklets-rsv.php, accessed June 4, 2015; Thuesen, *In Discordance with the Scriptures*, 100–103.

27. Nothdurft, "Text and Translation," 76–77.
28. Eric North, "The Constitution, 1900–1966," ABS Historical Essay 13, Part II, 1973, ABS Archives, New York, 26–31.

Chapter 21

1. Edwin H. Robertson, *Taking the Word to the World: 50 Years of the United Bible Societies* (Nashville, TN: Thomas Nelson, 1996), 94–95; *Bible Society Record* (hereafter *BSR*) 108:6 (August 1963), 88–89.
2. "ABS Percentage of UBS World Service Program," spreadsheet formulated for the World Service Budget Statements of the United Bible Societies, in the possession of John Erickson, Crawford, Nebraska (used with permission).
3. *BSR* 108:7 (September 1963), 104–105.
4. *BSR* 109:2 (February 1964), 26–28; 110:9 (November 1965), 144–145.
5. *BSR* 110:2 (February 1965), 18–20.
6. Kevin M. Kruse, *One Nation Under God: How Corporate America Invented Christian America* (New York: Basic Books, 2015), 205, 228–237.
7. Mary Peabody to ABS, August 16, 1966, Robert Taylor Papers, RG 18.07, Box 2, Folder 4, ABS Archives, New York; Dr. F. O. Holtham to ABS, November 2, 1966, Folder 8.
8. William B. Davis to ABS, September 15, 1966, Robert Taylor Papers, RG 18.07, Box 1, Folder 3, ABS Archives, New York; Fred Spitzhoff to Laton Holmgen, September 10, 1966, Box 2, Folder 6, ABS Archives, New York; Mary Silvia to ABS, January 12, 1966, Box 2, Folder 6; Memo: James Nettinga to Robert Taylor, March 24, 1966, Box 10, Folder 1.
9. Robert Taylor to William Davis, n.d., Robert Taylor Papers, RG 18.07, Box 1, Folder 3, ABS Archives, New York; Homer Ogle to Mary Silvia, January 20, 1966, Box 2, Folder 6.
10. *BSR* 111:1 (January 1966), 5.
11. *BSR* 111:2 (February 1966), 26–27; Memo: Robert Taylor to Dr. McCombe, September 7, 1966, Robert Taylor Papers, RG 18.07, Box 9, Folder 11; Robert Taylor to Fred Spitzhoff, September 20, 1966, Box 2, Folder 6.
12. *Annual Report of the ABS* (New York: ABS, 1967), 11, 76–77.
13. Ibid., 19.
14. *Annual Report of the ABS* (1968), 24–25; (1970), 26–27, 37 92.
15. *Annual Report of the ABS* (1968), 18, 19; (1970), 46, 8; (1972), 57.
16. *Annual Report of the ABS* (1966), 9.
17. *Annual Report of the ABS* (1965), 10; *BSR* 110:7 (September 1965), 2; *Annual Report of the ABS* (New York: ABS, 1969), 36.
18. *Annual Report of the ABS* (New York: ABS, 1961), 50–51.
19. *Annual Report of the ABS* (1968), 32; (1969), 8, 16.
20. *BSR* 114: 1 (January 1969), 7–9.
21. Mary Cordato, "Women's Involvement in the Bible Cause: 1816 to the Present," ABS Historical Working Papers Series, Working Paper 1993-1, 1993, ABS Archives, New York, 25, 27–29; *Annual Report of the ABS* (New York: ABS, 1965), 14, 115–116; (1970), 28; *BSR* 110:2 (February 1965), 28. In 1971, the Division of Women's Activities was created to bring more order to the labors of female volunteers on behalf of the Society, *Annual Report of the ABS* (New York: ABS, 1971), 142–143.
22. *BSR* 108:6 (August 1963), 85; 109:9 (November 1964), 130–131. In October 1964 the ABS opened a Distribution Center in Wayne, New Jersey, *BSR* 110:1 (January 1965), 10.
23. *BSR* 110: 9 (November 1965), 148; 110:10 (December 1965), 154–155, 164.
24. *BSR* 111:1 (January 1966), 8–9.
25. Billy Graham, An Address Delivered at the 150th Annual Meeting of the American Bible Society, May 12, 1966, ABS Archives, New York.
26. *Annual Meeting of the ABS* (New York: ABS, 1966), 16–19.

Chapter 22

1. Pius IX, "The Syllabus of Errors Condemned by Pius IX," www.papalencyclicals.net/Pius09/p9syll.htm, accessed June 7, 2015; *Annual Meeting of the ABS* (New York: ABS, 1946), 96; Ivan Nothdurft, "The American Bible Society and Roman Catholicism, 1816–1879," ABS Historical Essay 23, Part VII, Vol. 1, n.d., ABS Archives, New York, 6, 9, 15, 24, 25.

2. Ivan Nothdurft, "The American Bible Society and Roman Catholicism, 1816–1879," ABS Historical Essay 23, Part I, ABS Archives, New York, 68–92, 107–115, 118; 121–129.

3. Second Vatican Council, "Unitatis Redintegratio," November 21, 1964, www.vatican.va/archive/hist_councils/ii_vatican_council/documents/vat-ii_decree_19641121_unitatis-redintegratio_en.html, accessed June 8, 2015.

4. Pope Paul VI, "Dogmatic Constitution on Divine Revelation (*Dei Verbum*), November 18, 1965, www.vatican.va/archive/hist_councils/ii_vatican_council/documents/vat-ii_const_19651118_dei-verbum_en.html, accessed June 7, 2015.

5. *Bulletin of the United Bible Societies* 60 (1964), 182–183; Laton Holmgren, "Church Leaders Conference: Driebergen, Holland, June 22–24, 1964," Laton Holmgren Papers, RG 18.08, Box 21, Folder 21, ABS Archives, New York.

6. Oliver Beguin, *Roman Catholicism and the Bible* (London: United Bible Societies, 1963); Ivan Nothdurft, "The American Bible Society and Roman Catholicism, 1816–1879," ABS Historical Essay 23, Part VII, Vol. 2, n.d., ABS Archives, New York, Appendix A, 3–19; *New York Times*, November 9, 1966, 8.

7. *New York Times*, November 16, 1966, 34; Walter M. Abbott, SJ, Nothdurft, "The American Bible Society and Roman Catholicism, 1816–1879," Vol. 1, 135.

8. *New York Times*, November 9, 1966, 8; November 16, 1966, 34.

9. Nothdurft, "The American Bible Society and Roman Catholicism, 1816–1879," Vol. 1, 142–144; "The American Bible Society and Roman Catholicism, 1816–1879," Vol. 2, Appendix G, 45–48.

10. Nothdurft, "The American Bible Society and Roman Catholicism, 1816–1879," Vol. 1, 141–143.

11. Ibid., 145–147.

12. United Bible Societies and Secretariat for Promoting Christian Unity, *Guidelines for Interconfessional Cooperation in Translating the Bible* (London: W. H. Rickinson & Son, 1968).

13. Walter Abbott, *The Shape of the Common Bible* (Vatican City: Secretariat for Promoting Christian Unity Information Service, 1968).

14. Ibid.

15. *Bible Society Record* 114:4 (April 1969), 74.

16. Ibid.

17. Arthur Mattilla to ABS, December 19, 1966, Robert Taylor Papers, RG 18.07, Box 2, Folder 1, ABS Archives, New York; Robert Taylor to Arthur Matilla, December 28, 1966.

18. C. B. Mudner to ABS, November 13, 1966, Robert Taylor Papers, RG 18.07, Box 2, Folder 1, ABS Archives, New York; Robert Taylor to C. B. Murner, November 18, 1966.

19. "Cooperation with the Roman Catholic Church: An Outline for Discussion Drawn from the Latin American Secretaries Consultation in Oaxtepec, Mexico, December 3–7, 1968," Laton Holmgren Papers, RG 18.08, Box 21, Folder 21, ABS Archives, New York.

Chapter 23

1. Rick Kennedy, e-mail to author, June 9, 2015.

2. Stan Brown, comment on the blog "The Way of Improvement Leads Home," September 22, 2014, www.philipvickersfithian.com/2014/09/on-writing-history-of-american-bible_17.html, accessed June 9, 2015; Gene Chase, e-mail to the author, June 9, 2015; blog post, "The Way of Improvement Leads Home," September 18, 2014, www.philipvickersfithian.com/2014/09/send-us-your-stories-about-good-news.html, accessed June 9, 2015;

Una Cadegan, e-mail to the author, June 9, 2015; Tom Van Dyke, e-mail to the author, June 9, 2015.

3. "A Word About the Good News," in *Good News for Modern Man* (Grand Rapids, MI: Zondervan, 1992), 694.

4. On Nida see Phillip C. Stine, *Let the Words Be Written: The Lasting Influence of Eugene Nida* (New York: Society of Biblical Literature, 2004); Phillip C. Stine, "Eugene A. Nida: Theoretician of Translation," *International Bulletin of Missionary Research* 32:1 (January 2012), 38–39; Eugene Nida, interview by Peter Wosh, Kennett Square, PA, July 28, 1989, ABS Archives, New York.

5. Matthew Black and William Smalley, ed., *On Language, Culture, and Religion: In Honor of Eugene A. Nida* (The Hague: Mouton, 1974), viii; Eugene Nida, *Fascinated by Languages* (Amsterdam: John Benjamins, 2003), 2; Nida interview; Stine, "Eugene A. Nida," 38–39. On Nida's connection to Wycliffe see William Svelmoe, *A New Vision for Missions: William Cameron Townsend, The Wycliffe Bible Translators, and the Culture of Early Evangelical Faith Missions, 1917–1945* (Tuscaloosa: University of Alabama Press, 2008), 258–260.

6. Eugene Nida, *Good News for Everyone: How To Use the Good News Bible (Today's English Version)* (Waco, TX: Word Books, 1977), 13; Ronald F. Youngblood, "Good News for Modern Man: Becoming a Bible," *Christianity Today*, October 8, 1976, 14–17; Philip Towner, interview by John Fea, February 4, 2015, New York, NY.

7. David Neff, "Interview: Eugene Nida on Meaning-full Translations," *Christianity Today*, October 7, 2002, www.christianitytoday.com/ct/2002/october7/2.46.html, accessed June 9, 2015.

8. Peter Wosh, "Today's English Version and the Good News Bible: A Historical Sketch," RG 53, Box 2, ABS Historical Essays, 10–15, 1987, ABS Archives, New York, 1.

9. Ibid.; Erroll Rhodes, "Text and Translation: English Version, 1931–1966," ABS Historical Essay 16, Part VI-B, 1968, ABS Archives, New York, 14–15; Neff, "Interview: Eugene Nida."

10. Erroll Rhodes, "Text and Translation: Principles and Problems, 1931–1966," ABS Historical Essay 16, Part VI-A, 1968, ABS Archives, New York, 24–25, 67–68.

11. Rhodes, "Text and Translation: English Version, 1931–1966," Part VI-B, 69–70, 72.

12. Ibid.; Obituary, Robert Galveston Bratcher, *Society of Biblical Literature* website, www.sbl-site.org/publications/article.aspx?ArticleId=863, accessed June 9, 2015.

13. Nida, *Good News for Everyone*, 46.

14. L. D. Burnett, "Signs of the Times," *U.S. Intellectual History Blog*, October 19, 2013, http://s-usih.org/2013/10/signs-of-the-times.html, accessed June 9, 2015.

15. Ivan Nothdurft, "Distribution in the USA, 1967–1971," ABS Historical Essay 14, Part IX, 1974, ABS Archives, New York, 5, 10, 18, 22, 38–A, 83; *Bible Society Record* (hereafter *BSR*) 112:1 (January 1967), 10; *New York Times*, November 3, 1971, 49.

16. *New York Times*, November 3, 1971, 49; *Grand Prairie (TX) Daily News*, May 16, 1969, 3; *BSR* 111:4 (April 1966), 62; 114:8 (October 1969), 150; *The Index-Journal* (Greenwood, SC), November 7, 1970, 4; *BSR* 113:1 (January 1968), 11.

17. Neff, "Interview: Eugene Nida"; *BSR* 114:8 (October 1969), 150.

18. John Reumann, "Good News for Modern Man: The New Testament in Today's English Version," *Journal of Biblical Literature* 86: 2 (June 1967), 234–236; R. W. Danker, "Review of *Good News for Modern Man*," *Concordia Theological Monthly* 39:3 (March 1968), 216; Donald Ebor, "Review of *Good News for Modern Man*," *Church Quarterly Review*, 1:1 (1968), 66–67.

19. Nida, *Good News for Everyone*, 10, 114, 116–117, 118; Rick Kennedy to author, June 10, 2015.

20. Ebor, "Review of *Good News for Modern Man*," 67; Ivan Nothdurft, "The American Bible Society and Roman Catholicism, 1816–1879," ABS Historical Essay 23, Part VII, Vol. 1, n.d., ABS Archives, New York, 156–158; Nothdurft, "Distribution in the USA, 1967–1971," 45–46.

21. Nida, *Good News for Everyone*, 116–117; Billy Graham to Laton Holmgren, July 26, 1969, Papers of Laton Holmgren, RG 18.08, Box 1, Folder 11, ABS Archives, New York; Ivan

Nothduft, "Distribution in the USA, 1967–1971," ABS Historical Essay 14, Part IX, 1974, ABS Archives, New York, 20–21; *BSR* 115:1 (January 1970), 12–13.

22. H. Rhys, "Review of *Good News for Modern Man*," *St. Luke's Journal of Theology* 11:3 (1968), 110–111; Bruce M. Metzger, "Review of *Good News for Modern Man*," *Princeton Seminary Bulletin* 60:2 (1967), 67–68; Zane Clark Hodges, "Review of *Good News for Modern Man*," *Bibliotheca Sacra* 126:501 (January–March, 1969), 86–87.

23. Georgena Anderson to ABS, September 29, 1975, Alice Ball Papers, RG 18.10, Box 3, Folder 1, ABS Archives, New York; E. O. Hilty to ABS, September 26, 1975; Hariet DeJong to ABS, October 22, 1975; Rev. and Mrs. James Harrison to ABS (October 3, 1975); Rev. Thomas E. Koon to ABS, October 15, 1975; *BSR* 120:8 (October 1975), 40.

24. T. Jeffrey Delp to ABS, June 17, 1975, Alice Ball Papers, RG 18.10, Box 3, Folder 1, ABS Archives, New York; Brad Allman to ABS, June 7, 1975; Rebecca Marchand to ABS, September 12, 1975; Arthur Whitney to Rebecca Marchand, n.d.

25. *Gastonia (NC) Gazette*, June 29, 1970, 10; Nida, *Good News for Everyone*, 11.

Chapter 24

1. ABS, "Highlights in the Development of the Bible in *Today's English Version*," unpublished manuscript, ABS Library Working Papers, n.d.

2. ABS interview with Roger Bullard, n.d., ABS Archives, New York, 1–12, 15–16, 18.

3. ABS interview with Roger Bullard, 1–12, 31–32, 55, 60, 61.

4. Laton Holmgren, "Notes on Translations from Difficult Passages," Laton Holmgren Papers, RG 18.08, Box 10, Folder 8, ABS Archives, New York.

5. Ibid.

6. Ibid.

7. Robert Bratcher to Eugene Nida, June 17, 1974, Laton Holmgren Papers, RG 18.08, Box 10, Folder 10, ABS Archives, New York. On the Missouri Synod and the inerrancy of the Bible see James C. Burkee, *Power Politics and the Missouri Synod* (Minneapolis: Fortress, 2013).

8. Bratcher to Nida, June 17, 1974, Laton Holmgren Papers, RG 18.08, Box 10, Folder 10, ABS Archives, New York; Robert Bullard to Bratcher, June 21, 1974.

9. Laton Holmgren to Robert Bratcher, June 21, 1974, Laton Holmgren Papers, RG 18.08, Box 10, Folder 10, ABS Archives, New York.

10. Heber Peacock to Robert Bratcher, Laton Holmgren Papers, RG 18.08, Box 10, Folder 10, ABS Archives, New York.

11. Eugene Nida to Robert Bratcher, July 1, 1974, Laton Holmgren Papers, RG 18.08, Box 10, Folder 10, ABS Archives, New York.

12. Eugene Nida to Howard Clark Kee, January 27, 1975, Laton Holmgren Papers, RG 18.08, Folder 11, ABS Archives, New York. In 1981, at a seminar in Dallas sponsored by the Southern Baptist Convention's Christian Life Commission, Bratcher remarked publicly, "Only willful ignorance or intellectual dishonesty can account for the claim that the Bible is inerrant and infallible." He continued: "No truth-loving, God-respecting, Christ-honoring believer should be guilty of such heresy. To invest the Bible with the qualities of inerrancy and infallibility is to idolatrize it, to transform it into a false god." When Bratcher's words made it into several national newspapers through the syndicated United Press International, many Evangelicals and Southern Baptists (one of the largest contributors to the ABS) stopped donating to the ABS. Bratcher eventually resigned from the ABS, but continued to work as a consultant for the United Bible Societies until his retirement in 1995. He had violated one of the cardinal rules of the ABS by speaking publicly about his personal views of the Bible. Bob Allen, "Robert Galveston Bratcher, 1920–2010," *Christian Century*, August 10, 2010, 17; *New York Times*, June 17, 1981, A20.

13. Laton Holmgren to Eugene Nida, January 30, 1975, Laton Holmgren Papers, RG 18.08, Folder 10, ABS Archives, New York; Thomas Zimmerman to Laton Holmgren, January 27, 1975, Folder 11.

14. Robert Bratcher to TEV OT Committee, February 17, 1975, Laton Holmgren Papers, RG 18.08, Folder 11, ABS Archives, New York.

15. Ibid.
16. Warner Hutchinson to John Dean, February 24, 1975, Laton Holmgren Papers, RG 18.08, ABS Archives, New York.
17. Laton Holmgren to Ulrich Ficke, March 18, 1975, Laton Holmgren Papers, RG 18.08, ABS Archives, New York; Eugene Nida to Warner Hutchinson, April 16, 1975.
18. Robert Bratcher to Eugene Nida, November 6, 1975, Laton Holmgren Papers, RG 18.08, ABS Archives, New York; Eugene Nida to Robert Bratcher, November 19, 1975.
19. ABS, "Highlights in the Development of the Bible in *Today's English Version*"; "Good News Bible Endorsements, 1977–1978," Laton Holmgren Papers, RG 18.08, Box 2, Folder 13, ABS Archives, New York.
20. Lucian Legrand, "*The Good News Bible*: A Reaction from India," *Translator* 29 (1978), 331; D. F. Payne, "Review of *Good News Bible: Today's English Version*," *The Evangelical Quarterly* 49:3 (July–September 1977), 180, 183; Ainslie J. McIntyre, "Review of *The Good News Bible*," *Scottish Journal of Theology* 31:2 (1978), 190–191; Edward Greenstein, "Theories of Modern Bible Translation," *Prooftexts* 3:1 (January 1983), 14, 17; Michael David Coogan, "Review of *The Good News Bible*," *America* 136:9 (March 5, 1977), 197.
21. "Quotes about the *Good News Bible*, June 1978," Latin Holmgren Papers, RG 18.08, Box 2, Folder 13, ABS Archives, New York.
22. Alice Klykes to ABS, July 14, 1975, Alice Ball Papers, RG 18.10, Box 3, Folder 1, ABS Archives, New York; Joseph Jezowski to ABS, November 18, 1975; John Reimer to ABS, January 5, 1977, Laton Holmgren Papers, RG 18.08, Box 2, Folder 11, ABS Archives, New York.
23. K. E. Kroecker to ABS, January 15, 1976, Alice Ball Papers, RG 18.10, Box 3, Folder 1, ABS Archives, New York.
24. Harold Lindsell to Thomas Johnson, April 27, 1978; Laton Holmgren Papers, RG 18.08, Box 2, Folder 15, ABS Archives, New York.
25. Eugene Nida to Arthur Borden, March 21, 1978, Laton Holmgren Papers, RG 18.08; Eugene Nida to Thomas Johnson, June 6, 1978; Donald Scheimann, "Another Translation: Another Disaster," *Concordia Theological Quarterly* 42:2 (April 1978), 168–169.
26. Eric North to Laton Holmgren, September 10, 1974, ABS General Secretary Papers, RG 18.00, Box 8, Folder 7, ABS Archives, New York.

Chapter 25

1. Quoted in Peter N. Carroll, *It Seemed Like Nothing Happened: America in the 1970s* (New Brunswick, NJ: Rutgers University Press, 1990). For another perspective on the 1970s see Edward Berkowitz, *Something Happened: A Political and Cultural Overview of the Seventies* (New York: Columbia University Press, 2007).
2. *Annual Report of the ABS* (New York: ABS, 1974), 117; *Bible Society Record* (hereafter *BSR*) 120:1(January 1975), 35; *Annual Report of the ABS* (New York: ABS, 1979), 56.
3. *Annual Report of the ABS* (New York: ABS, 1977); 30, 31, 33; (1979), 30, 32; (1980), 34; (1973), 20, 30–31; (1974), 34–35; (1970), 41; (1973), 43; (1984), 36.
4. *Annual Report of the ABS* (New York: ABS, 1970), 8; (1973), 23; (1978), 24; John Erickson, interview by John Fea, Crawford, Nebraska, March 17, 2015; *BSR* 117:2 (February 1972), 5; 125:5 (May 1980), 10; 125:8 (October 1980), 5; 125:6 (June–July 1980), 6.
5. *Annual Report of the ABS* (New York: ABS, 1979), 24; Erickson interview; *BSR* 118:9 (November 1973), 6–10.
6. *BSR* 118:8 (October 1973), 4–17; 120:8 (October 1975), 21.
7. Erickson interview; *Annual Report of the ABS* (New York: ABS, 1974), 27–28; (1980), 24; (1979), 25; (1983), 27; (1975), 32; (1981), 24.
8. *Annual Report of the ABS* (New York: ABS, 1972), 124; (1977), 34.
9. Mary Cordato, "Women's Involvement in the Bible Cause: 1816 to Present," ABS Historical Working Paper 1993-1, 1993, ABS Archives, New York, 58–60; *BSR* 103:4 (April 1958), 58–59; Anne Braude, "Women's History *Is* American Religious History," in Thomas A. Tweed, ed. *Retelling U.S. Religious History* (Berkeley: University of California Press, 1997), 87–107.

10. *Annual Report of the ABS* (New York: ABS, 1972), 124; (1973), 55; (1974), 38; (1976), 50–52; (1982), 36–37.
11. Cordato, "Women's Involvement in the Bible Cause," 163, 164; Robert Taylor to ABS General Officers, interoffice Memo on "Unwritten Policies," June 3, 1970, 7. Copy presented to the author by John D. Erickson on June 14, 2015.
12. Cordato, "Women's Involvement in the Bible Cause," 105–111.
13. *Annual Report of the ABS* (New York: ABS, 1973), 55; (1974), 38.
14. ABS Art Department to "Whoever Assembles This Display," interoffice memo, July 1981, Alice Ball Papers, RG 18.11, Box 2, Folder 1, ABS Archives, New York.
15. Ellen Cummiskey to Alice Ball, interoffice memo on "California Scripture Courtesy Center Visit," June 23, 1982, Alice Ball Papers, RG 18.11, Box 2, Folder 1, ABS Archives, New York.
16. Ivan Nothdurft, "The American Bible Society and Roman Catholicism, 1816–1979," ABS Historical Essay 23, Part VII, n.d., ABS Archives, New York, 187–188, 197, 214, 311.
17. *BSR* 118:3 (March 1973), 22; *Annual Report of the ABS* (New York: ABS, 1970), 45; (1977), 29; (1978), 26; (1979), 31; (1980), 30–31; (1981), 28; (1973), 19; *BSR* 125:1 (January 1980), 13; *Annual Report of the ABS* (New York: ABS, 1972), 31; Nothdurft, "The American Bible Society and Roman Catholicism, 1816–1979," 222, 235, 245, 268, 269, 270; *Annual Report of the ABS* (New York: ABS, 1970), 43.
18. Nothdurft, "The American Bible Society and Roman Catholicism, 1816–1979," 228; *Annual Report of the ABS* (New York: ABS, 1979), 30; *BSR* 124:1 (January 1979), 26.

Chapter 26

1. David Hollinger, *After Cloven Tongues of Fire: Protestant Liberalism in Modern American History* (Princeton, NJ: Princeton University Press, 2013), 11–12. For a good overview of this period in American Evangelicalism see Steven P. Miller, *The Age of Evangelicalism: America's Born-Again Years* (New York: Oxford University Press, 2014).
2. "ABS National Division: Long Range Planning, July 1986," General Secretary Papers, RG 18.00, Box 1, Folder 2, ABS Archives, New York.
3. Ibid.
4. Clyde Taylor to Robert Taylor, October, 1968, Laton Holmgren Papers, RG 18.08, Box 2, no folder number (titled "EFMA/IFMA/ABS Correspondence, 1968–1969"), ABS Archives, New York.
5. Robert Taylor to Clyde Taylor, October 22, 1968, Laton Holmgren Papers, RG 18.08, Box 2, no folder number (titled "EFMA/IFMA/ABS Correspondence, 1968–1969"), ABS Archives, New York.
6. Laton Holmgren to Eugene Nida, August 7, 1969, Laton Holmgren Papers, RG 18.08, Box 2, no folder number (titled "EFMA/IFMA/ABS Correspondence, 1968–1969"), ABS Archives, New York; Eugene Nida to Laton Holmgren, August 18, 1969.
7. Francis Steele, "Principles of Bible Translations," August 1969, Laton Holmgren Papers, RG 18.08, Box 2, no folder number (titled "EFMA/IFMA/ABS Correspondence, 1968–1969"), ABS Archives, New York.
8. Laton Holmgren to Eugene Nida, August 14, 1969, Laton Holmgren Papers, RG 18.08, Box 2, no folder number (titled "EFMA/IFMA/ABS Correspondence, 1968–1969"), ABS Archives, New York; Peter J. Thuesen, *In Discordance with the Scriptures: American Protestant Battles Over Translating the Bible* (New York: Oxford University Press, 1999), 146–152. For an insider's history of the New International Version see Richard Kevin Barnard, *God's Word in Our Language: The Story of the New International Version* (Colorado Springs: International Bible Society, 1989).
9. Eugene Nida to Laton Holmgren, August 1969, Laton Holmgren Papers, RG 18.08, Box 1, no folder number ("EFMA/IFMA/ABS Correspondence, 1968–1969"); Oswald Hoffman to Eugene Nida, November 10, 1978, General Secretary papers, RG 18.00, Box 8, Folder 1, ABS Archives, New York; Eugene Nida to Oswald Hoffman, November 30, 1978.

10. Laton Holmgren, "Memo to Overseas Colleagues (UBS) on Evangelicals and the Bible Cause, May 5, 1970," Laton Holmgren Papers, RG 18.08, Box 1, no folder number ("EFMA/IFMA/ABS Correspondence, 1970").

11. Laton Holmgren, "Evangelicals and the Bible Cause," June 4, 1970, Laton Holmgren Papers, RG 18.08. Box 1, Folder 3, ABS Archives, New York; Laton Holmgren to Clyde Taylor, May 11, 1970, Laton Holmgren Papers, RG 18.08, Box 1, no folder number ("EFMA/IFMA/ABS Correspondence, 1970").

12. "Key 73: A Continental Call," *Christianity Today,* November 19, 1971; "Getting it Together for Jesus," *Christianity Today,* June 7, 1972, 16–17; *New York Times,* April 17, 1972, 14; Finding Aid, Records of Christianity Today International, Collection 8, Billy Graham Center Archive, Wheaton, IL, www2.wheaton.edu/bgc/archives/GUIDES/008.htm, accessed June 15, 2015; "NAE: Key 73 a Key Issue," *Christianity Today,* May 12, 1972, 34–35.

13. "Presbyterians Bolt COCU, Reject Key 73," *Christianity Today,* June 9, 1972; William Newman and William D'Antonio, "'For Christ's Sake': A Study of Key '73 in New England," *Review of Religious Research* 19:2 (Winter 1978), 139–140; *New York Times,* September 2, 1973, 23.

14. *Annual Meeting of the ABS* (New York: ABS, 1973), 7, 18; *Bible Society Record* (hereafter *BSR*) 118:1 (January 1973), 5, 23, 26; 118:3 (March 1973), 35.

15. *BSR* 118:4 (April 1973), 26; *New York Times,* September 2, 1973, 23; Carl F. H. Henry, "Looking Back at Key 73," *Reformed Journal* (November 1974), 6; "Key 73 and Constantine," *Christian Century,* January 2–9, 1974, 4–5.

16. "Key 73 and Constantine," 5; Henry, "Looking Back at Key 73," 6, 10, 11.

17. Billy Melvin to Wade Coggins, Jack Frizen, Paul Steiner, Arthur Gay, Robert McIntyre, and Paul Toms, 1983, Alice Ball Papers, RG 18.10, Box 3, Folder 12, ABS Archives, New York.

18. Ibid.

19. John Erickson, interview by John Fea, Crawford, Nebraska, March 17, 2015.

20. Erickson interview; *BSR* 114:10 (December 1969), 196; 115:2 (February 1970), 19; 115:3 (March 1970), 35; 116:7 (August–September 1971), 139.

21. Kevin M. Kruse, *One Nation Under God: How Corporate America Invented Christian America* (New York: Basic Books, 2015), 72, 75, 91.

22. *Annual Report of the ABS* (New York: ABS, 1974), 8, 31–32.

23. *Annual Report of the ABS* (New York: ABS, 1975), 39–40.

24. *Annual Report of the ABS* (New York: ABS, 1976), 39, 40; *BSR* 119:7 (August–September 1974), 11; 121:9 (November 1976), 17; 121:5 (May 1976), 25; 121:3 (March 1976), 25.

25. See, for example, Joel Carpenter, *Revive Us Again: The Reawakening of American Fundamentalism* (New York: Oxford University Press, 1997).

Chapter 27

1. *New York Times,* October 28, 1996, D1.

2. *New York Times,* November 2, 1996, 22.

3. Interoffice Memo, Robert Taylor to ABS General Officers, on "Unwritten Policies," June 3, 1970, sent to author by John Erickson, June 14, 2015; John Erickson, interview by John Fea, Crawford, Nebraska, March 17, 2015.

4. Erickson interview.

5. Erickson interview; Eugene Habecker, interview by John Fea, Taylor University, Upland, Indiana, March 26, 2015.

6. Habecker interview.

7. Habecker interview; Eugene Habecker, Report to the Board of Trustees, November 1991, personal papers of Eugene Habecker, shared with author on February 7, 2015, 2; Eugene Habecker, Report to the Board of Trustees, February 1992, personal papers of Eugene Habecker, shared with author on February 7, 2015, 7.

8. Habecker interview; Robert Briggs, interview by John Fea, March 11, 2015; Global Scripture Impact Website, www.gsimpact.org/about.html, accessed June 16, 2015.

9. Habecker interview.
10. Erickson interview.
11. Edwin H. Robertson, *Taking the Word to the World: 50 Years of the United Bible Societies* (Nashville, TN: Thomas Nelson), 1996, 9; Ivan Nothdurft, "The ABS and Other Societies Abroad," ABS Historical Essay 24, Part IV, n.d., ABS Archives, New York, 92–93.
12. Habecker interview; Peter Wosh, *Spreading the Word: The Bible Business in Nineteenth-Century America* (Ithaca, NY: Cornell University Press, 1994), 176. The British and Foreign Bible Society went through a similar transition around the same time. See Matthew Engelke, *God's Agents: Biblical Publicity in Contemporary England* (Berkeley: University of California Press, 2013), 10–12.
13. Lamar Vest, interview by John Fea, Pentecostal Theological Seminary, Cleveland, Tennessee, March 30, 2015.
14. Ibid.; Eugene Habecker, Report to the Board of Trustees, May 2000, 3; "Report of the Vision Task Force: The Mission and Vision of the American Bible Society for the Third Millennium," 2001, unpublished copy presented to author by Lamar Vest on March 30, 2015, 3.
15. Report of the Vision Task Force; Robert Hodgson, interview by John Fea, Columbia, Missouri, March 25, 2015; ABS website, www.americanbible.org, accessed June 16, 2015; Vest interview.
16. Hodgson interview.
17. *Holy Bible: African American Jubilee Edition* (New York: American Bible Society, 1999).
18. Hodgson interview.
19. David Burke, interview by John Fea, Morristown, New Jersey, March 11, 2015; David Burke, "Text and Context: The Relevance and Viability of the Bible Society's Movement's Fundamental Principle—'Without Doctrinal Note and Comment'—Past, Present, and Future," *UBS Bulletin* 194/195 (2002), 299–329.
20. Burke interview; Lea Velis, interview by John Fea, ABS, New York, March 15, 2015; Habecker interview; "Say a Prayer," *Forbes*, December 9, 2002, www.forbes.com/forbes/2002/1209/182.html, accessed June 17, 2015.
21. Nida Institute for Biblical Scholarship website, www.nidainstitute.org, accessed June 17, 2015; "Translation: A New Journal," *Translation* 1:1 (2011), 5; Philip Towner, interview by John Fea, ABS, New York, March 7, 2015.
22. Habecker interview. Habecker estimated that when he arrived over 70 percent of the Board of Managers was affiliated with the mainline denominations. When he left the ABS in 2005, he added, the board had only one more mainline Protestant than it did evangelical Protestant.
23. Habecker interview.
24. Habecker interview; Hodgson interview; Velis interview; Briggs interview.
25. IRS Form 1990 for 2004, 2005, 2006, provided by American Bible Society.
26. Habecker interview; Barclay Newman, ed. *Creating and Crafting the Contemporary English Version: A New Approach to Bible Translation* (New York: ABS, 1996); *Annual Report of the ABS* (New York: ABS, 1995), 5.
27. Habecker interview; Velis interview; *Bible Society Record* 146:8 (October–November 2001), 1–20.
28. Habecker interview; Vest interview; Eugene Habecker, Report to the Board of Trustees, May 2003, personal papers of Eugene Habecker, shared with author on February 7, 2015, 2.

Epilogue

1. Geof Morin, interview by John Fea, March 10, 2015. On the global expansion of evangelicalism see Donald M. Lewis and Richard V. Pierard, ed. *Global Evangelicalism: Theology, History & Culture in Regional Perspective* (Downers Grove, IL: IVP Academic, 2014). A similar shift toward evangelicalism, in the form of the Emerging Church movement, has taken place in the British and Foreign Bible Society. See Matthew Engelke, *God's*

Agents: Biblical Publicity in Contemporary England (Berkeley: University of California Press, 2013), 18–32.

2. Robert Hodgson, interview by John Fea, Columbia, Missouri, March 25, 2015; Vest interview, March 30, 2015; Habecker interview, March 26, 2015; *New York Times*, May 18, 2008, www.nytimes.com/2008/05/18/technology/18gordo. html?pagewanted=all, accessed June 17, 2015.

3. Vest interview, March 30, 2015; Roy Peterson, interview by John Fea, American Bible Society, New York, March 23, 2015; "American Bible Society Dismisses Doug Birdsall as President," *Christianity Today*, October 7, 2013, www.christianitytoday.com/gleanings/2013/october/american-bible-society-douglas-birdsall-lausanne.html, accessed June 18, 2015.

4. Peterson interview; Morin interview.

5. Nida Institute for Biblical Scholarship, "Scripture Engagement Description," unpublished document in possession of author, received from Geof Morin, American Bible Society, on March 19, 2015, 2.

6. Nida Institute for Biblical Scholarship, "Scripture Engagement Description," unpublished document in possession of author, 6.

7. Morin interview; Peterson interview; American Bible Society, "State of the Bible Survey," www.americanbible.org/features/state-of-the-bible-2015, accessed June 18, 2015.

8. Morin interview; American Bible Society, "ABS Strategic Plan FY 2016 to FY 2025," unpublished document in possession of author, 6.

9. Morin interview.

10. Peterson interview; Morin interview.

11. John Fea, "The Bible Cause's Ironic Move to Philadelphia," *Christianity Today*, February 27, 2015, www.christianitytoday.com/ct/2015/february-web-only/american-bible-society-ironic-move-to-philadelphia.html, accessed June 18, 2015.

INDEX